MINOR PROPHECY

Religion in North America

Catherine L. Albanese and Stephen J. Stein, editors

MINOR PROPHECY

Walt Whitman's
New American Religion

DAVID KUEBRICH

INDIANA UNIVERSITY PRESS

Bloomington and Indianapolis

Manufactured in the United States of America

Library of Congress Cataloging-in-Publication Data

Kuebrich, David

Minor prophecy : Walt Whitman's new American religion / David Kuebrich.

p.   cm. — (Religion in North America)

Bibliography: p.

Includes index.

ISBN 0–253–33191–9

1. Whitman, Walt, 1819–1892—Religion.   2. Religious poetry, American—
History and criticism.   3. United States—Religion—19th century.
I. Title. II. Series.

PS3242.R4K84   1989

811′ .3—dc19   88–45756

CIP

1   2   3   4   5   93   92   91   90   89

To the Memory of My Parents

I do not despise you priests:
My faith is the greatest of faiths and the least of faiths,
Enclosing all worship ancient and modern, and all between ancient and modern.

—"Song of Myself," 1855

The Great Construction of the New Bible. Not to be diverted from the principal
object—the main life work—the three hundred and sixty-five.—It ought to be
ready in 1859 (June '57).

—*Notes and Fragments*

I too, following many, and followed by many, inaugerate a Religion—I too go
to the wars.
I may be that I am destined to utter the loudest cries thereof, the conqueror's
shouts,
They may rise from me yet, and soar above every thing.
. . . .
My comrade!
For you, to share with me, two greatnesses—And a third one, rising inclusive
and more resplendent.
The greatness of Love and Democracy—and the greatness of Religion.

—"Proto-Leaf," 1860

When I commenced, years ago, elaborating the plan of my poems, and continued
turning over that plan . . . one deep purpose underlay the others, and has underlain it and its execution ever since—and that has been the religious purpose. . . . It [religion] is, indeed, too important to the power and perpetuity
of the New World to be consign'd any longer to the churches. . . . It must
be consign'd henceforth to democracy *en masse*, and to literature. It must
enter into the poems of the nation. It must make the nation.

—The 1872 Preface

Then still a purpose enclosing all, and over and beneath all. Ever since what
might be call'd thought, or the budding of thought, fairly began in my youth-
ful mind, I had had a desire to attempt some worthy record of that entire faith
and acceptance ("to justify the ways of God to man" is Milton's well-known
and ambitious phrase) which is the foundation of moral America.

—"A Backward Glance O'er Travel'd Roads," 1888

CONTENTS

FOREWORD

It is not often that Walt Whitman, the "good gray poet," is considered in religious terms. Indeed, David Kuebrich's fine study is the first book that we know to offer an extended analysis of Whitman and his work from the perspective of religious studies. There are, of course, a number of reasons for the neglect. Whitman's reputation for "barbaric yawp" hardly invited Victorian religious inquiry beyond condemnation for sexual frankness. Later critics mellowed on that score, but—in the division of labor that characterizes American universities—Whitman became the property of literature departments while scholars of religion looked elsewhere for subject matter. From the side of these scholars, an American poet, unschooled in theological tradition, untutored in systematic religious thought, neither overtly pious nor strongly identified in a public way with organized religion, did not compel attention.

Now David Kuebrich has changed that. Working with the skills of both religious *and* literary analysis, he probes Whitman's work with sensitivity and insight. Kuebrich discovers a poet akin in many ways to the classical mystics, a soul thirsting for the divine and speaking his need in the language of lover yearning for beloved. It is in this general context that Kuebrich treats Whitman's "homosexual" passages, his celebrations of "manly love," and his suggestive language of touch and intimacy. It is also in this context that Kuebrich reads Whitman as the minor prophet of a new American religion. For Kuebrich, Whitman's often-cited patriotism, his keen sense of loss at the assassination of Abraham Lincoln, his vision of the stature and status to be reached by the democratic republic, all need to be set in the expansive world of the poet's reach for divinity.

Kuebrich is the first to admit that Whitman's new American religion did not have much of a following. From the perspective of organization, it was a failure from the start. Even the poet's language militated against a movement, for his words formed an initiatory barrier, argues Kuebrich, that kept out all but an elite cadre of fellow-seekers. Accepting Whitman's religion meant hard intellectual and spiritual labor. It demanded sharpened intuitive faculties, an ability to penetrate the silence that surrounded the poet's coded "sounds." But Kuebrich does not measure religious cogency in numerical or institutional terms. That Whitman never took overt steps to "found" an organization is clear. That he nonetheless dreamed of leading the vanguard of a spiritual company that would bring America to her true divine measure becomes clear in Kuebrich's reading.

Demonstrating that measure, Kuebrich provides a gloss on the expansionism of Whitman's era, illuminating its spiritual side. In doing so he masterfully inserts the poet in a nineteenth-century popular religious world that includes millennialism and spiritualism, perfectionism and evangelical enthusiasm. Not everyone who follows Kuebrich's account will find this book easy going. Whitman's "barrier" of words perforce remains; and Kuebrich, as meticulous textual analyst, quotes extensively from the poet's works. Still, readers who persevere will be richly rewarded. Not only will they discover a powerful minor prophecy in Whitman's words, but also they will continue the task of recovering the religious heritage contained in American literature, a recovery too important to be left exclusively to literary critics.

We applaud David Kuebrich for his persistence and care in introducing the religious Whitman to a religious studies audience. His book, we believe, will contribute to a new generation of Whitman studies. On the literary side, these studies will avoid preoccupation with, for example, Whitman's sexual orientation. On the religious side, they will move past organizational and denominational categories to consider spiritual tenor and import.

These directions are all to the good. Not that Whitman's sexual orientation is insignificant (indeed, some readers may judge for various reasons that Kuebrich gives Whitman's alleged homosexuality too short shrift). And not that religious organization is an unimportant measure of vitality. But a balanced picture will present these factors alongside others. Alert to the poet's complexity, we are indebted to David Kuebrich for helping us reach a fuller, more nuanced understanding of the Whitman legacy. We are also indebted to Kuebrich for pointing in a direction that encourages further work in recovering the religious message of American literature.

Catherine L. Albanese
Stephen J. Stein

ACKNOWLEDGMENTS

No one can do research on Whitman without developing a warm appreciation for earlier Whitman scholarship. A number of works proved especially valuable to me, prominent among them Gay Wilson Allen's critical biography, *The Solitary Singer*, and his discussion of Whitman scholarship in *The New Walt Whitman Handbook*; Roger Asselineau's two-volume study of the development of Whitman's personality and work, *The Evolution of Walt Whitman*; James E. Miller, Jr.'s analysis of Whitman's vision in *A Critical Guide to "Leaves of Grass"*; and Harold Aspiz's *Walt Whitman and the Body Beautiful*, an investigation of Whitman's interest in nineteenth-century physiological and medical lore. Of course, one's thanks must also be extended to the general and individual editors of *The Collected Writings of Walt Whitman*.

In the process of writing and revising this study, I have become indebted to a number of individuals. Professors Giles Gunn and Edward F. Grier provided thoughtful criticism in responding to an earlier draft submitted for publication. I am also grateful for numerous improvements suggested by the general editors of this series, Professors Catherine Albanese and Stephen Stein. Mary Blackwell and her staff of typists at the George Mason University Office of Support Services deserve thanks, as does Lauren Bryant of Indiana University Press who was an extraordinarily helpful and cheerful editor. Years ago Professor Robert Streeter improved my understanding of Whitman and his historical context as I worked on my dissertation at the University of Chicago. To Professor James E. Miller, Jr., I reserve my deepest thanks for directing my dissertation with a judicious mixture of criticism and encouragement and for providing advice and support during both my graduate studies and subsequent career.

MINOR PROPHECY

I

RECONSIDERING WHITMAN'S INTENTION

"A little group are to signalize here on the prairies by the Wabash, the day that gave us the most divine of men."[1] This statement would not be noteworthy as a Christian's declaration of his plans to commemorate the birth of Christ. It is remarkable, however, because its author was not a Christian but a Whitmanite, the day referred to is not December 25 but May 31, and the "most divine of men" is not Christ but Walt Whitman.

Harvard professor Bliss Perry helped establish Whitman's reputation among academic critics by declaring that no American poet seems "more sure to be read, by the fit persons, after one hundred or five hundred years."[2] Horace Traubel, Whitman's close friend and the biographer of his last years, penned a scorching rebuttal. Reviewing Perry's book, he charged that the professor from Cambridge failed to realize that *Leaves of Grass* was "valuable for its religious rather than its esthetic inspiration"; and he condemned Perry's critical weighing of the respective merits of Keats and Whitman: "You might just as well set off Shake-speare against the Bhagavad Gita."[3]

A book that Traubel would have found more to his liking was Will Hayes's extended analogy of Whitman and Christ, *Walt Whitman: The Prophet of the New Era.*[4] The chapter titles indicate how the comparison informs the study; the first is "The Christ of Our Age" and others include "The Carpenter of Brooklyn," "A Friend of Publicans and Sinners," and "The Least of These My Brethren."

These items remind us that many of Whitman's earliest readers and critics hailed him as a religious prophet. For them, the *Leaves* was more than literary art; it was sacred scripture. These disciples created a loose confederation of groups, The Walt Whitman Fellowship: International, committed to the dissemination of the new religion of *Leaves of Grass*. Chapters were established, among other places, in New York, Philadelphia, Boston, Chicago, Atlanta, Knoxville, Toronto, and Bolton, England. But the Whitman cult was never large and in the 1920s it disappeared. The chief disciples had died and their places were taken by more academically oriented scholars. Religious enthusi-

asm had gradually given way to the more detached perspective of the professional critic.

Today's scholarship, looking back upon the enthusiasts, credits them with
providing important biographical materials and with pioneering the effort to
collect Whitman's prose and poetry in the ten-volume *Complete Writings* of
1902. However, the disciples' assessment of Whitman is judged naïve or inane,
if not insane. Perry dismissed the disciples as "hot little prophets," and both
the label and the judgment have endured. In the view of Charles R. Willard,
the historian of Whitman's American reputation, the demise of the enthusiasts
took the critical discussion out of the hands of rather peculiar individuals and
established it on "the plane of sane and traditional literary criticism."[5] More
recently, Gay Wilson Allen has asserted that although not all of the disciples
were "crackpots," nevertheless they were most likely to be "emotionally unsta-
ble, of uncertain sexual psychology, or subliterary minds who applied too literally Whitman's injunctions against literary conventions."[6]

But it seems to me that these early Whitmanites deserve a more sympathetic
evaluation. Certainly they made their mistakes. They overvalued Whitman in
likening him to such major religious founders as Christ or the Buddha. A more
serious shortcoming was their method of proclamation. Their writings, often
poignantly confessional and always insistently hagiographic, were insufficiently exegetical. Yet of all Whitman's critics, it is these early enthusiasts who
have most clearly perceived the nature and purpose of the poet's labors. Whitman did want to begin a new religion. He wanted his poetry to serve two functions: to promote the spiritual development of his readers and to provide them
with a coherent vision which would integrate their religious experience with
the dominant modes of modern thought and action—science, technology, and
democracy. It was these aspects of Whitman's effort that attracted his early
followers. "For me the reading of his poems is truly a new birth of the soul,"
testified Anne Gilchrist, widow of the Blake biographer Alexander Gilchrist.[7]
University of Chicago professor Oscar Lovell Triggs found in *Leaves of Grass*
"a new and modernized theology"; it was "the one book of considerable importance . . . that breaks utterly with feudal forms and assumes the processes
of democracy, and that is at the same time intentionally religious in basic purpose."[8] And it was Whitman's vision, declared the English scholar John
Addington Symonds, that enabled him "to comprehend the harmony between
the democratic spirit, science, and that larger religion to which the modern
world is being led."[9]

In the process of saving Whitman from the adulation of the early disciples,
academic criticism lost sight of the prophetic purpose that constitutes the heart
of Whitman's lifelong poetic effort. Rejecting the notion that Whitman's poetry is to be understood as an attempt to create a new religion, modern criticism
has developed three (sometimes overlapping) views toward the issue of
Whitman's spirituality. One approach, which is most clearly present in the psychoanalytic studies of Whitman, assumes that an author's religious language

is really something other: namely, the symbolic manifestation of the distorted desires of the id. Consequently, this criticism denies that there is any important religious dimension in the *Leaves*.[10] Another, which might be termed the "phases" approach, views Whitman's assertion of a fundamental religious purpose and prophetic self-image as the fabrication and posturing of an older, chastened, and complacent poet. This body of criticism, which now dominates Whitman studies, asserts that in the late 1850s Whitman underwent a personal crisis, precipitated by a homosexual affair, which radically altered the tone and content of *Leaves*. Whitman affirmed the emotional liberation and reality of his new sexual identity; but at the same time this new self-understanding forced him to reexamine the Transcendental faith in a unified cosmos, spiritual correspondences, and immortality that was present in his earlier poetry. In the process, the former buoyant optimism gave way to metaphysical doubting and a tragic melancholy which characterizes the poetry of the second stage (lasting from approximately 1859 to 1868). Then in the third and final stage, bowing to the emotional legacy of the war years, physical infirmity, a decline in genius, and a wider public acceptance, an older and more conventional Whitman set about writing new poems and revising the *Leaves*. He deleted some poems, altered others, and rearranged the overall order in an effort to obscure what he now perceived to be the waywardness of his middle years. It was only this later Whitman that tried, in hindsight, to invest his poetry with a religious purpose and to adopt the posture of a prophet of a new democratic faith. The task of the critic became one of saving the genuine Whitman from this later inauthentic poet-prophet and the scholarship that had assisted in perpetuating this image of the poet.[11] The third approach to Whitman acknowledges the presence of a religious theme in the various editions but unwittingly misinterprets it in two important respects. It distorts the character of Whitman's spirituality by treating it as a set of intellectual convictions rather than a special transhistorical mode of consciousness that gives rise to certain recurring religious values and beliefs; it also depreciates the importance of Whitman's religious faith by presenting it as just one of several themes in the *Leaves* rather than seeing it as constituting an emotional substratum that pervades and integrates the various themes into a unified symbolic vision.[12]

My purpose is to engage in a scholarly quarrel with these current views of Whitman and to propose a revisionist interpretation, one that tries to resurrect the earlier prophetic reading of Whitman's intention and to establish it at the center of Whitman studies. But to do this a new approach must be adopted which enables the critic to make a close analysis of Whitman's spirituality. In the present study, I have attempted to do this in three complementary ways. First, I have turned to existing phenomenological studies of religion for initial working definitions of certain key elements of Whitman's religion, for example, his notion of the soul, the basic structure of his religious cosmology, and his theory of religious symbolism. I have also employed a phenomenological approach, as a supplement to a traditional close reading of the text, to interpret what might be termed the epiphanic passages in some of Whitman's major poems because I believe that it is only by analyzing the religious experience underlying these passages that we can understand the poems themselves and see how they are informed by the poet's larger vision. Second, I have tried to relate Whitman's poetry to several currents of religious and political thought in antebellum culture which provided the basis of, and early inspiration for, his belief in a future religious democracy. Finally, rather than viewing the *Leaves* as an anthology of discrete poems or clusters of poems, I feel that the individual poems must be seen as the parts of a coherent religious myth. Perhaps Whitman's new religion was never articulated to the complete satisfaction of either himself or his readers. Nevertheless Whitman did arrive at a unified religious vision during the process of writing the first edition of the *Leaves*, and he continued to elaborate that vision throughout the rest of his life. The individual poems and sections of the *Leaves* are informed by this new religion and they cannot be considered in isolation.

Let me begin to discuss my use of the phenomenology of religion by distinguishing between several stages of religious activity. The primary level is the perception of the sacred in nature and history and the externalization of these experiences in religious symbols. At a secondary level is theology, or the systematic reflection upon the symbols of a particular religious tradition, which gives rise to creeds, doctrines, and moral codes. In addition, there are also the activities of religious institutions which attempt, by means of liturgy and instruction, to preserve and disseminate the experiences and ideas of the first two levels. Whitman was not concerned with—in fact, he was distrustful of— ritual and ecclesiastical institutions, and while his poetry does have moral and theological dimensions, these are subordinate elements. The *Leaves* deals mainly with the primary level of religion; accordingly, the interpreter must begin by investigating the nature and forms of Whitman's religious experience.

In analyzing the experiential dimension of Whitman's spirituality, his natural experience and spiritual beliefs should be viewed as a continuum rather than a dichotomy. For the mystic or profoundly religious personality insists, and Whitman strives to make fresh demonstration of this fact, that spiritual experience comes not from avoiding this world but rather through engaging it more fully. Whitman felt that the natural, if fully experienced, gave off intimations of the supernatural. Practically speaking, this means that a poem in the *Leaves* that seems merely to depict an encounter with nature (e.g., with the sun or stars) or a fellow human (e.g., the love relationships in "Calamus") may be pregnant with religious meaning. Therefore, the interpreter's task is a demanding one: to discern and explain those processes of consciousness whereby Whitman's sensory experience affected deeper layers of his psyche, subtly instilling a sense of supernatural realities. The critic must also disclose the nature and meanings of the various symbols Whitman used to express his spiritual insights and show how he attempted to organize his symbols into a rationally consistent and coherent vision. In short, the interpreter must elucidate Whitman's mental universe. When faced with this difficult undertaking, it is helpful to draw upon the scholarship and methodology of phenomenologists of religion.[13]

One reason for this arises from the novelty of Whitman's world view. In attempting to create a post-Christian myth, Whitman rejected the inherited religious vocabulary. When he does give expression to forms of religious experience that are present in Christianity, as he often does, he clothes them in new symbols and transforms them by adapting them to modern thought. The *Leaves*, with its emphasis upon the religious significance of nature, includes modes of religious experience and expression not present in the Judaeo-Christian tradition, like terrestrial or astral symbolism, which a critic only familiar with Western religion can easily misconstrue or even overlook altogether. One way to develop a broader understanding of religion is through the study of existing phenomenological descriptions of forms of religious experience that occur in other religious traditions. Obviously if the author studied is a Romantic poet like Whitman, it is especially important to be sensitive to the nature of religious symbolism and the essential meanings that various segments of nature have had in humankind's religious history. These descriptions can help the critic recognize and interpret these forms of religious experience when they appear in the *Leaves*.

A second reason for using this scholarship results from Whitman's distinctive method. In 1941, F. O. Matthiessen lamented the lack of an "adequately detailed scrutiny" of even such a major poem as "When Lilacs Last in the Dooryard Bloom'd."[14] Matthiessen himself never provided this close analysis of Whitman's achievement; and in the succeeding decades, although the *Leaves* has received more intensive scrutiny, it has continued to prove itself strangely resistant to a close reading. This resistance derives from the large contribution which the *Leaves* expects from the reader. Whitman devised a method in which he intentionally did not give full expression to many of his ideas. Instead he provided only "hints" or "suggestions" (the terms are his), and along with these he made existential demands upon the reader which were to lead to the full realization of what was merely hinted at in the text. This existential element in Whitman's poetic is one of the major reasons he considered the *Leaves* a new experiment in poetry, and the result is that the interpreter is left in a pretty fix. She or he finds that a close analysis of the language is insufficient; one must also somehow bring to the text those meanings which the poet intended but did not express. Phenomenological scholarship can provide some of these meanings, for it rather fully describes many recurring elements of religious life which Whitman merely suggests. Consequently, these descriptions can frequently be used to supplement the interpreter's understanding of the text.[15]

While the major tradition in Whitman studies has repudiated the idea that
Whitman wished to limn a myth for a new spiritual era, a small group of critics, notably Malcolm Cowley, James E. Miller, Jr., Thomas Crawley, and more
recently George Hutchinson, have emphasized Whitman's spirituality and prophetic intentions. But for the most part these studies have been hampered by
too narrow a notion of religion and also by speaking of religion as if it occurred in a historical vacuum. For instance, Malcolm Cowley, in his often cited
essay on the mysticism in "Song of Myself," declares that the poem is "hardly
at all concerned with American nationalism, political democracy, contemporary progress or other social themes"; and he further de-Americanizes Whitman with the subsequent assertion that most of his doctrines "belong to the
mainstream of Indian philosophy."[16] With the introduction of the study of
American literature into Indian universities, this judgment has received still
further development, finding its best expression in V. K. Chari's *Whitman in
the Light of Vedantic Mysticism.*[17] Cowley and Chari are correct in their observation that the *Leaves* and Vedantism both utilize a dynamic of knowing which
gives the subject a sense of participating in a more real spiritual order and consequently leads him or her to hold the material world to be less real or illusory.
But what both scholars present as a unique parallel is actually a fundamental
pattern of religious experience, one found not only in the *Leaves* and Vedantism but also in Christianity and many other religions. Whitman was a mystic
who gave expression to modes of experience which, in their essential forms,
are transhistorical and therefore have parallels in other traditions, but he was
also an antebellum American who subscribed to contemporary ideas about
science, religion, and literature and their role in the developing American
republic—and these ideas find expression in his poetry.

There is also an implicit ahistoricism in Miller and Crawley which stems
in part from an earlier formalistic style of criticism which deemphasized the
work's historical context and in part from their ahistorical use of ideal models
for interpreting Whitman's religion (Underhill's stages of Christian mysticism
and the biblical Christ-figure respectively).[18] Neither of these studies attempted
to relate Whitman's spirituality to mid-nineteenth-century American culture.
Benefiting from the interdisciplinary and historical nature of current literary
studies, Hutchinson employs a much more sophisticated hermeneutic, aptly
drawing upon current anthropological and historical-phenomenological studies for an understanding of the nature and function of religion. While accepting
the notion of transhistorical or ideal forms of religious experience, Hutchinson
is careful to insist that these are always historically conditioned. However,
Hutchinson's study is insufficiently historical, ignoring, for instance, the influence of such major historical currents as science and evolutionary thought on
Whitman's spirituality; as a consequence, he distorts Whitman by exaggerating his similarities with the shaman of archaic and traditional cultures.[19]

Three bodies of thought are especially important for an understanding of
Whitman's spirituality and its relation to contemporary American culture. The

first of these, which might be termed the Romantic religious world view (which includes but is not limited to American Transcendentalism), provided Whitman with a poetic and a basic religious cosmology. The second, the newly developing evolutionary thought in geology, astronomy, and biology, not only gave Whitman a process understanding of the natural world but also inspired him to make new formulations of divine immanence and human immortality. Third are the closely paired doctrines of perfectionism and millennialism that in some manner or another, ranging from scholarly theological treatises to more popular expression in the writings of reformers, communitarians and practitioners of various forms of medical and spiritual pseudosciences, permeated mid-nineteenth-century American culture and provided the source of Whitman's particular versions of these beliefs: his call for a new superior race of Americans and his dream of a future religious democracy. There are, of course, numerous helpful discussions of Whitman's debts to Emerson, evolutionary science, and the liberal political ideas of his day. I have not tried to trace over these well-charted paths but rather to call attention to the largely overlooked but crucial influence of antebellum Evangelical ideas and some of their more popular derivatives. This sheds new light upon Whitman's use of Emerson and other sources. Furthermore, it provides a better understanding of certain important religious themes in Whitman's poetry and helps to disclose the fundamental structure and unity of his vision.

"No one can know *Leaves of Grass* who judges it piecemeal," Whitman warned (*Camden*, II, 116). He asserted that his poems constituted a "totality" or "ensemble" or "massings" and claimed that they possessed a controlling "atmosphere" or an "orbic" quality.[20] But these words are not very illuminating; furthermore the Whitman scholar learns that unfortunately one cannot always take the poet's word as gospel. Yet Whitman so insistently cautions that his poetry must be read as a whole that these warnings cannot be ignored as yet another example of the "good gray poet's" annoying capacity for the sustained, artful fib. Rather Whitman's search for appropriate terms to suggest the unity of the *Leaves*, along with the novelty of the poems themselves, points to the need to develop an interpretive method that corresponds to the uniqueness of Whitman's text. As Gay Wilson Allen has stated: "The great [unresolved] problem in interpreting the poems . . . is to find a suitable context, some pattern of ideas, philosophy, religion, or psychology in which such terms as 'self,' 'soul,' 'spirit,' 'identity,' 'sex,' 'death,' etc., have interrelated meaning."[21]

Foiled in their efforts to find such a context, most critics have concluded that none exists. For instance, Hyatt H. Waggoner has recently asserted that Whitman's themes are "raw, crude, impure . . . impossible to fit into any coherent system of thought."[22] In a longer and more nuanced discussion of this issue, Roger Asselineau argued that Whitman began with "no idea of the way in which he was to organize this rich material [the themes of the *Leaves*] and

compose his book" and that any order "found in the later additions was imposed from the outside; it represents an intervention posterior to the act of
creation."[23]

Asselineau is certainly correct in rejecting the claims of Whitman's
disciples—claims inspired by Whitman himself—that the *Leaves* has a perfect
structural unity, having been planned as carefully as a grand cathedral with
each poem "designed and written with reference to its place in an ideal edifice."[24] But Asselineau moves too far in the counter direction, exaggerating the
disunity of the *Leaves*. Whitman did begin with a unifying principle and
the *Leaves*, from first edition to last, is informed by a coherent world view.
This did not provide Whitman with an architectonic structure for his constantly growing book of poems, but it did provide his poetry with intellectual
coherence.

In order to disclose the unity of the vision and the relations between its
themes, it is crucial, in addition to attending to Whitman's background and
the structure of his religious experience, to recognize that he employs a special
vocabulary of spiritual terms and symbols to express the intricacies of his spiritual vision. In making this point I am not referring to Whitman's penchant
for neologism but to the much more important fact that Whitman subtly invests what seems to be ordinary language with a level of mystical meaning.
Such words as "real," "new," "athletic," "touch," "love," "secret," "limitless," (and other '-*less*' words), "aroma," "tally," "whispers," "pulse,"
"power," "pride," "urge," "want," "yearnings"—the list could be made much
longer—have religious significance. These terms are never explicitly defined,
but their meanings are learned by examining their usage throughout the
Leaves. Similarly, Whitman consistently uses certain natural and historical
facts—for example, the waters, the stars, the grass—as symbols of spiritual
truths. With each usage the reader is only provided a few hints about the symbol's meaning, and to interpret the symbol it is necessary to accumulate the
hints from a variety of passages.

The consistency of Whitman's vocabulary and symbolism arises from his
unified vision. In the years between 1848 and 1855, as Whitman went through
his metamorphosis from newspaper editor to poet-prophet, he fashioned a new
religious world view which consisted of five interrelated parts: a religious cosmology, a religious psychology or theory of the soul, a program or set of existential demands for the soul's development, a millennial interpretation of history, and a coherent set of religious symbols. All of these are, in their essential
structures, traditional religious elements, but Whitman modernized them by
adapting them to the theories of evolutionary science and contemporary American political and religious thought. By integrating these traditional elements
with modern culture, Whitman arrived at a vision in which the evolution of
nature and the instinctual and emotional longings of humanity are seen as
manifestations of an immanent divinity in its upward ascent toward reunion
with its transcendent source, and the course of history is viewed as a movement

toward the universal redemption of humankind—a divinely ordained global drama in which the United States, because of its material wealth, democratic institutions, and new Whitmanian religion, would play a decisive role for centuries to come. During the period of his poetic maturity Whitman undoubtedly changed his mind about many things, but the basic structure of his vision, the notion of a deity whose immanent nature courses its way upward through all of creation toward its transcendent source, remained constant.

By not paying sufficient attention to Whitman's religious experience and language, scholarship has failed to perceive how the individual poems combine to elaborate a coherent religious vision. And the practice of analyzing the poems independently of one another as if they were not parts of a larger system but only units in an anthology has compounded that initial error. This has frequently led to interpretations that seriously distort Whitman's intention.

In analyzing the *Leaves*, I have used the final edition, complying with Whitman's own judgment that this was his preferred and authorized text. My purpose is to disclose the unified world view that informs the poetry as Whitman bequeathed it to posterity, but at the same time to show, because it is crucial to an understanding of both the poetry and Whitman's conception of his vocation, how less elaborate forms of this same vision—the same religious psychology, cosmology, and complex of millennial ideas—informed the earlier editions.[25] My examination of the evidence shows that Whitman had developed most of the principal features of his world view before 1855 and that all of them find at least rudimentary expression in the 1855 Preface and "Song of Myself." Whitman may or may not have weathered a crisis in the late 1850s, perhaps involving issues of a political, sexual, and vocational nature, but there is no evidence for asserting, as many critics have, that he lost his Transcendental faith and belief in personal immortality in these years. Nor is there any basis for arguing, as some critics have, that Whitman only later, in the years after the Civil War, began to conceive of himself as a religious prophet. It is true that during these later decades Whitman's poetry becomes less concrete, less sensuous, less personal, and is no longer animated by its earlier psychological tension and close engagement with the historical process. As a consequence, it loses much of its earlier vitality, the spirituality is more abstract, and the prophetic intentions more explicit. But this should be seen as a diminution of power and not as an effort to superimpose a newly conceived religious purpose upon the earlier poetry. In sum, there is a good deal more unity both in the *Leaves* and in Whitman's vocation and career than current criticism acknowledges.

The next two chapters describe the structure of Whitman's religion: how he ordered his religious experience into an evolutionary version of a traditional religious cosmology (chapter 2), and how he integrated this process cosmology with a theology of history that incorporated two of the most pervasive religious themes of antebellum culture, millennialism and perfectionism (chapter 3).

Chapter 4, on Whitman's style, elucidates the existential dimensions of his poetic and relates these to his theory and practice of symbolism. Chapters 5, 6, and 7 interpret respectively Whitman's announcement of his new faith and introduction of himself as a poet-prophet in "Song of Myself"; his belief in immortality in his two great poems on death, "Out of the Cradle Endlessly Rocking" and the "Lilacs" elegy; and his purposes for including two sequences of love poetry, "Children of Adam" and "Calamus" (chapter 7). The closing chapter considers Whitman's utility, assessing the extent to which his aesthetic and the poetry itself provide materials for a school of democratic literature.

Needless to say, this study does not illuminate every jot and tittle of the *Leaves*. Indeed, I argue at places that Whitman's suggestive method and intentionally ambiguous treatment of certain issues make it sometimes impossible to provide objective, fully convincing interpretations. However, if my thesis is correct that Whitman should be read as attempting to begin a modern religion, then my discussion of the structure of his vision does provide a new conceptual framework for the critical study of his poetry. My point is that Whitman's religious views are not just one theme that can be discussed in isolation and arranged alongside discussions of his other themes, for example, his treatment of politics, science, sex, and death, but that his religious ideas constitute a coherent world view that informs the other themes and integrates them with one another. Consequently, the interpreter's first task is to elucidate the structure of Whitman's vision. This in turn allows for a substantially closer reading of the individual poems and a more accurate critical portrait of the poet. The image of Whitman that finally emerges is, like that of the early enthusiasts, the figure of a prophet. But whereas theirs was a major religious founder, mine is that of a mere "would be" founder: a founder who failed in his chief ambition of creating a new religion, but in the process earned himself a lasting place in American poetry and also perhaps should be recognized, as I argue in the final chapter, as a minor prophet of a needed American civil faith.

In addition to providing a revised understanding of the *Leaves* as a religious text, I have also wanted to indicate its possible relevance to several areas of religious studies. For instance, in discussing the poet's symbolism, I have attempted to show how he adapted certain traditional religious symbols to modern culture by investing them with new elements of form and meaning. This aspect of Whitman's achievement perhaps deserves the attention of the historian of religions who is concerned to trace the changes symbols undergo as they appear in new historical contexts. Similarly, scholars in religious studies discuss the nature of myth, its feasibility in a scientific age, and the possible form it might assume. They may, therefore, be interested in Whitman's attempt to create a coherent set of symbols which would wed religion and modern science. Whitman's undertaking is also relevant to the recent interest in American civil religion. The new public faith Whitman presents for the United States rests upon a Transcendental metaphysics that is unacceptable to contemporary Americans, but perhaps there are elements of his poetic and theory of democracy that might provide both inspiration and materials for the creation of a new national vision to promote political and cultural revitalization.

After referring to my differences with the dominant scholarly view of the nature and purpose of Whitman's art, I also want to express my indebtedness to other critics. I have repeatedly drawn upon their work to enrich my understanding of Whitman's biography and poetry. Usually I have explicitly acknowledged my borrowings; where I have not, I trust they are evident to the specialists. My goal has been to make a judicious use of existing studies, combining the findings of earlier analyses with the insights offered by my religious reading in order to provide a comprehensive overview of Whitman as poet-prophet. In writing an interdisciplinary study that attempts to speak to scholars of literature and religion as well as to the interested general reader, I have encountered the unavoidable problem of writing for a diverse audience. I have tried to resolve this difficulty by giving the beginning student of Whitman or the scholar from another discipline a general introduction to Whitman and some of the central issues of Whitman scholarship.

II

A NEW RELIGION

FUSING THE REAL AND
THE MODERN

> Religion, Poetry, Honor belong to the Reason; to the real, the absolute.
>
> —Emerson to his brother Edward, 1834

> With what joy I begin to read a poem which I confide in as an inspiration. . . . This day shall be better than my birthday: then I became an animal; now I am invited into the science of the real.
>
> —Emerson, *The Poet*

Religious experience is of special intensity or power. So rather than speaking of the "holy," the religious person often, as these quotations from Emerson indicate, simply speaks of the "real." On the basis of his extensive investigations, the distinguished phenomenologist of religion Mircea Eliade has concluded that "the *sacred* is equivalent to . . . *reality*" and therefore the distinction between the sacred and profane is often expressed as "an opposition between *real* and *unreal* or pseudoreal."[1] A religious system attempts to define, legitimate, and preserve this experience of the real. In a desire to make sense of these moments of heightened reality, the religious personality has been led again and again, regardless of the historical situation, to formulate an elementary cosmology which distinguishes between the real and the unreal and defines the purpose of life to be the pursuit of the real. The religious person, according to Eliade, "always believes that there is an absolute reality, *the sacred*, which transcends this world but manifests itself in this world, thereby sanctifying it and making it real. He further believes that life has a sacred origin and that human existence realizes all of its potentialities in proportion as it is religious—that is, participates in reality."[2]

It would be fruitful to study four writers of the American Renaissance—Emerson, Thoreau, Hawthorne, and Whitman—in terms of this religious cosmology, for their art attempts to legitimate their sense of the real, to distinguish it from the illusory, and to disclose the moral pathways to reality. But at present I merely want to indicate, as preface to an analysis of Whitman's religion-constructing activities, how this cosmology appears in a letter Hawthorne wrote to his fiancée, Sophia Peabody (whom he already addresses as his wife):

> Belovedest, I have not yet wished you a Happy New Year! And yet I have—many, many of them; as many, mine own wife, as we can enjoy together—and when we can no more enjoy them together, we shall no longer think of Happy New Years on earth, but look longingly for the New Year's Day of eternity. . . . Oh, how I love you, belovedest wife!—and how I thank God that He has made me capable to know and love you! Sometimes I feel, deep, deep down in my heart, how dearest above all things you are to me; and those are blissful moments. It is such a happiness to be conscious, at last, of something real. All my life hitherto, I have been walking in a dream, among shadows which could not be pressed to my bosom; but now, even in this dream of time, there is something that takes me out of it, and causes me to be a dreamer no more. Do you not feel, dearest, that we live above time and apart from time, even while we seem to be in the midst of time? Our affection diffuses eternity round about us.[3]

Hawthorne's consciousness is arrested by the power of love. This is "real"; in comparison, the natural world seems illusory, a mere "dream of time." In fact, this experience is so real that he imagines it to be an anticipatory understanding here "in the midst of time" of a higher spiritual realm that he will enter into at death, "the New Year's Day of Eternity." Thus Sophia's shy but eloquent suitor conceives of his love as more than a psychological state; it is also a form of metaphysical wisdom—a revelation of a transcendent reality that he will know more fully in the afterlife.

To these sentiments, Whitman would respond with a hearty "Amen." Although he employs fresher language and a more enigmatic style, this same set of ideas informs his vision. *Leaves of Grass* is, at its most fundamental level, an existential poetry of the "real"—a term Whitman uses more often than "sacred" or "holy." Whitman interpreted and validated this level of experience by formulating a rather traditional religious world view which might be termed the "inner cosmology" of his vision.

The evidence suggests that Whitman had acquired the major ideas for this cosmology, from sources perhaps too general and vague ever to be precisely defined, by the beginning of his journalistic career in the early 1840s, before he was influenced by Emerson. Later Whitman became more familiar with Emerson's ideas so that by the late 1840s and early 1850s, when Whitman began to elaborate the religious vision of the *Leaves*, Emerson's essays undoubtedly served him well, providing not only a cogently reasoned version of the Romantic religious world view but also a definition of the poet as religious prophet which gave Whitman needed encouragement in his desire to project himself as the founder of a new religion. But one part of Whitman's religious cosmology is not derived from either religious romanticism in general nor, in its specific features, from Emerson in particular—namely, his new understanding of God's immanent presence in the creation as an ongoing process of progressive spiritual evolution from the prime matter of the universe to the soul's ongoing development in the afterlife.

This chapter analyzes the principal features of Whitman's experience of the real, the structure of his inner cosmology, and the means by which he adapted the latter to evolutionary thought. Apart from providing evidence for the above-mentioned general comments about Whitman's sources, I have not tried to provide a study of historical influences but rather to explain the inner dynamics and underlying unity of Whitman's religion.[4] In citing paragraphs from Whitman's writings which illustrate the elements of his cosmology, my criteria of selection have been economy and clarity. It is unnecessary to record the presence of these fundamental categories in each of the editions because they are the very form or habits of consciousness which constitute Whitman's spirituality. As the discussion in chapter 4 shows, Whitman's mode of symbolic "seeing," present in all the major poems, presupposes this fundamental cosmology.

I

Whitman's theory of the soul provides a starting point for approaching his notion of *the real* and reconstructing his religious world view. For the poet, the soul enjoyed a paradoxical status: it was an ultimate reality and yet, or in fact, because of this, it was also an unfathomable mystery. An enigmatic passage from a notebook in which Whitman jotted down ideas and early drafts later used in the *Leaves* presents an audience invoking the "Tongue of a million voices," presumably the poet, for his "tale of the soul." Despite his ability to name what remains mysterious to others, he is forced to confess his inadequacy: "I am vast . . . and my work is wherever the universe is—but the Soul of man! the Soul of Man!—To that, we do the office of the servants who wake their master at the dawn" (*NPM*, I, 105).

Yet if the soul's hidden recesses defied even a prophet's power of divination, Whitman did nevertheless have some beliefs about the soul which he held throughout his adult life. As the twenty-two-year-old editor of the New York *Aurora* he wrote two articles which clearly indicate that even at this early date (April 20 & 23, 1842), before he had read Emerson seriously, Whitman had already developed, at least in embryo, most of the ideas that would characterize his mature understanding of the soul.[5] One article, contrasting the "toiling aspirant for wealth" with the "poor poet, with ashy cheek," shows Whitman's

familiarity with those tenets of Romanticism which proclaimed the book of
nature as the symbol of a higher spiritual realm and the soul of the poet as
the best interpreter of the divine text: "Poor though he [the poet] be in worldly
wealth, he has a soul which in Nature's volume reads a lesson which imparts
content, nay, highest happiness. That is a holy volume . . . and he to whom
God gave the soul to comprehend it, and to love its varied pages, is the happiest
of his race." During his earthly sojourn, the poet "casts his eye upon morn's
mantling blushes, the retreating mists, and opening flowers, and is well satisfied"; and at life's end "he wakes—aye, *wakes* to revel in the glories of that
world beyond the veil."⁶ The other entry presents a much more significant
foreshadowing of the understanding of the soul Whitman presents in the
Leaves:

> But the soul's life! The soul—so grand and noble in its capacities, so thirsty
> for knowledge, so filled with the germs of illimitable progress—the soul, that
> has such awful powers, is endued with such quickness, such judgment, such abil-
> ity of thinking strange and unearthly thoughts, such a desire of assimilating itself
> to perfection and godlike purity, such insatiable anxiousness to discover hidden
> things, such unfathomable good will for its fellows, such undying faith in the
> efficiency of truth, and such towering ambition, that it may well be lost in won-
> der at itself. O, what venturesome mariner shall launch forth, and explore it,
> and take a plummet in his hand and sound its depths?
>   And part of the life of the soul is *love*; for the chambers of the heart are pleas-
> ant as well as costly. Things of surpassing fairness are there—thoughts that glow
> and dazzle—benevolence—innocent and holy friendship. Among their windings,
> restless and sparkling like rays of sunshine, lurk a hundred promptings and capa-
> bilities for delight. They are planted by God—and he who would stifle them is
> a bigot and a fool.⁷

Despite the many marks of conventionality, these passages bear too much of
Whitman's personal imprint to be dismissed as mere newspaper filling or the
insincere parroting of Romantic clichés. Here we already have the exclamatory
style, reverential tone, some of the associated terms and imagery—"germs,"
"mariner," "plummet," "satisfied"—and all the major ideas used to describe
the soul in the *Leaves*: its mysterious depth and divinely implanted yearnings—
especially for love, immortality, and divinity itself; its ability to discern the
spiritual meanings of nature; its insatiable desires and yet moments of satisfaction; its great pride, unlimited potential for development, and immortal nature.
    These various ideas about the soul, developed in greater depth and detail
in Whitman's subsequent experience and writings, are treated in other parts
of this study, but it is helpful at this point to analyze one of these beliefs: the
soul's apprehension of nature as symbol of spirit. Existing phenomenological
studies emphasize that the experiencing of a segment of the external world as
holy entails two factors.⁸ First, it is an especially intimate encounter. The
knowing subject overcomes the customary sense of separation from the known

object and feels a sense of psychological union with the inner depths of that which is known. Whitman believed that humans could experience the world in two ways: with the senses and the intellect and with these faculties plus the soul. The soul was the faculty of religious experience and it enabled the human consciousness to enter into the inner life of external objects:

> The soul or spirit transmutes itself into all matter—into rocks, and can live the life of a rock—into the sea, and can feel itself the sea— into the oak, or other tree—into an animal, and feel itself a horse, a fish, or a bird—into the earth—into the motions of the suns and stars—. (NPM, I, 57)

Second, phenomenological studies also point out that because religious experience activates this deeper dimension of consciousness, it establishes itself in the mind of the subject as an especially meaningful form of knowledge. Engagements with the outer world of this deep, unitive nature give the religious man the sense of participating in a level of being which, although immaterial, is nevertheless felt to be more real than the natural order. Whitman had this sense of a more important form of knowledge in his encounters with certain objects and events which, when experienced by his soul, spoke to certain deep-seated desires. For instance, when he experienced the star-filled heavens, the nocturnal whisperings of the ocean waves, or the scent of the calamus grass while alone in nature with his senses-cum-soul, these natural phenomena induced in him a state of consciousness which resolved his fear of death. At such moments he felt that the depths of his psyche participated in an infinite, eternal order; and this realization or "lived" sense of something infinite and eternal within himself assured him of his immortality. Experiences of this type convinced Whitman that properly perceived, the objects and events of the external world matched the soul part for part: "Strange and hard that paradox true I give, / Objects gross and the unseen soul are one" ("A Song for Occupations," ll. 101–102).

Since the soul's engagements with the outer world spoke to the very core of Whitman's being, he felt that these experiences provided knowledge superior to mere sensory experience.

> O the joy of my soul leaning pois'd on itself, receiving identity through materials and loving them . . .
> My soul vibrated back to me from them, from sight, hearing, touch, reason . . .
> The real life of my senses and flesh transcending my senses and flesh,
> My body done with materials, my sight done with my material eyes,
> Proved to me this day beyond cavil that it is not my material eyes which finally see.
>
> ("A Song of Joys," ll. 98–102)

It is the poet's interpretation of this "real life" of the senses which gives rise to the fundamental elements of his world view. His imagination was seized by the seemingly greater reality of these powerful feelings. This led him to posit a trinity of beliefs, so mutually dependent that one cannot analyze them in terms of a causal sequence, which gave primacy to this especially meaningful order of experience.

One part of this triad is a belief in an immanent divinity. Whitman could not conceive of these experiences as subjectively induced psychological states. They were too real to be dismissed as fanciful, so he judged them to be moments of communion with an intangible spiritual order that had a greater reality than the natural world. This led him to assert that the physical world was immanent with spirit; every external fact was the vehicle for an "eidólon," or a spiritual meaning that was more important than sensory knowledge, even the most refined empiricism:

> Beyond thy lectures learn'd professor,
> Beyond thy telescope or spectroscope observer keen, beyond all mathematics,
> Beyond the doctor's surgery, anatomy, beyond the chemist with his chemistry,
> The entities of entities, Eidólons.
>
> ("Eidólons," ll. 61–64)

At the same time, this more real order of experience also caused Whitman to affirm the immortality of the soul. These deep-seated realizations were simply too powerful not to endure. It was inconceivable that such reality could be subject to death and decay:

> Of your real body and any man's or woman's real body,
> Item for item it will elude the hands of the corpse-cleaners and pass to fitting spheres,
> Carrying what has accrued to it from the moment of birth to the moment of death.
>
> ("Paumanok," ll. 181–83)

He believed that the religious experiences which man "accrued" in this life developed the soul or "real body." These spiritual realizations informed or "identified" the soul and thus prepared it for the transcendent spiritual order which it would know more fully after death. Thus Whitman cautioned his readers to "Think of the Soul" because that "body of yours gives proportions to your Soul somehow to live in other spheres" ("Think of the Soul," l. 2).

This introduces the third member of the trinity: Whitman's belief in a transcendent divinity.[9] This last notion gave intellectual coherence to the other two, providing formal and final causes for the correspondence between the human soul and the outer world. Why did the meanings of nature and history match the needs of the soul? Because the human race and the rest of creation had proceeded from a common spiritual source. Humans were born with spiritual needs which could only be fulfilled by the soul's participation in the attributes of divinity. God, in his immanent nature, incarnated these attributes of himself in nature and history. Thus the external world existed, ultimately, for one reason: to lead the soul back to its creator.

Consistent with his positing of a more real spiritual order, Whitman depreciated the reality of the natural world. This established a crucial paradox in his thought: the external world which is celebrated with such loving enthusiasm is also declared unreal:

> To the cry, now victorious—the cry of sense, science, flesh, incomes, farms, merchandise, logic, intellect, demonstrations, solid perpetuities, buildings of brick and iron, or even the facts of the shows of trees, earth, rocks, &c., fear not, my brethren, my sisters, to sound out with equally determin'd voice, that conviction brooding within the recesses of every envision'd soul—illusions! apparitions! figments all! True, we must not condemn the show, neither absolutely deny it, for the indispensability of its meanings; but how clearly we see that, migrate in soul to what we can already conceive of superior and spiritual points of view, and, palpable as it seems under present relations, it all and several might, nay certainly would, fall apart and vanish. (*Democratic Vistas, PW,* 417–18)

Whitman was not a strict idealist, denying that things had a matter-of-fact existence. But he did assert that this world was but a dim version of a higher spiritual realm. The transcendent was eternal; this world was subject to change and would perhaps eventually pass away. The world of the spirit was absolute, existing for its own sake. This world was subordinate; in itself it was of no importance, but existed for the sake of its spiritual meanings—for the sake of exercising and developing the human soul. "I thought the things of Nature," Whitman wrote, "as in the main suggestive and gymnastic—not great because of objects or events themselves, but great in reference to a human personality and for identity and needful exercise" (*NPM,* IV, 1463–64).

This perspective informs Whitman's understanding of the purpose of human existence. This life was but a prelude, a period in which the soul prepared itself for the more real life to come:

> But what is life but an experiment? and mortality but an exercise? with reference to results beyond. (Preface, 1872, *PW,* 459)

> . . . the purpose and essence of the known life, the transient,
> Is to form and decide identity for the unknown life, the permanent.
> ("To Think of Time," 8)

The poet's task was to assist in this preparation. He was to lead his readers from an experience of the sensible to an awareness of the suprasensible divinity which was the source of it all:

> I have tried to show what I could of practical, materialistic, visible life, with an indication throughout of something beyond it all. I believe thoroughly that the main meaning of all the material world is the invisible and spiritual world, the immortality of the future; and back of it all is what I may call the almighty.[10]

Here a caveat might be mentioned. Of course it would be wrong to etherealize Whitman and view him as espousing an otherworldliness that disparaged human existence. He was no angel, but a nineteenth-century American who walked neck-deep in animal juices. But he believed that in a full experiencing of the natural, one became aware of the spiritual; and he felt that in leading his readers to the fullness of their humanity, he would convince them of their more than human destiny:

> I say I bring thee Muse to-day and here,
> . . . .
> Whatever forms the average, strong, complete sweet-blooded man or woman,
>   the perfect longeve personality,
> And helps its present life to health and happiness, and shapes its soul,
> For the eternal real life to come.
>
> ("Song of the Exposition," 7)

To sum up, Whitman's "inner cosmology" is a coherent group of interrelated ideas which defines the God-human-world relationship. Briefly outlined, it asserts: there is a God who transcends this world and yet is also immanent in it; nature and history are ultimately significant for their spiritual meanings; and human existence is a period in which the soul discovers God's presence in this world and thereby prepares itself for an afterlife in which it will know God more fully. There is nothing novel in these ideas; as Eliade's earlier statement suggests, this basic world view is quite common in the history of religions. Whitman's only departure from this statement is his affirmation of immortality, and this is a common religious belief, one which easily emerges from the experience of the "real." Also it might be noted that these ideas were readily accessible to the poet. Theism, a belief in immortality, and the view of this life as a preface to the next are all present in the Christianity and deism Whitman absorbed in his childhood. Neither deism nor Christianity emphasizes the idea that every natural fact is a religious symbol, but Christian mysticism quite often does; and certainly the discovery of God in nature was a staple element of Romanticism. Yet Whitman did not merely inherit these ideas. He tested them afresh in his experience, making them his own; and he often couched them in a new language and adapted them to his historical situation, as he struggled to create a modern religion.

II

Whitman did, however, make one major alteration in this traditional cosmology. He adapted it to process thought for he felt that a belief in purposeful, progressive development was essential to a correct understanding of nature, history, and the realm of the afterlife. Geology, astronomy, biology, history—all affirmed that this world, from its lowest level of inorganic matter to its culmination in the soul of contemporary man, was infused with a principle of incessant, meaningful development. In "Going Somewhere," Anne Gilchrist,

the British disciple who came to America to marry Whitman but eventually
realized that they would be camerados merely of the spirit, is depicted as bid-
ding adieu to her prophet with this profession of their shared faith:

> ... "The sum, concluding all we know of old or modern learning, intuitions
> deep,
> "Of all Geologies—Histories—of all Astronomy—of Evolution, Metaphysics all,
> "Is, that we all are onward, onward, speeding slowly, surely bettering,
> "Life, life an endless march, an endless army, (no halt, but it is duly over,)
> "The world, the race, the soul—in space and time the universes,
> "All bound as is befitting each—all surely going somewhere."

This process world view cannot be understood apart from Whitman's conception of a divinity who is both immanent and transcendent. God's immanent
nature performed two functions: it upheld the material universe, imbuing all
of nature and humanity with a spiritual essence and it impelled nature and
history to ever higher levels of perfection as it worked its way upward to its
transcendent source.

In notes for an intended lecture on religion, we see Whitman struggling for
an apt metaphor to describe the workings of divine immanence:

> There are in things two elements fused though antagonistic. One is that bodily
> element, which has in itself the quality of corruption and decease; the other is
> the element, the Soul, which goes on, I think, in unknown ways, enduring for-
> ever and ever.
> The analogy holds in this way—that the Soul of the Universe is the Male and
> genital master and the impregnating and animating spirit—Physical matter is Fe-
> male and Mother and waits barren and bloomless, the jets of life from the mas-
> culine vigor, the undermost first cause of all that is not what Death is.—
> (*Workshop*, p. 49)

In the *Leaves*, however, Whitman most frequently uses a "pulse" metaphor
to describe how divine immanence sustains the universe. God's transcendence
is compared to a central source of energy or life, analogous to a heart, and
his immanence to pulses of blood or energy which animate the creation. Thus
in "You Tides with Ceaseless Swell" the poet perceives the periodic movement
of the tides, as they are controlled by the unseen influence of the moon, as
a symbol of the intangible spiritual power or "unseen force" (l. 2) which pervades and vitalizes the world. He addresses it, asking: "What central heart—
and you the pulse—vivifies all?" (l. 4). Similarly, in "Proud Music of the
Storm" divine transcendence is compared to a "great organ" (l. 33) and
"strong base" (l. 38) which provides the "hid footholds of the earth" (l. 34);
and the "pulsations" from the base refer to the divine immanence which is
"Bathing, supporting, merging" the musical creation, that is, the entire universe (ll. 38–39). In a related use of this imagery, Whitman affirms his belief
that divine love informs the world by speaking of a "Love, that is the pulse

of all, the sustenance and the pang" ("The Mystic Trumpeter," l. 32). But "pang" clearly introduces the second function of God's immanent nature. The term belongs to what may be called Whitman's vocabulary of the divine urge: his use of such words as "urge," "dissatisfaction," "longing," "yearning," "pining," "burning," "need," "want," "curiosity," and "love" to indicate the inherent spiritual force which impels the creation to return to its source. This understanding of divine immanence receives its most succinct expression in "A Persian Lesson" where God or "Allah," who is "immanent in every life and object," is described as the "urge and spur of every life," the "invisible need of every seed," and the "central urge in every atom" which instills every item in the universe with the desire to "return to its divine source and origin."

Whitman believed that this immanent urge provided motive and direction to nature in its evolutionary ascent into higher forms. For instance, he states that there are "Unseen," "infinite," "unborn" buds in every square or cubic inch" which are "Urging" the universe "slowly, surely forward" ("Unseen Buds"); or again, he declares that the earth carries within it the "seed perfection" which unerringly directs its "mystic evolution" toward the good ("Song of the Universal," ll. 7 & 20). In similar manner, in "Song of Myself" it is to God's immanent governance of the evolutionary process that Whitman alludes when he speaks of the "Urge and urge and urge, / Always the procreant urge of the world" (ll. 43–44); and by the end of the poem it becomes clear that he believed that divine immanence had impelled nature's advancement from the "huge first Nothing" (l. 1153) to its culmination in human beings.

According to Whitman's evolutionary religious cosmology, every object in the universe possessed a developing immortal soul. In "To Think of Time" he asserts that "every thing without exception has an eternal soul! / The trees have, rooted in the ground! the weeds of the sea have! the animals!" (ll. 117–18); and in "Song of the Redwood-Tree" he declares: "(. . . *I bear the soul befitting me, I too have consciousness, identity, / And all the rocks and mountains have, and all the earth,*") (ll. 29–30). The process of spiritual evolution was an incessant series of spiritual alterations and advances in which the immortal soul attained to higher and higher levels of development as it pursued its evolutionary ascent through increasingly more complex levels of inorganic, animal, human, and finally post-human spiritual life. Accordingly Whitman could speak of his own imminent death as just one more transition in the unending series of translations and promotions that characterized the soul's existence: "I receive now again of my many translations, from my avataras ascending, while others doubtlessly await me" ("So Long," l. 67).

At the human level, this divine force manifested itself in the instinctive desires of the soul—desires for sex, love, freedom, immortality—which could only be satisfied through the soul's participation in divinity. Whitman maintained that these desires dictated human existence; every life was the story of an individual's attempt, wittingly or unwittingly, to fulfill the cravings of his soul:

> Ever the undiscouraged, resolute, struggling soul of man;
> (Have former armies fail'd? then we send fresh armies—and fresh again;)
> ....
> Ever the soul dissatisfied, curious, unconvinced at last;
> Struggling to-day the same—battling the same.
>
>   ("Life")

History was the record of humanity's slow but steady advance in its unceasing warfare with the material, political, and psychological impediments to a full spiritual life; and as poems such as "Passage to India" and "Thou Mother with Thy Equal Brood" indicate, Whitman could envision the day when all of humanity's accomplishments, the virtuous activity, the heroism, the science and technology, the art and the religion, would culminate in the creation of a perfect world. Then the soul would emerge victorious from the long war. The first whole human would make her or his advent, and history would come to glorious fulfillment. Human existence would be a perfect prayer—a life of union with divinity.

However, even if history were brought to a grand culmination with humanity's earthly apotheosis, the soul's development would not be complete. For Whitman believed that the progressive movement of nature and history was both fact and symbol, and as symbol, it indicated not only that the soul was immortal but also that it continued to develop in the afterlife: "Of the progress of the souls of men and women along the grand roads of the universe, all other progress is the needed emblem and sustenance" ("Song of the Open Road," l. 183). The "roads" of the universe were "grand" because there were no dead ends; the progress of the soul was a "journey ever continued" (Thoughts-2: "Of Waters, Forests, Hills"), an "endless march" ("Going Somewhere"), a "perpetual journey" ("Song of Myself," l. 1202). Often Whitman seems vague about the destination of souls after their human death and merely asserts that they pass to "other spheres" ("A Song of Joys," l. 142, "The World Below the Brine," "By Blue Ontario's Shore," l. 49) or "fitting spheres" ("Starting from Paumanok," l. 182). But other passages indicate that these "spheres" are stars or stellar systems. For instance, "Song of the Open Road" states that the constellations "suffice for those who belong to them" (l. 11), and "Song of Prudence" refers to things "well thought or said this day on any part of the globe, or on any of the wandering stars, or on any of the fix'd stars, by those there as we are here" (l. 33).

Evolutionary theory and democratic thought led Whitman to a new understanding of immortality and the divine-human relationship. He conceived of the afterlife as a process in which the soul attained to successively higher levels of illumination and participation in the divine consciousness. This crucial idea receives its most important and effective expression in the climactic sections of "Song of Myself," where the poet employs the new evolutionary theories of geology and astronomy to redefine the meanings of two traditional religious symbols, mother earth and the stars, perceiving the evolution of the former and the expansion of the latter to reveal the soul's immortality and ongoing development. This belief in humanity's infinite potential for spiritual development, combined with the poet's democratic sentiments, prompted him to promise to put over his readers "no master, owner, better, God, beyond what waits intrinsically in yourself" ("To You," l. 17). God is never presented in the *Leaves* as a master or king, symbols appropriate to a feudalistic or monarchical culture but not to a democratic one. Instead Whitman depicts the soul as continuing to develop until it ultimately becomes God's coequal, thus meeting with him "on perfect terms" ("Song of Myself," l. 1199) or as a younger brother who has his "Elder Brother found" ("Passage to India," l. 222). Thus modern science and democratic thought enabled the poet to arrive at a new, and in his mind more exalted, understanding not only of this world but also of the afterlife.

With the soul's post-human ascent toward divinity, we have traced Whitman's theory of progress full circle. It begins with the materials of the universe proceeding out of a transcendent deity as its immanent expression of itself. From the outset, the creation is divine and instinct with the desire to return to its transcendent source. This divine longing subsequently directs the evolution of nature and the movement of history toward the creation of perfect religious personalities who will be the ideal citizens of Whitman's religious democracy. After death, the human soul continues its development, perhaps ad infinitum, with the goal of becoming equal to God or a god itself.

The progressive advance of nature and history, whether perceived as fact or as religious symbol, disclosed that humans would attain to higher levels of development, both in this life and the next, than had previously been suspected. The work of the modern poet was to use this awareness to reinterpret God and the symbolic manifestation of divinity (the "eidólons") in nature and history:

> The prophet and the bard,
> Shall yet maintain themselves, in higher stages yet,
> Shall mediate to the Modern, to Democracy, interpret yet to them,
> God and eidólons.
>
> ("Eidólons," ll. 69–72)

Whitman would maintain himself in "higher stages" than previous inspired bards; by wedding a traditional religious world view with the intellectual currents of modernity, he would disclose the world to possess new, hitherto unthought of, dimensions of spiritual significance.

In attempting to adapt his religious system to evolutionary theory Whitman could not, as he could with the more traditional aspects of his cosmology, derive his ideas from the general thought of his time and the specific formulations of Emerson. Of course, Whitman could draw upon current scientific theories of evolution, but these writings did not provide the doctrines for his process theology but rather posed the challenge of how to reconcile a traditional religious cosmology with a scientific understanding of the natural world. In resolving this problem it seems likely that Whitman took up certain tentative statements or suggestions from Emerson's essays about the soul's evolution through different stages of natural existence and gave them a more literal and definite interpretation. But Emerson provides no support for Whitman's peculiar views on immortality; on this point, the disciple departed from the intellectual pathways of his master.

Emerson perhaps implies the presence of souls in at least the subhuman levels of animal life and their ongoing development through the higher forms of life in the verse epigraph to "Nature": "And, striving to be man, the worm / Mounts through all the spires of form." In "Nature" (*Essays: Second Series*) he asserts that even plants "grope ever upward towards consciousness" and that maples and ferns will advance until they "come to consciousness."[11] A passage from Emerson's essay "The Conservative" may be the source for the "pulse" metaphor Whitman uses to describe the activity of divine immanence:

> Consider it [the present order of society] as the work of a great and beneficient and progressive necessity, which from the first pulsation of the first animal life, up to the present high culture of the best nations, has advanced thus far.[12]

But unlike Whitman, Emerson never attempts to develop a consistent theory of spiritual evolution. In fact, in "The Method of Nature" Emerson explicitly denies his ability to provide a "natural history of the soul":

> I cannot tell if these wonderful qualities which house to-day in this mortal frame, shall ever re-assemble in equal activity in a similar frame, or whether they have before had a natural history like that of this body you see before you.[13]

Furthermore, as this quotation indicates, Emerson did not share Whitman's belief in the soul's post-human evolution or even his belief in personal immortality. As Emerson's thought matured, he increasingly conceived of immortality as a qualitative rather than a temporal state. According to this view, immortality was the existential sense of participation in God's eternal nature which humans could know in moments of heightened religious experience. In an effort to be faithful to the character of the "eternal now" of his spiritual experience, which transcended the secular categories of past, present, and future, Emerson rejected the popular doctrine of the immortality of the soul as a fundamental misunderstanding of the nature of spiritual existence:

> The moment the doctrine of the immortality [of the soul] is separately taught, man is already fallen. In the flowing of love, in the adoration of humility, there is no question of continuance. No inspired man ever asks this question, or condescends to these evidences. For the soul is true to itself, and the man in whom it is shed abroad, cannot wander from the present, which is infinite, to a future, which would be finite.[14]

By the time Whitman composed the first edition of the *Leaves*, he was too well read in Emerson and too sensitive to the nuances of Emerson's spirituality to misunderstand Emerson's views on immortality. But Whitman was unwilling to accept the idea of the dissolution of one's personal consciousness. So rather than interpreting his mystical moments of eternity as emotionally sufficient in themselves, he instead regarded them as preludes of a more real future life.

Whitman's theory of death and his great poems on death are discussed in a later chapter, but at this point it is appropriate to relate his rather novel conception of immortality to the historical milieu from which it emerged. Most recent critics have read Whitman as rejecting immortality, and only Professor Allen has rightly called attention to Whitman's notion of the soul's ongoing development and suggested that this idea might be derived from contemporary astronomical theory.[15] There is perhaps insufficient evidence ever to determine the precise sources of this article of Whitman's belief but it is clear that Whitman was forming his vision in a transitional period when religious thinkers were making the first attempts to reconcile older religious beliefs with new scientific theories and, not surprisingly, the discoveries in astronomy about the extent and evolution of the celestial universe led a few enthusiasts to conceive of immortality as a process of unending growth. For instance, new astronomical reports of the immensity of the heavens had led the eighteenth-century Swedish seer, Emanuel Swedenborg, with whose thought Whitman had some familiarity, to assert there were "myriads of worlds, and myriads of earths" in our universe, all of which were inhabited by humans, and after death the souls of all who had lived justly passed on to heaven where they were "continually advancing in wisdom."[16] Considering Whitman's keen interest in astronomy, it seems likely that he would have encountered the ideas of the prolific and widely read Christian astronomer and moral philosopher Thomas Dick (1784–1857) whose various works had been published in numerous editions by the early 1850s. Contemporary astronomical theory indicated to Dick that "the soul of man appears to be capable of making a perpetual progress towards intellectual and moral perfection."[17] Some aspects of Dick's understanding of immortality differ from Whitman's, but an 1838 work by the lesser-known C. S. Rafinesque, *Celestial Wonders and Philosophy*, presents a theory that closely resembles the position eventually expounded in the *Leaves*. The vastness of the sidereal realm, the seemingly infinite number of stars, and the phenomenon of stellar evolution prompted Rafinesque to redefine the stars' symbolic meaning. The "splendid Hieroglyphs" revealed not merely the old religious idea that "IMMORTALITY is the lot of all" ("A NEW REVELATION direct from HEAVEN") but also the new truth that there are many heavens and that the human soul will enjoy "joyful changes, mutations of life and love, ever leading to improving perfectible economies of existence."[18]

Whitman's notion that human souls would eventually become gods could have been derived from the Mormons. This idea is found in "The Book of Abraham" which Joseph Smith published in 1842 and also in Smith's famous funeral sermon for King Follett delivered at Nauvoo, Illinois, shortly before the Mormon prophet's assassination.[19] But if Whitman was familiar with this Mormon doctrine, it is more probable that he would have learned about it either from the New York newspapers, which reported on the Mormons extensively in the early 1840s, or from one of numerous books such as John Cook Bennett's *The History of the Saints: or, An Expose of Joe Smith and Mormonism* which attacked the claims of Smith and his followers.[20]

The new spiritualist movement, which was strongly influenced by Swedenborg's teachings, is another possible source of influence. For instance, Andrew Jackson Davis, the "Poughkeepsie Seer," maintained that the soul progressed eternally through subsequent worlds, each with numerous planes or stages of existence, but it never—contrary to Whitman's view of the soul's eventual loving union with God—attained to the seventh or final sphere, the seat of the Godhead or "Infinite Vortex" of love and wisdom. Davis's prophecies received wide attention in the popular press in the decade before 1855. Various of his books went through several printings during this period, and two were published by Whitman's friends and distributors of the *Leaves*, the phrenologists Fowler and Wells.[21]

Whitman's new understanding of immortality was probably not original and certainly not unique, but what was unique to Whitman's theory was the degree to which it was integrated into a larger process theology that provided a detailed and coherent interpretation of the universe consistent with contemporary science. It is around the idea of the soul's development that Whitman united his religious cosmology with his spiritual interpretation of history and his view of the afterlife. According to his cosmology, both the course of evolution and the individual objects and events of this world served to develop the soul; according to his philosophy of history, the dominant elements of American society, science (with its attendant technology) and democracy, delivered humans from external oppression and thereby enabled them to attain to higher levels of spiritual development. Thus evolution and history collaborated in the soul's earthly development, and in the afterlife the soul would, as Whitman declares in "The Soul's Procession," continue to grow "in the Spirit of God in greater space."[22]

III

INTERPRETING HISTORY'S MEANING

WHITMAN'S POST-CHRISTIAN
MILLENNIALISM

The reader of Whitman's journalism and other prose writings on the nature of American society is struck by the marked difference between the America described in the prose and the vision of America outlined in the *Leaves*. Readers familiar only with the poetry have sometimes charged that Whitman was constitutionally incapable of seeing evil in either his fellow humans or American institutions. But the prose clearly discloses Whitman's painful awareness of severe flaws in the national character and of social evils that permeated both New York City and the larger body politic. Critical of what he perceived to be a growing materialism, Whitman's newspaper editorials of the 1840s pronounced the "strife for gain" as the "greatest evil" of the American people and asserted that an "unholy wish for great riches enters into every transaction of society, and more or less taints its moral soundness." Central to all of Whitman's social criticism was a concern for the white working class. He called for shorter hours for young clerks in retail stores, raged out against employers who docked the pay of their unskilled laborers, and lamented the exploitation of female domestics. Observing the large number of poor young women in Brooklyn and New York, he placed the blame squarely upon the "miserably low rate of wages paid for women's work" and then extended his criticism to include the growing ranks of women factoryworkers in New England and New Jersey. Addressing New York's urban housing problem in 1856, Whitman advocated the creation of model housing for the "great mass of poor [who] live in insufficient tenements" which eroded family life and fostered fornication and prostitution. Although his concern was more for the dignity of the white worker than the plight of the enslaved black, Whitman consistently editorialized against the extension of slavery into new territories, lashed out at the failure of authorities to enforce laws prohibiting the slave trade, and criticized politicians for sacrificing democratic principles to party concerns, special interests and personal advancement. Prose writings after the Civil War continue to criticize an appalling absence of public virtue and question the adequacy of American economic arrangements. In *Democratic Vistas* Whitman denounced the "depravity of the business classes" and the widespread "corruption, bribery, falsehood, mal-administration" in municipal, state and national governments (*PW*, II, 370). In his later years he increasingly worried over the maldistribution of wealth and intensifying conflict between capital and labor. The most pressing problem was a matter of "social and economic organization, the treatment of working people by employers, and all that goes along with it." Unless this was resolved, he feared that the United States might, "like the countries of the Old World," create "vast crops of poor, desperate, dissatisfied, nomadic, miserably-waged populations" so that the republican experiment would prove "at heart an unhealthy failure" (*PW*, II, 527-28).

Yet none of these urgent social problems receive direct treatment in Whitman's new order of democratic poetry. Here he was not concerned to describe the America he observed as a New York journalist, worker in the Washington bureaucracy and Union hospitals, and aging Camden social observer. Instead he wanted to depict the ideal nation and people that comprised his mythic understanding of America's divine promise. In light of the tragedy and emotional trauma that plagued the family household during his early development, and Whitman's subsequent life-long brooding over the health of the American body politic, it is probable that the boundless national faith expressed in the *Leaves* is in part the product of a fearful personality that, finding no immediate political solutions to the dizzying array of social ills, finally sought refuge in the hope for a millennial future that would justify the present. But these considerations must be balanced by a recognition of the positive and realistic elements in Whitman's faith. On a psychological level, it seems that he always found security in his relationship with his mother. Furthermore, upon careful examination Whitman's faith appears not so much an evasion of reality as a highly original and thoughtful synthesis of various important religious and political beliefs that characterized the contemporary culture.

Whitman's optimism was undoubtedly fed by the tangible surface realities of his historical situation. In early nineteenth-century America, there were the indisputable facts of large-scale geographical expansion, technological development, and demographic growth. The ideological legacy of early American nationalism, with its utopian political rhetoric, also fueled Whitman's faith, and he was impressed by the indications of progressive development in the new theories of evolution in geology, astronomy, and biology.[1] Furthermore, it seems that by the later 1860s he had adopted Hegel's notion of history as an ascending movement in which the cultures of Asia and Europe would find their fulfillment in America where they would be fused into a higher synthesis. But Whitman's belief in historical progress is more than a combination of post-Revolutionary nationalism and the Victorian faith in material advancement reinforced by evolutionary science and Hegelian philosophy. Another source of Whitman's historical optimism, certainly the earliest source and I believe always the most important, was the peculiar fusion of American nationalism and Christian millennialism that developed into a widespread public faith during the decades between the American Revolution and the Civil War.

The American fascination with the millennium had its historical roots in the theology of national mission developed by the New England Reformed tradition, but in the early decades of the nineteenth century it spread both throughout the nation and beyond official denominational structures into the various movements for moral and political reform, the communitarian experiments, and new "scientific" and religious fads which promised to renovate society and redeem the human race. Usually the millennial era was interpreted in a Christian framework as the promised latter-day glory, but sometimes Christianity itself was seen as a stage in humanity's religious growth, one that needed to be transcended by a universal or natural religion so America could fulfill its mission of establishing the kingdom of God on earth and the human race could perfect its God-given nature.

Although scholarship has not related Whitman's poetry to this body of thought which informed so much of nineteenth-century American culture, it is virtually certain that Whitman was repeatedly exposed to it in the religious programs he attended as a child and young adult. In addition Whitman clearly absorbed a version of this Protestant millennialism from the temperance movement and the pages of the liberal Democratic organ, *The United States Magazine and Democratic Review*. Later he would also have become familiar with the millennialism associated with such pseudoscientific theories and heterodox religious movements as phrenology and spiritualism, both of which enjoyed widespread popularity during the years in which he labored upon the early editions of the *Leaves*.

The possible sources for Whitman's millennial views are so numerous that it is impossible to do more than call attention to the more likely lines of influence. However, it can be said with certainty that this antebellum tradition of religious nationalism provided Whitman with both his notion of America as a nation chosen by God to be a model to the world and his view of American history as a progressive movement toward an imminent millennial future. Furthermore, an analysis of Whitman's early millennialism indicates that this tradition provided the ultimate foundation, as well as the closest parallels, for two of Whitman's other major themes: his belief in the possibility of producing a new race of perfect women and men and his dream of a future religious democracy—that is, of a holy nation whose citizens, united with one another in a spirit of mystical affection, would live free of external constraints because of their voluntary obedience to the laws of God. Also, as becomes evident in subsequent chapters, an awareness of Whitman's millennial perspective is a prerequisite for understanding the significance of all of Whitman's poems. To assert this is not to argue that each poem bears a millennial theme but rather to recognize that the idea of progress—both evolutionary and historical— toward a millennial future informs Whitman's vision and that all his poems must be placed within this context. Yet in spite of his use of the categories of Christian millennialism, Whitman replaced the biblical theology and vocabulary with his own religious language and ideas. For this reason it seems appropriate to call his theory of progress a post-Christian millennialism.

In this chapter I discuss Whitman's millennialism in relation to antebellum millennialism and its corollary doctrines of spiritual perfectionism and religious republicanism. These three ideas must be discussed together not only because they are essential elements of Whitman's notion of history, and thus of his basic world view, but also because they are so intimately related that no one of them can be understood apart from the others. I have cited numerous examples of these beliefs and developed some of them in considerable detail in order both to suggest the widespread currency of these ideas, hence their likely influence upon Whitman, and to develop a context that illuminates the similar ideas in Whitman's poetry. Furthermore, I want to provide a corrective to the conventional view that Whitman derived his philosophy of history from Hegel. Far from being German imports, the principal elements of Whitman's theory of history were part and parcel of his native culture; they were, in fact, non-Christian versions of the most widespread and vital ideas of antebellum Protestantism.[2]

In tracing the origin and evolution of Whitman's millennialism, I inevitably raise again the thorny problem of the nature and degree of Whitman's indebtedness to Emerson. My judgment is that while Emerson was the most important single influence upon Whitman's development as a poet-prophet, he was not the earliest or most important source for the ideas that gave rise to Whitman's particular version of religious nationalism. In fact, the main corpus of Emerson's writings do not espouse the type of millennial and perfectionist beliefs that inform Whitman's poetry.

American Millennialism

Far from being a static doctrine, Christian millennialism has assumed different forms in keeping with the character of differing historical situations. While building upon the traditions of Jewish apocalyptic and New Testament prophecy, John's highly symbolic prophecies in the Book of Revelation provided Christianity with its first full-fledged vision of the end times. John's eschatology, often termed apocalyptic millennialism, projected a dramatic scenario for the brief remainder of world history which included the imminent visitation of startling natural and preternatural phenomena, the return of Christ and his saints and their victory over the Antichrist, the establishment of God's kingdom on earth for one thousand years, and finally a brief period in which Satan would be again released upon the world before encountering his final defeat.

Successive generations of Christians anxiously awaited this welcome resolution to world history, but after centuries of frustrated expectation, the church embraced the new viewpoint, most fully developed by Augustine, that the millennial predictions in Revelation were allegorical and not historical, referring to the individual believer's, and not the world's, ultimate triumph over the Antichrist. Augustine's allegorical millennialism became the official doctrine of the Roman church during the Middle Ages and Renaissance; and it continued to be maintained by Lutheran, Calvinist, and Anglican reformers of the sixteenth century, although these reformed churches did provide a peculiarly Protestant gloss upon some of John's symbols in order to legitimate the Reformation: references in Revelation to "Babylon" and the "beast" were now read as names for the Roman Church and the papacy.

A third type of millennialism was developed by some seventeenth-century English biblical scholars who revived the primitive church's belief in a coming earthly millennium, but with a crucial change: the advent of the millennial era, formerly conceived of as an apocalyptic event that dramatically reversed the process of history, was now described as an ongoing process of individual conversions and social amelioration. According to this doctrine of progressive millennialism, the approach to the end times had begun with the Reformation, which substantially weakened the dominion of the Antichrist, and history was now rapidly moving toward its consummation.

Whereas apocalyptic millennialism, often termed pre-millennialism or millenarianism, denied historical progress and expected Christ to come before the millennium, progressive millennialism was optimistic about the historical situation and its potential for improvement, and it placed the Second Advent at the end of the thousand years of blessedness when Christ would come to vanquish Satan after his brief re-emergence. This progressive post-millennialist viewpoint became widespread among British and American Protestants during the eighteenth century, and despite notable exceptions such as the pre-millennialism of William Miller and his followers in the 1840s, most antebellum American millennialism was of a progressive nature.[3]

It was Jonathan Edwards, the most articulate and influential apologist of the Great Awakening, who first provided American Protestantism with a full-fledged theory of a progressively realized millennium. In the series of sermons that adumbrated the ideas for his unfinished *History of Redemption*, he argued that the promised golden age of Christian fulfillment would be brought about gradually by the ordinary processes of spreading the gospel. Later, in *Some Thoughts Concerning the Present Revival of Religion in New England* (1742), Edwards proposed that the final days might be rather near at hand and he revived the earlier Puritan notion of American chosenness, assigning to events in America a primary role in the history of the world's redemption. Edwards saw the hand of God guiding history from the Reformation ("the first thing that God did towards the glorious renovation of the world") and the discovery of America ("about the time of the Reformation, or but little before") to the Puritan emigration ("consider the circumstances of the settlement of New England") and on to the Great Awakening and then the millennium ("what is now seen in America [the religious revival] . . . may prove the dawn of that glorious day").⁴

Rather than declining with the waning of religious enthusiasm in the late 1740s, millennialism became more widespread, at least in New England, because it attached itself to the spirit of British nationalism in England's war against France. New England ministers transferred the symbolism of the Antichrist from the Roman Church to the French government as the agent of political oppression and Catholic religion. After the close of the Seven Years War in 1763, Americans were appalled to discover that now the British government itself, having been undermined by corruption from within, had joined league with Satan. In the emerging Revolutionary conflict, Americans, especially New Englanders, used the categories of millennial thought previously applied to France to the new struggle for independence from England, and in the process some of them redefined their understanding of America's role in the world's redemption so that it included the preservation of not only true Christianity but also civil liberty.⁵ For instance, as John Adams surveyed the Christian era, he saw the people oppressed by a confederacy of two tyrannical systems, the "canon and the feudal law." The people suffered until "God in his benign providence raised up the champions who began and conducted the Reformation" which was nothing other than a popular revolt against this dual yoke. The Puritan emigration continued the movement for civil and religious liberty: "It was not religion alone, as is commonly supposed; but it was a love of universal liberty, and a hatred . . . of the infernal confederacy before described, that . . . accomplished the settlement of America." And now Adams saw Great Britain aiming at "an entire subversion of the whole system of our fathers, by the introduction of the canon and feudal law into America."⁶ Whereas Edwards had envisioned true Protestantism as the essence of the latter-day glory, the Revolutionary generation increasingly wedded the idea of freedom to the doctrine of a progressive millennium until republican liberty itself became both a prerequisite for and a fundamental element of the latter-day glory.

The successful revolution and institution of a republican government heightened America's sense of chosenness and provided the occasion for its public theologians to elaborate the relationship of the nation's millennial heritage to its new political system. Preaching to the Connecticut General Assembly in 1783 on the "political welfare of God's American Israel," Ezra Stiles, president of Yale, pointed to several evidences of America's divinely ordained destiny: a burgeoning population, the abolition of feudalistic land policies, checks against arbitrary government, and "Liberty, civil and religious." The last was crucial; the United States would be a model society and prime agent of the world's millennial destiny precisely because civil and religious liberty provided the right conditions for the flowering of true Christianity: "while Europe and Asia may hereafter learn that the most liberal principles of law and civil polity are to be found on this side of the Atlantick [sic], they may also find the true religion here depurated from the rust and corruption of ages, and learn from us to reform and restore the church to its primitive purity." Religion would be "depurated" because free speech and religious toleration would allow it to "receive its last, most liberal, and impartial examination."[7]

Civil and religious liberty, with the added elements of material abundance and technology, all found to an unprecedented degree in the new republic, became the commonplace justification for nineteenth-century America's millennial faith. In his often delivered sermon, "A Plea for the West," Lyman Beecher asserted that the millennium could not "come to pass under the existing civil organization of the nations." Rather it was "by the march of revolution and civil liberty, that the way of the Lord is to be prepared." And to the question: "from what nation shall the renovating power go forth?" the answer was, of course, that only the United States was "blessed with such experimental knowledge of free institutions" and the "pecuniary and moral power to evangelize the world."[8]

In the antebellum period, millennialism pervaded virtually every aspect of American Protestantism. Charles Grandison Finney, who shared honors with Beecher as the most eminent evangelist of the Second Great Awakening, sometimes would imprudently declare: "If the church will do all her duty, the millennium may come in this country in three years."[9] Even the sober-minded, non-evangelical William Ellery Channing was convinced that if Christians would reject the harsh, inscrutable deity of the Calvinists for the fatherly God of the Unitarians, this would "transform the world. Then will the new heaven and the new earth be created."[10] Millennial interest was so widespread among American Protestants that George Bush, writing in 1832, could proclaim: "No phraseology in prayer, in preaching, in the religious essay, or in the monthly-concert address is more common than that of *millennial* state, *millennial* reign, *millennial* purity, *millennial* glory, & c."[11]

Other currents in antebellum culture drew upon this Protestant tradition and developed it in new directions. Communitarian experiments, reform organizations, the peculiar American enthusiasm for health fads and the new half-sciences of phrenology and spiritualism—all these activities were, more often than not, conceived of as means to the millennium. For instance, according to the Grahamite American Physiological Society, which expounded the doctrines of health reformer Sylvester Graham concerning proper diet and sexual conduct, "the millennium can never reasonably be expected to arrive, until those laws which God has implanted in the physical nature of man are, equally with his moral laws, universally known and obeyed."[12] The prophets of spiritualism used millennialism as a philosophical basis for their new religion and in turn provided support for it. Mediums defended the authenticity of their occult power by explaining that as society progressed toward the millennial state, earth became more akin to heaven, thus facilitating communication between the two spheres. In some instances, celestial spirits, in response to the questions of earthly interlocutors, even gave their stamp of approval to schemes of political reform advanced as sure routes to the millennium.[13]

Millennialism in Whitman's Writings

The most notable feature of Whitman's early use of this millennial tradition is that he extends the process of politicizing the millennium. The Protestant faith is not mentioned, and political liberty, not piety, is the essence of the millennial character. In the early journalism, Whitman's understanding of historical progress might be considered a secular ideology except for the fact that he conceives of humans as creatures of God and America as designated by God to introduce a new era of freedom. Later, during the period in which he composed the early editions of the *Leaves*, Whitman's millennialism underwent a sea-change as he developed an evolutionary religious cosmology, an understanding of America's special mission based upon its political liberties and material wealth that closely resembled the Protestant interpretation of America's millennial role, and a dynamic religious psychology and new definition of the divine-human relationship that made individual spiritual development the essential ingredient for bringing about the millennial era. In his later years, Whitman's sense of millennial expectation became somewhat less intense, but he never gave up on his hope that the United States, guided by the new religion of the *Leaves*, would redeem the past by ushering in a new age of the spirit and attendant form of social organization that would, in effect, be the grand culmination of universal history.

In addition to the strong likelihood of Whitman's becoming acquainted with millennialist thought from such general sources as conversation and newspapers, it is most probable that he was introduced to these ideas by preachers and teachers in church programs he attended as a child and young adult. He was a student of the new Sunday school movement, first attending at Episcopal Saint Ann's in 1828, later at a Dutch Reformed school, and possibly at a Presbyterian church and Sunday school in 1832 or 1833.[14] Organized in 1824, the American Sunday School Union was but one unit of a larger phalanx of Protestant organizations being marshalled to evangelize the United States and the world (for example, the American Board of Commissioners for Foreign Missions, established in 1810; the Education Society, 1815; the Bible Society, 1816; the Colonization Society, 1817; the Tract Society, 1824; the Sabbath Union and the Home Missionary Society, 1828). These groups often used millennial imagery to motivate their armies of volunteer workers and to define their final objective. The possibility of Whitman's having received millennialist ideas from his Sunday school experiences is suggested by the fact that when the interdenominational American Sunday School Union was founded in 1824 it adopted as its motto two millennial verses from Isaiah: "The wolf shall dwell with the lamb, and the leopard shall lie down with the kid; and they shall not hurt nor destroy in all my holy mountain: for the earth shall be full of the knowledge of the Lord" (11:6, 9).[15] The first issue of the Union's publication for teachers, The *American Sunday School Magazine*, began by pronouncing Sunday schools the most efficient instrument for bringing about the millennium: "The period is rapidly hastening, when the praises of the Almighty will be the employment of nations. To this glorious consummation does every measure tend which bears the impress of divine approbation. Clothed with the experience of more than forty years, Sunday schools are brought to this unerring test, and receive the sanction of divine wisdom, which pronounces them '*very good*.' The varied schemes of Christian philanthropy are at once the hope and glory of our age: but of all she has devised to reclaim our fallen race; no one comes vested with higher pretensions to our favor, or more imperious demands upon our best service, than the one for which we now plead [the American Sunday School Union]."[16] Besides going to Sunday school, Whitman, either as a boy or young man, also observed revival services at the Methodist church on Sands Street in Brooklyn.[17] This was another likely source of exposure to millennialist ideas, for during this period revival ministers, in addition to bringing new souls into the churches, also directed converts into the new voluntary societies where they might assist in the final reformation of the world.[18]

In his early adulthood, after assuming the editorship of the New York *Aurora* in March, 1842, Whitman attended services at various local churches and reported some of his experiences.[19] Since this was a time of widespread revival and reform activity, Whitman probably heard some ministers exhort their congregations to work for the coming millennium. That his journalistic reports on the churches contain no allusions to this may be explained in part by the fact that these articles are largely devoid of doctrinal content. It seems that Whitman wanted to avoid ruffling the varied theological feathers of his readers. His personal convictions may also have made him disinclined to spread the idea of a specifically Christian version of the millennium, for other articles Whitman wrote in the *Aurora* indicate that he hoped for a coming millennium, but that he did not conceive of it in Christian terms.

A frequent attender of church services during the late 1840s when he began jotting down ideas for the *Leaves*,[20] Whitman often wrote articles for the Monday *Daily Eagle* which described the church he had visited the previous day.[21] Whitman was an admirer of Henry Ward Beecher who, like his father, Lyman, and brother, Edward, was a fervent millennialist. In 1849 Whitman attended a revival that Beecher conducted at the new Plymouth Church,[22] and in 1850 he wrote a sympathetic article on Beecher's preaching style for the Brooklyn *Daily Advertizer*.[23] Whitman is also believed to be the author of a series of articles on the Brooklyn churches which appeared in the *Advertizer* in 1850.[24] So it is most likely that he was hearing millennialist ideas preached from various pulpits during the period in which he began to write the *Leaves*.

By the time Whitman had assumed the editorship of the *Aurora*, he was also a reader and contributor to *The United States Magazine and Democratic Review* whose liberal editor, John L. O'Sullivan, espoused a theory of democracy that blended liberal republicanism and the American Protestant sense of chosenness. Labeling democracy as both the "cause of Humanity" and the "cause of Christianity,"[25] O'Sullivan defined it as essentially a faith in human-kind's ability to organize itself in terms of "the *voluntary principle*, the princi-ple of *freedom*."[26] He also conceived of America as having a special God-given role in world history: "to carry forward the noble mission entrusted to her of going before the nations of the world as the representative of the democratic principle and as the constant living exemplar of its results."[27]

In a March 30, 1842, *Aurora* editorial entitled "Defining Our Position," Whitman argued, in language less Christian than O'Sullivan's but with a simi-lar emphasis upon the American experiment in freedom, that the United States should not imitate European culture because America had a "higher and holier destiny, a more worthy mission." There was "in this republic the advantages and the capacities, for evolving the Great Problem—the problem of how far Man, the masterpiece of cunningest Omniscience, can have his nature per-fected by himself, and can be trusted to govern himself." America might serve as an example to other nations, "spreading to the gaze of the world, the glori-ous spectacle of a continent peopled by *freemen*."[28] Here in rudimentary form are expressed the central ideas that later inform Whitman's notion of America as a religious democracy. Blessed with material abundance and republican liberties ("the advantages and capacities"), America has a sacred mission: namely, to determine for the world how far humans can perfect themselves and thus be trusted to live free from governmental restraints. Implicit in this editorial is the belief that the United States is appointed by God to bring into the world a new era of human fulfillment and freedom.

This point is made more clearly several years later, in 1846, when Whitman, as editor of the Brooklyn *Eagle*, explicitly presents the United States as the agent for the liberation of humanity:

> For the time will surely come—that holy millennium of liberty—when the 'Vic-tory of endurance born' shall lift the masses of the down-trodden of Europe, and make them achieve something of that destiny which we may suppose God intends eligible for mankind. And this problem is to be worked out through the people, territory, and government of the United States.[29]

In his 1846 *Eagle* editorials on the Mexican War, Whitman invoked this no-tion of America's divinely appointed role to justify U.S. expansionism. An in-crease of United States territory was an "increase of human happiness and lib-erty." Mexico with "her superstition, her burlesque upon freedom, her actual tyranny by the few over the many" did not provide a political environment in which citizens could become more free and perfect. In short, what had Mex-ico "to do with the great mission of peopling the New World with a noble race? Be it ours, to achieve that mission!"[30] The military conflict was itself pro-ducing signs of an "ameliorated humanity" and Whitman, drawing upon the millennial imagery of Isaiah 2:4, asks if it is not a step toward the end times: "the advent of that holy era when all swords shall be beat into plough shares and spears into pruning-hooks?"[31]

Whitman's temperance novel, *Franklin Evans*, demonstrates his familiarity with one contemporary use of millennial language. As the temperance crusade grew it became closely associated with revival activities and millennialist aspirations, and many temperance workers began to make exaggerated spiritual claims for their cause. Signing the temperance pledge was often accepted as visible evidence of conversion, victory over the bottle ("demon rum") was identified with the final defeat of Satan, and world-wide abstinence with the universal redemption of humankind and the fullness of the latter days.[32] Whitman draws upon this alliance of temperance and millennialist themes in his novel when the protagonist, Evans, has a vision of the United States twenty years in the future celebrating what "appeared to be some general holyday." The dream scene celebrates the liberation of the last person from enslavement not only to alcohol but also to the "Snake-Tempter." Exulting in humanity's final victory over sin, one character proclaims: "Now man is free! He walks upon the earth, worthy the name of one whose prototype is God! We hear the mighty chorus sounding loud and long, Regenerated! Regenerated!"[33] It is unclear how sincere Whitman was in his support of the temperance movement[34]—certainly he did not favor total abstinence—but *Franklin Evans* does provide clear evidence of his familiarity with antebellum millennialism as it appeared in the temperance literature of the period.

As Whitman began composing passages for the *Leaves* in the late 1840s, his millennialism received further support from his growing interest in phrenology. Criticism emphasizes that Whitman was attracted to phrenology because it provided a faculty psychology, seemingly grounded in medical science, that he could use in his poetry, and because he received a needed tonic for his self-confidence and emerging identity as a poet from one or more flattering readings of the bumps and contours of his cranium. But another important ingredient in phrenology's appeal was the encouragement and support it provided to Whitman's millennial hopes.[35]

In July 1849 when he strolled into the Nassau Street office of Fowler and Wells, America's most eminent "practical phrenologists," to have his head read, he had been clipping and underlining articles about phrenology for three years. Some of these were from the nation's leading phrenological publication, the *American Phrenological Journal*, whose editor, Orson Squires Fowler, regularly expressed a millennial faith in articles with such titles as "Progress," "Human Progress," and "Progression, A Law of Nature." Whitman may have read Fowler's long response to a reader who did "not at all doubt the truth and coming reality of prophetic predictions," but wondered if the millennium were not in fact still a very distant prospect. Fowler replied that although he had "unequivocally argued a prospective millenium from that law of 'progression' set forth in this and preceding volumes," he had never asserted when it would be completed. Nevertheless, since the "millenial perfection" was to be achieved by "human agency in co-operation with this progressive principle established by the Deity," then it could be achieved soon for "it was left for *man* to say *when.*" Fowler admitted that it was true that progressive developments in the past had "been exceedingly gradual," but he was "strongly inclined to the opinion that these changes will be much more rapid hereafter than they have been heretofore." Calling attention to the rapid advances of recent years—"see what five years have done! Then what will twenty more do?"— Fowler predicted the millennium would occur "within our own life time," and he promised to elaborate further upon this in a series of articles on Republicanism that would show the "influence of civil liberty on human progression" and provide "additional evidence that these changes are close at hand, and may even surprise us by the suddenness of their advent."[36]

Over the next two years Fowler presented the proposed articles which described "the declaration of our Independence as the SECOND great event [Christianity was the first] or era of human destiny." The American revolution had not only freed the people from the oppression of aristocratic institutions and values, but also set in motion a process that would regenerate their very beings: it was "'the great salvation' of our race—physically, intellectually and morally." From America republicanism and total regeneration were destined to spread rapidly throughout the world: "Nothing can now arrest—nothing even retard—that complete revolution which is now regenerating our race, and ushering in the millennium."[37] Perhaps of special interest to Whitman was Fowler's prediction of a new universal religion that would be democratic in character, open to modern science, and vital to the life of the people:

> Though we shall have no new principles of religion, for these principles are as immutable as the throne of God, yet we shall have a new interpretation and practice of them. Its perversions will be obviated, and its intrinsic beauties, now cloaked under sectarian deformities and monstrosities, be developed, and beautify, instead of deteriorating mankind. It will not then, as now, interdict progression, but be its mighty lever. It will not then, as now, consist in nominal professions, but in the habitual PRACTICE of goodness. It will not then, as now, assume a proud, touch-me-not, aristocratic air. . . . It will not then, as now, be pompous and gaudy . . . but will seek out the poor and degraded, and educate their intellects, while it calls forth their souls in holy aspirations.[38]

Whitman was also interested in animal-magnetism or mesmerism, especially after 1848 when its vocabulary and concepts were embraced by the new spiritualist movement which claimed to communicate with departed souls who now existed in higher spiritual realms. In addition to providing a proof of human immortality, the advent of spiritualism itself was seen as a significant step toward the millennium, a clear sign that humans were now more intellectually and spiritually advanced than in previous ages. Probably no spiritualist would have interested Whitman more than Andrew Jackson Davis, who used his widespread recognition as a "philosophical" spiritualist to outline how the United States might be reorganized to effect the millennium. In his best-known book, *The Principles of Nature, the Divine Revelations, and a Voice to Man-*

kind, which was published in 1847 and went through eleven editions by 1852, the long-winded Davis stressed that the progressive evolution of nature and movement of history had brought America to the dawn of the millennial era; all that was now needed was a just distribution of the nation's wealth: "For all must repent, or, in other words, receive the conviction that distributive justice must pervade the social world before God's kingdom can come, and his will be done on earth as it is in heaven—or throughout all the spheres of celestial happiness."[39]

Like others who longed for the latter days, Davis saw the signs of the times as pregnant with apocalyptic import: "The great movements of the day are all advancing the public to this desirable consummation. The efforts for the abolition of slavery; those for the repeal of capital punishment; the reform of prison discipline; the temperance reformation . . . and finally the movements among every nation of the earth, both social, scientific, and spiritual—all proclaim the approach of this sublime era." And of course the United States would play the decisive role in this stupendous drama: "Our country, its interests, wealth, and government, are fearfully in a peace-destroying war, the result of which will be a powerful reaction on every mind . . . . The era is nigh: the judgment-day when wisdom shall predominate, will soon arrive; and this will banish ignorance, error, prejudice, and fanaticism, from the earth. A general revolution is at hand."[40]

There can be no doubt that both phrenology and spiritualism had a considerable influence upon Whitman during the years in which he was composing the first edition of the *Leaves*. He conceived of them as valid new sciences and wanted to incorporate, albeit with a studied vagueness, their general principles in his poetry.[41] Earlier, in August 1842, he had written in the *New York Sunday Times* that he had ceased to be "a devout disbeliever in the science of animal Magnetism" and declared that it "reveals at once the existence of a whole new world of truth, grand, fearful, profound, relating to that great mystery, in the shadow of which we live and move and have our being. . . ."[42] In the 1855 Preface he declares the "anatomist, chemist, astronomer, phrenologist, spiritualist . . . are the lawgivers of poets" (*PW*, II, 448), and his own review of the 1855 *Leaves* in the *American Phrenological Journal* describes the poet as "pregnant with the deductions of the geologist, the astronomer, the great antiquary, the chemist, the phrenologist, the spiritualist. . . ."[43] The technical vocabulary of both "sciences" are sprinkled throughout the *Leaves*, most prominently in the use of such mesmeric terms as "magnetic" and "electric" to describe spiritual relations and states and such phrenological terms as "amativeness" to describe love between the sexes and "adhesiveness" as a synonym for male comradeship.

In addition to millennialism, Whitman was also attracted to these two pseudosciences by a number of other ideas that were associated with them. Phrenology, especially as promoted by the Fowler brothers and Wells, stressed human improvability and perfectibility. Like Whitman's journalism and later writings, their lectures, books, and journals advocated enlightened views in the areas of education, penology, sexuality, temperance and diet, women's dress, and women's rights in general. The many parallels between Davis's spiritualism and Whitman's vision can be only briefly suggested. Both believed in evolutionary progression, including the notion that everything in the universe, even inorganic matter, had an internal spiritual principle that incessantly ascended to higher stages of spiritual organization. Concerning the soul, both maintained that its intuitions were the highest form of knowledge, that it could read the symbols of God in nature, that it was capable of union with God, and that it would progress eternally after death. In politics, both championed greater sexual equality and the cause of the working class. Both believed that American democracy, now leading the march of history, would introduce a higher form of spiritual democracy (Davis's term was "harmonial autocracy") characterized by absolute personal freedom and social harmony. Both espoused a doctrine of progressive revelation, and each proclaimed himself the prophet of a new spiritual vision that would liberate religion from creeds, priests, and religious institutions. Clearly the seer from Poughkeepsie and the poet from Paumanok had kindred visionary souls, and it seems likely, given Whitman's strong interest in spiritualism, that he was familiar with the ideas of this most famous of spiritualists.[44]

All these religious, political, and "scientific" currents must be kept in mind when considering the millennialism of Whitman's poetry and the issue of Emerson's influence. Clearly, Whitman had a rather fully developed millennial theory of history before he read Emerson closely. Furthermore, unlike these sources of influence, Emerson did not provide Whitman with a clear endorsement of his early millennialism, for as was true of his views about spiritual evolution in nature, Emerson's ideas on historical progress were guarded and intentionally somewhat vague. Sometimes, as in "Self-Reliance," Emerson explicitly rejects a belief in historical progress: "Society never advances. It recedes as fast on one side as it gains on the other."[45] Instead of dreaming of the future perfect world of the millennialists, a world that was to be built in part by human advancements in politics, technology, and economics, Emerson was more inclined to think of recovering the primordial garden of myth by restoring to the soul the powers it had allegedly lost in the course of history: "The problem of restoring to the world original and eternal beauty, is solved by the redemption of the soul."[46] In "History" Emerson does not develop the idea of historical progress but instead the notion that history may be read as a texture of religious symbols and thus the "world exists for the education of each man."[47] For Emerson, unlike most of his contemporaries, a democratic form of government was not better or higher, but only more appropriate for the times: "In this country, we are very vain of our political institutions. . . . They are not better, but only fitter for us."[48] Nor in Emerson's estimate were the current programs for moral and political reform to be considered efficient engines of progress: "Our young people have thought and written much on labor and reform, and for all that they have written, neither the world nor themselves have got on a step."[49] In "Experience" Emerson does eventually profess a vague faith in progress, but his is not the idea of progress of the progressive millennialists who believed they could read the course of historical development and usher in the millennial era by their own conscious efforts. Instead Emerson asserted that the "results of life [of one's individual efforts] are uncalculated and uncalculable";[50] his belief in progress was merely a faith that eventually, because of the guidance of a superintending spiritual force, the seemingly disparate, conflicting activities and goals of the human race would merge so that all would "one day be *members*, and obey one will."[51]

Although Emerson repeatedly called for a new cultural system and representative personality for the American people, he did not conceive of these as the culmination of history and the perfection of human nature. He anticipated not the end times but only new or different times. His point was that life in the United States was characterized by fresh material and intellectual realities and that these needed to be ordered by new institutions and informed by a new religious vision: "There are new lands, new men, new thoughts. Let us demand our own works and laws and worship."[52] The quondam Unitarian minister asserted that this needed cultural revolution required a new faith derived from fresh revelation. In his Sunday evening address honoring the six graduating seniors of Harvard Divinity School, he noted the "universal decay and now almost death of faith in society," and declared that "the need was never greater of new revelation than now."[53] In "The Poet" Emerson emphasized that the inspired bard was to be the agent of this new revelation, depicting him as the founder of a new religion: "All that we call sacred history attests that the birth of a poet is the principal event in chronology." In a graceful exciting closure, he summoned "the timely man, the new religion, the reconciler, whom all things await."[54]

Whitman felt the force and excitement of these ideas, but in adapting Emerson's lines to his own purposes he gave them a new slant by combining his mentor's call for a poet-prophet with his own long-standing millennialism. The result was the post-Christian millennialism that informs Whitman's later writings, appearing not only in the poetry of the *Leaves*, but also in the prose of various prefaces, the unpublished political tract entitled "The Eighteenth Presidency!" and *Democratic Vistas*, all of which anticipate an imminent spiritual revolution which will inaugurate a new religious era in which history and humanity reach their divinely ordained culmination.

Whitman based his mature millennial faith, developed in the years in which he composed the first edition of the *Leaves*, upon America's existing political and economic achievements. Like Lyman Beecher, Orson Fowler, and other proponents of millennialism, Whitman was also convinced of America's special role in the cosmic drama of redemption by the fact that the United States had apparently already removed so many obstacles to human development. He makes this point repeatedly, but perhaps most clearly in *Democratic Vistas* where he asserts that American society had passed through "two grand stages of preparation-strata." The first was political: the "putting on record the political foundation rights of immense masses of people." The second was technological and material: "wealth, produce, labor-saving machines, iron, cotton, local, State and continental railways." But as important as these stages were, they were of no significance in themselves; their function was merely to liberate the citizenry from material want and political oppression and thereby provide the opportunity for them to realize their spiritual potential. The first two stages were to find their fulfillment in a third: "a sublime and serious Religious Democracy" (*PW*, 409-410).[55] Accordingly, Whitman offered the following assessment of the American political system: "For it is not that democracy is of exhaustive account, in itself. Perhaps, indeed, it is, (like Nature,) of no account in itself." It derived significance from giving the citizenry freedom and opportunity for self-realization: "and now, impediments removed, to stand and start without humiliation, and equal with the rest; to commence . . . the grand experiment of development, whose end, (perhaps requiring several generations,) may be the forming of a full-grown man or woman—that *is* something" ("Democratic Vistas," *PW*, 380).

The transition to Whitman's ideal spiritual democracy was to be brought about by a new order of religious poetry that would nurture a cultural revolution. The millennial basis of this new religion, first presented in the long beginning poem of the 1855 *Leaves* (later entitled "Song of Myself") is discussed in chapter 5, but its principal idea may be briefly indicated by analyzing a series of notes Whitman wrote in the mid-1850s for an intended set of lectures on religion. In these Whitman rejects the existing Christian denominations as inappropriate for America: "who does not see that the outward & technical religious belief of the sects of this age is a mere crust crumbling everywhere under our feet? Who does not know that with all these churches, ministers and all the surface deference paid to the sects the souls of the people need something deeper and higher—have irrevocably gone from those churches" (*Workshop*, p. 42). Christianity and other existing faiths were not inherently bad, for they had "done the work that was for them [to do]" (*NPM*, VI, 2086), but they were now dated and Whitman refers to them as "passing chrysalis Religions" (*NPM*, VI, 2082), suggesting that they kept the human soul in a protected and quiescent state appropriate for earlier historical periods. But now political liberty and abundant material resources had given Americans a new sense of possibility. The people were "awake" and wanted more than the "mummeries" offered by the churches (*NPM*, VI, 2076); they needed a "real athletic and fit religion" (*NPM*, VI, 2061), that is, a religion that would help them to realize their full spiritual potential.

Central to this new religion was a new understanding of human existence that made humans into gods:

> The whole scene shifts.—The relative positions change.—Man comes forward inherent, superb,—the soul, the judge, the common average man advances,—ascends to place.—God disappears.—The whole idea of God, as hitherto, for reasons, presented in the religions of the world, for the thousands of past years . . . disappears.—(*NPM*, VI, 2097)

In this passage it seems that Whitman is developing a theology like the one Wallace Stevens formulates in "Sunday Morning," which denies the existence of a transcendent deity. But there is a crucial difference, for Whitman rejects not a belief in God but in the "idea of God" as presented in previous religions. Conceiving of the divine images of Christianity and all other religions as unconscious, partial projections of spiritual capabilities inherent in human nature, Whitman would destroy these idols by disclosing their source to be the impulses of the divinity inherent in the human spirit. But above humans there was still the high God who was the ultimate source of the entire creation, including humanity. Yet Whitman's understanding of the human soul as an expression of divine immanence and his notion of the soul's continuing development in the afterlife combined to make the distance between humans and God a difference of degree and not of kind. In due season, any human soul was "eligible to advance onward to be as supreme as any—I say that all goes on to be eligible to become one of the Supremes" (*NPM*, VI, 2043). Whitman's new religion would not deny God but would rather frcc the American people from the spiritual repression inherent in previous religions by informing them of the breathtaking fact that they could now realize their full humanity and ultimately become "one of the Supremes."

In sum, Whitman's view of contemporary history and his belief in a millennial future emerge out of his conviction that, as a result of existing political and material achievements, a new religious vision could now bring about the absolute liberation of humanity and disclose vistas of boundless possibility to each man and woman. In order to nurture this new race of humans, Whitman's vision had to free the American people from their major forms of psychological repression. Consequently, the major themes of Whitman's poetry may be briefly listed as a strategic assault upon what he considered to be the principal strongholds of repression. To liberate his readers from the fear that human existence was without meaning, Whitman would show that both evolution and history revealed a divinely ordained movement toward perfection in which death was merely a passage to a new and higher life. To free them from a socially induced sense of inferiority, he would announce an absolute democracy in which the average woman and man would, for the first time in history, be able to realize their inherent possibility. To deliver them from sexual repression, he would proclaim the sanctity of the body and passions; and he would release males from estrangement from their deepest selves and other men by encouraging masculine friendship as the highest form of religious experience.

It is hard to extract isolated passages from Whitman's writings which do justice to the complexity of his millennial faith because, as becomes evident in the rest of this chapter and the ensuing analysis of the *Leaves*, millennialism is not one item in Whitman's philosophy of history but the very form of his vision. Nevertheless it is perhaps helpful to attempt a brief overview of Whitman's millennialism in order to indicate how this idea continued to inform his poetry throughout his lifetime.

Whitman introduced the millennial message of his poetry with the 1855 Preface, which proclaims America the appropriate arena for the redemption of the race. All that is needed is a new order of poetry to acquaint the citizenry with their limitless potential for spiritual development. The introduction announces that the nation's culture and manners, while still held back by the vestiges (the "slough") of previous political, social, and religious systems, are on the verge of a radical transformation. Free of oppression and artificial constraints, American life is close to conforming with the divinely implanted laws of human nature: "Here is action untied from strings. . . . Here is the hospitality which for ever indicates heroes. Here the performance, disdaining the trivial" (*PW*, 435). Clearly America was ordained to house a vastly improved people, for its geographical expanse and natural grandeur would appear "monstrous without a corresponding largeness and generosity of the spirit of the citizen" (*PW*, 435–36). The beginning movement closes with Whitman's definition of America's purpose: it is ultimately not to be known for its fine cities or the "returns of commerce" or "shows of exterior victory" but for "the realization of full-sized men" (*PW*, 436–37).

To this country, brimming with potential and poised for change, Whitman introduces his figure of the God-like poet. He holds "steady faith" in a "time straying toward infidelity" (*PW*, 437); he "hardly knows pettiness and triviality" (*PW*, 438); he is "complete in himself" (*PW*, 438), "the one complete lover" (*PW*, 441), and is "himself the age transfigur'd" (*PW*, 454). This divine figure will elevate his compatriots with a vision that liberates them from all inherited modes of thought and conduct that deny their infinite potential or desecrate the human spirit: "There is not left [in his vision] any vestige of despair, or misanthropy, or cunning, or exclusiveness . . . and no man thenceforward shall be degraded for ignorance or weakness or sin" (*PW*, 438). The poet will launch his readers on the path to perfection: "A great poem is no finish to a man or woman, but rather a beginning" (*PW*, 455). He takes people "into live regions previously unattain'd" so that there "shall be a man cohered out of tumult and chaos—" (*PW*, 456). The reader is to realize that she or he is equal to the poet and capable, ultimately, of becoming a God: "The messages of great poems to each man and woman are, Come to us on equal terms. . . . We are no better than you. . . . Did you suppose there could be only one Supreme? We affirm there can be unnumber'd Supremes" (*PW*, 445).

In concluding Whitman predicts that a new order of poets will arise to sing this vision of human perfectibility and that they will replace existing religions: "There will soon be no more priests. Their work is done. A new order shall arise, and they shall be the priests of man, and every man shall be his own priest." Resplendent in their new sense of self-worth and absolutely confident of the goodness of their world, they "shall not deign to defend immortality or God, or the perfection of things, or liberty, or the exquisite beauty and reality of the soul." From America this faith would radiate to "the remainder of the earth" (*PW*, 456).

This proclamation of an approaching millennial dawn is repeated with further elaboration in the long opening poem, "Song of Myself" (see chapter 5), which Whitman uses to present the cardinal ideas and announce himself as the first prophet of the new religion which would transform the people, institutions, and culture of America and, ultimately, the world. The poem continues to make the major statement of the opening movement of subsequent editions where its intended purpose is to establish Whitman as the poet-prophet of a new faith and America as the agent of the world's millennial destiny.

Coming so quickly after the first edition, the 1856 *Leaves*, with its twenty new poems, contains little that adds to our understanding of Whitman's millennial outlook. Perhaps the most notable statement occurs in the Preface. Whitman, decrying the absence of sex in the writings of "savants, poets, historians, biographers, and the rest," asserts that "the courageous soul, for a year or two to come, may be proved by faith in sex."[56] This suggests that he thought that at least one major obstacle to the millennium, sexual repression, could be speedily removed. Later, as he wrote "Children of Adam" and "Calamus" for the 1860 *Leaves*, Whitman believed that he was composing programs to improve American physiology and liberate heterosexual love and repressed male tenderness, thus taking several large strides down the path to perfection.[57]

In the 1860 edition Whitman's belief in America's millennial mission prompts him to propose a new historical chronology. Going one step beyond Fowler and others who conceived of a course of history in which the most crucial advances toward the end times were the birth of Christ and the American Revolution. Whitman suggests that history's pivotal event was not the life of Christ but the Declaration of Independence. Thus the initials "T.S." or "The States" and "These States" are used to indicate the year of the book's publication—"Boston, Thayer and Eldridge, Year 85 of The States, (1860–61)" —and the dates of a number of poems: for example, "Europe, the 72nd and 73rd Years of These States." In the years after the Civil War Whitman identified most closely with Lincoln, conceiving of himself, like Lincoln, as playing a key role in the preservation of the Union and the emancipation of its people, but in the latter 1850s he entertains the notion of himself as a poetic Washington bringing about the spiritual liberation made possible by the earlier political one: "Washington made free the body of America for that was first in order. Now comes one who will make free the American soul."[58]

But there was no immediate amelioration of American character or culture in response to Whitman's bold summons. Americans did not become less money-minded or develop a greater commitment to the commonweal. Social distortions brought on by the burgeoning capitalist system continued, and the possibility that Whitman's sacred union might fall into civil war became increasingly ominous. So with no evidence of the anticipated spiritual revolution, Whitman was forced to acknowledge a lethargy of the national spirit, but he pronounced it temporary and continued to predict an imminent awakening:

> Then I will sleep awhile yet, for I see that these States sleep, for reasons;
> (With gathering murk, with muttering thunder and lambent shoots we all duly
>   awake,
> South, North, East, West, inland and seaboard, we will surely awake.)
>
> ("To the States," 1860)

Yet despite this postponement of hope, Whitman was still convinced, as he proclaims in "A Broadway Pageant" (1860), that all the struggles and achievements of the past would find their justification in the new society that was taking shape in the United States and would then spread from this center outward around the globe:

> And you Libertad of the world!
> You shall sit in the middle well-pois'd thousands and thousands of years,
> ....
> The box-lid is but perceptibly open'd, nevertheless the perfume pours copiously
>   out of the whole box.
> ....
> Were the centuries steadily footing it that way, all the while unknown, for you,
>   for reasons?
> They are justified, they are accomplish'd, they shall now be turn'd the other way
>   also, to travel toward you thence,
> They shall now also march obediently eastward for your sake Libertad.
>
> (Section 3)

For Whitman, America's geographical position was a fit emblem of its spiritual meaning. Human culture had moved westward from Asia through Europe to America where it not only completed its circular movement around the globe but also fulfilled the purpose of the long historical process.

With the coming of the Civil War, Whitman initially interpreted the excitement surrounding the Union effort as the long-awaited national awakening:

> I waited the bursting forth of the pent fire—on the water and air I waited long;
> But now I no longer wait, I am fully satisfied, I am glutted,

> I have witness'd the true lightning, I have witness'd my cities electric.
> ("Rise O Days from Your Fathomless Deeps," ll. 43–45)

Later the war's long scarlet course and Lincoln's assassination curbed Whitman's enthusiasm, but it nevertheless remained a fact that the Union, the repository of all millennial hopes, had survived. This enabled Whitman to incorporate the war and his war poems into his millennial vision by, among other things, adding the introductory poem "To Thee Old Cause" (1871) which affirmed that the recent "strange sad war" was fought for the "eternal march" of the "old cause," by which Whitman meant the freedom and perfection of the race. Furthermore, the crucial fact about Lincoln's death, as Whitman interpreted it for his millennial vision in the "Lilacs" elegy (discussed in chapter 6), was not the assassination itself, but the fact that Lincoln's life had been preserved until the end of the war, enabling him to guide the Union through the national crisis so that it could continue to pursue its divinely ordained destiny.

In the years after the Civil War, Whitman's sense of expectation became more tempered but he never lost his faith that American society would soon inaugurate some basic transformation, even consummation, of the course of history. The 1872 Preface again asserted that nations and civilization were "closing up, toward some long-prepared, most tremendous denouement" in which the United States were "unquestionably designated for the leading parts," for in America "history and humanity seem to seek to culminate" (*PW*, 460). Throughout the 1870s Whitman proclaimed America, the ideal spiritual America he defined in his poems, to be the purpose of universal history.[59] It is pronounced the "scheme's culmination" ("Song of the Universal," l. 43) and the *"purpose of all,"* where would appear the *"culminating man"* ("Song of the Redwood-Tree," ll. 56 & 53). In "Thou Mother With thy Equal Brood," the ship of American democracy floats not for itself alone but for the sake of all of history: "Earth's *résumé* entire floats on thy keel O ship, is steadied by thy spars, / With thee Time voyages in trust, the antecedent nations sink or swim with thee" (ll. 51–52). From America would unfold the millennial future, with a regenerated humanity living in perfect harmony with God, envisioned in "The Mystic Trumpeter" (Section 8):

> Marchers of victory—man disenthral'd—the conqueror at last,
> Hymns to the universal God from universal man—all joy!
> . . . .
> War, sorrow, suffering gone—the rank earth purged—nothing but joy left!
> The ocean fill'd with joy—the atmosphere all joy!

Yet the millennial theme in the poetry of the 1870s and 1880s is dulled. For various reasons the earlier immediacy and expectation give way to a settled tone more akin to ecclesiastical litany than revolutionary manifesto. Having suffered a stroke in 1873, Whitman was physically wasted. In the aftermath of the war, he perhaps harbored the long-term numbing depression that overtakes many who either experience the worse ravages of combat or attend to those who have. In addition to physical and psychological impediments, there were political factors that tempered Whitman's voice. During his political formation in the 1830s and 1840s he embraced a liberal Democratic ideology that was implicitly anarchic in its emphasis upon individual freedom and responsibility and anticipation of a progressive reduction of governmental control. The poetry of the 1850s and 1860s heightened the perfectionist and millennial tendencies present in his earlier thought, but then the Union victory failed to usher in the anticipated political parousia. God's chosen nation had been preserved; slavery, which violated American principles and robbed manual labor of its dignity, had been eliminated. But with these threats removed, there emerged in greater clarity another obstacle to the people's advancement: the power of the capitalist class. Whitman's perfectionist and millennial creed had always had an economic basis. It assumed that in America, for the first time in history, the masses would be free from want. But what if this material foundation were removed by the political and economic power of the wealthy? One possible solution was to call for new governmental regulation, but Whitman never considered this option seriously because it violated essential tenets of his faith. Having forged a political vision that called for a heightened self-regulation that would be nurtured by a new poetic vision, Whitman was unable to develop an alternate conceptual framework that allowed for an adequate response to this new problem "of social and economic organization" ("The Tramp and Strike Question" [1882], *PW*, 527). Faced with this dilemma, Whitman's response was to wish the difficulty away by treating it as a passing stage rather than a structural problem. So in the 1880s he continued to reiterate his theory of stages of American development. For the past century, the United States had provided "the first general aperture and opening-up to the average human commonalty [sic] . . . the eligibilities to wealth and wordly success and eminence." Now there would "certainly ensue other stages" for it would soon be "fully realized that ostensible wealth and money-making, show, luxury, &c., imperatively necessitate something beyond—namely, the sane eternal moral and spiritual-esthetic attributes" and these will finally "make the blood and brawn of the best American individualities" (*PW*, 530).

With this comforting outlook, Whitman did not have to revise his vision, but only repeat his earlier millennial message and wait for a new awakening of the national spirit. Time would prove that the nation was still on its ordained millennial course. To the end Whitman continued to insist that epochal events of nineteenth-century America would justify the past and redeem the world. Thus a small poem of 1890, "On, on the Same, Ye Jocund Twain," sums up Whitman's understanding of America history and his four decades of poetic effort. Democratic nation and democratic poet (the "Jocund Twain")

had resolutely marched onward together, ever disclosing the working out of
the divine will through the course of American history:

> I chant my nation's crucial stage, (America's haply humanity's)—the trial great,
>   the victory great,
> A strange *eclaircissement* of all the masses past, the eastern world, the ancient,
>   medieval,
> Here, here from wanderings, strayings, lessons, wars, defeats—here at the west
>   a voice triumphant—justifying all.
>
> ("On, on the Same, Ye Jocund Twain!")

Millennialism and Perfectionism

The Protestant commitment to the idea of a progressively realized millennium required a positive theory of human nature and a belief in the possibility of widespread moral improvement that was antithetical to the received
Calvinism, with its emphasis upon moral depravity and predestination,
which had dominated two centuries of American religious thought. Accordingly, in the three decades before the Civil War, the most important change
in antebellum Protestant theology was a transition from Calvinism to Arminianism, and the attendant emergence of a radical emphasis upon Christian
perfection.

Of the Evangelicals, it was Charles Grandison Finney who marshalled the
most popular assault upon Calvinism. Although an ordained minister in the
Presbyterian Church, which officially embraced Calvinism, Finney, with a
near-awesome disdain, dismissed the Westminster Confession, the credo of
American Calvinists, as a "wonderful theological fiction."[60] A product of his
busy, pragmatic times, Finney developed and practiced a theology of revivalism
which in its energy and operational simplicity rivaled Davy Crockett's dictum
for the conduct of politics: "Be sure you're right and then go ahead." With
his Calvinistic perspective, Jonathan Edwards could only account for the revivals and numerous conversions of the First Great Awakening by attributing
them to the miraculous workings of God's mysterious providence. Finney, the
"Father of Modern Revivalism," in promoting the Second Great Awakening,
denied the need of waiting for God to shower down his grace. For Finney, a
revival of religion was not a miracle but the inevitable product of correct methods: "The connection between the right use of means for a revival and a revival
is as philosophically sure as between the right use of means to raise grain and
a crop of wheat."[61] Rejecting Calvinism's emphasis upon predestination and
human passivity in the conversion process as a doctrine of "cannot-ism,"
Finney insisted that religion "is something to do, not something to wait for,"[62]
thus giving his followers a personal responsibility for their spiritual welfare

that was consistent with their new experiences of political citizenship and economic individualism.

Finney instructed young converts not to aspire merely to be "as good Christians as the old church members," but to "aim at being holy" and not rest satisfied till they were "as perfect as God." "Perfect as God" and "perfect obedience to the law of God"—with phrases such as these Finney delineated his image of the true Christian.[63]

When this doctrine of perfectionism received its first clear exposition in a series of sermons Finney delivered in New York City in the winter of 1836–37, his New School colleagues (the Presbyterian and Congregational ministers who, influenced by the theology of Yale's Nathaniel Taylor were trying, as rapidly as discretion would allow, to move their denominations to a softer Calvinism and beyond to Arminianism) greeted his position with the same drawn faces that Andrews Norton and other Unitarian moderates would, in the succeeding year, receive Emerson's Divinity School Address, and for the same reason: both groups feared their efforts to effect a more moderate theological reform would be rejected as a result of their association with the radicalism of brash upstarts.

Yet Finney's call for perfection was far from being the cry of a lone eccentric; it proved to be but one voice of a growing chorus. In a series of six sermons published in 1835, the Reverend Edward Beecher, son of Lyman and president of Illinois College, proclaimed that the "glorious advent of the kingdom of God is near at hand" and that what "the exigencies of the age" now required was a "COMPLETE, FULLY-DEVELOPED, AND WELL-BALANCED holy character."[64] Accordingly, he encouraged his audience to "aim at the standard of entire perfection: and no one should aim at any thing lower."[65]

In the late 1830s and early 1840s exponents of perfectionism also arose among the experimental religious communities and those striving for radical political reform. Perfectionist aspirations led John Humphrey Noyes to found his community at Putney, Vermont (later relocated at Oneida, New York). As a means of spreading his new light to others, Noyes first outlined his views in the community's organ, *The Perfectionist*, and they were later reprinted in 1838 as *The Way of Holiness*. The foundation of Noyes's theology was his dating of the Second Coming and the beginning of the Christian dispensation not with the life of Christ but with the fall of Jerusalem in A.D. 62. Accordingly, it was possible for nineteenth-century Christians to attain to even higher levels of holiness than had been realized by the leaders of the early Church, for the apostles and disciples lived in the "*latter-day glory of Judaism*" without benefit of the New Covenant. Arguing that Paul, although "living in the mere dawn of the dispensation of the second coming," had nevertheless "preached and practiced perfect holiness," Noyes proclaimed to his readers how "*much more* may we, living in the nineteenth century of that dispensation, believe and confess that Christ has made an end of sins."[66]

Like Noyes, the pacifist and abolitionist leader William Lloyd Garrison also believed that Christ's second coming was a spiritual event that had occurred in the first century and that made it possible for subsequent Christians to live free of sin. Perfectionism was the converse side of Garrison's commitments to non-resistance and abolitionism. An editorial entitled "Perfection" in *The Liberator* of October 15, 1841, took to task a presbytery in upstate New York that had published a statement opposing the new belief in perfectionism. Such a position was, in Garrison's mind, tantamount to making "a Christian life compatible with a military profession . . . with enslaving a portion of mankind . . . with a participation in all popular iniquities." The traditional Christian doctrine of humanity's inherent sinfulness was in fact an acceptance of sin and an obstacle to social reform. Therefore, Garrison instructed his readers that instead of "assailing the *doctrine*, 'Be ye perfect, even as your Father in heaven is perfect,' let us all aim to establish it, not merely as theoretically right, but as practically attainable."[67]

Perfectionism was not restricted to a few noted ministers, communitarian leaders and reformers. In the three decades before the Civil War, the number of seekers after perfection increased dramatically in all the major Protestant denominations, especially in the cities.[68] The year 1858, marked by a great nation-wide revival that effected half a million conversions, was a watershed in the acceptance of perfectionist ideas.[69] Preachers of perfect holiness were invited to speak at daily prayer meetings which developed almost spontaneously in Chicago, Philadelphia, New York, and nearly every Northern town and city. Finney, who served as a professor of theology and president of Oberlin College from 1835 until his death, had not been a sought-after speaker in the East during the two decades following his espousal of perfectionism in the winter of 1836–37, but his ideas received a warm welcome when he preached in New York and other Eastern cities during the revival of 1858. For the rest of his life, he and Asa Mahan, a second pillar of Oberlin perfectionism, found ample opportunity to spread their gospel throughout the country.[70] Finney's successful second hearing attests to the fact that perfectionist ideas had taken root among large sectors of American Protestantism in the 1840s and 1850s. Many a Christian had digested sermons and pored over books expounding texts such as Matthew 5:48, "Be ye therefore perfect, even as your Father which is in heaven is perfect," and II Corinthians 13:11 "Be perfect, be of good comfort, be of one mind, live in peace."

As with millennialism, the Protestant churches and Protestant-inspired communitarian and reform activities provided both the seedbed and strongest support for perfectionist views, but a belief in human perfectibility also extended into other areas of American culture, including phrenology and spiritualism. Fowler's articles on human progress in the *Phrenological Journal* were regularly punctuated with apostrophes to the spirit of perfectionism:

Our world is to be reformed and made a perfect Paradise. Depravity is to be comparatively banished. All human virtues are to grow in the utmost luxuriance. Illimitably and incalculably is mankind to become perfected and happy.[71]

O humanity, how low thou art sunken! But how heaven-high it is thy destiny to rise! Man! thy capacities are angelic! thy nature is divine—made even in the image of God! And thou are yet to become his worthy children—to be like Him.[72]

Our race is to be illimitably improved, and republicanism is to improve it. Every species of human ill and evil is to be done away, and to republicanism, mainly, I look as that grand instrumentality by which "old things shall pass away, and all things become new."[73]

Andrew Jackson Davis could conjure up similar language to describe humanity after they had adopted his spiritual views and reorganized society to establish distributive justice. Then virtue and morality "will bloom with an immortal beauty"; the "formerly-misdirected race of man" would be "elevated, refined, and perfected" and everyone would be brought "to the fulness [sic] of the stature of a PERFECT BEING!"[74]

In marked contrast to this emerging perfectionism, Emerson, in keeping with his non-millennial view of history, does not expound a theory of human perfectibility. In fact, in "Self-Reliance," he explicitly denies this possibility, asserting: "No greater men are now than ever were" and "Not in time is the race progressive."[75] Emerson's theology theoretically allows for the perfect integration of the individual human will with the divine will, but Emerson believed that in reality this only occurred in a rare individual such as Christ. So whereas Whitman looked forward to a new race of perfect religious personalities, Emerson called for a new Christ, or great man, who would serve as a model personality for modern American culture, and he expected everyone else to be imperfect imitations of this ideal.

Like other millennialists, Whitman also subscribed to an attendant theory of human perfectibility, and his confident prophecy of a new race of men and women is but one instance of the widespread spiritual optimism that characterized American religion in the period before the Civil War. Whitman's perfectionism could have developed independently of external influence, a natural outgrowth of his earlier millennialism. Yet it is certain that Protestantism also nurtured Whitman's perfectionism at least indirectly, through the mixture of progressive political sentiments and Protestant political theology that Whitman received from O'Sullivan's *Democratic Review*. And in light of Whitman's interest in religion and his frequent church attendance during the period in which perfectionist teachings were becoming increasingly prominent, it is likely that he would have encountered this new doctrine directly both in his reading and his encounters with church people. Later his ideas about human perfectibility would be reinforced by phrenology, spiritualism, and other schemes and fads that promised to elevate the human race.

As was the case with Whitman's millennialism, the seeds of his mature doctrine of perfectionism were also present in his early journalism. As already noted, in an *Aurora* editorial Whitman asserted that America's mission was to determine "how far man, the masterpiece of cunningest Omniscience, can have his nature perfected by himself." There is also an implicit perfectionism in Whitman's editorials for the Brooklyn *Daily Eagle* which speak of the "great mission of peopling the new world with a noble race" and of Americans achieving "something of that destiny which . . . God intends eligible for mankind." In the six years following his newspaper career while Whitman labored over the first edition of the *Leaves*, he came to a new appreciation of just how cunning Omniscience had been in creating its masterpiece. In the process of integrating his earlier perfectionism with his new understanding of the universe as a process of divine immanence incessantly evolving upward toward reunion with its transcendent source, Whitman's former rudimentary faith in perfectionism now took the form that throughout the long course of evolution and history it had been divinely ordained that America would produce a new race of women and men by creating the conditions that would allow them to realize fully the immanent divinity latent within them. We have already noted how Whitman emphasizes humanity's potential for divinity in the writings of the 1850s—the 1855 Preface, "Song of Myself," and the lecture notes on religion. This theme is continued in the later writings, and Whitman was careful to give it special emphasis in the sequence of poems that he first arranged to introduce the *Leaves* in 1871 and that he continued to use (with additional poems) in all subsequent editions. It is an example of this perfect or culminating individual—formed and regulated by the unobstructed energies and laws of God's immanent nature—which Whitman introduces in the opening poem of the *Leaves*: "Cheerful, for freest action form'd under the laws divine, / The Modern Man I sing" ("Onc's-Self I Sing").

Whitman intended for the *Leaves* to be the manifesto of humanity's final liberation from the impediments to perfection. In the book's second poem, "As I Ponder'd in Silence," the genius of Old World poetry sternly confronts the upstart American singer, admonishing him for attempting to enter the ranks of the world's great poets with a subject matter unbefitting an epic bard:

> *. . . What singest thou? it said,*
> *Know'st thou not there is but one theme for ever-enduring bards?*
> *And that is the theme of War, the fortune of battles,*
> *The making of perfect soldiers.*

But Whitman, who later explains that he doffs his hat "to nothing known or unknown" ("By Blue Ontario's Shore," l. 237), stands undaunted. His is a truly heroic subject, he responds; for he too sings of a war, "*a longer and greater one than any*," of which the wars of previous poets, and his own Civil War, were mere segments and symbols:

> . . . *the field the world,*
> *For life and death, for the Body and for the eternal Soul,*
> *Lo, I too am come, chanting the chant of battles,*
> *I above all promote brave soldiers.*

Whitman will sing of the warfare throughout history, in which men and women, impelled by the divinity within them, have incessantly struggled to free themselves from everything that inhibited their development. Four poems later, the poet states that it is to this cause, a cause "Deathless throughout the ages, races, lands" for which "all war through time was really fought," that he dedicates his poetry:

> To thee old cause!
> . . . .
> These recitatives for thee,—my book and the war are one,
> Merged in its spirit I and mine, as the contest hinged on thee,
> As a wheel on its axis turns, this book unwitting to itself,
> Around the idea of thee.
>
> ("To Thee Old Cause")

In the book's fourteenth poem, "To a Certain Cantatrice," the nature of this cause, which has not yet been fully described, is made more explicit; it is "the good old cause, the great idea, the progress and freedom of the race." In "By Blue Ontario's Shore" it is further defined as "the great Idea, the idea of perfect and free individuals" (l. 154). In short, Whitman's poetry is dedicated to, and informed by, his desire to liberate and perfect the human race in what he conceived of as history's decisive period.

Like other millennialists, Whitman conceived of his perfect men and women as religious; his writings always indicate that religion completes human nature. For instance, in his lecture notes, he defines religion as a "curious something, the crown of life and being, the lumine of the soul, without which all else is darkness" (*NPM*, VI, 2042). In "Democratic Vistas" he outlines a model personality for the future use of the American people. Completing this personality, and without which Whitman felt it would remain "but an amputation," was to be an "all penetrating Religiousness" that would allow man "to enter the pure ether of veneration, reach the divine levels, and commune with the unutterable" (*PW*, 398–99). Similarly, in *November Boughs*, he states that in the "making of a full man, all the other consciences, (the emotional, courageous, intellectual, esthetic, &c.,) are to be crown'd and effused by the religious conscience" (*PW*, 648). The many references in the *Leaves* to a radically new humanity—for example, "A new race dominating previous ones and grander far" ("Paumanok," l. 249) and a "thousand perfect men and women"

("Offerings")—refer to the citizenry of Whitman's envisioned religious democracy who, already freed from material and political oppression by American abundance and freedom, have now also been liberated in spirit by the poet's new religion and thus are fit participants in the new spiritual age.

Like that of the evangelicals, Whitman's proposed means of producing perfect people was to convert the masses to a vital religious faith. But in contrast to evangelical Christians, who conceived of conversion as the regeneration of fallen human nature by divine grace, Whitman naturalized the process of conversion, conceiving of it as the natural development of the spiritual potential present in all humans. "I will see," he wrote, "whether there is not . . . a religion, and a sound religious germenancy in the average human race . . . a germenancy that has too long been unencouraged, unsung, almost unknown" (1872 Preface, *PW*, 462). This new religion would differ from eighteenth-century deism or natural religion, which was largely a rational affair, in that it would address the deepest affective or instinctual levels of personality, the soul or immanent divinity present in all men and women.

There was a previously unimaginable confidence that verged on spiritual pride in Finney's exhortation to be "perfect as God." Yet as we have seen, Whitman is even more audacious; instead of proclaiming to his readers that they can become as perfect as God, he charges them to become gods. The *Leaves* repeatedly sounds the theme that humans can undergo an apotheosis simply by realizing their inner divinity. Whitman inflates with ecstatic self-satisfaction at this possibility: "To be this incredible God I am!" ("Song at Sunset," l. 29). His prophetic mission is to depict images of divine men and women as models for his readers: "to chisel with free stroke the heads and limbs of plenteous supreme Gods, that the states may realize them walking and talking" ("Myself and Mine"). Freed from all the shackles of the past, humans would now bring their spirits to full actualization and worship their own divinity. Thus Whitman speaks of his new order of poets as "priests of man" (*PW*, 456), and he declares that he can survey the gods of former religions and discover "as much or more in a framer framing a house" ("Song of Myself," 41).

Millennialism and Republicanism

In many respects the period between the Revolution and the Civil War was a time of special challenge and opportunity which entailed an unprecedented amount of individual freedom: freedom from government imposed from above; freedom from mandatory membership in a state-supported church and the right to belong to any church or no church, to be an active member of the laity, and in some denominations to be a minister, even without laboring to get professional training; freedom from the tyranny of place, and family and community control—the chance to move to new areas and begin afresh; freedom from the traditional society's ascriptive hierarchy, which locked each member into a fixed social class, and the opportunity for economic and social mobility. It was, in theory and to an extraordinary degree in practice (at least for white males), the freedom to think and act for oneself and carve out one's own destiny. Yet at the same time these new waves of liberty were accompanied by troubling undertows that gave rise to considerable anxiety, for they occurred in the midst of a rapid process of capitalistic modernization, characterized by unregulated urban growth, technological innovation, the creation of new national and international markets, and marked social stratification. Traditional social relationships were disrupted, older values were giving way to a growing competitive and commercial spirit, and the idea of a classless republic seemed increasingly tenuous. In addition, regional differences between the North and the South were becoming accentuated. Both the presence of slavery and the possibility of disunion were deeply troubling to a society officially committed to the principles of freedom and equality. These contradictions were all the more threatening to those Americans nursed upon the mythic understanding that the preservation and dissemination of these republican values were part of their nation's divinely ordained mission.[76]

The earlier optimism that characterized the millenialism of the beginning decades of the nineteenth century was never extinguished, but by the 1840s and 1850s an uncharacteristic mood of concern and attendant shrillness crept into many of the calls for perfection and glorious pictures of the coming latter days. As the course of American development took unexpected detours in response to unanticipated developments and imperfectly understood social forces, the complex of millennial ideas assumed new social burdens. In addition to inspiring the citizenry to work for reform and promoting social cohesion, they also provided needed assurance about the future. The millennial picture of a society whose members, united in loving fellowship, lived in free obedience to the will of God was especially attractive to many antebellum Americans because it seemed to provide a solution, consistent with a republic's commitment to individual freedom, to the problem of how to allow for a free citizenry and yet maintain the political unity and public morality necessary for the state's well-being.

According to the dominant line of public discourse, America's social problems were not fundamentally economic or structural, and they were not to be solved by the creation of new economic institutions or regulations that would diminish individual liberty. Solutions of this nature were not widely entertained, in fact they were scarcely conceived of, because of their apparent incompatibility with political and economic individualism. The American habit of mind was to think in terms of freedom and individual morality; the social challenge before the American people was essentially an experiment in freedom—an experiment to determine to what extent a society could organize itself in terms of independent citizens operating free of traditional social and institutional restraints. "In no part of the world has so little depended on the

Ruler and so much on the people," wrote Dartmouth professor Charles B. Hadduck. "Never before has the experiment been made to determine, with how little power the ends of society may be attained,—how little we must submit to be controlled, and how far we are capable of governing ourselves."[77]

Massachusetts legislator and educator Horace Mann was fond of citing the abolition of traditional restraints, which was accompanied by a constant trumpeting of new freedom, to convince his lecture audiences of the need for state-supported public education: "If republican institutions do wake up unexampled energies in the whole mass of a people, and give them implements of unexampled power wherewith to work out their will; then these same institutions ought also to confer upon that people unexampled wisdom and rectitude."[78] Warning that America was now raising the first generation to be molded under these new conditions of freedom, Mann, "with the deepest anxiety," asked his auditors, "what institutions exist among us, which at once possess the power and are administered with the efficiency requisite to save us from the dangers that spring up in our own bosoms?"[79] In Mann's eyes, the solution was, of course, to upgrade the public schools so they might produce a literate citizenry and inculcate the necessary moral and religious values.

Mann's position was a particular variant of a much larger body of political thought which sought to guide the development of the new social order by instilling the populace with internalized values and an unprecedented degree of moral rectitude. For Mann the means was public schools; others proposed to effect the same end through different or complementary agencies, for instance through the development of a national literature that would nourish democratic ideals or the growth of churches that would disseminate Protestantism and republicanism.

Like Mann, Finney also emphasized that republican governments required a virtuous and intelligent people. God providentially matched forms of government to the character of the people. If they were "extremely ignorant and vicious," he "restrained them by the iron rod of human despotism"; if they were "more intelligent and virtuous," he gave them "the milder form of limited monarchies"; if still more virtuous, he "established republics for their government." As a believer in progress toward perfection, Finney could conceive of the possibility of a "perfectly virtuous" citizenry; in which case the government would be "proportionally modified, and employed in expounding and applying the great principles of moral law";[80] that is, law would be internal not external and government would not exist to enact and enforce laws but to instruct people in the principles of religion and morality.

For Finney and many another proponent of revivalism, the best way to prevent democracy from degenerating into anarchy was to convert citizens to Christ and nourish their spirituality until they freely chose perfect obedience to the law of God. Revive piety and reform society was their formula for the millennium. "The great desideratum of the present age is not a plan of action," asserted the Reverend Edward Beecher. The plan was to use revivals to convert citizens who would then "organize all departments of society, in accordance with the law of God." Then people would choose God as their king and he would rule not "By compulsory power, but by the free, spontaneous, delightful, heart-felt choice of unnumbered millions."[81]

The dream of deriving the social order from the saintliness of the citizenry was not limited to the evangelicals. Selected to preach the annual election sermon for Massachusetts in 1830, William Ellery Channing chose to speak on the subject of spiritual freedom. Confessing his distrust of the body of American thought—which receives classic expression in Madison's famous Federalist essay on factions—that attempted to design institutions "to extract from them freedom, notwithstanding a people's sins" by balancing "Men's passions and interests against each other; to use one man's selfishness as a check against his neighbor's," Channing emphasized that there was "no substitute for virtue"[82] and no true freedom apart from the will of God: "That mind alone is free which, looking to God as the inspirer and rewarder of virtue, adopts his law, written on the heart and in his word, as its supreme rule, and which, in obedience to this, governs itself, exerts faithfully its best powers, and unfolds itself by well-doing in whatever sphere God's providence assigns."[83]

Progressive Democrats who subscribed to the principles of O'Sullivan's *Democratic Review* also believed in the possibility of organizing a society free from laws and governmental controls. In comparison to the ministers, O'Sullivan employed a more political vocabulary and rested his hopes for the new democracy less upon the churches than upon the persuasive power of a democratic literature and the democratic system itself as an arena for training citizens in the responsibilities of freedom. But the basis of O'Sullivan's faith, like that of the ministers, was a belief that God had implanted in human nature a potential for self-control that would, if fully realized, do away with the need for external controls. Starting with the maxim that the "best government is that which governs least," O'Sullivan argued that government should only provide "the single nucleus of a system of administration of justice between man and man." Pointing to the "perfect self-government of the physical universe," he stated that the "same hand was the Author of the moral, as of the physical world" and therefore human society could organize itself in terms of "the same fundamental principles of spontaneous action and self-regulation which produce the beautiful order of the latter." This "full and fearless faith in the Providence of the Creator," also "essentially involved in Christianity," was the "essence and the one general result of the science of political economy." America was not yet ready for the "full adoption" of these principles, but to pursue their implementation was "the noble mission entrusted to her." This "cheerful creed . . . of high hope and universal love" was unlike "all others, which imply a distrust of mankind" in that it rested upon the "natural moral principles" infused into the human race "by its Creator, for its own self-development and self-regulation."[84]

Perhaps it was from the *Democratic Review* that Whitman acquired the position that the Democratic Party stood for faith in human nature. As he explained in the *Eagle*, every nation had two classes of politicians. One of these, represented in the United States by the Whigs, "look upon men as things *to be governed*—as having evil ways which cannot be checked better than by law"; the other, represented by the Democrats, "wish to deal liberally with humanity, to treat it in confidence, and give it a chance of expanding, through the measured freedom of its own nature and impulses."[85] In his journalistic career, Whitman himself dealt "liberally with humanity," consistently urging a philosophy of freedom, small government, and few laws. In the *Aurora* he warned against excessive legislation, maintaining that laws not only failed to improve morality but also "hampered" the "holy cause of human progress,"[86] presumably because they deprived citizens of the opportunity to exercise self-control. An *Eagle* editorial entitled "Maxims for School Teachers," advised pedagogues: "Teach children to govern themselves."[87] Another observed that "unless men are laws unto themselves, statutes are useless, except for the purpose of protecting rights, property, personal safety, &c. from outrage."[88]

During his tenure as editor of the Brooklyn *Daily Eagle*, Whitman repeatedly insisted that the American democracy, if it were to be true to its republican nature and realize its God-given destiny, must increasingly derive its order and progress not from legislation but from the virtue of its citizenry: "Why, we wouldn't give a snap for the aid of the Legislature, in forwarding a purely moral revolution! It must work its way through individual minds. It must spread from its own beauty, and melt into the hearts of men."[89] As a source of this self-discipline, he advocated "the influence and example of home . . . well-rooted principles . . . a habit of morality."[90] He also hoped that the public discussion conducted by the American press would disseminate the liberal values needed for reform: "*It is to the discoveries and suggestions of free thought, of 'public opinion,' of liberal sentiments, that we must at this age of the world look for quite all desirable reforms, in government and any thing else.*"[91]

Later, in the years during which he forged the world view of the *Leaves*, Whitman's earlier belief in freedom probably received further encouragement from reading Emerson, whose Transcendentalism provided a non-Christian theological basis for dispensing with man-made law. Emerson could shock his audiences; he proclaimed: "No law can be sacred to me but that of my nature"[92] and "henceforward I obey no law less than the eternal law,"[93] because he believed that humans could, by realizing their inner divinity, unite their souls with the Oversoul and live in conformity to the laws of God. "We lie in the lap of immense intelligence, which makes us receivers of its truth and organs of its activity."[94] In "Politics," noting that the "tendencies of the times favor the idea of self-government, and leave the individual . . . to the rewards and penalties of his own constitution," Emerson chafes with moral dissatisfaction over the existing social arrangement with its reliance upon civil legislation and governmental enforcement: "We live in a very low state of the world, and pay unwilling tribute to governments founded on force."[95] Yet at the same time, a recognition of human weakness and social complexity also restrained him from asserting that internalized values were sufficient basis for a social order:

> There is not, among the most religious and instructed men of the most religious and civil nations, a reliance on the moral sentiment and a sufficient belief in the unity of things, to persuade them that society can be maintained without artificial restraints, as well as the solar system. . . .
>
> I do not call to mind a single human being who has steadily denied the authority of the laws, on the simple ground of his own moral nature.[96]

Although apparently tempted to make such a denial, Emerson instead limits himself to the observation that nevertheless "nature continues to fill the heart of youth with suggestions of this enthusiasm."[97] Again Whitman went beyond Emerson, for although unwilling to suggest that the existing legal system should be immediately discarded, he was nevertheless led by his belief in perfectionism and an imminent millennium to proclaim the possibility of an ideal future society in which man-made law would be unnecessary.

In developing the world view of the *Leaves* Whitman arrived at a theory of freedom which rooted his earlier political liberalism in a religious psychology which was in turn integrated into his larger religious vision. According to this new viewpoint, the human soul was a dynamic spiritual entity which, in attempting to realize its inherent divinity, constantly strove for higher levels of spiritual comprehension or perfection. If it were impeded in its development, the result was pathology and immorality. In a notebook for the 1855 edition, wickedness is defined as "the absence of freedom and health in the soul" (*NPM*, I, 65). Whitman cautioned: "Let everything be as free as possible.— There is always danger in constipation"; and he declared that "the schools and hospitals for the sick and idiots and the aged [should] be perfectly free" (*NPM*, I, 81).

Whitman could make such unequivocal endorsements of freedom because he conceived of perfect freedom as the fulfillment of human nature. Only the ideal religious personalities of the future would be perfectly free; these women and men would live in obedience to the spiritual laws of their nature and thus participate in a divinely ordained order. Whitman conceived of his future religious democracy as the "younger brother of another great and often-used word, Nature"; and the "lesson of Nature" was "the quality of Being, in the object's self, according to its own central idea and purpose, and of growing therefrom and thereto" (*PW*, 393–94). In a parallel with O'Sullivan's analogy between the natural world and the political order, Whitman conceived of a sociopolitical system that would allow the citizenry to live as freely as plants and animals in the realm of nature. Much more than a political right, this idea of freedom was a religious state of existence. Whitman wanted to add this spiritual dimension to the American notion of independence:

> The old men, I remember as a boy, were always talking of American independence. What is independence? Freedom from all laws or bonds except those of one's own being, control'd by the universal ones. To lands, to man, to woman, what is there at last to each, but the inherent soul, nativity, idiocrasy, free, highest-poised, soaring its own flight, following out itself? ("Democratic Vistas," *PW*, 410–11)

This conception of freedom also integrates Whitman's politics with his larger world view informed by the notion of an immanent-transcendent divinity. As the previous quotation indicates, Whitman's free individual would not be autonomous in a modern or secular sense; rather, in realizing the "laws or bonds" of the "inherent soul," the individual would become integrated with the "universal ones." That is, in bringing to consciousness or actualizing the seeds of divine immanence within human nature, the individual would integrate the laws of human nature with the attributes of divine immanence which ordered the rest of creation. This understanding of freedom is made explicit in the following passage in which Whitman distinguishes between autonomy and religious liberty:

> Great—unspeakably great—is the Will! the free Soul of man! At its greatest, understanding and obeying the laws, it can then, and then only, maintain true liberty. For there is to the highest, that law as absolute as any—more absolute than any—the Law of Liberty. The shallow, as intimated, consider liberty a release from all law, from every constraint. The wise see in it, on the contrary, the potent Law of Laws, namely, the fusion and combination of the conscious will, or partial individual law, with those universal, eternal, unconscious ones, which run through all Time, pervade history, prove immortality, give moral purpose to the entire objective world, and the last dignity to human life. ("Freedom," *PW*, 538)

Like Christian mystics who defined the highest state of spiritual development as a union of human and divine wills, Whitman also believed in the possibility of a fusion of human and divine natures. His notion of a religious democracy presupposes a race of such fully developed religious men and women.

In the *Leaves* Whitman's radical depreciation of law takes many forms and often seems to verge upon anarchy, but these statements are misunderstood if considered apart from his belief in a future race of spiritually perfect individuals who have replaced external restraints with inner imperatives so that they freely live in obedience to the laws of God. When Whitman asserts that he "places over you no master, owner, better, God," he adds "beyond what waits intrinsically in yourself" ("To You," l. 17). The future or "culminating" man of Whitman's dreams is not addressed as being free from law but as *"pois'd on yourself, giving not taking law"* ("Song of the Redwood-Tree," l. 56). In regard to the liberation of women from protective restrictions, Whitman was willing to expose them to the moral crudities of life because he imagined a future American woman possessed of perfect self-regulation: "She too is a law

of nature—there is no law stronger than she is" ("Song of the Broad-Axe,"
l. 248). Whitman could use a locomotive, full of power, proceeding with apparent abandon and yet surely adhering to its proper course, as the image of
his ideal individual:

> Roll through my chant with all thy lawless music, thy swinging lamps at night,
> Thy madly-whistled laughter, echoing, rumbling like an earthquake, rousing all,
> Law of thyself complete, thine own track firmly holding.
>
> ("To a Locomotive in Winter," ll. 19–21)

Because he anticipated a future citizenry capable of living in union with the
divine nature, Whitman adopted a non-Christian version of the optimistic position espoused by many of his Christian contemporaries: the solution to the
problem of modern republican freedom was that the old external constraints
were to be replaced by internalized spiritual restraints—by the law of God en-
graved upon the people's hearts. In "Democracy in the New World" Whitman heartily endorses this idea as expressed by the British theologian, Canon
Kingsley:

> "The ideal form of human society," Canon Kingsley declares, "is democracy.
> A nation . . . of free men, lifting free foreheads to God and Nature . . . knowing
> and doing their duties toward the Maker of the universe, and therefore to each
> other; not from fear, nor calculation of profit or loss, but because they have seen
> the beauty of righteousness, and trust, and peace; because the law of God is in
> their hearts. Such a nation—such a society—what nobler conception of moral
> existence can we form?"

After this statement, Whitman added: "To this faith, founded in the ideal, let
us hold—and never abandon or lose it" ("Democracy in the New World," *PW*,
529). Whitman could envision a "Race henceforth owning no law but the law
of itself" ("Race of Veterans"), and he could imagine cities "Where the men
and women think lightly of the laws" and "Where children are taught to be
laws to themselves" ("Song of the Broad-Axe," l. 125), because he anticipated
a future America that was fully integrated into the divine will: "Land in the
realms of God to be a realm unto thyself, / Under the rule of God to be a rule
unto thyself" ("Thou Mother With Thy Equal Brood," ll. 99–100).

Inspirationism and Whitman's Prophetic Vocation

Whitman's effort to combine an evolutionary religious cosmology and millennial faith in a new post-Christian religion seems disturbingly presumptuous
and might even be mistaken for evidence of megalomanic derangement. However, properly perceived, Whitman's ambitions to prophecy appear to be a
highly unusual but nevertheless sound response to his historical situation.
Whitman grew up in a period of religious ferment marked by an intense indi-

vidualism and the creation of new sects and belief systems, and his labors to forge a new myth should be seen as one manifestation of a third widespread feature of antebellum religion which historians of American religion term "inspirationism," that is, the belief in the possibility of arriving at either a new and markedly superior interpretation of old revelation or even developing a totally new revelation.[98] The evangelicals' reinterpretation of Scripture to support the new teaching of perfectionism, Emerson's call for a fresh revelation, the outbreak of spiritualism, and the founding of Mormonism are all examples of inspirationism, and the inspiration for *Leaves of Grass* is an instance of this larger phenomenon. Whitman flourished at a time when new faiths were called for and sometimes actually created, and his personal sense of calling seems to be a thoughtful assimilation of the peculiar confluence of religious and literary currents that fed into his early development and subsequent maturation. Various studies of Whitman's biography and reading indicate a number of sources from which he could have derived the concept of a poet-prophet and the need to create a new religion, and it is perhaps helpful to list some of the more important influences. An awareness of these does not make his decision to found a new religion any less startling or awesome, but it does make his sense of himself as an inspired prophet somewhat more understandable.

The seeds of Whitman's daring choice of vocation were firmly, even if unintentionally, planted by his family. His grandfather Whitman and his parents were admirers of the liberal Quaker leader, Elias Hicks, who fomented a split between Orthodox and Liberal (or Hicksite) Quakers in 1829. Hicks agreed with the Quaker belief that the meaning and application of Scripture was to be illuminated by the inner light of the human soul, but he went beyond orthodoxy with the Emersonian-like assertion that this light was of higher spiritual authority than the Bible and the source of all religious inspiration. As Allen points out, Whitman always felt a "bond of spiritual kinship" with Hicks who was also of Long Island working-class stock,[99] and in his old age Whitman wrote a biographical essay on Hicks in which he recalls his parents taking him at the age of ten—a reward for a day's good behavior—to listen to Hicks who was "very mystical and radical." Hick's significance, according to Whitman, was that he pointed "to the fountain of all naked theology, all religion, all worship . . . namely in *yourself*" ("Elias Hicks," *PW*, 638 & 627). Evidently, Whitman always retained a positive image of Hicks and his unorthodox doctrine must have been a welcome support to the fledgling poet when he wanted to proclaim himself the source of a fresh revelation. Whitman's father was also attracted to the militantly anti-Christian deism of Count Volney, Thomas Paine, and Frances Wright,[100] and Whitman inherited many deistic criticisms of Christianity—a distrust of priests and organized religion, a denial of Christ's divinity, an openness to non-Christian religions, and a concern to reconcile science and faith—that would lead him to feel the need for creating a new religion.

Later, as a young newspaper editor, Whitman reviewed Samuel Taylor Coleridge and Thomas Carlyle, who were esteemed by many American religious liberals as two of the most seminal minds of the period. He learned of the former's distinction between the "Understanding," which was responsible for practical information and logical thought, and the "Reason," which was capable of the immediate intuition of spiritual truth.[101] In the latter's *Sartor-Resartus* he read of a similar faculty of "Pure Reason" described as the source of religious revelation or the true scripture "whereof all other Bibles are but Leaves," and he must have thrilled to the prediction of Carlyle's protagonist, Professor Diogenes Teufelsdroeckh, that there would soon arise a new religious vision, the product of an inspired poet, the "Pontiff of the World ... who, Prometheus-like, can shape new Symbols and bring new Fire from Heaven."[102]

But even more important to Whitman's developing sense of vocation was the influence of Emerson, who domesticated Coleridge's epistemology and Carlyle's proposal for a new mythology by fusing them with America's persistent longing for a native literature. As noted earlier, Whitman probably became acquainted with Emerson's writings in 1842 , but the evidence suggests that Whitman developed, at least in embryo, many of the political and religious tenets of his mature faith before Emerson became a significant influence upon his thought. In the period in which Whitman composed the *Leaves*, however, Emerson became his chief mentor, providing him with theological ideas and spiritual insights and, of greater importance, a poetic that contained a theory of progressive revelation and called for a poet-prophet to provide America with a needed new religion. According to Trowbridge's recollection, Whitman told him, while conceding the importance of Emerson's influence ("I was simmering, simmering, simmering; Emerson brought me to a boil"), that he would have eventually found himself and written the *Leaves* without the assistance of Emerson's essays.[103] Perhaps, but surely the *Leaves* would then have been a different and lesser book, for Whitman would have had a less sophisticated understanding of religion and a less substantial basis for conceiving of himself as a prophet. One questions whether Whitman, without Emerson's encouragement, would have found the courage to announce himself as the founder of a new religion.

In sum, Whitman was the recipient of a radical Quaker tradition which transformed the doctrine of the inner light into a belief in the human soul as a potential source of fresh revelation. He was also a grandchild of the Enlightenment and the eldest son of American Transcendentalism, with full rights of primogeniture to the radical ideas which proceeded from the fusion of liberal Protestantism and Anglo-American Romanticism—ideas which prepared the way for a new religious prophet. Placed in this context, Whitman's attempt to begin a modern religion appears extraordinary but not unreasonable. In assuming the mantle of prophecy, he was fulfilling the traditional role of the liberal religious mystic who lives in a period of profound cultural transition. As the historian of religions Kees Bolle reminds us, it is the mystics, more than any other group, who have "contributed most to the formulation of new myths."[104] For reasons pertaining to both the content of the vision and the means for its dissemination, it was a virtual certainty that Whitman's attempt to establish a new religion would prove a failure. Yet it is an index not only of his optimism but also of his intellectual integrity and imaginative power that rather than ignore the religious implications of the Enlightenment or merely lament the inadequacies of the regnant mythology, Whitman, who is often condemned as anti-intellectual, tried to lay the foundation for a modern, rationally consistent religion.

IV

STYLE

FROM SILENCE TO SYMBOL

Much remains unsaid in *Leaves of Grass*; rather than fully articulating his ideas, Whitman merely "hints" and "suggests." In part, this was unavoidable, for he was confronted with the dilemma of the mystical poet who wants to sing of a dimension of life which surpasses human powers of expression. However, Whitman's silence was also strategic. Like Emerson, he emphasized religion as a matter of intuition rather than tuition, for he was not concerned to provide his readers with creed or doctrines but to effect their existential participation in his vision. Consequently, he developed a style which intentionally left many things unstated: "I swear I see what is better than to tell the best, / It is always to leave the best untold" ("Song of the Rolling Earth," ll. 102–103). In doing this Whitman wanted to prevent his audience from acquiring merely a conceptual knowledge of his faith; if the reader were to understand his hinted meanings, he would have to realize them in his own experience and thus be subject to their compelling power. Finally, Whitman's suggestive method also reflects his perfectionist and millennial orientation. He would not have demanded so much of his readers if he had not subscribed to the notion that perfect sanctification was possible and that the future religious democracies of America and the world demanded a new race of spiritual athletes who would strive for perfection.

For all of these reasons Whitman's poetic method includes a strong existential element. In addition to the language he employs, he also makes a series of claims upon his readers which, taken together, constitute a program to develop their souls and convince them that this world is immanent with spirit. Whitman's suggestive method requires such spiritually active readers. With this audience, Whitman could refer to a segment of the external world and merely suggest its spiritual meaning. The readers would then encounter this natural fact with their senses and souls; and this experience, combined with the poet's subtle commentary, would enable them to intuit the text's intended but not fully stated meanings.

I have attempted to explicate the religious functions of Whitman's existential demands by showing how they parallel the first two stages of the classical spiritual way of Christian mysticism. Since there is no evidence that Whitman studied this Christian tradition, I assume that the likenesses are a matter of independent development and arise from Whitman's and the Christian mystic's similar objectives. Both had the goal of drawing people out of their entangling webs of worldly pursuits and redirecting their energies toward spiritual development. The parallelism calls attention to the fact that there were various currents present in antebellum culture which Whitman could draw upon to create a program of spiritual development similar to that of the Christian mystical way.

After discussing how Whitman's existential claims develop the reader's soul so that it can experience the sanctity of the external world, the second part of this chapter discusses the dynamics of a particular, intense type of religious knowing: namely, religious symbolism. Influenced by new critical and Freudian theories of symbolism, some scholars fail to appreciate the importance of relating Whitman's symbols to their proper context, namely, the poet's religious cosmology and theory of the soul, in order to understand how they function in the poetry. The major epiphanies in the *Leaves* are also its most veiled "secrets." In such central poems and sequences as "Song of Myself," "Out of the Cradle," the Lincoln elegy, and "Calamus," Whitman wants the spiritually prepared reader's soul to encounter a particular natural fact as a religious symbol. At such moments, the reader is to have a religious experience that will enable him or her to realize the unstated spiritual truth that resolves the poem. Consequently, the critic must have a method for disclosing the poem's unwritten meaning. After explicating the nature of this problem and suggesting an interpretive method appropriate to the nature of Whitman's text, the final part of this chapter interprets Whitman's aquatic symbolism so that its meaning can be drawn upon later in analyzing some of the individual poems.

I

Both Whitman and many Christian mystics present a program for promoting the growth of the soul which entails a restructuring of the personality and a reorientation of one's energies and aspirations. In the Christian tradition, this first stage of the spiritual quest goes by the quaint yet awesome title of "Purgation," a process which involves both a mortification of selfish desires (or a weaning of oneself from the "ways of this world") and also a redirection of one's life in pursuit of spiritual values.[1] A similar twofold dynamic is present in Whitman. On occasion, he enjoins his reader to selflessness—though admittedly a selflessness of a peculiarly republican character. It is combined with a hardy independence, and unlike the Christian mystic, Whitman advocates self-denial not only because it promotes spiritual development and puts the good of others before self-interest, but also because it is a form of civic behavior that Whitman believed essential to a successful democracy:

> This is what you shall do: Love the earth and sun and the animals, despise riches,
> give alms to everyone that asks, stand up for the stupid and crazy, devote your
> income and labor to others, hate tyrants, argue not concerning God, have pa-
> tience and indulgence toward the people, take off your hat to nothing known
> or unknown, or to any man or number of men—go freely with powerful unedu-
> cated persons, and with the young, and with the mothers of families. (1855 Pref-
> ace, *PW*, 440)

And sometimes the poet harshly denounces the life devoted to worldly success;
for instance, in "Thought" (Of persons . . .), he describes those dedicated to
the attainment of "high positions, ceremonies, wealth, scholarships" as "sad,
hasty, unwaked somnambules" who are "full of the rotten excrement of
maggots."

But consistent with his characteristically positive attitude, Whitman spends
most of his time not in condemning worldliness but in encouraging his readers
to orient their lives in terms of lasting spiritual truths. "Song of Prudence" asserts that "Charity and personal force are the only investments worth any
thing" (l. 15); and "To Think of Time" reminds the reader that this life is but
a prologue for eternity:

> (I see one building the house that serves him a few years, or seventy or eighty
>   years at most,
> I see one building the house that serves him longer than that.)
> . . . .
> I swear I think there is nothing but immortality!
> That the exquisite scheme is for it, and the nebulous float is for it, and the coher-
>   ing is for it!
> And all the preparation is for it—and identity is for it—and life and materials
>   are altogether for it!
>
> (ll. 29–30 & 119–21)

Whitman views worldly pursuits not as immoral, but as relatively unimportant
activities which should be subordinated to one's spiritual development:

> What are you doing young man?
> Are you so earnest, so given up to literature, science, art, amours?
> These ostensible realities, politics, points?
> Your ambition or business whatever it may be?
>
> It is well—against such I say not a word, I am their poet also,
> But behold! such swiftly subside, burnt up for religion's sake,
> For not all matter is fuel to heat, impalpable flame, the essential life of the earth,
> Any more than such are to religion.
>
> ("Starting from Paumanok," 8)

These calls to be in this world but still not of it seem to draw upon several
anti-materialist traditions in antebellum culture. Of course, there was the general influence of Christianity and of Whitman's Quaker heritage in particular
with its emphasis upon a radical simplicity and service to others. The Revolu-

tionary tradition of civic virtue that Whitman learned from his father's admiration of Paine and Jefferson also encouraged avoiding luxury and engaging in service for the commonweal. In addition, the Romantic imperative to seek solitude in nature was a recognition of the need to relinquish or escape from worldly concerns in order to become attuned to more important spiritual realities. Finally, as M. Wynn Thomas has recently argued, the self Whitman celebrates in the *Leaves* is intended, in part, as a critical response to the increasingly acquisitive and competitive attitudes being engendered by developing urban-commercial capitalism.[2]

But mortification and the reorientation of the personality form only one-half of purgation. It also involves a transformation of the senses—not a denial, but a cleansing or purification. Regarding this point, one of the ablest students of Christian mysticism, Evelyn Underhill, states that "pure sensation" provides "one of the most accessible avenues" to union with God;[3] the beginner on the mystic way must "see more intensely, hear more intensely, touch and taste more intensely than ever before."[4] This requires adjusting the intellect and the will: freeing the former of customary expectations and preconceptions and the latter of the desire to have and to use. When this is accomplished the mystic perceives things in a simpler and more truthful way, which is termed a "simple seeing" or "sensation without thought."[5]

It is this fresh experiencing of the world which Whitman emphasizes at the beginning of "Song of Myself" (ll. 10–13):

> Creeds and schools in abeyance,
> Retiring back a while sufficed at what they are, but never forgotten,
> I harbor for good or bad, I permit to speak at every hazard,
> Nature without check with original energy.

And sections 24–29, in which he proclaims that "Seeing, hearing, feeling, are miracles" (l. 523) constitute a sustained rhapsody over the beauty of the world when simply perceived, that is, by senses unencumbered by self-interest and thought. Indeed, two key elements of Whitman's style, simplicity and suggestiveness, are designed to portray things as perceived in this innocent or uncorrupted manner. "Nothing is better than simplicity," he proclaimed in the 1855 Preface, because it allowed the poet to be "the channel of thoughts and things without increase or diminution" (*PW*, 444); and similarly Whitman's use of suggestion proceeds, in part, from his refusal to truncate or distort experience by making it conform to an intellectual system. Candid experience is primary, and then only after the reader has fully experienced some segment of the world does Whitman's voice subtly impose its suggestions of spiritual meaning.

This pure sensation sanctifies the world. Its impulses, uninterrupted by intellectual and practical considerations, penetrate those deeper layers of consciousness which both Whitman and the Christian mystic term the "soul": a substratum of consciousness which underlies the intellect, will, and senses. The result is the deeper, more intimate form of spiritual knowing which gives the religious person a sense of identity or union with a spiritual reality present in the natural world. Using the language of Christian mysticism, Underhill describes it as a "loving gaze," an "act of communion" which discloses a "fraternal link with all living things."[6]

When the Christian mystic encounters the world in this manner, he or she has reached the second stage of the mystical way, "Illumination," a form of contemplation which, according to Underhill, "the old mystics sometimes called the 'discovery of God in His creatures.'"[7] God left his "traces, trail, or footsteps" upon his creatures, asserted St. Francois de Sales, so that man's knowledge of the creation "seems no other thing than the sight of the feet of God";[8] similarly Thomas Traherne insisted that the "world is never enjoyed aright till you see how a sand exhibiteth the power and wisdom of God."[9] Whitman wished to lead his readers to this sacramental vision of the world. He would unite the souls of his readers with the creation:

> When the full-grown poet came,
> Out spake pleased Nature (the round impassive globe, with all its shows of day and night,) saying, *He is mine*;
> But out spake too the Soul of man, proud, jealous and unreconciled, *Nay, he is mine alone*;
> —Then the full-grown poet stood between the two, and took each by the hand;
> And to-day and ever so stands, as blender, uniter, tightly holding hands,
> Which he will never release until he reconciles the two,
> And wholly and joyously blends them.
>
> ("When the Full-grown Poet Came")

Then others would join in his psalm of praise, declaring with him: "I hear and behold God in every object" ("Song of Myself," l. 1281).

Some critics have maintained that Whitman's sensuous mysticism distinguishes him from Christian mystics who are alleged to deny the senses, but Christian mysticism uses a form of sensory, "illuminative" seeing to disclose the presence of God in nature. The real difference between the Christian mystic and Whitman is the latter's unrestrained blessing of human sexuality as a means to spiritual development and union with divinity. Of course, the religion of Romanticism, especially Emerson's emphasis upon correspondential vision, provided Whitman with the doctrine of God's incarnational presence in nature. In addition, as Arthur Wrobel has pointed out, various phrenological writers with whom Whitman was familiar reinforced this conviction by maintaining that a superb physiology with well-developed and well-regulated senses was a prerequisite for apprehending the spiritual laws that inform the creation. The soul, according to one health reformer and supporter of phrenology, "feels" through the senses.[10]

But neither Whitman nor the Christian mystic stop with a perception of divine immanence. Rather, both maintain that the human consciousness, in realizing the sanctity of the natural order, rises to an awareness of divine transcendence. This positing of a transcendent spiritual order is not pure speculation independent of experience, but rather is felt to be a faithful rendering of the full implications of experiencing the sanctity of the natural order. This world, properly perceived, gives off intimations of transcendence. The failure to follow this movement of thought from the sensible to the supersensible, is, in Christian mysticism, to mistake a stage of development with the final goal and thus to end the mystical quest prematurely, arriving at a mere nature mysticism.[11] In writing upon this aspect of mystical experience in *Democratic Vistas*, Whitman makes a similar point. He asserts that when nature is perceived not only with the senses but also with the "moral and spiritual consciences," then man learns of his "destination beyond the ostensible, the mortal." Thus Whitman describes natural facts as "parents" whose "legitimate heirs" are the "elevating and etherealizing ideas of the unknown" (*PW*, 417). It is this crucial dynamic of consciousness, this impulse toward transcendence, which establishes both Whitman and the Christian mystic as theists rather than pantheists.

In "Union," the third and final stage of the Christian way, the mystic achieves a sense of integration with the will of God. This stage is also present in Whitman's thought, where it is usually described, as it was in the preceding chapter, as a fusion of the "laws" of the human and divine natures. Also we might note that Whitman adapts mystical union, as he did the self-denial of the purgative stage of the mystical path, to his political concerns, making it an important source of social order and political unity. However, at present it suffices to observe that Whitman's poetic includes a program for the reader's spiritual development which corresponds to the purgative and illuminative stages of Christian mysticism. This enables him merely to make "suggestions" about segments of the natural world and yet be leading his reader to spiritual insights which defy a more direct means of communication. To speak of God in this most indirect and modest way was, in Whitman's mind, the proper procedure and highest end of religious art. Thus he told Traubel that he admired Millet's paintings for their "untold something behind all that was depicted— an essence, a suggestion, an indirection, leading off into the immortal mysteries." When Traubel replied that he appreciated the *Leaves* for the same quality, Whitman responded, "If you are right and if it is so. [sic] I take it as the glory, not the shame, of the best work—its essential crown, confirmation" (*Camden*, II, 407).

II

In an effort to make Whitman more amenable, or at least more understandable, to contemporary readers, modern scholarship has proposed two interpretations of the dynamics of Whitman's symbolic imagination. Influenced by

Ernst Cassirer's theory of symbolic modes and the new criticism's emphasis upon the autonomy of a work of art, Charles Feidelson, Jr., has argued that the literature of the American Renaissance arises from a special imaginative process which expresses itself through metaphor and synecdoche. According to Feidelson, this literature has no sign value; its symbols point neither inward to the poet nor outward to the external world. The writing of symbolic poetry is a pure act of the imagination in which the author discovers the possibilities of this particular mode of consciousness.[12] More recently, Edwin Haviland Miller and Stephen Black have used psychoanalytic theory to study Whitman's symbols. This approach also ignores the referential aspects of the poet's symbols and instead views them as symptoms of unconscious conflicts.[13] Neither of these theories elucidate either Whitman's own understanding of symbolism or the intended meaning of the various symbols in the *Leaves*. A better explanation is provided by scholarship in the phenomenology of religion which recognizes that religious symbolism presupposes the religious psychology and world view discussed in chapter 2.[14] On the subjective side, it demands an inner spiritual faculty or soul that is capable of perceiving the sanctity of the natural world. On the objective side, it requires a transcendent divinity that is also immanent in the world. The symbolic experience itself is an especially intense form of illuminative seeing in which the natural fact, perceived as symbol, unlocks or activates an instinct or need of the soul. In this process, the religious subject has the sense of simultaneously discovering a depth aspect of himself and an attribute of divinity. Accordingly, to the religious consciousness symbolic language is highly referential. It refers outward to a natural fact and an intangible spiritual fact: an aspect of God's transcendent nature that is also immanently present in the world. Furthermore, since this spiritual fact is experienced as an existential realization, the symbol also points to an inner structure of consciousness: it develops or reinforces a dimension of the soul.

This account of Whitman's theory of symbolic knowing is not a novel interpretation but rather a re-statement of what is often spoken of in scholarship on Emerson, Thoreau, and Whitman as "correspondential vision." Since this term is often used in vague ways, I have tried briefly to enumerate its principal elements. Also I have wanted to emphasize that for Whitman the religious symbol exists not in print but in the external world. Whitman believed that God made the real symbols by writing his attributes into nature and history. Experiencing the symbols was not an intellectual insight but a spiritual revelation—a deep, powerful feeling in which an element of the external world expressive of an aspect of divinity addressed the "soul." Whitman's symbolic method presupposes that his readers will be spiritually prepared (or have developed souls) so that they are capable of experiencing a fact as symbol and also that they will actually encounter the natural fact (e.g., the stars, the waters, the calamus grass) and be subject to its spiritual influence.

Two of Whitman's statements about his poetic practice are crucial to understanding his symbolic method:

> The word I myself put primarily for the description of them [poems] . . . is the word Suggestiveness. I round and finish little, if anything. . . . The reader will always have his or her part to do, just as much as I have had mine. I seek less to state or display any theme or thought, and more *to bring you, reader, into the atmosphere of the theme or thought—there to pursue your own flight* (emphasis added). ("A Backward Glance," *PW*, 724-25)

> I have not been afraid of the charge of obscurity. . . . Poetic style, when *address'd to the Soul*, is less definite form, outline, sculpture, and becomes *vista, music half-tints, and even less than half-tints*. True, it may be architecture; but again it may be *the forest wild-wood*, or the *best effects thereof, at twilight, the waving oaks and cedars in the wind, and the impalpable odor* (emphasis added). (1876 Preface, *PW*, 473)

Whitman does not spell out ("round and finish") the meanings of his symbols. Rather, consciously risking obscurity, he only brings the reader into the "atmosphere of the theme or thought," that is, he leads the reader to a natural fact and then uses his poetry to help create a delicate atmosphere ("less than half-tints" or "the impalpable odor") that will put the reader into a proper state of consciousness for arriving at the existential realization of the spiritual insight which Whitman intends for the natural fact to convey. So in interpreting one of Whitman's symbols the reader cannot extract its meaning directly from the text itself, but must instead infer its meaning from the nature of the natural fact (the meaning it seems suitable for conveying), and the mood created by the context Whitman creates around the symbol. Perhaps no other writer has expected so much of readers, demanding that they realize the poem's unexpressed meaning out of their own spiritual experience.

There are many ways in which this strategy of communication might break down. Readers might not submit to the spiritual discipline and they might not go into the world to have an immediate experience of the natural facts. Also, since some of Whitman's symbols such as the lilacs and calamus grass are not traditional and since others, although traditional, are expressed in fresh language and invested with new levels of meaning, readers cannot draw upon their knowledge of traditional religious symbols to recognize and interpret Whitman's use of symbols.[15] Much of the confusion that surrounds "Song of Myself" and Whitman's poems about death and manly love arises from the fact that Whitman's fresh symbolism and peculiar strategy of symbolic communication make it almost impossible for readers to discover his unstated but intended meanings. Briefly stated, the problem is to recognize when Whitman is using a natural fact as a symbol and what meaning he intends for it to convey.

There are no easy rules for determining this, but it is helpful to note that Whitman repeatedly employs two strategies. The first is his use of the shorelines. As we shall see in the ensuing discussion, Whitman perceived the shoreline as the symbol par excellence of the spiritual merging with the natural.

He frequently uses it as the setting for perceiving aspects of this world as symbol, and so the reader must concentrate whenever the poet takes up a position by the water. The second strategy might be called a "rhetoric of emanations." To suggest that the spiritual power of an external object or event is affecting his soul, Whitman uses terms which refer either to the most delicate and ethereal aspects of the natural world or to physical touching or embracing. This is why the *Leaves* is filled with references to aromas, scents, fragrances, and odors, to rustlings, whispers, hisses, murmurings, echoes, and to light touches, kisses, and embraces. There is no tidy way to sum up Whitman's use of this vocabulary, but a few examples will illustrate my point. To indicate the spiritual power of a sunset breeze, he speaks of it as "whispering" something "unseen" ("To the Sun-Set Breeze"); similarly, he suggests the influence of the stars upon his soul by declaring: "I hear you whispering there O stars of heaven" ("Song of Myself," l. 1299). To describe his spiritual union with the surrounding objects of nature in "Song of Myself" (l. 26), he speaks of them as providing "a few light kisses, a few embraces, a reaching around of arms." In these cases, the terms are used in a purely figurative sense; but at other times, as when the poet speaks of the "hissing" sea or the "aroma" of the calamus grass, the words refer to natural facts which are part of the symbolic experience and which are also used to symbolize the occult spiritual energies which are affecting the poet's soul.

Once it is determined that a fact is employed as a religious symbol, there is still the problem of discerning its spiritual meaning. Again there is no fully satisfactory way of doing this, but as I indicated in my introductory chapter, I feel the following methods are helpful. First, the *Leaves* must be read as a whole, that is, the interpreter must closely examine the language that surrounds the symbol not only in the particular poem at hand but throughout the *Leaves*, looking for recurring motifs and related patterns of meaning. Also, in addition to a close reading, it is necessary to make a phenomenological analysis by attempting to intuit the state of consciousness and accompanying existential realization to which Whitman tries to bring his reader. Finally, since some of Whitman's symbols are traditional in their essential structure, the reader can sometimes draw upon existing scholarship in the phenomenology of religion for an analysis of the symbol's recurring basic content in various historical contexts. With this in mind, the reader can then return to Whitman's language to discern additional nuances of meaning.

III

An analysis of Whitman's aquatic imagery will clarify my remarks about Whitman's symbolism and partially illustrate my interpretive method.[16]

From the influence of Judeo-Christian culture, most Westerners are familiar with the essential meanings of aquatic symbolism from various biblical narratives and themes; for example, "Genesis," where the waters precede the rest of creation; "Noah," where the universal flood destroys the creation in order to purify the world; and passages (such as Luke 3:3, in which John the Baptist preaches baptism by water for the remission of sin) where the waters serve as a symbol of purification and renewal. These uses of aquatic symbolism are, of course, not unique to the Bible, but characteristic of how water functions in a multitude of religious systems. They illustrate Eliade's conclusion that regardless of the religious framework in which it appears "the function of water is shown to be the same; it disintegrates, abolishes forms, 'washes away sins'— at once purifying and giving new life. Its work is to precede creation and take it again to itself."[17]

Whitman's practice conforms to this traditional usage. Water is repeatedly employed as a symbol of the divine source from which man and the rest of the creation proceed and to which they return after their death or dissolution. Thus the poet establishes his spiritual unity with the soil of Long Island by pointing to their common emergence out of the divine sea: "I too have bubbled up, floated the measureless float, and been wash'd on your shores" ("As I Ebb'd with the Ocean of Life," l. 42). In "Crossing Brooklyn Ferry," where he is concerned to develop a sense of mystical union with his audience, he reminds the future reader that they have both proceeded from the same spiritual source: "I too had been struck from the float forever held in solution" (l. 62). Conversely, after their finite existence, humans and the rest of nature are conceived of as flowing back into these mystic waters. In "To Old Age" human death and the soul's return to God is analogized to an "estuary that enlarges and spreads itself grandly as it pours in [sic] the great sea." The same comparison occurs in *Democratic Vistas*: "Mortal life is most important with reference to the immortal, the unknown, the spiritual, the only permanently real, which as the ocean waits for and receives the rivers, waits for us each and all" (*PW*, 403).

More frequently, however, Whitman compares dying to setting sail for a deep sea. Human existence is likened to a ship sailing in shallow waters or anchored near the shore. Within the context of this imagery, the lifting of the anchor symbolizes the soul's spiritual liberation at death, and the ship's passage into deeper, uncharted water symbolizes the emancipated spirit's transition into the afterlife and its newly acquired capacity for deeper participation in God's mysterious nature:

> Joy, shipmate, joy!
> (Pleas'd to my soul at death I cry,)
> Our life is closed, our life begins,
> The long, long anchorage we leave,
> The ship is clear at last, she leaps!
>   ("Joy, Shipmate, Joy")
>
> Put on the old ship all her power to-day!
> . . . .

> As we take to the open—take to the deepest, freest waters.
> ("Old Age's Ship & Crafty Death's")

Heave the anchor short!
Raise main-sail and jib—steer forth,
O little white-hull'd sloop, now speed on really deep waters,
. . . .
Sail out for good, eidólon yacht of me!
                                            ("Sail Out for Good, Eidólon Yacht!")

Whitman's frequent allusions to the sea as a mother is consistent with and expands these other meanings. The metaphor implies that one way of understanding the origins of the creation is to think of it as proceeding from God just as humans come forth from the maternal womb. Also this imagery suggests that God is a loving and caring divinity; and when the maternal sea in "Out of the Cradle" whispers the "delicious word death," Whitman is indicating that death should be viewed not with terror but instead as analogous to a mother's calling of her children back to herself.

With the sea symbolizing spiritual reality in Whitman's mental universe, the land represents the natural world, and the seashore assumes an important mediating function. It is a symbol of the mysterious frontier where the material order fuses with its spiritual source. In "Sea-Shore Fancies" the poet discusses the symbolic meaning of this boundary and its significance to his poetry:

> Even as a boy, I had the fancy, the wish, to write a piece, perhaps a poem, about the sea-shore—that suggesting, dividing line, contact, junction, the solid marrying the liquid—that curious, lurking something (as doubtless every objective form finally becomes to the subjective spirit,) which means far more than its mere first sight, grand as that is—blending the real and ideal, and each made portion of the other.
>
> (*PW*, 138-39)

The seashore exercised such a strong influence upon his psyche that he resolved to write a book expressing this "liquid, mystic theme." However, later he decided that it would not serve as the subject of his work, but rather as an "invisible *influence*, a pervading gauge and tally."

This retrospective commentary may not be strict autobiography, but it does elucidate the shoreline's symbolic meaning in the *Leaves* where it serves as a locus of spiritual perception and poetic inspiration. In numerous poems an important revelation occurs at the margin of waters. In "Out of the Cradle," it is at the beach that Whitman learns the meaning of death and achieves his birth as a poet. In "As I Ebb'd with the Ocean of Life," while walking the Long Island strand, the poet perceives the sea ("the ocean so mysterious") as the symbol of God's infinite and incomprehensible nature and he then becomes overwhelmed with the relative insignificance of himself and his poetic vision. In "By Blue Ontario's Shore," Whitman is at the shoreline when a phantom arises and demands from him the poem *"that comes from the soul of America"* (l. 4). In "When I Heard at the Close of the Day," the most intimate love poem in "Calamus," the poet lies with his lover on the seashore—and the sea, symbolizing the divinity, assures him of the sanctity of his love:

> And that night while all was still I heard the waters roll slowly continually up
>   the shores,
> I heard the hissing rustle of the liquid and sands as directed to me whispering
>   to congratulate me,
> For the one I love most lay sleeping by me under the same cover in the cool
>   night.
>
> ("When I Heard at the Close of the Day")

Lesser shorelines in the *Leaves* can also function in the same way. For instance, in "Calamus" when Whitman presents a form of spiritual love that is an anticipation of the divine love he will know after death, he plucks the symbol from a pond which he locates beyond the "gates" of this world, thus suggesting that it, like Thoreau's Walden Pond, possesses an otherworldly depth:

> Collecting I traverse the garden the world, but soon I pass the gates,
> Now along the pond-side, now wading in a little, fearing not the wet,
> . . . .
> And here what I now draw from the water, wading in the pond-side,
> . . . .
> And this, O this shall henceforth be the token of comrades, this calamus-root
>   shall.
>
> ("These I Singing in Spring," ll. 3, 4, 18, & 20)

The shoreline and waters are important elements in the spiritual ecology of the calamus plant.

Whitman's main use of aquatic symbolism is to suggest God's transcendent nature, but he also sometimes uses it as a symbol for spiritual purification and renewal. For instance, the poet's immersions in the sea combine all the above aspects of the sea symbolism. They entail a journey across the mystic dividing line and also a form of death and rebirth in which the poet returns to the divine source of his existence and emerges in a more pure or noetic state. Accordingly Whitman's immersion in the sea in "Song of Myself" (22) prepares him for and thematically foreshadows his ensuing claim to religious prophecy. Likewise, in "When I Heard at the Close of the Day," Whitman spiritually prepares himself to meet his comrade by bathing himself in the sea.

In a related use of this imagery, the poet describes his effort to sanctify the natural world as a sending of sea-sounds and sea-breezes onto the land. He indicates his desire to create a religious democracy in "Thou Mother with Thy Equal Brood" (l. 24), by stating that he will send "murmuring under, pervading all . . . the rustling sea-sound." Similarly, he promises to bless Lincoln's grave by sending "Sea-winds blown from east and west, / Blown from the Eastern sea and blown from the Western sea, till there on the prairies meeting" ("When Lilacs Last in the Dooryard Bloom'd," ll. 74–75).

As a concluding point, it should be noted that Whitman attempts to modernize his aquatic symbolism by adapting it to an evolutionary world view. In line with his process understanding of the universe, he conceives of the soul as engaged in an ever-continuing spiritual voyage. Thus Whitman depicts his readers as sailors of spiritual waters who emphatically exclaim that they are confronted with a "*boundless vista*" ("In Cabin's Ships at Sea"); and he depicts the soul's ongoing existence in the afterlife not as an arrival at a safe harbor but as an embarkation upon a deeper level of the divine consciousness:

> Oh little white-hull'd sloop, now speed on really deep waters,
> (I will not call it our concluding voyage,
> But outset and sure entrance to the truest, best, maturest;).
> > ("Sail Out for Good, Eidólon Yacht!")

After death, the soul would confidently sail on, realizing that its new voyage was but another exploration of the "seas of God."

> Sail forth—steer for the deep waters only,
> . . . .
> O my brave soul!
> O farther farther sail!
> O daring joy, but safe! are they not all the seas of God?
> O farther, farther, farther sail!
> > ("Passage to India," 9)

But this "modernization" of a traditional religious symbol is not very clearly exemplified in Whitman's aquatic imagery. It appears more dramatically in the climactic movement of "Song of Myself," which derives its significance from the fact that it presents the addition of a new religious meaning to two traditional symbols.

V

THE PRINCIPAL POEM

It is likely that no more than one or two hundred people, at the very most, read the 1855 *Leaves*, and with the exceptions of Emerson, who found "incomparable things said incomparably well," and Thoreau, who was convinced, at least by 1856, that the author had "spoken more truth than any American or modern that I know,"[1] few readers had the faintest inkling that the long first poem was Whitman's announcement of a new faith for a new era. During the process of composition, Whitman quietly wrote his verse, probably sharing his work with no one. Adrift in the seas of his mystical vision, he lost sight of the vast distance between his bold new orientation and that of even the most ardently millennial and perfectionist Christians, let alone of the even larger gap between his outlook and that of the legions of spiritually lukewarm Americans. In one respect Whitman's period of creative isolation and spiritual solipsism was his salvation. Fortified by his readings in Emerson and free from the critical response of others, he was able to sustain the needed courage to proclaim his audacious message. But this artistic isolation also had its liabilities. Out of touch with his potential audience, he could not anticipate the difficulties his readers would encounter and try to lessen the burden of understanding, nor could he prepare himself for the abysmal reception his book would receive.

From his post-Christian and perfectionist perspective, Whitman looked forward to a new generation of readers who, committed to the goal of fully realizing their inherent spirituality, would wrestle with his cryptic bible, forcing it to give up its secret meanings. Instead most who opened the *Leaves* found, not good news about the universe, but strange pages filled with long, unintelligible lines, which they rejected as rambling prose. The blame can not be entirely attributed to the dull wits of Whitman's audience, for except to a few fellow mystics of a similar Transcendental bent, the 1855 edition, consisting mainly of "Song of Myself" and "Sleepers," was largely unintelligible. Whitman had written a book of poetry informed by a coherent world view, but it was in a language that drew heavily upon the poet's new symbols and mystical terminology. This private vocabulary, when combined with the ineffable nature of the subject matter and the poet's suggestive method, added up to a strange new mental universe to which readers were not given a sufficient number of conventional signs to find their bearings. In starting his new religion through a new style of poetry, Whitman simply did not have a community of readers who shared his language and he failed to include a lexicon. In later editions, as he provided more poems and altered existing ones to elaborate and clarify his prophetic intentions, more readers, especially those inclining toward mysticism and free religion, were able to put some of the pieces of the linguistic puzzle together.

Yet even today "Song of Myself" (with the possible exception of "Sleepers") remains the most enigmatic of the major poems. It is surely a tribute to Whitman's power that scholars recognize it as the most important poem in American literature even though there is still no agreement about its meaning. For instance, four rather recent important studies—by Richard Chase, who reads the poem as a "comic drama of the self" which takes "the specific form of American humor," and by Edwin Hairland Miller, Stephen Black, and David Cavitch, who make psychoanalytic interpretations,—do not find the "Song" to be religious in its character and purpose. On the other hand, James E. Miller, Jr., Malcolm Cowley, Diana Middlebrook, and George B. Hutchinson all, though each in quite different ways, conceive of it as the extended depiction of a religious consciousness in complex interaction with the world. Miller describes it as the "dramatic representation of a mystical experience" which parallels the phases of Christian mystical development but differs from them in that it celebrates the senses and the self. Cowley describes its subject as "a state of illumination induced by two (or three) separate moments of ecstasy" and says that most of its teachings "belong to the mainstream of Indian philosophy." Middlebrook views it as "the personification of a theory of the Coleridgean imagination" with its ability "to bestow grace on ordinary life" and holds that Whitman's purpose is to "liberate common folk into their identities as poets of their own experience." And Hutchinson characterizes it as an ecstatic performance in which the shamanic poet-prophet resolves the riddles of human existence in a manner which heals himself and is exemplary for the larger culture.[2]

In keeping with my general understanding of Whitman, I also think "Song of Myself" is essentially a religious work, but rather than seeing the poem as an American outcropping of Indian religion, or as illustrating a timeless religious mode of being, or as a poetic version of a shamanic ritual, I believe it is more accurately viewed as presenting a new religion for the American people that embraces modern science, especially nineteenth-century evolutionary thought, and that emphasizes personal religious experience and spiritual development. The poem either implies or explicitly asserts the basic ideas of Whitman's evolutionary religious cosmology and millennialist faith. Its central religious tenet is that the universe is the creation of a loving transcendent God who is also immanently present in the evolution of nature and the progressive course of history. According to this world view all the facts of nature and history are religious symbols, expressive of divine immanence, and contributing elements in a divinely ordained cosmic movement toward perfection. Furthermore, since humans are infused with this immanent divinity, their basic instincts and longings (Whitman is especially concerned to include their sexual impulses) are divine, and humans can perfect themselves in this life by freeing themselves of all impediments to spiritual growth. And since this immanent divinity is impelled with the instinct to return to its transcendent source, then after its human existence, the soul continues to attain to increasingly higher levels of participation in divine transcendence.

Proclaiming his religious vision in America, where he believed the average person was already virtually free of political and material oppression, Whitman anticipated that his new faith would, by further freeing the American people of psychological and spiritual oppression, bring the citizenry to perfection and the society to its millennial fulfillment. Accordingly the poem bristles with the ecstatic energy of a prophet who is announcing the end times. What was now needed was for the people of America to realize that they lived in a perfect universe that was designed for their well-being:

> Do you see O my brothers and sisters?
> It is not chaos or death—it is form, union, plan—it is eternal life—it is Happiness.
> (ll. 1317–18)

Yet although "Song of Myself" is informed by Whitman's new religion, its theme is not only the revelation of this faith but also Whitman's presentation of himself as its founding prophet. The ideas of his new faith are developed in all his poems, but in this first major poem Whitman is especially concerned to establish himself as the prophet of a new world view who will lead the reader on into the rest of his vision. The poem's ubiquitous "I," as often observed, is not just Whitman's self but the representative modern personality. It is, in fact, Whitman's illustration in the character of himself, of his millennial personality or "culminating man," the perfect modern *homo religiosus*. But in addition to presenting this representative self, which readers might emulate and eventually equal, Whitman also presents himself as unique in that he has the sense of calling and requisite spiritual insight and poetic power to promulgate a new religion. So while the "I" begins by declaring himself representative, "what I assume you shall assume," he quickly goes on to assert that he has a special mission: "I, now thirty-seven years old in perfect health begin [to expound my vision], / Hoping to cease not till death." Throughout the poem Whitman assumes the role of a prophet-teacher who addresses his readers as disciples or students. It is Whitman in his role as seer who discloses the spiritual meaning of the grass (section 6) and other natural facts, who sounds the victory music of his faith and prepares a spiritual banquet for his readers (Sections 18 & 19). Again it is not the representative Whitman, but the poet-prophet who is so excited by encountering the world with his senses-cum-soul that he must transmute his experience into poetic vision (Sections 24–31). It is only the inspired poet who has the spiritual insight to "understand and interpret the large hearts of heroes" (l. 822) and the saving knowledge with which to pull up the "descending man" (l. 1011) and cure "the sick as they pant on their backs" (l. 1021). It is Whitman the creator of a new religion who promises that his vision incorporates the truths of the religions of the past (Sections 41 & 43), and it is the religious founder who translates the earth and stars into a fresh proof of human immortality (Sections 44–46). In sum, as Whitman introduces the doctrines of his new religion, he also proclaims himself to be the prophet of a new age of the spirit.

I find the poem to have seven parts which largely correspond to the divisions of earlier scholars, and I think the poem can be seen as consisting of four large overlapping movements.[3] In the introductory sections (1–6), the poet dramatizes the intensity and compelling power of his religious experience, emphasizing the extent of his illumination and the amplitude of his faith. Next, in the long middle part of the poem (Sections 7–38), he shows how his spiritual mode of being enables him to perceive the world as a sacred universe and thus inspires him, as he phrased it later, "to attempt some worthy record of that entire faith and acceptance ('to justify the ways of God to man' is Milton's well-known and ambitious phrase) which is the foundation of moral America" ("A Backward Glance," PW, 729). Throughout these two movements, Whitman repeatedly suggests that he is a bearer of salvation. In the third and climactic phase (Sections 39–45), Whitman (1) explicitly declares himself the founder of a new religion, (2) dethrones the divine images of previous religions and declares the divinity of the human spirit and its potential for unlimited development, and (3) modernizes two old religious symbols, mother earth and the starry heavens, into a new interpretation of human immortality by adapting them to the theories of evolutionary geology and astronomy. This act of symbol transformation clarifies the basis for the spiritual optimism of the preceding passages by providing fresh confirmation that God has, in his loving providence, designed the world with humanity's well-being in mind. At the same time, this demonstration of poetic power provides the reader with a solid earnest of Whitman's ability to create a spiritual vision which will reconcile traditional religious values with the main tenets of modern culture. The poem ends with a brief summation and conclusion (Sections 46–52).

Although "Song of Myself" is informed by a coherent world view, the poem itself does not, as I have suggested earlier, provide the general reader with enough information about this world view to interpret the poem as a self-contained whole. Instead it is first necessary to arrive at an understanding of some of Whitman's symbols, his mystical vocabulary, and the essential structure of his vision by studying the entire Leaves. Since this preliminary work has been done in the preceding chapters, I will now draw upon it in the ensuing discussion.[4]

I

In terms of our earlier discussion of the nature of religious experience and the stages of the Christian mystical way, we can thus summarize the poem's opening movement (sections 1-6): Whitman asserts that he is purging his senses and intellect so he can assume a religious or illuminated mode of being in which he experiences nature as sacred and symbolic, and he affirms his religious experience to be an especially powerful and satisfying form of knowledge which gives him a sense of union with divinity. Whitman does not provide a detailed reenactment of his own spiritual development but rather attempts to suggest, through a series of statements and succinct vignettes, the various dimensions of his spiritual life. At the same time, he begins to establish himself as a prophet by persistently suggesting that he has a saving knowledge to bestow upon his readers.

In the first section Whitman describes himself preparing to enter into spiritual communion with nature. Like the Christian mystics, his immediate objective is to detach himself from busy concerns and relax so that his soul will come forth ("I loafe and invite my soul"). His goal is to free his mind of conceptual systems which distort experience ("Creeds and schools in abeyance") so he can encounter the natural world truthfully ("Nature without check with original energy") and assimilate himself with the divine laws which inform the creation.[5]

The poet's ensuing rejection of houses with their "perfumes" further indicates his desire to escape from the distorting influences of contemporary civilization so that he can recover his primal self ("become undisguised and naked") and establish a fully sensuous and therefore spiritual relationship with nature:

> I will go to the bank by the wood and become undisguised and naked,
> I am mad for it to be in contact with me.
> The smoke of my own breath,
> Echoes, ripples, buzz'd whispers, love-root, silk-thread, crotch and vine,
> My respiration and inspiration, the beating of my heart, the passing of blood
>   and air through my lungs,
> The sniff of green leaves and dry leaves, and of the shore and dark-color'd sea-
>   rocks, and of hay in the barn,
> The sound of the belch'd words of my voice loos'd to the eddies of the wind,
> A few light kisses, a few embraces, a reaching around of arms.

(2)

Whitman cryptically indicates that he is experiencing the sanctity of nature by employing virtually his full lexicon—"Echoes," "ripples," "whispers," "sniff," "kisses," "embraces," "reaching around of arms"—for describing his soul's participation in, or perception of, the spiritual emanations of the natural order. (My point is not to deny the frank sexuality of Whitman's poetry, but to indicate that here and elsewhere in the *Leaves* he blesses sexual intimacy by using it as a symbol of the soul's relationship with divinity.) These relationships with nature provide the ties ("love-root, silk-thread, crotch and vine") which unite his soul to God. The references to inhalation and other vital activities symbolize those spiritual processes which enliven the poet's soul, inspiring him to utter a frank and natural poetry consistent with the spirit of nature itself: "the belch'd words of my voice loos'd to the eddies of the wind."

After having hinted at his spiritual illumination, Whitman obliquely introduces his salvific theme, promising the reader a treasure more valuable than material wealth and a form of knowledge superior to mere learning or aesthetic appreciation. In a passage whose full import becomes evident later, he indicates that he will lead the reader beneath the realm of appearances to an immediate relationship with the divine source of all being:

> Have you reckon'd a thousand acres much? have you reckon'd the earth much?
> Have you practis'd so long to learn to read?
> Have you felt so proud to get at the meaning of poems?
>
> Stop this day and night with me and you shall possess the origin of all poems,
> You shall possess the good of the earth and sun, (there are millions of suns left,)
> You shall no longer take things at second or third hand, nor look through the
>   eyes of the dead, nor feed on the spectres in books.
>
> (2)

In the next three sections (3-5), Whitman characterizes his faith. It defies verbal explanation ("To elaborate is no avail") and it is not a matter of intellectual understanding: "Backward I see in my own days where I sweated through fog with linguists and contenders, / I have no mockings or arguments, I witness and wait." It must be experienced to be understood; and having realized it existentially, the poet has found it more than satisfactory. His anxieties have been resolved and he approaches the universe with a solid confidence:

> Sure as the most certain sure, plumb in the uprights, well entretied, braced in
>   the beams,
> Stout as a horse, affectionate, haughty, electrical,
> I and this mystery here we stand.
>
> (3)

Whitman trusted in his religious experience and the insights arising from it because, as discussed in chapter 2, they possessed a special power or reality; they satisfied the needs of his soul. "The test of the goodness or truth of anything," he wrote in his notes, "is the soul itself—whatever does good to the soul, soothes, refreshes, cheers, inspirits, consoles" (*Workshop*, 49). This criterion of truth is affirmed in section three:

> (1) I am satisfied—I see, dance, laugh, sing;
> (2) As the hugging and loving bed-fellow sleeps at my side through the night,
>   and withdraws at the peep of the day with stealthy tread,

(3) Leaving me baskets cover'd with white towels swelling the house with their
    plenty,
(4) Shall I postpone my acceptation and realization and scream at my eyes,
(5) That they turn from gazing after and down the road,
(6) And forthwith cipher and show me to a cent,
(7) Exactly the value of one and exactly the value of two, and which is ahead?

Manuscript evidence indicates that Whitman repeatedly labored over line 2,[6] but its possible sexual implications need not concern us here. The importance of this passage for the present discussion is not the gender of the bedfellow or the nature (physical or Platonic) of the love intimated, but the fact that this love is especially meaningful or powerful and is interpreted as a religious experience. Whitman asserts that it provides the bread of real life (the "baskets cover'd with white towels"), and he carefully distinguishes it from a mere dream or passing enthusiasm or infatuation by stating that its benefits remain after the event itself (3). In the light of having experienced this life-giving reality, he incredulously asks if he should deny its validity ("postpone my acceptation and realization"), and instead discipline and redirect himself ("scream at my eyes" to "turn"), limiting his existence to merely rational and economic considerations (6 & 7). The question receives no answer because Whitman feels it needs none; he is sure that everyone would choose the powerful and real.

After making this explanation of the "truth" of religious experience, Whitman briefly depicts a former moment of profound mystical illumination in which he had a sense of his soul's perfect union with the divine nature:

(1) I believe in you my soul, the other I am must not abase itself to you,
. . . .
(2) I mind how once we lay such a transparent summer morning,
(3) How you settled your head athwart my hips and gently turn'd over upon
    me,
(4) And parted the shirt from my bosom-bone, and plunged your tongue to my
    bare-stript heart,
(5) And reach'd till you felt my beard, and reach'd till you held my feet.
(6) Swiftly arose and spread around me the peace and knowledge that pass all
    the argument of the earth,
(7) And I know that the hand of God is the promise of my own,
(8) And I know that the spirit of God is the brother of my own,
(9) And that all the men ever born are also my brothers, and the women my
    sisters and lovers,
(10) And that a kelson of the creation is love,
(11) And limitless are leaves still or drooping in the fields,
(12) And brown ants in the little wells beneath them,
(13) And mossy scabs of the worm fence, heap'd stones, elder, mullein and
    poke-weed.

(5)

The erotic language (2–5) functions in two ways; it suggests the intensity and completeness of the spiritual experience; also it sounds an important subtheme, the poet's desire to sanctify sexuality, because it implicitly states that sexual activity is not only a physical act but also a religious symbol which manifests how the soul longs for and unites with God.

In this moment of mystical attunement Whitman has a strong sense of his inner divinity (8) and his declaration that the "hand of God is the promise of my own" (7) is the poem's first veiled affirmation that the human soul continues to develop in the afterlife until it becomes the virtual equal of its creator. This part of the poem is also the first appearance in the *Leaves* of what might be termed Whitman's "passages of spiritual peace," that is, moments of intense religious experience characterized by a state of serene well-being (6) which convince Whitman that divine love is the ultimate reality of the universe (10) and that the experience of this love whether with the divinity directly, or through the mediation of natural facts or other humans, is the best proof of human immortality. In this state of mystical consciousness, the poet also recognizes the divinity immanent in his fellow humans (9) and in all of nature, even its most common and insignificant items: "leaves," "ants," "elder," and "poke-weed." Even these, like all natural facts, are "limitless" in a twofold sense: having the capacity to function as religious symbols, they open into or are revelations of the infinite spiritual ground of all being; also like everything else in Whitman's universe, they possess immortal souls that undergo "limitless" development as they continuously evolve into higher forms of life.

Finally, it might be noted that the shift from the past tense (1–6) to the present (7–13) is important. This particular experience is a past event, but because it spoke so powerfully to the poet's being, his faith endures. He can still confidently affirm: "I know."

Whitman proceeds, in an ingeniously crafted discussion of his perception of the symbolic meaning of things, to illustrate the "limitless" meaning of one common natural fact:

> A child said *What is the grass?* fetching it to me with full hands;
> How could I answer the child? I do not know what it is any more than he.
>
> (6)

But Whitman immediately shows that the grass reveals several levels of spiritual meaning. Its color is a symbol of the fact that humans are creatures of hope: "I guess it must be the flag of my disposition, out of hopeful green stuff woven." It is also a symbol of the love that informs the processes of nature: "I guess the grass is itself a child, the produced babe of the vegetation." It proves that God considers all humans as equals and thus endorses democracy, for the grass is a "uniform hieroglyphic" which reveals itself to everyone, "Sprouting alike in broad zones and narrow zones, / Growing among black folks as among white." As a symbol of democracy, it also reveals to Whitman that his spiritual vision should be open to all: "Kanuck, Tuckahoe, Congressman, Cuff, I give them the same, I receive them the same." Perhaps most important of all, in a passage that foreshadows Whitman's use of grass in "Calamus" and the "Lilacs" elegy, the grass is presented as a symbol of immortality: "The smallest sprout shows there is really no death."

In the most startling and charming part of this section, Whitman compares God to a flirtatious young woman and the grass is her perfumed handkerchief "designedly dropt":

> Or I guess it is the handkerchief of the Lord,
> A scented gift and remembrancer designedly dropt,
> Bearing the owner's name someway in the corners, that we may see and remark,
>   and say *Whose?*

The grass serves as a symbol of the fact that all natural facts are religious symbols which, when detected, acquaint the soul with God. With precious wit, Christian mystics speak of God's wooing or love match with the soul, but here Whitman is more playful and daring for he depicts God as coquettishly dropping a perfumed hankie smack in the way of his human creatures. One suspects that *She* might even walk the streets to solicit vagrant souls.

II

Whitman moves from a meditation upon this one natural fact to an enumeration in sections 7–17 of the items of America's natural landscape and of the manifold activities and enterprises of its heterogeneous population. These catalogs of Americana have raised two questions for critics: Are they poetry? What is their relationship to the larger poem? One defense of the catalogs' poetic character, which is also the probable inspiration for Whitman's use of this device, is Emerson's declaration in "The Poet": "Bare lists of words are found suggestive to an imaginative and excited mind." But more compelling to many modern readers than this article of Transcendental poetics is the fact that both the imagery and the diction of these passages often rise to a level of vivid, quintessentially American realism that has never been surpassed in its economy and originality. It is not without significance that when Randall Jarrell, in his often cited essay on Whitman's style, argued that Whitman was "a poet of the greatest and oddest delicacy and originality and sensitivity, so far as words are concerned,"[7] he drew most of his examples from the catalogs in "Song of Myself." But the other question of function has received less convincing answers, and I would argue that an analysis of Whitman's own statements about his art indicates that he intended for the catalogs to serve several complementary poetic, political and religious purposes in order to further his claim to being the prophet of a new religion that would unite and perfect the American people and convince them of the sanctity of this world.

In aspiring to establish himself as a national bard Whitman realized that he somehow had to include all the American people in his vision. This idea finds expression in the 1855 Preface when Whitman asserts that the new American poet must be "commensurate with a people" (PW, 741), and it receives further elaboration in his self-assessment in a "A Backward Glance": "I have wish'd to put the complete Union of the States in my songs without any preference or partiality whatever. Henceforth, if they live and are read, it must be just as much South as North—just as much along the Pacific as Atlantic—in the valley of the Mississippi, in Canada, up in Maine, down in Texas, and on the shores of Puget Sound" (PW, 727). This quotation provides one important reason why the catalogs are a potpourri of the American people with summary passages like the following in which Whitman proclaims himself a member of every American region:

> A Southerner soon as a Northerner, a planter nonchalant and hospitable down
>   by the Oconee I live,
> A Yankee bound my own way ready for trade . . .
> . . . .
> At home on the hills of Vermont or in the woods of Maine, or the Texan ranch,
> Comrade of Californians, comrade of free North-Westerners. . . .
>
> (16)

Another passage from this same retrospective essay, explains one of the catalogs' political purposes: "For grounds for 'Leaves of Grass' . . . I abandon'd . . . high, exceptional personages of Old-World song. . . . But [introduced in their stead] the broadest average of humanity and its identities in the now ripening Nineteenth Century, and especially in each of their countless examples and practical occupations in the United States to-day" (PW, 715). In keeping with his democratic politics and identification with the working class, Whitman wanted to celebrate not the exceptional person but the masses of ordinary people. Accordingly the catalogs contain long lists of average Americans in their "practical occupations": the omnibus driver, policeman, boatman, trapper, butcher-boy, blacksmith, carpenter, pilot, harpooner, spinning-girl, farmer, printer, machinist, mill-girl, etc. In addition to providing an economical means of embracing all of these women and men, the catalogs are also implicitly egalitarian because Whitman does not rank the occupations in some order of importance but places them all on equal footing. The contralto is paired with the carpenter (ll. 264–65) and the duck-shooter with the deacons (ll. 269-70); after the bride comes the opium-eater, followed by the prostitute, who precedes the president (ll. 303–308).

Whitman also wanted the catalogs to promote political unity among the diverse peoples and regions of the United States. According to the inherited wisdom of eighteenth-century political thought, a republic, which depended upon the voluntary commitment of its citizenry to the common good, was an inappropriate form of government for an extensive geographical area because regions within a vast republic would develop special customs and economic interests and these in turn would prompt secessionist movements and perhaps civil war. When the United States was formed in defiance of this prevailing theory, Madison, in Federalist Paper X, tried to settle fears about the wisdom of this venture by arguing that in a large republic enough factions would develop to cancel one another out. But fears of political disintegration were kept alive by the nation's transcontinental expansion and the growing hostility between the North and South.

Like many of his contemporaries, Whitman feared that the United States was too large and diverse to sustain itself as an enduring political entity, so even as late as his writing of "Democratic Vistas" (1867- 70), he still expressed his "fear of conflicting and irreconcilable interiors, and the lack of a common skeleton." To remedy this situation, he called for a national poetry which would establish the "only reliable identity, the moral and artistic one"; and he proposed that "two or three really original American poets . . . fusing contributions, races, far localities . . . would give more compaction . . . to these States, than all its Constitutions, legislative and judicial ties" (*PW*, 368). This passage further clarifies Whitman's use of catalogs to include representatives of all the nation's peoples and regions: he is not only proclaiming himself poet of all the people and declaring their equality but he is also enlisting his poetry as an agent of social cohesion.

Besides including all the people, Whitman also wanted to improve them, and so the catalogs are also designed to promote the readers' moral and spiritual development. Whitman felt that an active, hardy, independent, passionate life close to nature nourished the soul by freeing it from the repressive influences of an excessive intellectualism and artificial moral restrictions. Civilization tended to alienate the human spirit from its proper grounding in a healthy (in fact, divine) animal vitality. Speaking to this point in "A Backward Glance" Whitman asserted: "The educated world seems to have been growing more and more ennuyed for ages, leaving to our time the inheritance of it all." But this degenerative influence could be compensated for by recalling people to the "original inexhaustible fund of buoyancy, normally resident in the race" (*PW*, 725–26). Earlier, in the 1876 Preface, he declared that the ideal American personality was to be revitalized by the primal energies of nature and the human passions, enabling it to attain to a perfect integration of intellect and instinct; it was, in Whitman's words, to possess "the precious accumulations of the learning and experiences of the Old World . . . vitalized by the perennial influences of Nature at first hand, [and] . . . the passions, in all their fullest heat and potency, of courage, rankness, amativeness, and of immense pride." The American people would "reap from them the savage and sane nourishment indispensable to a hardy nation" (*PW*, 468–69). It is because of his faith in the restorative powers of nature that Whitman declares in the catalogs: "I am enamour'd of growing out-doors, / Of men that live among cattle or taste of the ocean or woods" (ll. 255-56); or again "Alone far in the wilds and mountains I hunt, / Wandering amazed at my own lightness and glee" (ll. 175-76).

This faith in nature is another reason why the catalogs are filled with hunters, farmers, fishermen, and sailors and briefly delineated scenes such as one of a trapper "drest mostly in skins, his luxuriant beard and curls protected his neck, he held his bride by the hand, / She had long eyelashes, her head was bare, her coarse straight locks descended upon her voluptuous limbs and reach'd to her feet" (ll. 187-88). Similarly, because Whitman believed in the "savage and sane nourishment" of the passions, including sexual desire, he describes without criticism "The youngster and the red-faced girl [who] turn aside up the busy hill" (l. 150) and makes a masterful condemnation of female sexual repression by tenderly portraying a woman burning with secret desire as she covertly gazes upon a group of young male bathers (ll. 199-216).

Whitman conceived of this use of nature and the passions to revitalize the personality as essentially a religious process. In the catalogs he gives his readers pictures of American life that he described in the 1855 Preface as "the roughs and beards and space and ruggedness and nonchalance that *the soul loves*" (emphasis added, *PW*, 435). In terms of my analysis of the mystical way in chapter 4, this appeal to the liberating energies of nature and the instincts should be seen as relating to the second half of purgation, which entails a freeing of the self from the tyranny of the mind's customary preconceptions and habits of thought so that one can experience "pure sensation" or "sensation without thought."

Whitman also uses the catalogs to convince his readers of the perfect sanctity of the universe. It was not enough, Whitman declared in the 1855 Preface, for the poet "to indicate . . . the beauty and dignity which always attach to dumb real objects," for people also expected him "to indicate the path between reality and their souls" (*PW*, 439). In the catalogs Whitman discloses two pathways: he implies that all the objects in the universe are religious symbols that feed the soul and he asserts that everything in the universe is an integral part of a divinely ordained program for the soul's development. The inventories of Americana are punctuated with reminders that all these items, like the grass discussed in the preceding section, were designed by God to be bearers of spiritual meaning. Reflecting upon the gaze of an ox, he ponders its meaning: "what is that you express in your eyes? / It seems to me more than all the print I have read in my life" (ll. 235–36). Or again, he suggests that the colors of two wood ducks are not accidental but have been designed by God to correspond to inner spiritual facts:

> I believe in those wing'd purposes
> And acknowledge, red, yellow, white, playing within me,
> And consider green and violet and the tufted crown intentional.
> (ll. 239–41)

And in response to the wild gander's call in the night, he states that he understands its meaning: "The pert may suppose it meaningless, but I listening close, / Find its purpose and place up there toward the wintry sky" (ll. 247–48). At the same time he insists that all these things are also good because they are in their proper places, advancing the world's amelioration:

> And [I] peruse manifold objects, no two alike and every one good,
> The earth good and the stars good, and their adjuncts all good,
>
> (ll. 134–35)

> (The moth and the fish-eggs are in their place,

> The bright suns I see and the dark suns I cannot see are in their place,
> The palpable is in its place and the impalpable is in its place.)
>
> (ll. 352–54)

These natural facts, Whitman affirms, are not the result of chance or the residue of blind forces; all have, as he states later, "some intricate purpose" (l. 382).

Whitman wanted his first set of catalogs to help provide a foundation for his millennial faith and belief in America's special mission by leaving his readers with the impression that he had considered all the ingredients of American life and found them sacred in themselves and elements of a cosmic plan designed by God. His ever-present, underlying poetic intention, as noted earlier, was to present "some worthy record of that entire faith . . . which is the foundation of moral America. . . . [To] formulate a poem whose every thought or fact should . . . connive at an implicit belief in the wisdom, health, mystery, beauty of every process, every concrete object, every human or other existence, not only consider'd from the point of view of all, but of each" ("A Backward Glance," *PW*, 729). Once Whitman converted the American people to this unrestricted faith, he could then go on to convince them of their inherent divinity and of America's "intricate purpose" in this cosmic drama of human redemption.

III

In the next enigmatic sequence (18-22) Whitman gives indirect expression to his millennial vision through two cryptic pairs of symbols. The movement begins with a set of traditional metaphors for spiritual salvation: military victory and a banquet. First, Whitman compares his poetry to victory music:

> With music strong I come, with my cornets and my drums,
> I play not marches for accepted victors only, I play marches for conquer'd and slain persons.
> . . . .
> I also say it is good to fall, battles are lost in the same spirit in which they are won.

I beat and pound for the dead,
I blow through my embouchures my loudest and gayest for them.

(18)

It was conventional in antebellum millennial rhetoric to conceive of Christianity's struggle against Satan and sin as analogous to a military conflict,[8] and Whitman draws upon this usage in describing his post-Christian vision of humanity's struggle for spiritual liberation. In promising music for this warfare, Whitman is pledging to provide his readers with a vision that will guide and sustain them in their efforts to develop their souls and establish an ideal spiritual democracy. In terms of his vision Whitman can assert that it is as good to fail as to succeed in this struggle because in both cases the participants develop their souls by giving expression to their divine impulses for freedom and perfection. In declaring that his "loudest and gayest" music is for the dead, Whitman is indirectly alluding to the fact that the boldest and most optimistic element of his new religion is his doctrine of immortality and incessant development.

The ensuing banquet imagery which stresses the inclusiveness of Whitman's faith alludes to the Last Supper and echoes passages in Luke emphasizing the universality of Christ's message.[9] In this way Whitman appeals to biblical precedent in proclaiming his extreme version of the period's widespread rejection of Calvinism's doctrine of a limited atonement that left most souls predestined for hell.

This is the meal equally set, this the meat for natural hunger,
It is for the wicked just the same as the righteous, I make appointments with all,
I will not have a single person slighted or left away,
The kept-woman, sponger, thief, are hereby invited,
The heavy-lipp'd slave is invited, the venerealee is invited;
There shall be no difference between them and the rest.

(19)

There is no place for a hell in Whitman's vision of a universe of constantly progressing souls. Instead he possessed a "quenchless faith," as he phrased it, in "salvation universal" ("Song of the Universal," ll. 58 & 61), but at the same time neither does Whitman propose an amoral philosophy of "anything goes" as this passage might be mistakenly assumed to imply. Rather he propounded a doctrine of "prudence suitable for immortality" (given its first articulation in the 1855 Preface) by which he meant that virtuous actions developed the soul and prepared it for a higher existence in the afterlife: "All that a male or female does that is vigorous and benevolent and clean is so much sure profit to him or her in the unshakable order of the universe and through the whole scope of it forever" (PW, 453–54). In contrast, vile or base actions restricted or distorted the human spirit, causing it to begin the next phase of its existence in a less developed spiritual state. The democratic or inclusive character of Whitman's faith comes from the fact that everyone is subject to this developmental spiritual economy and must participate on the same terms: "If the savage or felon . . . the greatest poet or savan . . . the President or chief justice is wise it is the same . . . if the young mechanic . . . if the prostitute is wise it is no more nor less. The interest will come round" (*PW*, 746–47). Whitman can advertise his meal as "equally set" for the wicked and the righteous because it is an article of his religion that every soul will receive the same nourishment for the same actions. With this egalitarian theme, Whitman hoped to give readers a sense of self-worth and possibility that would inspire them to work for their spiritual perfection.

These promises of salvation are supplemented by Whitman's use of terrestrial symbolism to declare his ability to disclose a sacred universe. Whitman first embraces the earth:

> Smile O voluptuous cool-breath'd earth!
> . . . .
> Far-swooping elbow'd earth—rich apple-blossom'd earth!
> Smile, for your lover comes.
> Prodigal, you have given me love—therefore I to you give love!
> O unspeakable passionate love.[10]
>
> (21)

This passage, which picks up and amplifies the theme of section 5 ("a kelson of the creation is love"), illustrates the need to relate a single instance of Whitman's symbolism to its recurring usage. Whitman perceived the earth as a significant symbol, "The mighty earth-eidólon" ("Eidólons"). Despite its role as provider of humanity's material needs, it was even more important for its spiritual meaning: "the whole earth and all the stars in the sky are for religion's sake" ("Starting from Paumanok," l. 106). The earth disclosed several important spiritual truths, but at this point Whitman calls attention to it as a symbol of God's providential love. Other poems reinforce this meaning: the earth is termed a "great mother" ("Song of the Rolling Earth," l. 41), it has "great charity" ("Kosmos"), and it is the "Earth of chaste love" ("Spontaneous Me," l. 14).

In a related use of terrestrial imagery Whitman also makes the earth a symbol of divinely ordained evolution. Since he conceived of higher forms of life as evolving out of the earth, he also saw the earth as a manifestation of the divine love which informed the evolutionary process in its movement toward higher forms of perfection. Thus he speaks of "Amelioration" as "one of the earth's words" ("Song of the Rolling Earth," l. 17) and exclaims: "The apple-shaped earth and we upon it, surely the drift of them is something grand" ("A Song for Occupations," l. 54). To Whitman's mind, one of the greatest proofs of the goodness of the universe and, consequently, of God's love, was the fact that the earth had nurtured the potential for human life throughout its long evolutionary ascent. Whitman hoped that the earth, when perceived as a religious symbol from an evolutionary perspective, would convince his readers that everything in the universe contributed to a universal process of purposeful development. This theme, elaborated later in sections 38 and 44, is not made explicit here, but it underlies Whitman's promise to return the earth's "prodigal" love.

Whitman provides further justification for his comprehensive love, which includes even what appears to be evil, in the next section's subtle aquatic symbolism:

(1) You sea! I resign myself to you also—I guess what you mean,
(2) I behold from the beach your crooked inviting fingers,
(3) I believe you refuse to go back without feeling of me,
. . . .
(4) Sea of the brine of life and of unshovell'd yet always-ready graves,
(5) Howler and scooper of storms, capricious and dainty sea,
(6) I am integral with you, I too am of one phase and of all phases.

(7) Partaker of influx and efflux I, extoller of hate and conciliation,
. . . .
(8) (Shall I make my list of things in the house and skip the house that supports them?)
(9) I am not the poet of goodness only, I do not decline to be the poet of wickedness also.

                                                                                    (22)

Whitman gives himself to the sea because he intuits its spiritual meaning (1). In keeping with the preceding discussion of Whitman's aquatic symbolism, it may be said that the sea symbolizes the divine reality which preserves ("brine of life") or supports ("house that supports") the creation ("lists of things" in the poem) and reabsorbs things after their finite existence (thus it has "unshovell'd yet always-ready graves"). The sea's desire for the poet (2 & 3) refers to the mystical love by which God calls humans to him/her, first through religious symbols and, ultimately, through death. Immersion itself suggests a temporary experience of perfect integration with divinity (6); it is an anticipation of the illumination the soul will know after death. In this momentary state of elevated consciousness, the poet is able to understand the underlying goodness in the seeming contradictions and evils of this world (7 & 9), and he can lovingly proclaim the wholeness and perfection of the universe.

                                        IV

In the next ten verse paragraphs (23-32) Whitman simultaneously sanctifies the human senses and instincts, especially sexuality. As in sections 1-6, but this time in greater detail, he clarifies the existential basis of his vision by showing how his religious faith arises out of his mystical or "illuminated" perception in which he experiences the world with senses "cleansed" of intellectual preconceptions and worldly aspirations. At the same time Whitman continues to develop his right to proclaim himself a prophet by repeatedly asserting that he is so possessed by the spirit that he can do nothing other. Overwhelmed by his sense of the perfection and sanctity of the universe, he has no choice but to heed Emerson's instruction to the poet and proclaim "It is in me, and shall out."

The celebration of the body as a means to religious experience is introduced carefully. For instance, Whitman endorses modern science "Hurrah for positive science! long live exact demonstration!" But he then quickly goes on to inform the "Gentlemen" of science that their objective truths are not the foundation of his vision: "Your facts are useful, and yet they are not my dwelling, / I but enter by them to an area of my dwelling" (23). At this point he also takes special pains to exorcise his readers of their dualistic orientation which divides the world into good and evil. Insistently, he brings forth items that have traditionally been termed ugly or evil, and gives them his benediction:

> Through me many long dumb voices,
> Voices of the interminable generations of prisoners and slaves,
> Voices of the diseas'd and despairing and of thieves and dwarfs,
> . . . .
> And of the rights of them the others are down upon,
> Of the deform'd, trivial, flat, foolish, despised,
> Fog in the air, beetles rolling balls of dung.
>
> (24)

Whitman ends this catalog by emphasizing the holiness of the human body, including the sexual organs:

> Through me forbidden voices,
> Voices of sexes and lusts, voices veil'd and I remove the veil,
> Voices indecent by me clarified and transfigur'd
> . . . .
> If I worship one thing more than another it shall be the spread of my own body,
>   or any part of it,
> Translucent mould of me it shall be you!
> Shaded ledges and rests it shall be you!
> Firm masculine colter it shall be you!
>
> (24)

This celebration of the body introduces the idea that it is sacred because it is the means by which the world comes into contact with the soul:

> I believe in the flesh and the appetites,
> Seeing, hearing, feeling, are miracles, and each part and tag of me is a miracle.
>
> Divine am I inside and out, and I make holy whatever I touch or am touch'd
>   from.
>
> (24)

Having thus affirmed the validity of religious truth and the sanctity of the body, Whitman is now ready to transfigure the flesh by demonstrating how his sensory experience gives rise to his religious vision. From the latter part of section 24 through 29, he dramatizes how his sensations of sight, hearing, and touch culminate in ecstasies of illumination so overwhelming that he is compelled to relieve his excited soul through poetic utterance.

Sight, supplemented by the activity of his soul, enables the poet to perceive the sunrise as a symbol of spiritual illumination and inspiration:

   (1) To behold the day-break!
   (2) The little light fades the immense and diaphanous shadows,
   . . . .
   (3) Something I cannot see puts upward libidinous prongs,
   (4) Seas of bright juice suffuse heaven.
   . . . .
   (5) The heav'd challenge from the east that moment over my head,
   (6) The mocking taunt, See then whether you shall be master!

                                                        (24)

   (7) Dazzling and tremendous how quick the sun-rise would kill me,
   (8) If I could not now and always send sun-rise out of me.
   (9) We also ascend dazzling and tremendous as the sun,
 (10) We found our own O my soul in the calm and cool of the daybreak.

                                                        (25)

The sun's ability to dispel the darkness suggests to Whitman the ease with which spiritual enlightenment resolves the dark or problematic elements of life, revealing them to have no more substance than "diaphanous shadows" (2). And he conceives of the early morning sun, while it remains below the horizon and shoots its rays upward into the heavens (3 & 4), as an analogue to the poetic act which also proceeds from something the poet "cannot see," the mysterious recesses of his soul, and which also sends upward "libidinous prongs" and "bright juices," that is, songs of passionate love and joy. Aware of this parallel, the poet feels taunted by the sun to create a spiritual revelation superior to its physical illumination (5 & 6). He can respond to this challenge because his soul has been awakened by the profound mystical experience described earlier in section five and referred to here in lines 9 and 10. Furthermore, he claims that he must respond because otherwise his consciousness would be overpowered by the psychic energies engendered by his experience (7 & 8).

Next Whitman turns to hearing ("Now I will do nothing but listen") and presents a brief catalogue of sounds which progresses through four levels: first are the sounds of nature, next of the human voice, then of machines, and finally of music, ending with a grand opera:

(1) I hear the train'd soprano (what work with hers is this?)
(2) The orchestra whirls me wider than Uranus flies,
(3) It wrenches such ardors from me I did not know I possess'd them,
(4) It sails me, I dab with bare feet, they are lick'd by the indolent waves,
(5) I am cut by bitter and angry hail, I lose my breath,
(6) Steep'd amid honey'd morphine, my windpipe throttled in fakes of death.[11]

(26)

At its most fundamental level of metaphoric meaning, this cryptic passage affirms the traditional mystical perception that the entire creation contributes to a cosmic harmony. In ascending through the sounds to their culmination in the rapturous music of a grand opera, Whitman's more explicit point—perhaps still not made sufficiently clear—is that all sounds become sacred music to his illuminated soul. As he states later in "That Music Always Round Me," "I hear not the volumes of sound merely, I am moved by the exquisite meanings." As with the sun in the earlier passage, the music also transports the poet's soul (2–4), so that he is on the verge of psychological dissolution (5 & 6); and Whitman's comparison of his song with the soprano's (1) suggests that he perceives the music, as he did the sunlight, to be presenting a challenge to his poetic power.

The passage on touch parallels the two preceding sequences. Whitman begins by implying that a mere touch can bring him to a new level of being: "Is this then a touch? Quivering me to a new identity." He depicts the power of touch by likening all tactile stimulation to sensations of sexual feeling: "My flesh and blood playing out lightening to strike what is hardly different from myself, / On all sides prurient provokers stiffening my limbs." These "provokers" are then described as raping the poet:

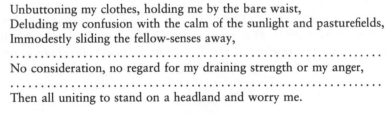

Unbuttoning my clothes, holding me by the bare waist,
Deluding my confusion with the calm of the sunlight and pasturefields,
Immodestly sliding the fellow-senses away,
. . . .
No consideration, no regard for my draining strength or my anger,
. . . .
Then all uniting to stand on a headland and worry me.

The sentries desert every other part of me,
They have left me helpless to a red marauder,
They all come to the headland to witness and assist against me.

(28)

This depiction of a frenzied poet, stripped and carried by touch to a headland, seems utterly without meaning until we recall that the seashore symbolizes the boundary where the finite merges with the infinite. Then it becomes evident that Whitman is obliquely stating that touch so transports his soul that it almost frees him from the natural world, plummeting him into the divine consciousness.[12] Once again sensation climaxes in a spiritual experience which brings the poet to the brink of consciousness: "You villain touch! What are you doing? My breath is tight in its throat, / Unclench your floodgates, you are too much for me."

Relief is found in sexual release, apparently brought on by masturbation ("my own hands carried me there"), and also, if I read Whitman's cryptic lines correctly, by poetic utterance:

(1) Blind loving wrestling touch, sheath'd hooded sharp-tooth'd touch!
(2) Did it make you ache so, leaving me?
(3) Parting track'd by arriving, perpetual payment of perpetual loan,
(4) Rich showering rain, and recompense richer afterward.
(5) Sprouts take and accumulate, stand by the curb prolific and vital,
(6) Landscapes projected masculine, full-sized and golden.

                                                                                    (29)

The passage indirectly refers to Whitman's sexual ejaculation: the semen "leaving me" (l. 2), the poet's "arriving" (l. 3) and the "showering rain" of semen (l. 4). But there is also an underlying triplicate analogy that likens Whitman's semen to showers of rain and to poetic utterances because all have the power to create new life. The semen and rain receive explicit comparison in the passage, but the analogy between sexual and poetic activity remains implicit here. It receives further development later in "Song of Myself" (40), where Whitman declares "On women fit for conception I start bigger and nimbler babes, / (This day I am jetting the stuff of far more arrogant republics)." And in "A Woman Waits for Me," Whitman informs his female readers that his poetry transmits the "stuff to start sons and daughters fit for these States, I press with slow rude muscle," and that he expects "perfect men and women out of my love-spendings" (ll. 28 & 36). The reference to receiving a "recompense richer afterward" (l. 4) is also evidence of the implicit analogy between Whitman's sexual and poetic activity. Earlier in the poem Whitman has promised to give back to the earth (l. 446) and to "repay" the divine sea (l. 453) the love that has been given to him by praising them in his poetry. Now he suggests that just as God's creation of the world was an act of love to humans that deserves repayment in kind, so he also is creating a new world and new humanity with his poetry, and for this act of love he expects to be repaid (the "recompense richer hereafter") with the spiritual love of his readers. "Lovers, continual lovers, only repay me," he declares in "City of Orgies"; and in a later part of "Song of Myself" he even suggests that just as he is helping his readers' souls to progress through the human stage of their development, so he expects them to return the favor at some later stage in their pilgrimage: "If you tire, give me both burdens, and rest the chuff of your hand on my hip, / And in due time you shall repay the same service to me" (ll. 1217–18).

In these passages, Whitman's spiritual realizations have been stimulated by segments of the outer world—a sunrise, grand opera, and erotic touches—that might easily engender deeply emotional, and thus soul-stirring experiences. But the poet then goes on to assert that every sight, sound, or touch, every sensory experience, regardless of how seemingly insignificant, is potentially a carrier of all spiritual truths and an experience of divinity:

> All truths wait in all things,
> They neither hasten their own delivery nor resist it,
> They do not need the obstetric forceps of the surgeon,
> The insignificant is as big to me as any,
> (What is less or more than a touch?)
>
> (30)

Whitman concludes this discussion by relating his belief in the soul's spiritual evolution through pre-human levels of existence to his understanding of the religious symbolism of nature. He asserts a correspondence between nature and his soul:

> I find I incorporate gneiss, coal, long-threaded moss, fruits, grains, esculent
>   roots,
> And am stucco'd with quadrupeds and birds all over.
> And have distanced what is behind me for good reasons,
> But call anything back again when I desire it.
>
> (31)

> They [natural objects] bring me tokens of myself, they evince them plainly in
> their possession.
>
> (32)

The reason, Whitman suggests, that he can perceive the meanings of these natural facts is because his soul, having passed through these forms of inanimate and animal life in its evolutionary ascent, still somehow retains their spiritual qualities in the depths of its being. Thus he can "call anything back," that is, recall its meanings, and it can serve as symbol or "token" of himself. According to this theorizing, the symbol's power to unlock a depth aspect of consciousness is actually a reactivating of a primitive instinct. Thus the poet colorfully refers to the objects of the outer world as the "reachers of my remembrancers" (l. 699).

V

The poem's fifth part (sections 33–38) resumes the catalogic style of the second movement. Again in an effort to establish himself as a national poet, Whitman shows that his vision includes all the objects, inhabitants, and activities of America's diverse geographical regions; again in his concern to nurture a race of perfect Americans, he appeals to the liberating and restorative powers of nature and the passions; and again in his desire to disclose the sanctity of the world, he suggests that everything has a sacred meaning:

> I fly those flights of a fluid and swallowing soul,
> My course runs below the soundings of plummets.
>
> I help myself to material and immaterial,
> No guard can shut me off, no law prevent me.
>
> I anchor my ship for a little while only,
> My messengers continually cruise away or bring their returns to me.
>
> (33)

Whitman's active and omnivorous ("fluid and swallowing") soul encompasses everything in the universe. It goes beneath the natural facts ("below the sounding of plummets") to discover their spiritual ("immaterial") truths. The facts of the world are symbols or "messengers" which report their meanings to his soul.

However, after this passage Whitman's style alters from a rapid listing of discrete items to the development of a series of pictures from American history which depict acts of heroism and suffering. At one level Whitman intends for these passages to further his claim to be a national bard by showing that he has the imaginative power to celebrate America's achievements and provide exemplary models for the citizenry. The call for native American archetypes to embody the ideals of the new nation had become a staple ingredient of early nineteenth-century criticism, and one of Whitman's notes, entitled "Caution," indicates that he found this reiterated plea tedious, but that he also appreciated its significance for his poetic effort: "Not to blaat [sic] constantly for *Native American* models, literature, &c, and bluster out *'nothing foreign,'*" he warns himself; and he continues: "The best way to promulge Native American models and literature is to supply such forcible and superb specimens of the same that they will, by their own volition, move to the head of all, and put foreign models in the second class—" (*NPM*, IV, 1588). At this point, in "Song of Myself," Whitman attests that he can provide such models from American history. "I understand the large hearts of heroes" (l. 822), he proclaims; then he quickly describes the intrepid skipper who rescued the surviving passengers of the storm-wrecked steamer *San Francisco* (33), the massacre of Captain Fanin and his company of high-mettled Texans (34), and the fighting pluck of John Paul Jones and his crew in their engagement with the British *Serapis* (35–36).[13]

However, as with the earlier catalogues, Whitman integrates the poetic and political concerns of these passages with his larger attempt to redeem the world. These heroic episodes with their accompanying injuries and deaths are intertwined with accounts of a wounded fugitive slave, a crushed fireman, a dying general, cholera patients, and miserable prisoners. In this tissue of suffering and death, the description of an amputation is typical of the whole:

> The hiss of the surgeon's knife, the gnawing teeth of his saw,
> Wheeze, cluck, swash of falling blood, short wild scream, and long, dull, tapering groan,
> These so, these irretrievable.
>
> (36)

Thus the issue of heroism is merged with the problem of evil, and this fifth movement functions to show that Whitman's faith, far from being a naive optimism, takes full cognizance of injustice and evil. "I am the hounded slave"; "I am the mash'd fireman"; "I am the man, I suffer'd, I was there," he asserts (33). After weaving this fabric of pain, the hitherto confident poet depicts himself crushed with his sense of human misery: "Askers embody themselves in me and I am embodied in them, / I project my hat, sit shame-faced, and beg" (37).

But even as Whitman has been composing these images of suffering, he has also been quietly laying the groundwork for a positive solution to the problem of evil. We gain insight into why Whitman selects these particular episodes of heroism and suffering by recalling a relevant passage from the 1855 Preface. "What do you think," Whitman asks, "is the grandeur of storms and dismemberments and the deadliest battles and wrecks, and the wildest fury of the elements, and the power of the sea . . . ?" And he answers that it is "that something in the soul which says, Rage on, Whirl on, I tread master here and everywhere . . . Master of nature and passion and death, and of all terror and all pain" (*PW*, 445–46). The passages of suffering in "Song of Myself" are selected and shaped to demonstrate not only his awareness of evil but also his conviction that the soul was superior to anything it might encounter, including death. To make this point, Whitman alludes to the "disdain and calmness of martyrs" and shows us sufferers who are masters of their fate: the dying general gasps, "*Mind not me—mind—the entrenchments*" (l. 870); although surrounded and without ammunition, the four hundred and twelve young men negotiate for an "honorable capitulation" (l. 879); and Captain John Paul Jones "composedly cries" from his burning vessel "*we have just begun our part of the fighting*" (l. 916). Whitman intended these instances of heroic defiance to the forces of repression, suffering, and death to reveal the soul's almost instinctive assertion of its immortality.

Furthermore, Whitman interweaves symbols of human immortality into his final description of agony and death by including along with the "Formless stacks of bodies" references to the "slight shock of the soothe of waves" and "Delicate sniffs of sea-breeze" and the "few large stars overhead" (36).[14] Here, as in sections 22 and 28, these references to the sea are subtle symbolic reminders of the loving divinity or spiritual sea which continues to support the soul after human death. Similarly the stars repeat the reference in section 21 to the "night of the large few stars" and look forward to the astral symbolism of sections 45 and 46 which constitutes the poem's most explicit assertion of immortality.

These implicit reminders of immortality receive reinforcement in section 38 as Whitman depicts himself regaining the *terra firma* of his faith:

> (1) Enough! enough! enough!
> ....
> (2) That I could forget the trickling tears and the blows of the bludgeons and hammers!
> (3) That I could look with a separate look on my own crucifixion and bloody crowning!
> ....
> (4) The grave of rock multiples what has been confided to it, or to any graves,
> (5) Corpses rise, gashes heal, fastenings roll from me.
> (6) I troop forth replenish'd with supreme power, one of an average unending procession,
> ....
> (7) The blossoms we wear in our hats the growth of thousands of years.[15]
>
> (38)

Drawing upon the imagery of Christ's crucifixion and resurrection, Whitman fuses the Christian doctrine of personal immortality (2–5) with his belief in evolutionary progress (6 & 7); and he now states the two-fold resolution to the problem of evil that undergirds the poem. Suffering and death are vindicated because the events of this life are not final but instead prepare the soul for a better existence in the afterlife. Furthermore, this world's evil smudges disappear when humans overcome their mistaken tendency to view things in isolation ("look with a separate look") and instead place them within the larger context of universal evolution. Given sufficient season, the cosmic process justifies itself, gradually ascending to forms of goodness and beauty: "The blossoms we wear in our hats the growth of thousands of years" (7). With this reaffirmation of his faith, Whitman again assumes his role as religious teacher: "Eleves, I salute you! come forward! / Continue your annotations, continue your questionings" (38).

VI

In the next seven sections (39–45) the earlier promises of salvation are accentuated as the poem reaches its climax:

> To any one dying, thither I speed and twist the knob of the door,
> Turn the bed-clothes toward the foot of the bed,

> Let the physician and the priest go home.
>
> (40)

> I am he bringing help for the sick as they pant on their backs,
> And for strong upright men I bring yet more needed help.
>
> (41)

> It cannot fail the young man who died and was buried,
> Nor the young woman who died and was put by his side,
> Nor the little child that peep'd in at the door . . .
> Nor the old man who has lived without purpose. . . .
>
> (43)

While emphatically asserting that he bears good tidings for all of humankind, Whitman explicitly introduces himself as the founder of a new religion that is "the greatest of faiths and the least of faiths, / Enclosing worship ancient and modern and all between ancient and modern" (43). In announcing this new synthetic or universal religion, Whitman gives expression to the dream of a small group of nineteenth-century liberal religionists, mainly Transcendentalists, who wanted to create a new Bible that would incorporate the best values of the world's various religious traditions.[16] His faith is the "greatest" because it will comprehend all the religions of the past:

> Magnifying and applying come I,
> Outbidding at the start the old cautious hucksters,
> Taking myself the exact dimensions of Jehovah.
> Lithographing Kronos, Zeus his son, and Hercules his grandson,
> Buying drafts of Osiris, Isis, Belus, Brahma, Buddha.[17]
>
> (41)

At the same time Whitman's new religion is the least of faiths because, believing that the divine figures of past religions were only projections of attributes of the human spirit, Whitman chooses to worship not one of these supernatural beings but the divinity inherent in his and every human soul:

> Accepting the rough deific sketches to fill out better in myself, bestowing them
>   freely on each man and woman I see,
> Discovering as much or more in a framer framing a house.
>
> (41)

Yet this belief in the soul's divinity constituted the core of Whitman's millennial faith because, as discussed earlier, it entailed both a belief in human perfectibility and in the soul's ongoing development in the afterlife. If Whitman could convince his readers of this fact, they would be willing to accept the strenuous demands of his religion and set about their pursuit of perfection and incessant development.

At this point the poem arrives at a critical juncture. Whitman's steadily increasing claims to a saving knowledge have culminated in his announcement of himself as the founder of a new and superior religion. Now to bolster his claim to prophethood and provide convincing grounds for his belief Whitman must persuasively demonstrate his spiritual genius and provide convincing proof of the vitality of his vision. To do this, he adapts two traditional religious symbols—mother earth and the celestial vault—to the newly developed evolutionary theories in biology, geology, and astronomy. To understand Whitman's meaning and the religious and cultural significance of this act of symbol transformation, it is helpful to view it from the perspective of the history of religions.

According to Mircea Eliade, religious man has universally experienced the earth as a creating and protecting mother. Eliade provides many examples, one of the most interesting of which comes from Smohalla, an American Indian prophet of the Umatilla tribe who refused to dig the earth:

> You ask me to plow the ground! Shall I take a knife and tear my mother's bosom? Then when I die she will not take me to her bosom to rest. You ask me to dig for stone! Shall I dig under her skin for her bones? Then when I die, I cannot enter her body to be born again. You ask me to cut grass and make hay and sell it, and be rich like white men! But how dare I cut off my mother's hair?[18]

Although Smohalla was Whitman's contemporary and compatriot, he lived in a traditional culture, and thus his evocation of mother earth—in addition to being beautiful in itself—provides a striking backdrop for appreciating Whitman's adaption of this experience of the telluric mother to evolutionary thought:

> Long I was hugg'd close—long and long.
>
> Immense have been the preparations for me,
> Faithful and friendly the arms that have help'd me.
>
> Cycles ferried my cradle, rowing and rowing like cheerful boatmen,
> . . . .
> Before I was born out of my mother generations guided me,
> My embryo has never been torpid, nothing could overlay it.
>
> For it the nebula cohered to an orb,
> The long slow strata piled to rest it on,
> Vast vegetables gave it sustenance,
> Monstrous sauroids transported it in their mouths. . . .
>
> (44)

Thus drastically science had altered the poet's understanding of his relationship to the soil on which he stands. No longer does he conceive of human life as a process of emerging from and returning to the earth in Smohalla's manner; nor does he conceive of himself and the earth as instantaneous creations by divine fiat as recorded in Christian scripture. Instead Whitman sees all development as linear, progressive evolution. Drawing upon Laplace's nebular hypothesis which pictured the planets, satellites, and sun of our solar system as condensing out of a formless body of gas (the nebula), Whitman describes the earth as having "cohered to an orb." Also, influenced by the contemporary theories of evolutionary geology and pre-Darwinian biology, Whitman views the "strata" as being gradually produced by a long series of geologic developments and humans as having ascended from lower stages of inorganic and organic existence.[19] Even with this evolutionary perspective, however, Whitman continues to perceive the earth as a religious symbol which still conveys its traditional meaning: it is still experienced as a nourishing and loving mother, reflecting the divine love underlying the creation. But Whitman invests the symbol with a new dimension of meaning—one that was inconceivable prior to the advent of evolutionary thought. Now the earth is a loving *terra mater* not only because it is a source of life and provides for the needs of human existence, but also because it has cared for human life (or something that had the potential to develop into human life) in its long passage through the incipient, inorganic stages of existence.

The significance of this act of symbol transformation becomes clearer when related to the astral imagery of the poem's ensuing section:

I open my scuttle at night and see the far-sprinkled systems,
And all I see multiplied as high as I can cipher edge but the rim of the farther systems.

Wider and wider they spread, expanding, always expanding,
Outward and outward and forever outward.

My sun has his sun and round him obediently wheels,
He joins with his partners a group of superior circuit,
And greater sets follow, making specks of the greatest inside them.

(45)[20]

The "far-sprinkled systems" and "farther systems" are accurate references to contemporary astronomical theory. In the late eighteenth and early nineteenth centuries Sir William Herschel (1738–1822), the founder of stellar astronomy and observational cosmology, while investigating the phenomenon of double stars among the fixed stars in an attempt to determine parallax, unexpectedly discovered the existence of binary stars, two stars revolving about each other in regular orbit due to gravitational influence. Thus Herschel showed that Newton's law of gravitational attraction applied not only to the solar system but to the distant heavens. Herschel also systematically swept the heavens with telescopes superior to any previously used for the study of faint objects; as a result, he raised the number of known nebulae from 100 to 2,500, resolved some nebulae into stars, and hypothesized that many distant nebulae were actually galaxies beyond our Milky Way.[21] Succeeding astronomers and natural theologians speculated that the galaxies were ordered both within themselves and with one another by mutual gravitational attraction. A universe of such grandeur and complexity could only be, they asserted, the product of infinite intelligence and power. Again and again mid-nineteenth-century astronomical discussions are punctuated with passages of religious meditation. Let me give but one example, from O. M. Mitchell's *A Course of Six Lectures on Astronomy*:

> If there be anything, then, that can lead us upward to the contemplation of the attributes of Him who sustains all things by the might of His power, it is the understanding of His works above. If you would know His glory, examine the infinite numbers of mighty suns that blaze about us. Multiply the hundred millions with which we are associated, by the thousands of other systems beyond us, and compute the result. . . . If there be not a conviction of Ommipotence here, then it is impossible for the human mind to comprehend it.[22]

Whitman shared these sentiments. For him, however, the new cosmology provided, in addition to a fresh confirmation of God's wisdom and power, a new understanding of the fact and nature of man's immortality. Consider his later musings upon the death of Thomas Carlyle (in February 1881):

> And now that he has gone hence, can it be that Thomas Carlyle . . . remains an identity still? In ways perhaps eluding all the statements, lore and speculations of ten thousand years—eluding all possible statements to mortal sense— does he yet exist, a definite, vital being, a spirit, an individual—perhaps now wafted in space among those stellar systems, which, suggestive and limitless as they are, merely edge more limitless, far more suggestive systems? I have no doubt of it. In silence, of a fine night, such questions are answer'd to the soul, the best answers that can be given. (*PW*, 253)

The tenor of Whitman's response to the starry heavens is typical of the traditional religious imagination. Eliade states that contemplation of the sidereal zones, because of their height, remoteness, and seemingly infinite expanse, has always impressed the religious consciousness with an awareness of transcendence, absolute reality, and eternity. In many religions, the souls of the dead are believed to ascend to these regions.[23]

But Whitman adds a new element to the religious understanding of the celestial vault. Perceiving the stars from the perspective of nineteenth-century astronomy, he intuits that these symbols of immortality reveal a spiritual fact which had gone unnoticed in previous "statements, lore and speculations": namely, that the distant astral systems exist for the soul's post-human habitation and edification. Furthermore, since Whitman also posits that the universe is constantly expanding, his understanding of the heavens leads him to believe that the soul's spiritual development does not, as such a religion as Christianity holds, cease after death. Rather the afterlife is an ongoing process of achieving successively higher levels of consciousness and, corresponding to these, ever more comprehensive degrees of integration with the cosmos, and hence with the divinity who manifests through it. It is this new realization which completes the climactic movement of "Song of Myself":

> There is no stoppage and never can be stoppage,
> If I, you, and the worlds, and all beneath or upon their surfaces, were this moment reduced back to a pallid float, it would not avail in the long run,
> We should surely bring up again where we now stand,
> And surely go as much farther, and then farther and farther.
>
> (45)

> This day before dawn I ascended a hill and look'd at the crowded heaven,
> And I said to my spirit *When we become the enfolders of those orbs, and the pleasure and knowledge of every thing in them, shall we be fill'd and satisifed then?*
> And my spirit said *No, we but level that lift to pass and continue beyond.*
>
> (46)

Both the soul and the universe were engaged in a process of seemingly endless expansion. Consequently, for Whitman the spiritual quest was truly a journey without end.

To sum up, this approach reveals a profoundly religious mind triumphantly reorienting itself in response to modern science. The result is a new understanding of divine providence which redefines the nature of immortality and the divine-human relationship. Whitman intended to convert readers with this feat of spiritual creativity, convincing them of the magnitude of his prophetic power and the validity of his vision. If the readers were brought to experience the stars and the earth in this new way, they would be convinced that the poet's vision of a divinely designed evolutionary cosmos was true and that his belief in man's immortality and ongoing development was indeed justified.

Yet despite its creative brilliance Whitman's ambitious peroration fails to achieve its desired effect. In later poems such as "Out of the Cradle," "Crossing Brooklyn Ferry," and the "Lilacs" elegy, Whitman effectively captures, to the extent that language can, the occult atmosphere of the natural facts—the bird's song and the sea, the evening sunlight on the East River and the May evening night—that induce the epiphanic moments which resolve the poems. As a result readers are subconsciously caught up into the poems' spellbinding power and they feel satisfied that these works have reached a resolution (even though they may have no clear sense of their final meaning). In contrast, at the climax of "Song of Myself" Whitman does not effectively exploit the resources of language to lure his readers into a mood that will move them to accept the intended but unstated meaning of his symbols. Instead he explicitly asserts the symbolic meaning and asks for the readers' tentative assent, or perhaps it is better to say that he expects the readers to now go out into nature and experience the earth and stars as religious symbols so that what they have received from the poem as a tuition will be transmuted by the occult energies of nature into a vital intuition.

A comparison of the ending of "Out of the Cradle" to the climactic passages just cited from sections 45 and 46 helps to demonstrate why the conclusion to "Song of Myself" is decidedly less effective. In the latter the conclusion is signaled by a single line at the beginning of section 44, "It is time to explain myself—let us stand up," which largely fails, as the history of the poem's reception demonstrates, to alert the reader to the significance of what is to follow. In contrast, note how much more carefully Whitman introduces his epiphany from the sea:

> A word then . . .
> The word final, superior to all,
> Subtle, sent up—what is it?—I listen;
> Are you whispering it, and have been all the time, you sea-waves?
> Is that it from your liquid rims and wet sands?

The repetition of "word," modified by "final" and "superior," give this passage the proper emphasis. Also the series of three questions, one of which is further emphasized by the use of dashes, further directs the reader's attention to the symbolic message from the sea.

Another difference is the apt use of language in "Out of the Cradle" to convey the mood which the sea induced in the poet's consciousness:

(1) Whereto answering, the sea,
(2) Delaying not, hurrying not,
(3) Whisper'd me through the night, and very plainly before daybreak,
(4) Lisp'd to me the low and delicious word death,
(5) And again death, death, death, death,
(6) Hissing melodious, neither like the bird nor like my arous'd child's heart,
(7) But edging near as privately for me rustling at my feet,
(8) Creeping thence steadily up to my ears and laving me softly all over,
(9) Death, death, death, death, death.

Whitman employs a series of devices—internal punctuation (ll. 1–3,6), the chant-like repetition of death (ll. 5 & 9), and eight participles (ll. 1, 2, 6-8) to recreate the steady rhythms of the sea. In addition, the words themselves, in both their denotations and their very sounds— "whisper'd," "Lisp'd," "Hissing melodious," "edging near," "rustling," "creeping," and "laving"— develop a mood of quiet and suggest a gentle, intimate leading of the human spirit to a moment of revelation. By these devices—and the soothing influence of the sea itself—Whitman wanted to seduce the reader into a sense of death as a gentle transition into a closer relationship with the divine source of all being.

But in contrast, examination of the above-cited passages from the climax of "Song of Myself" reveals that Whitman does not try to communicate a symbolic experience of the earth or stars per se but rather poeticizes evolutionary theory and invests it with a spiritual purpose. In place of striving to convey his mystical sense of the fecundity and nurturing power of the earth or the awe-inspiring beauty and grandeur of the stars, in a manner similar to his later description of the sea in "Out of the Cradle," Whitman instead, continuing the technique used in the earlier catalogic sections, inserts a passage between the terrestrial and astral symbols which reminds the reader that the universe is full of facts designed by a loving divinity to nurture the human soul:

> My lovers suffocate me,
> Crowding my lips, thick in the pores of my skin,
> Jostling me through streets and public halls, coming naked to me at night,
> Crying by day *Ahoy*! from the rocks of the river, swinging and chirping over
>   my head,
> Calling my name from flower-beds, vines, tangled underbrush,
> Lighting on every moment of my life,
> Bussing my body with soft balsamic busses,
> Noiselessly passing handfuls out of their hearts and giving them to be mine.
>
> (45)

Rapt with his joyful faith in the perfection of the universe and personal immortality, Whitman gives expression to his sense of being engulfed by symbols that address his soul with their proclamations of divine love. This ecstatic outpouring fits well with the tone of this phase of the poem, but neither this passage nor the descriptions of the evolution of the earth and heavens draw the reader into the compelling power of the symbolic experience itself. Throughout "Song of Myself" Whitman manages to fuse two potentially conflicting impulses: his wish to reconcile faith and reason by grounding his religion in evolutionary theory, and his desire to free his readers of conceptual systems so that he can lead them into a mystical mode of perception. The poem's conclusion suffers from the fact that at this crucial moment he chose to subordinate mystical impulse to scientific theory.

VII

The final sections (46–52) are both an end and beginning. They conclude Whitman's introduction of himself and his new religion, and they invite the reader to explore this vision further in the ensuing poems. As an ending, Whitman pithily repeats several of his more important points. For example:

> I have said that the soul is not more than the body,
> And I have said that the body is not more than the soul,
> And nothing, not God, is greater to one than one's self is.
>
> (48)

As a beginning, by employing a series of traditional metaphors for spiritual instruction and development, he establishes himself as a guide who will lead the reader upon a quest for spiritual perfection. He depicts himself as a loving and providing father and the reader as a child in need of spiritual sustenance:

> Sit a while dear son,
> Here are biscuits to eat and here is milk to drink.
>
> (46)

Or again, he is the trainer of spiritual athletes:

> I am the teacher of athletes,
> He that by me spreads a wider breast than my own proves the width of my own.
>
> (47)

He is the hardy and experienced pilgrim who supports his weaker and less experienced companion:

> Shoulder your duds dear son, and I will mine, and let us hasten forth,
> . . . .
> If you tire, give me both burdens, and rest the chuff of your hand on my hip.
>
> (46)

And he is the father who loves his spiritual children and encourages their development and autonomy:

> The boy I love, the same becomes a man not through derived power, but in his own right.
>
> (47)

In addition to the exhortations and encouragement expressed in these quotations, the poet entices the reader with more promises of the splendor that presents itself to those who perceive the world with the eyes of a fully developed soul.

> Long enough have you dream'd contemptible dreams,
> Now I wash the gum from your eyes,
> You must habit yourself to the dazzle of the light and of every moment of your life.
>
> (46)

He also underscores the importance of his message: "I do not say these things for a dollar or to fill up the time while I wait for a boat" (47); and he extends a series of directions and admonitions, for example:

> If you would understand me go to the heights or water-shore,
> . . . .
> No shutter'd room or school can commune with me,
> But roughs and little children better than they.
>
> (47)

> Failing to fetch me at first keep encouraged,
> Missing me one place search another,
> I stop somewhere waiting for you.
>
> (52)

It is all made to sound very solemn and serious. It is. The reader is being asked to choose for a new life and to work for self-perfection and the redemption of the nation and the race.

ANTICIPATIONS OF IMMORTALITY

"If maggots and rats ended us, then Alarum!
for we are betray'd."

—"To Think of Time"

In the Preface to the 1876 *Leaves* Whitman confides that he had planned to write a sequel to the *Leaves* devoted entirely to death, but that now, still suffering from the effects of a severe stroke (which occurred in January 1873), he must forego such an effort and instead conclude his existing work with a series of poems on "death, immortality, and a free entrance into the spiritual world" (*PW*, 466–67n). However, both Whitman's body and spirit rallied, enabling him to continue to revise and to rearrange his poems, and even to write some new ones, including new ones on death. The final edition of the *Leaves* includes the two masterworks, "Out of the Cradle Endlessly Rocking" and "When Lilacs Last in the Dooryard Bloom'd"; several lesser but excellent poems on death ("To Think of Time," "On the Beach at Night," and "Come Up from the Fields Father"); major poems in which death is an important theme ("Song of Myself," "Crossing Brooklyn Ferry," "Passage to India," and "The Sleepers"); and over 100 brief chants devoted to death.

Yet when it comes to the question What did Whitman believe about death? one is hard put to answer, for as Whitman himself admitted, he had no well-formulated theory. He fully acknowledged death's mystery, and, his statements about it are, accordingly, intentionally vague (*Camden*, II, 71). However, he does have what might be termed a "minimal position," consisting of several beliefs which he continually affirmed throughout his career. One of these is that death is good. It is "lucky to die," asserts the 1855 and each subsequent version of "Song of Myself" (l. 132). In 1860 Whitman writes of the "joy of death" ("Song of Joys," l. 139) and he refers to it in 1865 as a "strong deliveress" ("Lilacs," l. 147). The 1876 Preface describes death as "the greatest part of existence" (*PW*, 466n). Another belief is that in personal immortality.

In one of the anonymous reviews he wrote for the first edition, he declared that the author of *Leaves* "recognizes no annihilation, or death, or loss of identity."[1] The 1876 Preface asserts that the "idea of immortality, above all other ideas . . . is to enter into, and vivify, and give crowning religious stamp, to democracy in the New World." Death, pronounced a central theme of New World poetry (the "crown and point which all lives and poems should steadily have reference to"), is defined not as the soul's termination but as a transition to another stage of existence: "the justified and noble termination of our identity, this grade of it, and outlet-preparation to another grade" (*PW*, 466–67n). And as noted earlier, he brooded over the death of Carlyle in 1881, asking himself: "Can it be that Thomas Carlyle . . . remains an identity still?" And he answered: "I have no doubt of it." In his final years he still emphatically insisted to Traubel: "When I say immortality I say identity—the survival of the personal soul—your survival, my survival" (*Camden*, I, 149). Similarly, the poetry itself repeatedly asserts the indestructibility of the "real body" or soul and depicts the afterlife as a process of progressive development. This notion is present in "Song of Myself" from the first edition to the last, and it is affirmed in numerous other poems such as "Song of the Open Road" in 1856 (l. 11), "Song of Joys" in 1860 (ll. 9 & 142), "Passage to India" in 1871 (ll. 204–11), "Going Somewhere" in 1887 and "Sail Out for Good, Eidólon Yacht" in 1891.

It should also be noted that Whitman employs the word "death" in two ways: in its customary sense as the termination of life and in a boldly paradoxical usage to refer to the world the soul will know after its human existence. In this second usage, "death" might also be expressed as "the realm of death" and approximates the traditional meaning of the terms "God" or "heaven." This brings us to one more of Whitman's notions about death. It is, in its second sense, the purpose or fulfillment of the creation and human existence. Of the entire creation, only the soul is real; everything else exists to prepare it for death, that is, for the more real world of the afterlife: "But what is life but an experiment? and mortality but an exercise? with reference to results beyond" (1872 Preface, *PW*, 459).

Yet despite the abundant evidence of Whitman's belief in personal immortality, most recent criticism denies this point, and the great poems on death, "Out of the Cradle Endlessly Rocking" and "When Lilacs Last in the Dooryard Bloom'd," are interpreted as the poet's mature acceptance of the hard fact of human mortality.[2] It is this misreading of these poems, combined with a distorted understanding of "Calamus" (discussed in the next chapter), which forms much of the basis for the commonplace view that Whitman's career may be divided into three distinct phases—early animal-like optimism gives way to the collapsed faith of the middle period (1859–67) which is then covered over by the uninspired prophecy of the final two decades which attempts to insinuate a religious purpose into the earlier poetry.[3] My purpose in this chapter is to provide a close reading of "Out of the Cradle" and "Lilacs" which corrects the current critical misconception of these poems by showing how they reinforce Whitman's earlier belief in immortality.

Before turning to these two poems, however, let me briefly state several additional reasons why it seems untenable to view Whitman in these years as having experienced a life-shattering crisis that undermined his earlier healthy-minded belief. Other parts of the 1860 *Leaves* continue Whitman's efforts to develop a new civic faith; for instance, many poems in "Chants Democratic" aim to inspire the citizenry and galvanize the national will for future democratic struggles. Furthermore, as will be demonstrated in the next chapter, "Children of Adam" contains an affirmation of human sexuality and a program of eugenics which continue Whitman's earlier concerns to liberate the human spirit and create a more perfect race of Americans, and the new form of comradeship or "manly" love depicted in "Calamus" is not, even in the 1860 edition, presented as an obstacle to Whitman's faith but rather as its strongest support and crowning feature. Whitman's optimistic faith may have been tempered in the late 1850s and '60s by a number of factors: disappointment with the response to the first two editions of the *Leaves*, unsatisfactory personal relationships perhaps coupled with troubling questions about his sexual identity, intense political turmoil accompanied by the threat and then the reality of civil war, and the sense of reduced possibility that routinely comes with middle age. More life experience and frustrated expectations moderate the tone of the poetry in this period, but there are no grounds for asserting that Whitman repudiated his earlier world view. Whitman's poetic career is best understood not as a series of stages but as a continuous process of gradual change and development. In his last two decades, Whitman suffered a noticeable diminution of power, but after the early 1850s the essential structure of his religious vision remained constant.

The view that the major poems on death deny immortality is also incongruous with the fact that other new poems in the 1860 edition explicitly affirm immortality and the soul's ongoing development in other spheres:

> For not life's joy alone I sing, repeating—the joy of death!
> The beautiful touch of Death, soothing and benumbing a few moments, for reasons.
> Myself discharging my excrementitious body to be burn'd, or render'd to powder, or buried.
> My real body doubtless left to me for other spheres.
>
> ("A Song of Joys," ll. 139–42)

> Of your real body and any man's or woman's real body,
> Item for item it will elude the hands of the corpse-cleaners and pass to fitting spheres.
>
> ("Starting from Paumanok," ll. 181–82)

> I receive now again of my many translations, from my avataras ascending, while others doubtless await me.
> An unknown sphere more real than I dream'd, more direct, darts awakening rays about me, *So long!*
>
> ("So Long!" ll. 67–68)[4]

The problem posed by such passages is how to reconcile these affirmations of immortality with the great death poems which make no such explicit declarations. To do this it must be recognized that the *Leaves* contains two types of death poetry: brief chants or passages which proclaim immortality to the reader's intellect as a simple assertion of fact and more complex poems which make no explicit affirmations but instead try to move the reader's soul to an existential realization of this article of Whitman's faith. "Out of the Cradle" and the "Lilacs" elegy belong to this latter category, and to understand how a belief in immortality emerges in such poems, it is necessary to attend to the recurring problems in interpreting the *Leaves*: the special religious vocabulary and the subtle and intricate symbolism which must be derived from the larger vision. Furthermore, it is especially important to use a phenomenological method of intuition to grasp the spiritual truth that Whitman wishes to communicate but refuses to articulate. For the dramatic tension of each of these poems is resolved in a moment of epiphany in which the poet relies upon the occult influences of a natural scene, in combination with his own poetic power and spiritual suggestions, to induce in the reader an emotional state that provides an anticipatory experience of the afterlife and thus the strongest possible proof of immortality. Whitman does not declare his belief in immortality because he wants to force readers to develop the intended state of consciousness and thereby encounter the truth of their immortality in all of its compelling power. It is because critics have considered the poems in isolation and overlooked this existential element that they have read them as denying a belief in the soul's ongoing life.

"Out of the Cradle Endlessly Rocking"

The poem's opening movement (ll. 1–22) describes the mature poet's nocturnal journey to the seashore of Long Island. But closer examination discloses that the preamble refers not so much to the present as to the spiritually significant items and events of that earlier night which so impressed themselves upon the poet's consciousness that they, like the objects described in "There Was a Child Went Forth," became a part of the poet "for many years or stretching cycles of years" (l. 4). It is their enduring influence, the poet states, that now leads him back to the sea. The experience of the earlier night enabled and compelled Whitman, then a young boy, to become a poet. Now he returns seeking

fresh confirmation of his poetic vocation. There is a note of urgency, for
Whitman's project is, like Wordsworth's, to record a former sacred spot of
time; and just as Wordsworth wrote somewhat desperately, anxious to capture
his earlier formative moments before he lost his sense of their vital power, so
Whitman returns, "Borne hither, ere all eludes me, hurriedly" (l. 17), to this
hallowed place of his childhood, seeking the revitalization of a former revelation. But there is an important difference: whereas Wordsworth feared a loss
of insight, Whitman, on this occasion, fears a loss of faith.

The tortuous complexity of the poem's opening twenty-two line sentence
with its nineteen lines of multi-layered dependent phrases and clauses stacked
upon the subject, the "I" of line 20, emphasizes that all of the things
enumerated—the moon, the stars (the "shower'd halo"), the briers, the shadows, the fields, the sands, the song of the bird, the subsequent songs from the
poet's soul, and most of all, the sea—are simultaneously present to the poet's
consciousness. Since these things were intimately bound up with the dramatic
religious experience of that previous night which awakened the poet's soul,
they are present in his mind as more than conceptual memories; they are
modes of feeling, now being reactivated by the poet's intentional re-enactment
of the event which originally unlocked these aspects of his psyche. The poet's
task is to comprehend this rich complex of consciousness and to distill from
it suggestions, or prophecies, of the future life. In this creative activity, the poet
will "use" the "hints" from the external world which he has received in the
past and is now again receiving; yet, through the contribution of his imagination, he will also engage in the creative process of "swiftly leaping beyond
them" with an utterance that unites this world with the next (the "here and
hereafter"):

> Throwing myself on the sand, confronting the waves,
> I, chanter of pains and joys, uniter of here and hereafter,
> Taking all hints to use them, but swiftly leaping beyond them,
> A reminiscence sing.
>
> (ll. 19–22)

It is important to note that the poet has thrown himself onto the sand and
peers into the sea. This location (the juncture for Whitman of the real and the
ideal) from which he speaks in the poem indicates that he is concerned not
merely to record the former experience but to relive it so that he can, in re-
experiencing the sea's mystic undulations, feel once again that calm state of
spirit that earlier enabled him to understand the meaning of the sea when its
waves spoke to him "the word stronger and more delicious than any" (l. 14).

The opening sentence is also a virtual thesaurus of symbols of immortality.
With typical economy, Whitman refers to three natural cycles, the day ("midnight"), the moon ("half-moon"), and the seasons ("Ninth-month"), which
renew themselves after a period of death or darkness. The implicit assertion

is that man's spirit will similarly revive itself at the end of the life cycle. Also, the blackness of the night, which symbolizes death, is penetrated by the stars, symbols of immortality. Furthermore, the night itself, as it is developed in the *Leaves*, is a rich symbolism which is used, like the sea, to suggest the mysterious spiritual matrix from which the creation proceeds and to which it returns (see "Poets to Come," "The Sleepers," "From Pent-Up Aching Rivers," and "Youth, Day, Old Age and Night."). The allusion to the poet's having emerged from the "Ninth-month midnight" refers to his gestation in the maternal womb, but the darkness of the biological womb also symbolizes the spiritual fact that human life proceeds from a dark or mysterious spiritual source; and journey into the night, in both "Out of the Cradle" and the "Lilacs" elegy, is actually a brief return to the divine source of all being which provides the poet with an anticipatory realization of the life he will know after death.

The story of the two birds in the poem's second part (ll. 23–149) epitomizes human life. Their idyllic springtime with their nest, their eggs, and their joyous love which enables them to confront life with confidence (*"Singing all time, minding no time, / While we two keep together"*) [ll. 39–40] is symbolic of the human longing for emotional fulfillment and perfect love. The she-bird's ensuing death and the male's anguished cries, caroled day and night "thenceforward all summer" (l. 46), symbolize love's inevitable frustration and the subsequent frantic, unending search to recover an irrevocable loss.

But the male bird's song, although it does not bring back his mate, is not in vain. It achieves its primary function—the purpose, in Whitman's cosmology, of all natural facts—which is to communicate a spiritual truth from God to the human soul. Thus the child, who comes to realize the song's symbolic meaning, later asks if the song is not really addressed to him: "Demon or bird! (said the boy's soul,) / Is it indeed toward your mate you sing? or is it really to me?" (ll. 144–45).

The bare-headed and bare-footed boy—the bareness allows the boy to have a full sensory experience of the wind-carried aria and the waves of the sea—actually receives two complementary revelations. As the wind blows to his ears the echoes of the bird's declining lament, the imaginative, empathetic child, strategically standing at the shoreline with his feet in the ocean, also feels the sea's persistent rhythms and hears its hoarse moans and hisses. The boy's soul unites with the song and the sea; and this "trio" interacts to produce the ecstasy:

> The boy ecstatic, with his bare feet the waves, with his hair the atmosphere dallying,
> The love in the heart long pent, now loose, now at last tumultuously bursting,
> The aria's meaning, the ears, the soul, swiftly depositing,
> The strange tears down the cheeks coursing,
> The colloquy there, the trio, each uttering,
> The undertone, the savage old mother incessantly crying,

> To the boy's soul's questions sullenly timing, some drown'd secret hissing,
> To the outsetting bard.
>
> (ll. 136–43)

The boy realizes the bird's situation is also his, for he too yearns for love. With this recognition, his desire for love, previously latent or unconscious, is activated, and since love is, according to Whitman's religious psychology, the central impulse of the soul, this moment gives birth to the boy's soul. Now, as he explains in the ensuing lines, he is spiritually awake and understands the purpose of his existence ("Now in a moment I know what I am for, I awake" [l. 147]). This realization provides the future poet with one-half of his vision. It enables him to write poetry that will clarify the lives of his readers by revealing to them that they are informed with a longing for love, and that the purpose of their lives is to pursue this impulse ever more fully.

But this revelation contains within itself the need for further illumination. For the boy-turned-poet now wants to know the purpose of this insatiable yearning which, as he has seen with the bird, seems to be frustrated by death. So he seeks a clue or spiritual hint from the surrounding environment which will explain this mysterious "unknown want":

(1) Never more the cries of unsatisfied love be absent from me.
(2) Never again leave me to be the peaceful child I was before what *there* in the night,
(3) By the sea under the yellow and sagging moon,
(4) The messenger *there* arous'd, the fire, the sweet hell within,
(5) The unknown want, the destiny of me.

(6) O give me the clew! (it lurks in the night *here* somewhere,)
(7) O if I am to have so much, let me have more!

> (ll. 153–59, emphasis added)[5]

In this portion of the poem (ll. 150–73), the poet's reminiscence of the earlier night fuses with his present experience. The question was first raised "there" (2 & 4), that is, during the former night; but the poet has returned—indeed this is the purpose of his journey—to the sea to hear the "savage old mother" answer once again "here" (6) on the present night. The mature poet now recognizes, as the boy did earlier, that the sea has been responding to the question all along:

(1) Are you whispering it, and have been all the time, you sea-waves?
(2) Is that it from your liquid rims and wet sands?

(3) Whereto answering, the sea,
(4) Delaying not, hurrying not,
(5) Whisper'd me through the night, and very plainly before daybreak,
(6) Lisp'd to me the low and delicious word death,
(7) And again death, death, death, death.

(8) Hissing melodious, neither like the bird nor like my arous'd child's heart,
(9) But edging near as privately for me rustling at my feet,
(10) Creeping thence steadily up to my ears and laving me softly all over,
(11) Death, death, death, death, death.

(ll. 163–73)

The sea's answer or meaning, as throughout the *Leaves*, is that it symbolizes the transcendent divinity to which the soul returns at death. Furthermore, in keeping with Whitman's strategy of suggestiveness, the full significance of the sea's symbolic meaning is not made explicit but rather must be intuited from the effect Whitman presents it as having upon his soul. The ocean's recurrent, unhurried rhythms (4), as it melodiously hisses and rustles (8 & 9), envelops and calms the poet's spirit (10), and he interprets this state of emotional well-being to be a foretaste of the greater happiness he will know in the afterlife. From this experience he realizes that death is not the final frustration of love, as it seemed to the bird. Rather the frustration of earthly love casts the soul into a period of doubt which paradoxically resolves itself in faith by driving the soul to the realization that the true object or destiny of its love is the God of love it will know more fully in the afterlife. Thus "death," but death as the soul's transition, not its termination, is the answer to the "unknown want" of line 157. Whitman believed death would bring his soul into closer union with the "great Camerado, the lover true for whom I pine" (Song of Myself, l. 1200). He makes this same point more succinctly and clearly, in the small, later poem, "The Untold Want," which depicts the dying soul sailing out into the divine sea to have its desire for love finally clarified and satisfied: "The untold want by life and land ne'er granted, / Now voyager sail thou forth to seek and find."

This epiphany at the sea constitutes the necessary second half of Whitman's vision. It is, as he terms it, the "key" (l. 179), or crucial fact, in which all of his poems find their needed consummation. Whitman can now show that the spiritual yearnings depicted in his poems—yearnings which are all ultimately manifestations of the desire for love—are not erased by death and left ever unfulfilled. The revelation reassures the poet that he is not the tenant of an indifferent universe. Rather as the poem's central metaphor implies, a loving divinity attends to human needs, much as a loving mother cares for her cradled infant, and in death, this divinity calls its children back to itself. With this realization, Whitman's faith is restored, and he can depart from the sea and continue in the construction of his optimistic vision.

"When Lilacs Last in the Dooryard Bloom'd"

In mid-March of 1865 Whitman returned from Washington to his mother's home in Brooklyn to visit with his brother George on furlough from the Union forces. Lee surrendered to Grant on April 5 and the Whitmans rejoiced: the war was over, George would see no further fighting, and most of the family would spend Easter together. But with Easter Saturday morning came the newspaper reports of Lincoln's assassination, and the family spent the day, as Whitman later wrote, reading both regulars and extras, which they passed "silently to each other."[6]

Lincoln's death engendered thousands of public orations and poetic elegies, so it is not surprising that it inspired Whitman to attempt some sort of major expression. A presidential death, especially an assassination, required due public acknowledgment, but Lincoln's death elicited more than mere funeral commemorations. A public tragedy, one of seemingly unnatural and untimely character, was profoundly unsettling to a people who considered themselves the divinely appointed agent of the world's millennial destiny. It demanded a public religious interpretation. So the obsequies tended to be not only expressions of mourning but also exercises in public theology, and it is helpful to survey some of these as a context for the focus and meaning of Whitman's elegy.

For most commemorators of Lincoln's death, the crucial issue was its religious meaning. Starting with the assumption of a providential deity who superintended the events of this world, they were anxious to interpret the significance of this great sign—a sign whose meaning was made all the more awesome and enigmatic by the fact that the Union's recent victory had been interpreted by its public theologians as evidence of divine approval. Now in the midst of their victory celebrations and self-congratulation there arose the question of how to read this seeming manifestation of heavenly wrath. Typical of this line of thought is the eulogy of Senator Charles Sumner of Massachusetts, which began with the premise of a watchful divinity: "In the universe of God there are no accidents. From the fall of a sparrow to the fall of an empire, or the sweep of a planet, all is according to Divine Providence, whose laws are everlasting." Then Sumner posed the problem: "Perhaps never in history had this Providence been more conspicuous than in that recent procession of events, where the final triumph was wrapt in the gloom of tragedy. It will be our duty to catch the moral of this stupendous drama."[7]

As one might expect, such a difficult question received quite diverse answers. Some related it to the covenant theology they had used to understand the suffering of the war. The assassination was further atonement for the nation's violation of its special agreement with God which promised national prosperity in return for providing a model of republican Protestantism. In allowing slavery to continue, the United States had violated both the political and the religious provisions of this contract; as a result, God had scourged the sinful country with this horrible war. But even this was not enough; God's corrective justice required more. This is the view clearly, if infelicitously, expressed in the verse of R. H. Newell:

> 'Twas fitting the thunder of Heaven should roll,
> Ere cannon exultant had deafened the soul
> To what in all ages the maker hath taught,
> The pardon of sin is with suffering bought;
> . . . .
>
> Our honor forgot what was due to the slave.
> For still with the South must we share in the guilt.[8]

Similarly, Reverend Henry Smith of Buffalo asserted that the assassination "ought to teach us that God has had, and still has, somewhat against us also."[9]

Others interpreted the assassination as a divine mandate instructing the Union to replace Lincoln's inclination to forgive Southern leadership with a policy of stern justice. An editorial in the Buffalo *Express* declared that "conciliatory lenience" must now be replaced with "the iron hand of justice . . . ungloved with any tenderness whatever." "Perhaps," it went on, "in the great design of Providence . . . it was needful that this awful tragedy should be enacted, to steel the softened temper of the people."[10] Reverend Lord of the Buffalo Central Presbyterian Church surmised that God "has taken away the kind and amiable Chief Magistrate when he has done his work, and put a stern judge in his place"; and he added a menacing generality with a meaning sufficiently clear for his auditors: "And as surely as the Lord God Omnipotent reigneth, so surely he has something for Andrew Johnson to do."[11]

Another idea frequently cited in the memorials is the notion that God did not allow Lincoln's life to be taken before his earthly mission was completed. In a brief essay, Jacob Rhodes raised the thorny point that it was none other than the most valued man in the nation "whom God permitted the assassin to strike," but he then reminded himself and his readers that Lincoln's "work was done, a sad and toilsome but good and glorious work. His fame is assured for all time as the friend of right, and law, and liberty."[12] "Springfield's Welcome to Lincoln," read at the burial services, sounds the same note:

> Before the rebels struck the blow
> That laid thee in a moment low,
> God gave thy wish: it was to see
> OUR UNION SAFE, OUR COUNTRY FREE.[13]

Bryant made a similar point in one succinct line: "Thy task is done; the bond are free."[14] Emerson's address at the old meeting-house in Concord combines the idea that Heaven was using the assassination to consummate Lincoln's historic mission with the need to place the post-war government in stronger hands: "And what if it should turn out, in the unfolding of the web . . . that this heroic deliverer could no longer serve us; . . . and that Heaven, wishing to show the world a completed benefactor, shall make him serve his country even more by his death than by his life?" Outraged by the assassination, the government would now acquire an "unwonted firmness, to secure the salvation of this country in the next ages."[15]

Many eulogists felt that the nature and time of Lincoln's death demanded that they reaffirm their faith in the Civil War as a necessary, divinely ordained struggle in the United States' progressive realization of its millennial purpose. Buffalo's Reverend Lord reminded his audience that the same divinity who spared Lincoln until his work was done had also "planted this nation and sifted all Europe for three hundred years to colonize the New World with a peculiar people, a chosen generation and a royal priesthood, to furnish an example to the down-trodden nations for a free Church and a free State." God "could not suffer this purpose to be defeated." The Pilgrim and Puritan fathers "did not endure poverty and famine in the land of their exile, to have their divinely appointed work crushed under the head of a remorseless slaveocracy."[16] And Reverend Smith reassured his listeners that the Union victory was "in fact a part of those glorious triumphs by which the kingdom, and the greatness of the kingdom under the whole heaven, are to be given to the people of the Saints of the Most High God."[17] Lincoln's death was in the service of Protestant republicanism; he was, then, a martyr to the millennium. "Springfield's Welcome" credited the president with having preserved an exemplary Christian republic:

> A country where the Gospel truth
> Shall reach the hearts of age and youth,
> And move unchain'd in majesty,
> A model land of liberty![18]

A similar view of Lincoln and America as divinely ordained to bring a new dispensation of freedom to the entire world informs the "Historic Apostrophe" with which B.F. Morris concluded his memorial record of the nation's public obsequies:

> The oppressed people of all lands looked up to him
> As the annointed of liberty, and hailed in him the consecrated
> Leader of her cause
> . . . .
> He inaugurated a New Era in the history of mankind.[19]

I have dealt at some length with the various religious responses to Lincoln's death—atonement, mercy to justice, fulfillment of personal mission and millennialism—because Whitman also felt compelled to provide a religious interpretation, and an awareness of how his contemporaries made sense of the assassination helps us to understand the content of the "Lilacs" elegy. First of all, Whitman had no doctrine of personal guilt and his belief in America's chosenness does not contain the Protestant notion of punishment for failure to live up to the covenant. Accordingly, "Lilacs" does not point to the need for national atonement. It also seems, from Whitman's concern for the suffering survivors in section 15, which does not distinguish between the people of the North and the South, that Whitman, like Lincoln, favored a policy of forgiveness. Consequently, he could not interpret the assassination as a divine directive issued to divert the nation from a mistaken notion of leniency. But the poem does endorse the notion of fulfillment of one's calling. Like many of the eulogists, Whitman works to undo the seemingly untimely and meaningless aspects of Lincoln's death by stressing that he had completed his personal mission. Finally, the poem continues the *Leaves'* millennial theme, for the picture Whitman paints for Lincoln's tomb depicts a post-war America that has resumed its role of providing its citizens with the political and economic conditions necessary for them to perfect themselves and establish a religious democracy.

The poem is usually discussed in terms of three central symbols—the star, the lilacs, and the bird—and certainly these dominate the first nine of the poem's sixteen sections. Yet except for a brief reference to the bird in section 13, they are absent in sections 10–13 and the first eighteen lines of section 14. This part of the poem cannot be relegated to a subordinate position for in it the poet decides what "pictures" should "adorn the burial house," that is, he decides how to interpret Lincoln's death so as to reconcile it with his belief in God's providential care and America's special mission. The central element in this part of the poem is the poet's view of a harmonious and productive nation of workers on a tranquil spring evening, and it seems to me that this evening landscape should be seen as the elegy's fourth major symbol. Whitman's experience at this point in the poem constitutes an epiphany on the order of the revelations which resolve his other major poems.

The threnody's opening statement of intense mourning for the loss of a loved one ("I mourn'd and yet shall mourn with ever-returning spring," l. 3, and "thought of him I love," l. 6) is rather typical of other eulogies to Lincoln. But there are also some special grounds for the intensity of Whitman's sense of personal loss. Although it is unlikely that he had ever met Lincoln, he had seen him frequently. As he passed down Pennsylvania Avenue, the president often nodded to the poet. At the inauguration parade, just several weeks prior to the assassination, Whitman had once again noted the "old goodness, tenderness, sadness, and canny shrewdness" of Lincoln's face,[20] and later that same day he attended the public reception at the White House. Whitman undoubtedly felt a secret kinship with Lincoln, for he conceived of himself as being the president's poetic counterpart: both were commanders-in-chief of the American people in their struggle for freedom.

Two of the threnody's symbols, the star and the lilacs, were literal facts which Whitman associated with Lincoln's death. In the evenings succeeding the inauguration, he recorded in his notebook the "western star, Venus . . . has never been so large, so clear" as it then seemed before sinking beneath the horizon early in the night; it seemed a "miracle" which "suffused the soul." After the assassination, Whitman retrospectively interpreted the star's symbolic import, and he conveys this meaning in his elegy by means of his special religious vocabulary. Just as the mystical illumination of section 5 of "Song of Myself" occurred on a "transparent" summer morning, so this special evening is described as a "transparent shadowy night" and "cool transparent night" (ll. 57, 62). "Transparent" suggests a time in which spiritual meanings manifest themselves, and the oxymoron of the first phrase indicates the paradox of inner spiritual revelation in the physical and emotional darkness. On such nights, Venus had affected the recesses of Whitman's being; in terms of his mystical lexicon, it spoke a special meaning to his soul: "Now I know what you must have meant as a month since I walk'd"; "As I saw you had something to tell as you bent to me night after night" (ll. 56, 58).

In addition to emphasizing the star's revelatory appearance, Whitman also asserts that some mysterious cause prevented him from sleeping: "(for something I know not what kept me from sleep)" (l. 60); thus he took the nocturnal strolls that enabled him to experience the star's purpose. That Whitman makes a point of his inexplicable restlessness suggests that this combination of astral phenomenon and poet's insomnia should not be dismissed lightly by the reader. For the poet it intimated more than an interesting coincidence; it was quite possibly a divinely ordained conjunction. Of course, Whitman, whose soul was suckled on deism and who later imbibed full drafts of Transcendentalism, believed not in the constantly intervening God of the Puritans but in the post-Enlightenment conception of a deity whose purposes conformed to universal laws. But Whitman did, nevertheless, subscribe to the notion of a God of history who enacted his will through different nations in different historical periods. This God had chosen America to introduce the final phase of history. With these assumptions, Whitman, like his contemporaries, was inclined to see such a stupendous event as Lincoln's assassination, coming at the end of the nation's near-mortal agony, as nothing less than a divine intervention. If he believed this, he could entertain the idea that God might also have arranged for the nation's inspired bard—the bard who was to provide America with a new religious self-understanding—to have a personal epiphany which would disclose the meaning of Lincoln's death. Whitman is not so presumptuous as to claim this, but he does call attention to his mysterious sleeplessness, thus making it possible for his readers to draw this inference.

For Whitman, of course, this star, and every star, was a symbol of immortality; and it must have been personally significant that this star was Venus, the morning star, and therefore an especially strong sign of the soul's survival after death. But the star goes unnamed in "Lilacs," and Whitman associates it only with the death of the president from the West ("O powerful western fallen star!" l. 7), leaving implicit its connotations of resurrection and immortality. Instead, it is the lilac which serves as the vehicle for these positive themes. When Whitman returned to Washington either on Easter Sunday evening or the following morning, the city's lilacs were already in bloom; at Wednesday's funeral, sprays of lilac banked the presidential bier. But the lilac was selected for the poem not because of these historical facts but because its characteristics made it an appropriate emblem for the poem's dual themes of love and immortality. Its meaning, like that of Whitman's other major symbols, is defined and reinforced by a larger pattern of recurring imagery. The "heart-shaped leaves" are mentioned three times (ll. 13, 16, 193) and it is described as "blooming perennial" (l. 5) and as the "lilac that blooms the first" (l. 51) of the spring flowers. Described as "tall- growing" (l. 13) and "perennial" (l. 5) with "delicate" blossoms and "perfume strong" (l. 14), the lilac bush becomes closely related to the "tall," "perennial," "scented," "delicate" calamus grass ("Scented Herbage of My Breast"), the *Leaves'* primary symbol for the spiritual love that is man's best proof of immortality. In turn, the calamus grass is a hardy breed of the grass described in "Song of Myself," 6, as a symbol of immortality. So there is a unified motif running from the "hopeful green stuff" of the "Song" through "Calamus" and the "lilac-scent" and "Fifthmonth grass" of "Out of the Cradle" to the "rich green" leaves of the lilac bush in the Lincoln elegy.

Hailed as the poet's "dear brother" (l. 24) and "dearest brother" (l. 102), the hermit thrush, which serves as the poem's third major symbol, represents the inspired poet who can fathom the mystery of death and affirm, in eloquent and reassuring tones, a faith in the afterlife. Unlike the mockingbird of "Out of the Cradle," the thrush is not an afflicted singer. From his secluded recess in the swamp, the nocturnal songster praises death and the mysteries of the primal night. The serene tones of his song reflect an important fact about the poem: Whitman, the bird's "brother" and translator, is grieved by Lincoln's death but he is not bewildered as he was in "Out of the Cradle." The bird's confident song is an affirmation of divine love and human immortality, and the fact that Whitman hears the bird's reassuring tones indicates that he still maintains, at least at an intellectual level, his faith that Lincoln's death was ultimately neither a personal nor a national tragedy. "Out of the Cradle" is a poem of emotional loss and metaphysical questioning, raising the issue of life's meaning and resolving it with a fresh proof of immortality. In contrast, the "Lilacs" elegy is a poem of emotional loss and political concern; in order for Whitman to arrest his sense of sorrow he must invest Lincoln's death with political meaning by reconciling it to America's sense of chosenness. Only then will the poet be able to accept the bird's song at an emotional level and join him in his praise of death.

During the poem's first nine sections, as Whitman describes the funeral train and elaborates the symbolism of the star and lilacs, he refrains from going to the swamp where his spirit might unite with the bird's. Three times he states that he is held back by his grief (ll. 10, 69–70, 106). In order to free himself of his emotional pain, Whitman stresses that he must resolve the question of how to memorialize Lincoln's death:

O how shall I warble myself for the dead one there I loved?
And how shall I deck my song for the large sweet soul that has gone?
And what shall my perfume be for the grave of him I love?

(ll. 71–73)

O what shall I hang on the chamber walls?
And what shall the pictures be that I hang on the walls,
To adorn the burial-house of him I love?

(ll. 78–80)

The poet's answer begins with a prelude in response to the first set of questions (ll. 71–73) in which he draws upon the *Leaves'* recurring use of aquatic imagery as a symbol of divinity. His "perfume" for the grave will be:

Sea-winds blown from east and west,
Blown from the Eastern sea and blown from the Western sea, till there on the
    prairies meeting,
These and with these and the breath of my chant,
I'll perfume the grave of him I love.

(ll. 74–77)

In effect, Whitman promises to fuse his verse with the winds from the divine sea, that is to interpret and bless Lincoln's death with inspired poetry.

After this preface, Whitman decides to "adorn the burial-house" with pictures of the peaceful and prosperous society—a society ripe with the promise of new life—that he looks out upon in the peaceful spring evening:

Pictures of growing spring and farms and homes,
With the Fourth-month eve at sundown, and the gray smoke lucid and bright,
With floods of the yellow gold of the gorgeous, indolent, sinking sun, burning,
    expanding the air,
With the fresh sweet herbage under foot, and the pale green leaves of the trees
    prolific,
In the distance the flowing glaze, the breast of the river, with a wind-dapple here
    and there,
With ranging hills on the banks, with many a line against the sky, and shadows,
And the city at hand with dwellings so dense, and stacks of chimneys,
And all the scenes of life and the workshops, and the workmen homeward re-
    turning.

(ll. 81–88)

The scenes of productive farms and urban workers in the midst of a bountiful nature constitute a picture of the ideal America, for which, in Whitman's mind, the Civil War was fought. Whitman left the Democrats for the Free Soil Party and later endorsed the Civil War not for the sake of freeing Southern slaves— though he did strongly oppose slavery—but to preserve the dignity of the common people who would be laborers and farmers in the new lands of the West. "The young men of the free States," he argued in the Brooklyn *Daily Eagle*, "must not be shut out from the new domain . . . by the *introduction* of an

institution which will render their honorable industry no longer respectable."
Slavery was of benefit to the privileged Southern aristocrat, to "the one out
of thousands," but it was "destructive to the dignity and independence of all
who work, and to labor itself." Therefore Whitman called "upon every mechanic of the North, East, and West" and most of all "upon *the farmers*" to
oppose the extension of slavery so they would remain "'free and independent'
not only in name but also by those social customs and laws which are greater
than constitutions."[21]

As long as they were unfettered by political oppression and had dignified
work, Whitman was confident the ordinary people could, especially when encouraged and guided by a vital national literature, become his dreamed-of race
of "full grown men and women." By furnishing the presidential tomb with this
picture of a secure, healthy nation, Whitman is asserting his faith that America
is once again free to pursue its ordained mission. Thus Lincoln's death was
not untimely; he had been preserved until he had preserved the Union, and
now it could proceed to become the great religious democracy of Whitman's
dreams.

In analyzing this picture of American life, it is important to observe that it
is an evening scene, and it is followed in the next section with a brief song
of praise to the cycle of day which culminates in the "eve delicious" and "welcome night" (l. 97). In fact, as we learn at the beginning of section 14, the
entire poem up to line 120 is the poet's reflection at the close of a spring day:
"now while I sat in the day and look'd forth, / In the close of the day with
its light and the fields of spring." It is the feeling of calm and completion engendered in the poet's soul by the sunset and evening stillness that arrests
Whitman's mourning and allows him to perform his poetic obsequies. At this
point, the mood of the poem is akin to the "solemn stillness" mentioned at
the beginning of Gray's "Elegy" or to the "deep solemnity" of night that
Wordsworth describes as requiring "small internal help" to take "possession
of the faculties" (Prelude, VII). The evening nourishes in Whitman a sense of
calm well-being like that he felt at the sea in "Out of the Cradle" or when
his spirit rested in manly love: "For how calm, how solemn it grows to ascend
to the atmosphere of lovers, / Death or life I am then indifferent" ("Scented
Herbage," ll. 13–14). Once again the poet's intended meaning is not made explicit, but he expects the readers, drawing upon their own experiences of viewing peaceful spring landscapes in the evening calm, to realize that his soul is
enveloped in a spirit of peace and assurance which he interprets as an anticipatory experience of the peace and love he will know in the afterlife.

It seems appropriate to speak of this picture of a revitalized democracy in
the quiet of the spring evening as the poem's fourth major symbol, for it engen-
ders in the poet the complex state of emotional fulfillment which frees him
from his mourning, resolves his political anxiety, and gives him a living conviction of God's providential care for Lincoln and America. Having attained this
spiritual renewal, Whitman is now able, as the funeral train imposes itself upon

the tranquil scene before him, to integrate Lincoln's death, symbolized by the train's dark cloud of smoke, with the darkness of the night, comforting symbol of the afterlife. Taking the "thought of death" (l. 121), the fearful thoughts associated with Lincoln's assassination, in one hand, and the "sacred knowledge of death" (l. 119), his present mystical intuition of immortality in the other, he retires to the swamp.

At this point we see the typical Whitmanian pattern of movement to a shoreline for a crucial revelation: "Down to the shores of the water, the path by the swamp in the dimness" (l. 124). Whitman undoubtedly selected the setting of a swamp because its moist, dark, lushness made it an apt emblem of the mysterious spiritual matrix which he conceived of as the source of all life.[22] The swamp's "shadowy cedars and ghostly pines" (l. 125), traditional symbols of immortality, suggest that the human spirit survives in the ineffable primal night of death, symbolized here by the actual night, described as the "hiding receiving night that talks not" (l. 123).

Through an inimitable control of rhythm, arising from a masterful use of present participles and repetitions, and an alliterated diction laced with o's, l's, n's, and s's, Whitman attributes to the bird a soothing, liquid eulogy that continues the mood of serene well-being and presents death as life's welcome fulfillment. As in "Out of the Cradle," the transcendent divinity is personified as an attentive mother ("*Dark mother always gliding near with soft feet,*" l. 143) who calls the soul back to herself; and again ocean imagery is used to suggest the infinite God of love to which the soul returns:

> . . . *I joyously sing the dead,*
> *Lost in the loving floating ocean of thee,*
> *Laved in the flood of thy bliss O death.*
> (ll. 147–50)

The last three stanzas of the bird's psalm make the poem's central point: since the primary purpose of this world is to prepare the soul for a more real afterlife, man's death consummates the creation. Fittingly, the bird's joyous carol closes with a brief catalog of the world; carefully included are three of Whitman's major symbols of resurrection and immortality—the fecundity of the earth, the star-filled night, and the ocean with its whispering waves—which show that this world, by its very nature and structure, points to the fact of immortality, and thus exists for the sake of a more real spiritual order:

> *From me to thee [Death] glad serenades,*
> *Dances for thee I propose saluting thee, adornments and feastings for thee,*
> *And the sights of the open landscape and the high-spread sky are fitting,*
> *And life and the fields, and the huge and thoughtful night.*
>
> *The night in silence under many a star,*
> *The ocean shore and the husky whispering wave whose voice I know,*

And the soul turning to thee O vast and well-veil'd death,
And the body gratefully nestling close to thee.

Over the tree-tops I float thee a song,
Over the rising and sinking waves, over the myriad fields and the prairies wide,
Over the dense-pack'd cities all and the teeming wharves and ways,
I float this carol with joy, with joy to thee O death.

(Section 14)

In "floating" over the land and sea, the song comprehends the entire creation and dedicates it to death, that is, to the realm of the afterlife. For every natural fact is, of course, a spiritual symbol which serves to prepare the soul for its life after death. In this sense, death is, as Whitman exclaims in "Calamus," "what it [the creation] is all for" ("Scented Herbage of My Breast," l. 37).

The poet's spirit, rapt by the bird's song, is held fused with the spirit of death. As he listens, he is reassured by the realization that all of the Civil War dead, both Union and Confederate, have been delivered into the serene mode of existence in which he is presently participating. Thus he becomes convinced that it is not for them that he should mourn, but for the survivors—the living who still suffer as he did prior to this experience:

I saw the debris and debris of all the slain soldiers of the war,
But I saw they were not as was thought,
They themselves were fully at rest, they suffer'd not,
The living remain'd and suffer'd, the mother suffer'd,
And the wife and the child and the musing comrade suffer'd,
And the armies that remain'd suffer'd.

(Section 15)

With this understanding, Whitman departs from the swamp, but the insights he has had into the mystery of death, his "retrievements out of the night" (l. 198), are retained in his consciousness and expressed in his elegy. Whitman's catharsis is completed not only by his renewed faith in America's destiny and man's immortality but also through his poetic activity which has enabled him to enshrine Lincoln's death in his vision as an enduring symbol—a symbol which would reconcile his readers to the death of Lincoln, to the deaths of the slain soldiers, and to the fact of death itself.

VII

THE ECSTASY AND QUIET OF RELIGIOUS LOVE

Thoreau visited Whitman in New York in the fall of 1856, and, after some initial reservations, pronounced the Long Island poet to his liking, as he did also his poetry. "We ought to rejoice greatly in him," he said. But there was one matter about which he did not rejoice—Whitman's candid treatment of the human body and heterosexual love. "It is as if the beasts spoke," Thoreau complained.[1] Other Victorians agreed. A London reviewer of the 1855 edition declared that Whitman's "indecencies stink in the nostrils" and a reviewer for the *Christian Examiner* censured the 1856 *Leaves* as an "ithyphallic audacity."[2] When Whitman went to Boston in 1860 to oversee the printing of the third edition, Emerson advised him against publishing "Children of Adam," arguing that the explicit sexuality would unnecessarily restrict his audience; and Sophia Thoreau, Mrs. Emerson, and Mrs. Alcott all refused to allow this pollutor of the Pierian spring to be invited to their homes. The *Leaves* continued to elicit such reactions, although with decreasing frequency, throughout the nineteenth century.

Twentieth-century readers have responded differently. Comfortable with "Children of Adam," they have been intrigued, sometimes shocked, and, increasingly, some have been inspired, by the seemingly homosexual sentiments of "Calamus." Edward Bertz, a German physician familiar with both Whitman's poetry and the pioneer psychological studies of sexuality, began the discussion of Whitman's alleged homosexuality in 1905 by arguing that Whitman was a homosexual and that this was the key to understanding "his work, his personality, and his gospel." A debate ensued, chock-full of ideological commitment and testy repartee. Bertz, swimming in the heady currents of positivism, characterized the argument as a conflict between faith and science: "Merrill and Cassares [defenders of Whitman's heterosexuality] represent the first; I the second. And when faith and science enter into conflict, science triumphs in the end." Leon Bazalgette retorted that Whitman was best understood not by the "foremost scholars" but by "idlers and children." To this, Bertz administered the quietus: "'Idlers and children' know the 'good gray poet' . . . not by mystical intuition, but through physical contact."[3]

Subsequent discussion of "Calamus," although characterized by less animus and more critical acumen, has continued along the tracks of this earlier controversy. Some scholars, such as James E. Miller, Jr., and Gilberto Freyre, have argued against the homosexual interpretation;[4] however, a much longer list of critics, including Newton Arvin, Mark Van Doren, Clark Griffith, Stephen Whicher, Roger Asselineau, Gay Wilson Allen, Malcolm Cowley, Edwin Haviland Miller, and Arthur E. Golden, read the sequence as homosexual love poetry.[5] In the last ten years, the homosexual reading has been even more strongly asserted by Robert K. Martin, Joseph Cady, Alan Helms, Karl Keller, and Jimmie Killingsworth.[6] Unlike earlier readings which either treated the alleged homosexuality as a pathological aspect of Whitman's personality and a minor and detracting theme in the *Leaves*, or sometimes, as in the case of Griffith and Whicher and those who drew upon their scholarship, as compelling Whitman into a traumatic reassessment of his earlier Transcendental optimism, these more recent studies see the homosexuality as integral to Whitman's mature self-realization and as a positive and central element of his vision. For instance, Martin argues that Whitman's homosexuality is "the source of his art, the center of his book, and the foundation of his political theory." And "Calamus" is "the heart of *Leaves of Grass*, as well as the root; it is Whitman's book of [homosexual] self-proclamation and self-definition."[7] For this group of critics Whitman acquires a new claim to cultural significance and inventive genius: he is the first self-proclaimed homosexual in modern literature, and in the process of so defining himself in a homophobic society, he succeeded in forging appropriate artistic strategies of simultaneous revelation and concealment for subtly communicating a positive image of a gay sensibility to other gay readers.

At present, a reconsideration of both "Children of Adam" and "Calamus" is overdue. An adequate interpretation of Whitman's love poetry must underscore two facts: the love celebrated in each sequence, as is true of all instinctive and emotional energy in Whitman's religious psychology, is an expression of divine immanence seeking reunion with its transcendent source; and the realization of this love is a religious experience—an anticipatory reunion with God which gives the soul a preview of the afterlife.

When the theme of comradeship is properly located in the larger religious and political purposes of the *Leaves*, much of the scholarship regarding Whitman's alleged homosexuality appears to be seriously flawed. It becomes evident that the experience of manly love does not lead Whitman to a crisis of belief but rather is the essence and culmination of his faith. The more recent scholarship which interprets the "Calamus" motif as a celebration of gayness repeatedly distorts the poetry by attempting to discuss Whitman's alleged gayness as a separate theme that can be considered apart from his religious vision. It is perhaps impossible to resolve whether or not Whitman intended for his poetry to endorse homosexuality, but when adequate attention is given to the religious dimensions of "Calamus," much of the evidence currently cited to support a gay reading becomes questionable or unconvincing.[8]

"Children of Adam"

Scholarship has had little to say about "Children of Adam," the notable exception being Harold Aspiz's discussion of how the sequence makes use of contemporary perfectionist eugenic theories. As Aspiz suggests, Whitman's celebration of heterosexual love is consistent with then-current medical lore, especially popular versions of Larmarckian theory. It seems likely that Whitman's desire to nurture a superior race of men and women prompted him to draw upon these theories which postulated the possibility of significant evolution between one generation and the next. The first half of the formula for rapid evolutionary progress required parents to develop superior physical characteristics through proper diet and exercise. The second called for fully natural and passionate sexual relations to insure that the parents' improved traits would be transmitted to their offspring.[9]

As a complement to Aspiz's reading, I now want to demonstrate how the sequence contributes to Whitman's religious vision and to indicate the various strategies he uses to disclose the sanctity of the body and its desires and thereby free his readers from sexual repression that would impede their physical and spiritual development. Generally speaking, it may be said that Whitman's world view—his commitment to human perfectibility and America's millennial future, his religious interpretation of evolutionary progress, and his denial of evil in the cosmos—required him to proclaim the beauty, perfection, and even divinity, of human sexuality. At the same time his psychology of religious experience led him to interpret sexual desire as a spiritual longing and sexual release and fulfillment as a form of religious ecstasy and a proof of human immortality.

Whitman asserted that the "universe has one complete lover, and that is the greatest poet" (1855 Preface, *PW*, 441), and in saying this he was not referring to romantic or sexual love, but to a love that he felt toward the world as a consequence of his belief in the perfection of the creation. To be the greatest lover was also to be one who sings with "unrestricted faith" ("Starting from Paumanok," l. 97) in God, in immortality, in the course of evolution, in the special mission of American democracy, in the goodness of human nature, and, not least of all, in the goodness of human sexuality. The enemy was faithlessness, in whatever form it might assume, including what Whitman referred to in his famous epistolary preface to Emerson as "infidelism about sex":

> Infidelism usurps most with foetid polite face; among the rest infidelism about
> sex. By silence or obedience the pens of savans, poets, historians, biographers,

and the rest, have long connived at the filthy law . . . that what makes the manhood of a man, that sex, womanhood, maternity, desires, lusty animations, organs, acts, are unmentionable and to be ashamed of. . . . This filthy law has to be repealed. . . . Of women just as much as men, it is the interest that there should not be infidelism about sex, but perfect faith.[10]

Regardless of whatever achievements the human race made in technology, government, and other areas of human culture, Whitman was convinced there could be no perfect American personality and no millennial era unless humans freed themselves of repressive sexual conventions.

Whitman's simplest argument for the propriety of a frank treatment of sex in literature was merely to point to the undeniable fact that human sexuality was the source not only of human life but also of human souls and, indirectly, of humanity's moral and spiritual values. A philosophy was "cowardly and rotten," he asserted, that could not "publicly name, with specific words, the things on which all existence, all souls . . . all beauty, all purity, all sweetness, all friendship, all strength, all life, all immortality depend."[11] Thus in "Children of Adam" Whitman instructs his female readers to be proud of their sexuality because they created both bodies and souls: "Be not ashamed women, your privilege encloses the rest, and is the exit of the rest, / You are the gates of the body, and you are the gates of the soul ("I Sing the Body Electric," ll. 66-67). Similarly, speaking of the procreative role of the male, Whitman asserts that out of him shall come "countless immortal lives with countless embodiments and enjoyments" ("Electric," l. 115), that is, the innumerable souls of his progeny that will continue to develop in the afterlife.

The title of the sequence, with its allusion to the creation of Adam, reminds the reader of the traditional doctrine that the body is the handiwork of God. Whitman's belief in evolution and historical progress, in conjunction with his millennialism, caused him to invert the biblical mythology and place the garden and the creation of the first true or complete human beings at the end of history. In "Children of Adam" Whitman further develops this idea by assuming the role of an antebellum slave auctioneer who, in the process of pointing out the beauties and perfection of the human body, makes the practice of selling people seem even more immoral by reminding his readers that human beings, when viewed from the perspective of modern science, are all the more invaluable for being the end product of eons of evolutionary activity:

> Gentlemen look on this wonder,
> Whatever the bids of the bidders they cannot be high enough for it,
> For it the globe lay preparing quintillions of years without one animal or plant,
> For it the revolving cycles truly and steadily roll'd.
> ("I Sing the Body Electric," ll. 98–101)

Whitman's philosophical monism, which denied the possibility of evil in the chain of being below the level of humans with free will, also required him to declare the perfection of the body and human sexuality. He introduces this idea in the sequence's short opening poem:

> . . . all [is] beautiful to me, all wondrous,
> My limbs and the quivering fire that ever plays through them, [exists] for rea-
> sons, most wondrous.
>
> ("To the Garden the World")

Later, the idea, developed at length earlier in "Song of Myself," that everything in the universe is both sacred in itself and contributes to the cosmic harmony is extended to include the human body and its sexuality:

> She [the female] is in her place and moves with perfect balance,
> . . . .
> The male is not less the soul nor more, he too is in his place,
> . . . .
> The man's body is sacred and the woman's body is sacred,
> No matter who it is, it is sacred . . .
> . . . .
> Each has his or her place in the procession.
>
> (All is a procession,
> The universe is a procession with measured and perfect motion.)
> ("I Sing the Body Electric," 5 & 6)

Because the poet's earliest note about the composition of "Children of Adam" speaks of it as a "string of Poems" which will celebrate the "amative love of woman—the same as *Live Oak Leaves* [later entitled "Calamus"] do the passion of friendship for man," one critic has seen them as a camouflage intended to conceal the homosexual tenor of "Calamus."[12] But this judgment overlooks the fact that the sequence is not only consistent with, but essential to, Whitman's vision. Having prophesied a future millennium of perfect freedom, having defined the human instincts as an expression of divine immanence, and having pronounced all things perfect, Whitman had to liberate and bless human sexuality. Otherwise there would have been a large lacuna in his bible. Silence on this subject would be construed as the poet's dumb confession that the world was not thoroughly sacred and that man could not trust the deepest impulses of his being. Whitman had to reject Emerson's suggestion that the sequence be deleted. As he later explained to Traubel: "When I tried to take those pieces out of the scheme the whole scheme came down upon my ears; He [Emerson] did not see the significance of the sex element as I had put it into the book and resolutely there stuck to it—he did not see that if I had cut sex out I might just as well have cut everything out—the full scheme would no longer exist—it would have been violated in its most sensitive spot" (*Camden*, I, 351).

In addition to declaring human sexuality an incarnation of divine immanence and an element in God's cosmic design, "Children of Adam" also presents the body and sexuality as an important source of religious experience. For instance, in "I Sing the Body Electric" Whitman emphasizes that the body is a religious symbol which nourishes the soul. In section 2 he lists the bodies of numerous ordinary Americans as they appear in everyday life:

> The sprawl and fullness of babes . . .
> . . . .
> The bending forward and backward of rowers . . .
> . . . .
> The march of firemen in their own costumes, the play of masculine muscle
> through clean-setting trowsers and waist-straps.

This is followed by a twelve-line vignette of an octogenarian patriarch "of wonderful vigor, calmness, beauty of person" (l. 35). These passages convey a sense of the beauty and dignity of the human form, but they also make the further point that mere perception of the body can be a religious experience that satisfies the soul:

> I have perceiv'd that to be with those I like is enough,
> . . . .
> To be surrounded by beautiful, curious, breathing, laughing flesh is enough,
> . . . .
> There is something in staying close to men and women and looking on them,
> and in the contact and odor of them, that pleases the soul well,
> All things please the soul, but these please the soul well.
>
> (Section 4)

The style is indirect and works by understatement, but nevertheless the repetitions direct our attention to Whitman's main point that merely experiencing the human body gives him a sense of spiritual satisfaction and well-being that is akin to the spiritual fulfillment that characterizes many of the major epiphanies in his poetry.

The symbolism of the body is amplified in the ensuing section which presents the gender characteristics of each sex as symbols of spiritual truths which give further satisfaction to the soul:

> As I see my soul reflected in Nature.
> As I see through a mist, One with inexpressible completeness, sanity, beauty,
> See the bent head and arms folded over the breast, the Female I see.
>
> (ll. 72–74)

The poet's perception of the female form gives rise to feelings of wholeness, well-being, and beauty which he interprets as the soul's participation in these attributes of divinity. Similarly, the male form reveals the divine attributes of power and self-sufficiency:

> The male is not less the soul nor more, he too is in his place,
> He too is all qualities, he is action and power,

. . . .
The full-spread pride of man is calming and excellent to the soul.
                                                    (ll. 75–76 and 80)

After these illustrations of how aspects of the body function as symbols, the
final section of the poem employs the catalogic technique of "Song of Myself"
to suggest that the parts of the body are both sacred and symbolic, so that
each reveals a corresponding spiritual dimension of the soul: "Oh I say these
are not the parts and poems of the body only, but of the soul, / Oh I say now
these are the soul!" (ll. 163–64).

In contrast to the sense of calm and spiritual satisfaction arising from experiencing the body as symbol, sexual activity affected the soul in another way.
In terms of Whitman's dynamic religious psychology, the passions and instinctual drives were not only biological and psychological forces but also forms
of spiritual energy which excited and liberated the soul by freeing it from artificial moral constraints and excessive intellection. Accordingly, sometimes when
Whitman describes the soul free of sexual repression, he presents it as being
reborn in nature, thereby suggesting that the sexually liberated soul would be
so fully realized that it would, like plants and animals, freely live in perfect
accord with its God-given nature:

> Singing the true song of the soul fitful at random,
> Renascent with grossest Nature or among animals.
>   ("From Pent-Up Aching Rivers," ll. 14–15)

> . . . absolv'd from previous ties and conventions, I from mine and you from
> yours!
> To find a new unthought-of nonchalance with the best of Nature!
>   ("One Hour to Madness and Joy," ll. 12–13)

Of nature's many "influences" upon the soul, one that receives attention in
"Children of Adam" is the influence of winds and storms which Whitman saw
as performing the same spiritual function as sexual passion. These natural phenomena were symbols of God's power and freedom which, amongst other purposes, sometimes served to liberate and animate the soul, inducing a state of
illumination or ecstasy. For instance, in "By Blue Ontario's Shore" Whitman
explains how the seashore winds inspired his ecstatic vision by freeing his soul
from its bodily ties:

> Thus by blue Ontario's shore,
> While the winds fann'd me . . .
> I thrill'd with the power's pulsations . . .
> Till the tissues that held me parted their ties upon me.
>   (ll. 316–19)

Similarly, in "Proud Music of the Storm" it is the nocturnal storm with the
"Blast that careers so free" (1. 2) that provides the setting and inspiration for

Whitman's vision of "Poems bridging the way from Life to Death" (l. 163). For Whitman, sexual passion was the incarnation of a spiritual force analogous to that expressed in storms and it served an analogous spiritual function. Like the winds and storm, the sexual drive, which Whitman describes as the "furious storm through me careering" ("From Pent-Up Aching Rivers," l. 30) also served to carry the soul to a moment of freedom and ecstasy:

> One hour to madness and joy! O furious! O confine me not!
> (What is this that frees me so in storms?
> What do my shouts amid lightnings and raging winds mean?)
>   ("One Hour to Madness and Joy," ll. 1–3)

But what, Whitman asks, is the basis or meaning of this elemental, all-consuming desire for freedom that the soul experiences in storms and sexual passion? The question receives no direct answer because Whitman intends to puzzle the reader momentarily and thereby lead him or her to a paradoxical proof of human immortality. Just as Whitman interpreted the defiance of the hero and martyr in the face of death as an inherent proof of the soul's immortality ("Song of Myself," sections 33-36), and just as he conceived of the soul's desire for unending love as a promise that it would encounter a higher love in the afterlife ("Out of the Cradle"), so he also believed that the sense of power and freedom that humans felt in the presence of storms or under the influence of sexual passion, once it was reflected upon and properly understood, would be seen as evidence that the soul was to know a greater power and freedom after death.

In the last analysis, for Whitman sexual experience is religious experience which acquaints humans with a higher level of reality and provides them a taste of the afterlife. Sexual activity is presented as a way to give birth not only to new bodies and souls but also to the souls of the participants. Thus Whitman speaks of "life that is only life after love" ("Spontaneous Me," l. 14). Drawing upon his recurring use of the waters as a symbol of divinity, Whitman describes sexual activity as a form of religious experience by describing it as a temporary immersion in the sea of God's spirit which results in a person being born again:

> . . . after the child is born of woman, man is born of woman,
> This is the bath of birth, this the merge of small and large, and the outlet again.
>   ("I Sing the Body Electric," ll. 64–65)

Similarly, speaking of the joy his soul finds when he merely touches the flesh of others, he declares, "I do not ask any more delight, I swim in it as in a sea" ("I Sing the Body Electric," l. 49). Having had these sexually induced experiences of divinity, Whitman conceives of his sexual desire as being at bottom a desire for the perfect joy and fulfillment that the soul will only know from fuller participation in divinity in the next life. Accordingly, sexual desire is actually a desire to ascend to a higher level of spiritual existence: "To ascend, to leap to the heavens of the love indicated to me! / To rise thither with my inebriate soul!" ("One Hour to Madness and to Joy," ll. 20–21).

Yet if Whitman found it necessary to unbind man's sexual instincts and pronounce them sacred, he did not find it necessary to define the forms that this emancipated sexuality would assume. The pictures of ideal sexual freedom suggest an absence of all restraint:

> To find a new unthought-of nonchalance with the best of Nature!
>> ("One Hour to Madness and Joy," l. 13)

> (O that you and I escape from the rest and go utterly off, free and lawless,
> Two hawks in the air, two fishes swimming in the sea not more lawless than
>> we.)
>> ("From Pent-Up Aching Rivers," ll. 29–30)

But in encouraging man to mix with "the best of Nature," Whitman does not advocate licentiousness. The "lesson of Nature," as defined in "Democratic Vistas," was the quality of Being, in the object's self, according to its own central idea and purpose, and of growing therefrom and thereto—not criticism by other standards, and adjustments thereto" (PW, 394). The reader was to free his sexuality from restrictive conventions so that he would become acquainted with the impulses of his own being. Believing these to be divine, the poet felt that action flowing from them would possess its own gracefulness and order.

Regarding the three major forms of sexual behavior traditionally forbidden by Christianity—masturbation, extramarital sexual relations, and homosexuality—the sequence approves of the first, is intentionally vague about the second, and ignores the third. In Whitman's cultural milieu, both conventional wisdom and professional medical judgment vehemently condemned masturbation. According to the judgment of Sylvester Graham, "self-pollution" was "by far the worst form of venereal indulgence," causing dyspepsia, physical debility, impairment of the "intellectual and moral faculties," insanity, premature death, and suicide.[13] In contrast, Whitman presents masturbation as natural, denying that it is either sinful or detrimental to physical or mental health. After describing the "young man all color'd, red, ashamed, angry" with "pulse pounding through palms and trembling encircling fingers," the poet condemns not the act but the "consequent meanness of me should I skulk or find myself indecent, while birds or animals never once skulk or find themselves indecent" ("Spontaneous Me," ll. 34, 39).

When Whitman swears "the oath of the inseparableness of two together, of the woman that loves me and whom I love more than my life" ("From Pent-up Aching Rivers," l. 31), he appears to favor a traditional marital relationship of faithful partners. Aspiz argues that Whitman's views on marriage conform to the medical lore of the time which maintained that chastity before and in marriage was essential to the proper begetting of children.[14] There is supportive evidence for this contention in both Whitman's poetry and prose. For instance, "Song of the Broad-Axe" praises "the well-married young man and woman, / The roof over the supper joyously cook'd by the chaste wife, and joyously eaten by the chaste husband, content after his day's work" (ll. 223–24). In an early fictional piece, "The Half-Breed," the illegitimate child of Father Luke and the Indian girl is born deformed, a "half-idiot, half-devil."[15] But the *Leaves* is not always so clearly conventional in its treatment of sexual conduct. It contains several passages that seem to view the traditional norm of limiting sexual activity to marriage as unnatural and to call for greater liberation:

> Give me the drench of my passions, give me life coarse and rank,
> To-day I go consort with Nature's darlings, to-night too,
> I am for those who believe in loose delights, I share the midnight orgies of young
>   men.
>
> ("Native Moments")

In "Once I Pass'd through a Populous City," there is no hint of remorse or condemnation in Whitman's depiction of a transient sexual affair:

> . . . I remember only a woman I casually met there who detain'd me for love
>   of me,
> Day by day and night by night we were together . . .
> I remember I say only that woman who passionately clung to me,
> Again we wander, we love, we separate again.

Yet unlike such contemporaries as Josiah Warren, who advocated free love in his various communitarian experiments on Long Island and elsewhere, or John Humphrey Noyes, who opposed exclusive relationships in favor of carefully controlled "complex marriages" between consenting members of the Oneida community, Whitman makes no such direct assault upon the institution of marriage.[16] Instead he takes a more moderate course of merely suggesting the possibility of greater freedom while intentionally avoiding ethical prescriptions. In this respect his treatment of sexual norms parallels his treatment of political freedom. In both cases he calls for externally imposed restraints to be replaced by the laws of human nature in union with the divine nature; and in neither instance does he attempt to define precisely how this freedom should express itself. He only provides ideals of freedom and fulfillment which are intended to orient and inspire.

"Calamus"

John Addington Symonds was an ardent disciple of Whitman. He was also a homosexual and in several letters over a period of nearly two decades he diplomatically raised the issue of whether "Calamus" was intended to encourage homosexuality. Finally, in 1890, Whitman responded, vehemently denying any such purpose. In *Walt Whitman: A Study*, Symonds gave a carefully conditioned public acceptance to this denial, at the same time noting how some of the poems might be read as expressions of homosexuality and that Whitman's response might be a revisionist reading of "Calamus." Writing to Edward Carpenter in early 1893, Symonds expressed this viewpoint more forcefully in what has since become a frequently cited letter in Whitman scholarship. "I wrote in the Summer of 1890," Symonds relates, "asking him what his real feeling about masculine love was, & saying that I knew people in England who had a strong sexual bias in such passions, felt themselves supported & encouraged by Calamus." Symonds then quotes several passages from Whitman's response which expressed outrage and bewilderment at Symonds's suggestion. As a postscript, Whitman made reference, apparently in an attempt to prove his heterosexual inclinations, to having fathered six children and refers to a grandchild: "fine boy writes to me occasionally—circumstances (connected with their benefit and fortune) have separated me from intimate relations." Concerning this postscript, Symonds tells Carpenter: "It struck me when I first read this p.s. that W. W. wanted to obviate 'damnable inferences' about himself by asserting his paternity."[17] Subsequent criticism has extended Symonds's response, judging the postscript to be the ruse of an embarrassed and more cautious older poet who wanted to camouflage the homosexuality of "Calamus."

It is unfortunate that criticism has not equally attended to another passage in Whitman's letter to Symonds which instructs him upon how to read the *Leaves*: "L of G is only to be rightly construed by and within its own atmosphere and essential character—all of its pages & pieces coming strictly under *that*."[18] This advice is still timely, especially in regard to "Calamus," for no segment of the *Leaves* has suffered more from being considered apart from the "atmosphere and essential character" of the entire work. When "Calamus" is placed within the context of Whitman's larger religious vision, it becomes clear that its fundamental level of meaning is not a gospel of homosexuality but of a mystical love which the religious personality traditionally affirms to be the soul's proper sustenance and best means of union with divinity. Whitman's repressed homosexuality played an important, perhaps indispensable, role in the genesis of "Calamus," but the love he celebrates may involve no conscious sexual (i.e., genital) dimensions. It serves three important functions, all of which are religious, but for the purpose of the analysis, I shall term them the spiritual, the political, and the poetic.

The Spiritual

"Calamus" opens with Whitman announcing his withdrawal from the public world:

(1) In paths untrodden,
(2) In the growth by margins of pond-waters,
(3) Escaped from the life that exhibits itself,
(4) From all the standards hitherto publish'd, from the pleasures, profits, conformities,
(5) Which too long I was offering to feed my soul,
(6) Clear to me now standards not yet publish'd, clear to me that my soul,
(7) That the soul of the man I speak for rejoices in comrades,
(8) Here by myself away from the clank of the world,
(9) Tallying and talk'd to here by tongues aromatic,
(10) No longer abash'd, (for in this secluded spot I can respond as I would not dare elsewhere,)
(11) Strong upon me the life that does not exhibit itself, yet contains all the rest,
(12) Resolv'd to sing no songs to-day but those of manly attachment,
(13) Projecting them along that substantial life.

("In Paths Untrodden")

Again the poet has retired to a shoreline for religious reasons. He has left the superficial activities and values of the world of appearances (the "clank" of the "life that exhibits itself") so that his spirit may become integrated with a more real spiritual order ("the life that does not exhibit itself, yet contains all the rest"). At the pondside, his soul experiences the revelatory power of the waters and is "talk'd" to by the scented calamus grass (9). This gives the poet sufficient insight and fortification to depict a new type of love which, unlike the pleasures and goods of the natural world (4 & 5), satisfies the hunger of his soul (6 & 7); and he promises (12) to project images of this love "along that substantial life" referred to in lines 11 and 13, thus indicating that the meaning of these love poems will only be understood by spiritually developed readers whose souls participate in this level of spiritual reality.

In contrast to this religious reading, Cady and Martin interpret the poet's retreat as a withdrawal from the dominant heterosexual culture so that he will have the freedom and courage to proclaim the new standard of homosexual love.[19] According to this view, the poem's basic opposition between the "life that exhibits itself" and the "life that does not exhibit itself" contrasts Whitman's unfulfilled life in the heterosexual culture with his more satisfying experience of homosexual love. Perhaps the strongest point of this reading is its explanation for Whitman's use of "abash'd" and "dare" (l. 10) as referring to the feelings of shame he has acquired from the dominant culture and the courage he needs to proclaim himself in a homophobic society. But this usage can be accounted for without resorting to a homosexual interpretation for Whitman may simply be stating that as a person reared in a society that condemns expressions of tenderness between males as unmanly or homosexual, he feels shame and fear in calling for intense affection between men.

Furthermore, a reading which makes the homosexual theme primary distorts two important elements in the poem. The invisible life that "contains all the rest" cannot adequately be explained as a reference to homosexual culture (How does it "contain" everything else?), but it can be understood as the spiritual realm, that is, the transcendent and immanent deity that informs the creation. Also, Whitman's description of the "life that exhibits itself" as devoted to "pleasures, profits, conformities" is not a fitting way to characterize heterosexual society in contrast to a homosexual culture, but it is an apt way to distinguish a life devoted to conventional, worldly concerns, which are ultimately unsatisfying, from a life devoted to spiritual development which can satisfy the infinite desires of the soul. This spiritual reading is supported by a parallel passage from "Starting from Paumanauk" (8), composed late in 1859 or early 1860 when Whitman was at work on "Calamus" #1,[20] which also contrasts the "ostensible realities" of this world to the greater reality of religious experience:

> What are you doing young man?
> Are you so earnest, so given up to literature, science, art, amours?
> These ostensible realities, politics, points?
> Your ambition or business whatever it may be?
>
> It is well—against such I say not a word, I am their poet also,
> But behold! such swiftly subside, burnt up for religion's sake,
> For not all matter is fuel to heat, impalpable flame, the essential life of the earth,
> Any more than such are to religion.

The crucial issue posed by the second poem, "Scented Herbage of My Breast," is why Whitman links the themes of love and death. For Griffith and Whicher the answer is that a recognition of his deepest love as unnatural and unsanctioned engendered in Whitman a profound sense of alienation which destroyed his earlier Transcendental cosmology and belief in immortality. Cady and Martin interpret death as a metaphor for Whitman's conversion from the unsatisfying values of heterosexual culture to the new reality of homosexual love.[21] But these readings reflect the current critical misunderstanding of Whitman's poetry on death. In "Scented Herbage" Whitman associates his love with death not because his love is unproductive and tragic but because, as in "Out of the Cradle," he interprets the experience of love to be an anticipatory understanding of the greater love the soul will know after death in its new relationship with its "Camerado true," the loving God who is the only satisfactory object of its desires. The poem's controlling idea is accurately suggested in a passage of a letter Whitman wrote to Bernard O'Dowd in 1891: "Concluding with love & best respects to you . . . what we hold to & pass each other is pure sentiment, good will &c. (am not sure but such things are the best proof of immortality)—."[22] In "Scented Herbage" the calamus grass is established as the symbol of a form of love that instills an existential realization of death as a transition to a higher level of spiritual existence and fulfillment.

In the poem's opening movement (ll. 1–21), Whitman describes himself experiencing the religious meaning of the calamus grass. By referring to it as the "Scented herbage of my breast" and "blossoms of my blood," he shows that his consciousness is fused with the inner spirit of the plant so that he perceives its symbolic meaning. References to the plant's "Perennial roots" and its annual renewal indicate that this grass, like the grass in "Song of Myself," 6, is a symbol of immortality; and just as Whitman indicated in the "Song" that he did not fully understand the meaning of the grass, so now he states: "Oh I do not know what you [the calamus leaves] mean there underneath yourselves." Faced with this mystery, the poet must, in part, depend upon the power of the natural fact to reveal its spiritual meaning to his readers: "I permit you to tell in your own way of the heart that is under you." The ensuing lines merely hint at how the grass reassures Whitman of his triumph over death, and so it is again necessary to attempt to intuit his unexpressed meaning:

> Yet you are beautiful to me you faint tinged roots, you make me think of death,
> Death is beautiful from you, (what indeed is finally beautiful except death and
>   love?)
> O I think it is not for life I am chanting here my chant of lovers, I think it must
>   be for death,
> For how calm, how solemn it grows to ascend to the atmosphere of lovers,
> Death or life I am then indifferent, my soul declines to prefer,
> (I am not sure but the high soul of lovers welcomes death most,)
> Indeed O death, I think now these leaves mean precisely the same as you mean.

The grass functions as a symbol of immortality because it stands for a type of love which induced in Whitman a "calm" and "solemn" state of consciousness akin to what he felt in the epiphanic moments of his two great poems on death. This made him "indifferent" to death because he felt that he was already experiencing it; he believed that this tranquility of spirit was an anticipation of the afterworld.

In the poem's second part (ll. 21-end), the poet announces that he will no longer describe his experience of the calamus plant but rather will distill its meaning: "Emblematic and capricious blades I leave you, now you serve me not, / I will say what I have to say by itself." He then declares that the love symbolized by the grass has given him such a strong sense of the afterlife that he can now write poems that will make death "exhilarating." Again, as in the first poem, Whitman distinguishes between finite and transcendent levels of reality; and having had the sense of participating in a more real spiritual order, he realizes that this present life and world find their meaning and fulfillment in the next:

> (1) For now it is convey'd to me that you [Death] are the purports essential,
> (2) That you hide in these shifting forms of life, for reasons, and that they are
>   mainly for you,
> (3) That you beyond them come forth to remain, the real reality,

(4) That behind the mask of materials you patiently wait, no matter how long,
(5) That you will one day perhaps take control of all,
(6) That you will perhaps dissipate this entire show of appearance,
(7) That may-be you are what it is all for. . . .

The greater reality of this love has convinced the poet that the natural world is transient ("shifting forms of life") and unreal (a "mask of materials" or "show of appearance"). Its importance derives from the fact that it contains hidden within itself (2) the attributes of the transcendent spiritual order which exist there "for reasons," namely, to serve as symbols which will prepare the soul for the "real reality" or transcendent realm which it will know after death.

As presented in "Scented Herbage" and throughout "Calamus," comradely love is important because of its power to soothe man's spirit and fortify his faith. Thus in a later poem, "Of the Terrible Doubt of Appearances," Whitman presents himself beleaguered by doubts:

That may-be reliance and hope are but speculations after all,
That may-be identity beyond the grave is a beautiful fable only,
May-be the things I perceive, the animals, plants, men, hills, shining and flowing waters,
The skies of day and night, colors, densities, forms, may-be these are (as doubtless they are) only apparitions. . . .

And it is the love of comrades which convinces him that he is cared for in this world and that his belief is indeed well-founded:

To me these and the like of these are curiously answer'd by my lovers, my dear friends,
When he whom I love travels with me or sits a long while holding me by the hand,
When the subtle air, the impalpable, the sense that words and reason hold not, surround us and pervade us,
Then I am charged with untold and untellable wisdom, I am silent, I require nothing further,
I cannot answer the question of appearances or that of identity beyond the grave,
But I walk or sit indifferent, I am satisfied,
He ahold of my hand has completely satisfied me.

In experiencing this love, the poet's soul is fulfilled, and he accordingly describes himself as "satisfied," the same term he uses in "Song of Myself" (3), where he characterizes his religious experience as being too real to be doubted. A passage from one of the notebooks provides a useful gloss to the meaning of "satisfied": "We know that sympathy or love is the law over all laws, because in nothing else but love is the soul conscious of pure happiness, which appears to be the ultimate resting place, and point of all things."[23] The love of comrades provided Whitman with his strongest experience of the "real." Accordingly, it was this experience, more than any other, which convinced him that the depths of his psyche could actually participate in a transcendent level of reality. This world of "appearances" might pass away, but the soul and the "real reality" ("Scented Herbage") would never be subject to death or dissolution.

In the third poem, "Whoever You Are Holding Me Now in Hand," Whitman presents a set of moral demands for understanding him and becoming his ideal reader and lover. Again the pursuit of conventional values is contrasted to the quest for spiritual perfection:

> You would have to give up all else, I alone would expect to be your sole and
>   exclusive standard,
> Your novitiate would even then be long and exhausting,
> The whole past theory of your life and all conformity to the lives around you
>   would have to be abandon'd,
> Therefore release me now before troubling yourself any further, let go your hand
>   from my shoulders,
> Put me down and depart on your way.

Furthermore, the reader must study the *Leaves* alone in the midst of nature:

> . . . in some wood for trial,
> Or back of a rock in the open air,
> (For in any roof'd room of a house I emerge not, nor in company,
> And in libraries I lie as one dumb, a gawk, or unborn, or dead).

It is only to the person who is willing to do these things, that Whitman promises his love:

> Here to put your lips upon mine I permit you,
> With the comrade's long-dwelling kiss or the new husband's kiss,
> For I am the new husband and I am the comrade.

The purpose of Whitman's solitary retreat into the realm of nature in the opening movement of "Calamus," and in this poem in particular, are clarified by a passage from a brief essay he wrote in 1861 which he apparently intended for use as an introduction to the *Leaves*. After declaring that he will not "school man in virtues, nor prove anything to the intellect . . . nor sing amours or romances, nor the epics of signal deeds," Whitman explains that he wants instead to have an intimate conversation with the reader in the midst of nature's restorative atmosphere and free from the false values of the world:

> . . . from me to you, whoever you are, we twain alone together a conference,
> giving up all my private interior musings, yearnings, extasies [sic], and contradic-
> tory moods, reserving nothing. A conference amid Nature, and in the spirit of
> Nature's genesis, and primal sanity. A conference of our two Souls exclusively,
> as if the rest of the world, with its mocking misconceptions were for a while
> left and escaped from. (*NPM*, IV, 1452)

In this passage, as in the third "Calamus" poem, Whitman is dealing with the psychological dynamics of spiritual conversion. He hopes that the influence of

nature, in combination with the guidance, encouragement, and promises ten-
dered by the poet's intimate voice, will inspire the reader to embrace his call
to become a new person and work for a new society. At the same time he exploits the timeless or non-temporal character of religious experience (as perceived by the religious consciousness) to establish a sense of union with his
spiritually active readers. Just as a sense of mystical union with Christ sustains
dedicated Christians, especially when their religious values lead them into
conflict with the values of the surrounding culture, so Whitman intended
for the members of his new religious faith to find in him their chief inspiration and dearest comrade. For him, the ideal poet-reader relationship was
a bond of mystical love between souls who, having recognized the limited
nature of such worldly goals as status, power, and wealth, now supported one
another as they pursued their spiritual development in this and succeeding
existences.

Readers have found the most perplexing aspect of the poem to be Whitman's
warnings about how difficult his message is to understand and the dangers involved in trying to discover within one's own experience his suggested but unstated meaning:

> But these leaves conning you con at peril,
> For these leaves and me you will not understand,
> They will elude you at first and still more afterward, I will certainly elude you,
> . . . .
> Nor will the candidates for my love (unless at most a very few) prove victorious,
> Nor will my poems do good only, they will do just as much evil, perhaps more,
> For all is useless without that which you may guess at many times and not hit,
>   that which I hinted at;
> Therefore, release me and depart on your way.

According to the homosexual reading, Whitman can only hint at the nature
of his manly love because homosexuality could not be openly discussed, and
the warnings serve to provide a "realistic account of the difficulties implicit
in a commitment to a program of social change as wide-reaching as that of
homosexual liberation."[24] But again, as with the opening poem, it is important
to recall Whitman's concern to distinguish secular concerns which can be
grasped by the intellect and senses and the greater reality of the spiritual life
which defies expression and can only be known by the soul. In terms of this
religious perspective, Whitman cannot name his love because it partakes of this
ineffable spiritual reality, and he dare not try lest he risk misleading his readers
by allowing them to mistake a mere intellectual understanding as sufficing for
the reality itself. Instead Whitman emphasizes that to understand him fully the
readers must completely reorient their lives, rejecting conventional values and
embarking upon a process of spiritual development. They are enticed to take
up this quest by the promise of Whitman's highest love, but at the same time
they are realistically warned of the price they must pay and of the likelihood

that they will misunderstand the signs and become lost along the way. In this manner Whitman calls attention to the gravity of the demand he is making upon his readers.

To emphasize the spiritual nature of "manly" love is not to ignore the importance of passionate human love in "Calamus." As always in the *Leaves*, the spiritual is birthed and nurtured by the natural. In fact, many of the "Calamus" poems have no explicit religious dimension. For instance, "Behold This Swarthy Face" merely describes how the poet greets other men with a kiss, and "What Think You I Take My Pen in Hand?" depicts "two simple men" kissing farewell at a pier. But in keeping with Whitman's method, these poems have an unstated religious purpose. Readers were to imitate these "types" of love, and to relate their experience to the spiritual hints provided in the *Leaves*. Then they would come to understand the emotions induced by their acts of friendship and love as revelations of a higher world. For Whitman the natural is always to find its fulfillment in the transcendent, and it is the transcendent form of manly love which receives emphasis in the opening poems of "Calamus."

The fourth poem, "For You Democracy," introduces the sequence's political theme (discussed later), but then in the next poem, "These I Singing in Spring," Whitman again depicts the mystical nature of his manly love as he establishes the calamus plant as one of the key symbols of his new religion. Resuming the theme introduced in the opening poem of journeying to a pond-side, he now indicates that this symbolizes a movement into a transcendent spiritual realm by describing himself as passing beyond the "gates" or boundaries of the natural world: "Collecting I traverse the garden the world, *but soon I pass the gates*, / Now along the pond-side, now wading in a little, fearing not the wet" (emphasis added). In the ensuing lines the poet presents himself in the solitude of nature where he feels himself to be in mystical union with the souls of absent friends and lovers, some of whom are living and others dead:

> Far, far in the forest, or sauntering later in summer, before I think where I go,
> Solitary, smelling the earthy smell, stopping now and then in the silence,
> Alone I had thought, yet soon a troop gathers around me,
> Some walk by my side and some behind, and some embrace my arms or neck,
> They the spirits of dear friends dead or alive, thicker they come, a great crowd,
>   and I in the middle.

In this passage Whitman is clearly using language of physical love to suggest a spiritual love between souls so intensely passionate that it transcends the barriers of space and time and even death itself.

Having created this context, he institutes the calamus grass as the symbol of the highest form of spiritual love. Its special importance is signified by the fact that he pulls it directly from the water and offers it only to those who can love as he has loved:

And here what I now draw from the water, wading in the pond-side,
(O here I last saw him that tenderly loves me, and returns again never to separate
    from me,
And this, O this shall henceforth be the token of comrades, this calamus-root
    shall,
Interchange it youths with each other! let none render it back!)
. . . .
Indicating to each one what he shall have, giving something to each;
But what I drew from the water by the pond-side, that I reserve
I will give of it, but only to them that love as I myself am capable of loving.

The calamus is reserved for a spiritual elite. Its symbolic meaning is only open
to those developed souls who, like Whitman, have learned to experience
human love not just as an emotion but also as a form of metaphysical truth:
an experience which unites the soul with God.

But why select the calamus grass as the appropriate natural fact for symbolizing this love? In explaining his choice in a letter to Moncure Conway in
1867, Whitman described calamus as a "very large & aromatic grass, or rush,
growing about water-ponds in the valleys—[spears about three feet high]
—often called 'sweet flag'—grows all over the Northern and Middle States";
and he stated that the "recherché' or ethereal sense of the term, as used in my
book, arises probably from the actual Calamus presenting the biggest & hardiest kinds of spears of grass—and their fresh, aquatic, pungent bouquet."[25]
From the properties Whitman ascribes to the plant, it is easy to understand
his decision. For Whitman, every upward-shooting blade of grass proclaimed
man's victory over death ("The smallest sprout shows there is really no death,"
"Song of Myself," 6) and so these "biggest & hardiest . . . spears of grass"
might fittingly symbolize a love which convinced man of his immortality; their
pungent aroma could suggest this love's intangible and yet compelling power;
and naturally growing at the water's edge, the calamus grass would indicate
this love's ability to link the natural (the land) with the transcendent (the
waters).

Of course the tall-leaved calamus can also be interpreted as a phallic symbol,
and it has frequently been pointed out that in "Song of Myself" Whitman likens the calamus root to the penis and testes: "Root of wash'd sweet flag! timor-
ous pond-snipe! nest of guarded duplicate eggs!" (l. 535). However, a more
relevant passage, since it occurs in the same sequence, for determining the symbolic meaning of calamus appears in "Scented Herbage," where the roots and
leaves are presented as a symbol which fuses Whitman's love with his belief
in immortality:

Scented herbage of my breast,
Leaves from you I glean, I write, to be perused best afterwards,
Tomb-leaves, body-leaves growing up above me above death,
Perennial roots, tall leaves, O the winter shall not freeze you delicate leaves,

Every year shall you bloom again, out from where you retired you shall emerge
again.

(ll. 1–5)

Furthermore, even if at one level the calamus is to function as a phallic symbol,
it does not necessarily follow that Whitman intends it as an encouragement
of homosexual love. As the unique bond shared by all men, the phallus is an
appropriate symbol of male comradeship, and as a source of physical generation, it reinforces the theme of immortality.

In an intended preface written in the 1860s Whitman succinctly states his
hope that the *Leaves* will provide readers with a vital religious faith: "Sweet
FAITH, beyond all lore and riches in the world, may somewhere somehow by
the path I lead you, among these leaves, an odorous glistening blossom, appear, O friend and become yours" (*NPM*, IV, 1479). It is not by accident that
the imagery he uses to refer to religious faith is close to that used to describe
the calamus plant in "Scented Herbage": "Oh I do not know whether many
passing by will discover you or inhale your faint odor . . . / O slender leaves!
O blossoms of my blood!" Whitman consistently uses odors to suggest the intangible nature of spiritual experience, and it is appropriate that he speak of
both faith and his calamus love as blossoms because both are the ultimate fruit
or beauty of his poetry. Furthermore, any adequate interpretation of "Calamus" must relate the sequence to Whitman's effort to establish a new religion
because the love Whitman celebrates in "Calamus" provides both the existential basis and ultimate fulfillment of his faith. As later poems in the sequence
make clear, Whitman conceives of this love as arising primarily out of experiences of intense love between men, but in these opening poems which set the
context for "Calamus," the emphasis is on the transcendent aspects of this
love. It acquaints the soul with a higher or otherworldly realm, presents an
existential proof of immortality, and establishes a mystical bond between poet
and reader and the living and the dead.

So, in the last analysis, what is the spiritual function of "Calamus"? A brief
analysis of the function of love in mystical religion suggests that the "Calamus"
sequence is quite in keeping with other mystical texts on love, for mystics always stress that love is the soul's best means to the transcendent. For instance,
in the "Symposium," Socrates instructs his listeners that "in the attainment
of this end [God and immortality] human nature will not easily find a better
helper than love. And, therefore, also, I say that every man ought to honour
him [Love] . . . and walk in his ways."[26] Similarly, the Apostle John states: "No
man hath seen God at any time. If we love one another, God dwelleth in us"
(John 1:4, 12). In light of the spiritual content of "Calamus" and Whitman's
familiarity with Plato and the Bible, it seems reasonable to assume that he had
this mystical evaluation of love in mind when he maintained in the sequence's
eighth poem, "The Base of all Metaphysics," that underlying Platonism, Chris-

tianity, and German Idealism, three systems that predicate an ideal realm of the spirit, is the "dear love of man for his comrade, the attraction of friend to friend." This poem, added to the *Leaves* in 1871, is sometimes seen as a prime example of Whitman's later effort to conceal his unconventional ways by superimposing a religious dimension upon the earlier poetry. But as has been indicated by this analysis of the introductory movement, "Calamus" was always replete with spiritual meaning. The addition of this poem does not give the sequence a new content but rather clarifies and reinforces its spiritual meanings. Here Whitman presents the comradeship of "Calamus" as a recurring or transhistorical pattern of religious experience. He suggests that it is the state of consciousness induced in the soul by comradeship, more than anything else, which provides the basis for man's belief in the existence of a higher spiritual order. In this notion, we have Whitman's primary purpose in "Calamus": to lay down human love as the existential cornerstone of his new religious edifice.

The Political: Whitman's Mystical Union

Beginning with the early enthusiasts, American critics have stressed the importance of comradeship to democracy, a theme introduced in the sequence's fourth poem, "For You O Democracy." Whitman announces that he will "make the continent indissoluble" by planting "companionship thick as trees along all the rivers of America." The motif is continued in "I Hear It Was Charged Against Me," "I Dream'd in a Dream," "A Leaf for Hand in Hand," "To the East and to the West," "A Promise to California," and "The Prairie-Grass Dividing." As these titles reveal, Whitman was especially concerned to include the western states; in the last-mentioned poem he uses the prairie grass, perhaps because calamus does not grow in the West, as a symbol of comradeship:

> The prairie-grass dividing, its special odor breathing,
> I demand of it the spiritual corresponding,
> Demand the most copious and close companionship of men.

Not surprisingly, Marxist critics have also emphasized the political significance of Whitman's comradeship. For instance, the Brazilian scholar Gilberto Freyre, who has made the best Marxist reading of Whitman, argues that the "Calamus" love, because it transcends class distinctions and national boundaries, provides the requisite emotional basis for a democratic society and, ultimately, a global fellowship. Searching for antecedents of Whitman's doctrine of love, Freyre, in passing, likens it to Saint Francis of Assisi's notion of spiritual brotherhood.[27] The comparison is more appropriate than Freyre's discussion suggests, for although Marxist and non-Marxist critics do not make this point, even the political theme in "Calamus" has a religious basis and purpose.

It has close parallels with American Protestantism's notions of the elect nation and the coming millennium, and it is an integral part of Whitman's post-Christian millennialism.

Although many of Whitman's Christian contemporaries drew upon millennial imagery as a motivating ideal, they nevertheless kept the primary emphasis upon individual and social reform as a means to the millennium and did not become preoccupied with writing or relishing lengthy disquisitions on the pleasures of the kingdom. However, when they did briefly characterize the coming era, it was often depicted as a godly community of loving fellowship. According to Lyman Beecher, when the citizens of the republic would become subjects of the government of God, their hearts would be inscribed with the "law of universal and impartial love."[28] His son Edward described the impending "renovation of the world, and its union in the love of God" as a time in which "all the institutions of all nations [will be based] on the great principles of the law of love."[29] Joseph Berg promised that the "heart of Christian charity will expand under the breathings of the love of God . . . reaching out in the gushings of purest sympathy to gather in the outcast and the perishing."[30] In espousing his glad tidings of universal perfectionism, William Arthur declared, "Humanity may be sanctified! Communities of men may be reared who shall dwell in peace and love, and earth may become a mirror of heaven."[31] With greater reserve, Yale theologian Samuel Harris explained that the "law of the kingdom is the law of love"; its members become a "brotherhood, united in fellowship by their common faith in Christ, and are workers together with God to extend his kingdom through the world."[32]

Whitman is engaging in a similar type of millennial futurism in "Calamus" which images forth a future with "companionship thick as trees along all the rivers of America" ("For You O Democracy") and with the "institution of the dear love of comrades" established in "every city of these States" ("I Hear It Was Charged Against Me"). What is unique in Whitman's understanding of the relationship between love and the millennium is that he conceives of this love as something more than a quality of the renewed individual and an ingredient of the new age; it is also essential to the well-being of a democracy. Indeed, Whitman felt that "Calamus" was so crucial to American unity that on one occasion he asserted the sequence was mainly important for its political significance; it was by "the beautiful and sane affection of man for man" that the United States were to be "most effectually welded together, intercalated, anneal'd into a living union" (*PW*, 471). Spiritual comradeship, in combination with perfectionism and a shared national religious vision, was the solution to the republican problem of how to allow for individual liberties and yet maintain a cohesive society.

The political unity of Whitman's future religious democracy would ultimately derive from its being a spiritual community. Just as Christianity teaches the doctrine of all believers being united in a mystical body with Christ as its head, so Whitman propounded the notion of a corporate mysticism in which he was the timeless center of mystical sympathy. "Calamus" was to "arouse and set flowing in men's and women's hearts, young and old, endless streams of living, pulsating love and friendship, directly from them to myself, now and ever" (1876 Preface, *PW*, 471). These bonds of love would not be subject to the constraints of death: "I cannot be discharged from you! not from one any sooner than another! / O death! O for all that, I am yet of you unseen this hour with irrepressible love" ("Starting from Paumanok," l. 212). While Protestants saw themselves as receiving spiritual sustenance from Christ in their efforts to establish the heavenly city in America, Whitman dreamed of future generations who would turn to him for inspiration, guidance, and support as they worked to build a godly republic:

> With firm and regular step they wend, they never stop,
> Successions of men, Americanos, a hundred millions,
> One generation playing its part and passing on,
> Another generation playing its part and passing on in its turn,
> With faces turn'd sideways or backward towards me to listen,
> With eyes retrospective towards me.
>
> ("Starting from Paumanok," ll. 31–36)

The Poetic: An Electric, Athletic, Secret, and Manly Love

The relationship the *Leaves* is most concerned to promote is a love between souls, especially between the soul of the poet and his readers. This theme is introduced in the book's third poem, "In Cabin'd Ships at Sea," where the poet announces that his love is "folded" (l. 21) in each of his chants, and it recurs frequently thereafter. The informing image of the small poem, "As I Lay with My Head in Your Lap Camerado," typifies the intimacy that Whitman sought in the poet-reader relationship. Ultimately, the souls of the two, regardless of their separation in time, were to become fused in an intense mystical love: "We never met, and ne'er shall meet—and yet our souls embrace, long, close and long ("Thanks in Old Age"). Throughout "Calamus" Whitman works to develop this spiritual bond with his readers. By my count, twelve of the poems are primarily, if not exclusively, concerned with this theme. Some, such as "Roots and Leaves" and "Western Boy," provide instruction and make demands which will promote this relationship. Others, like "Not Heat Flames Up and Consumes," the enigmatic "Earth, My Likeness," and "Full of Life Now," intrigue, encourage, and tantalize the reader with cryptic hints and promises of the mysterious love that lies hidden in the *Leaves*, waiting to be realized by the spiritually developed reader. But to understand many of these poems, it is again necessary to attend to the poet's mystical vocabulary. The "Calamus" love is characterized as "electric," "athletic," and "secret"; terms which, if separated from the context of the *Leaves*, as they often have been in previous criticism, seem to mean little more than "passionate," "unmentionable," and "physically robust" respectively and appear to refer to a forbidden form of physical love. However, for Whitman, these terms most often convey spiritual meanings. In addition, Whitman's use of the term "manly," although it does not have religious significance, does carry ethical and political connotations overlooked in Whitman scholarship.[33]

Whitman's use of electrical terms is undoubtedly borrowed from contemporary mesmerists and spiritualists.[34] By 1850 mesmerism, in vogue the two preceding decades, was on the decline, but its electrical theory and terminology were incorporated by the new social fad and heterodox religion of spiritualism which reached a peak of popularity in the decade before the Civil War. According to mesmeric and spiritualist lore, the entire universe was permeated by a highly rarified electrical fluid which had its source in God. This "PRIMAL matter, which is electricity," asserted the popular mesmeric lecturer John Bovee Dods, is the "natural atmosphere or substance" which emanates from God.[35] God was "positive" to the world, so electricity flowed from deity to the rest of the creation. In turn, the "positive" mesmerist could induce a trance in the less highly charged or "negative" clairvoyant. Similarly, in spiritualism "positive" spirits of the higher realm activated the electricity of the less highly charged humans with whom they communicated.[36]

In all cases, spiritual communication involved the discharge of subtle electrical energies. Andrew Jackson Davis repeatedly described spiritualism as a form of electrical intercourse with spiritual beings: it was "a 'Jacob's ladder', composed of magnetism and electricity ... reaching into Heaven, upon which angels descend and ascend, bringing 'tidings of great joy'."[37] In 1853 Judge John Edmonds of the New York Supreme Court reported in what became one of the most popular treatises on spiritualism that the spirit of Francis Bacon instructed him on how best to communicate with departed loved ones. The secret was to "let the electric bond which connects life with death vibrate with emotions of love, of truth, of good and noble aspirations"; then the "returning current shall bring back to your consciousness the certainty that you are surrounded by those whose thoughts accord with your thoughts."[38]

Perhaps Whitman did not subscribe to this literal belief in a universal electrical fluid, but he found this electrical language an apt metaphor for spiritual force or energy. For instance, he speaks of God's transcendence and immanence as constituting a "joyous, electric all" ("As They Draw to a Close"). Within the context of this metaphor, the inspired poet, the poet who is in union with divinity, is depicted as possessing an electrified soul: "Held by this electric self out of the pride of which I utter poems" ("As I Ebb'd with the Ocean of Life," l. 7) and the poet's task is to transmit this spiritual electricity to others. In proclaiming his intention to transfigure the flesh, Whitman states that he will make bodies "electric" and "discorrupt them, and charge them full with the charge of the soul" ("I Sing the Body Electric," ll. 1 & 4). Or again, he speaks of his desire to create a religious democracy as the creation of an electrified national soul: "Think not our chant, our show, merely for products gross or lucre—it is for thee [America], the soul in thee, electric, spiritual!" ("Song of the Exposition," l. 236).

This view of the poet as a transmitter of spiritual energy must be kept in mind when interpreting the "electric" love of "Calamus." For example:

> O you whom I often and silently come where you are that I may be with you,
> As I walk by your side or sit near, or remain in the same room with you,
> Little you know the subtle electric fire that for your sake is playing within me.
> ("O You Whom I Often and Silently Come")

In light of Whitman's usage, the "subtle electric fire" of these lines clearly has religious meaning: it refers to the intangible spiritual energy or love which unites poet to reader as their souls fuse in their mutual participation in the divine reality.

Whitman's frequent comparisons of spiritual activity to athletic exercise reflect the sharp emphasis upon self-improvement in antebellum religion. In a period in which religious leaders routinely exhorted their listeners to strive for spiritual perfection, references to arduous spiritual activity were not uncommon. Finney proclaimed to his audiences: "All the powers of the soul are strengthened by exercise" and "If you are deficient in a particular grace, exercise that."[39] William Arthur described the early Christians as addressing God with "prayers which importuned and wrestled with an instant and irrepressible urgency."[40] In narrating her spiritual autobiography, Phoebe Palmer used the same metaphor, speaking of herself as "for a long time wrestling earnestly with God."[41] In characterizing the sanctified soul, William Boardman, like Whitman, presents it as driven by a burning active love: "The spirit in him will be love; a constraining fire in his bones; he cannot but be active."[42]

Whitman's use of "athletic" builds upon his notion of this world as an arena for exercising and developing the soul. His anticipated religious democracy would require spiritually active citizens—citizens which he described in "Thou Mother with Thy Equal Brood" as a "larger, saner brood of female, male . . . athletes, moral, spiritual" (l. 84). Believing that the American churches failed to promote this spiritual activity, Whitman called for their replacement by a "real athletic and fit religion" (*NPM*, VI, 2061). In his effort to initiate this vital religion through a new order of poetry, he called for poems which would require of the reader an "exercise, a gymnast's struggle" (*PW*, 425); and he proudly proclaimed of his own poems that there was "naught made complete by me for you, but only hinted to be made by you by robust exercise." For this reason, in "Starting from Paumanok" Whitman asserts that his poetry must be "wrestled with" (l. 235), and in "Song of Myself" he presents himself as a "teacher of athletes" (l. 1234).

This use of athletic imagery continues in "Calamus" where, in the opening poem, the poet promises to project "types of athletic love." Later he emphasizes this love's dynamic and spiritual nature by describing it as "Ethereal, the last athletic reality" ("Fast Anchor'd Eternal O Love!"). And, as we shall see, the poet declares in "Earth, My Likeness" that "an athlete is enamour'd of me, and I of him" because he chose to communicate the truths of his vision through a method which left subtle hints to guide the active reader to the realization of the intended meanings. Readers of the *Leaves* must, of course, be athletic to discover Whitman's most important spiritual meanings. He termed these "secret" in part because they defied linguistic expression and in part because he chose to communicate them through a method in which he, rather than futilely straining to express his insights, left subtle hints to guide the active reader to the realization of the intended meaning. One of the poet's "secrets," perhaps his most important one, is the mystical love hinted at in "Calamus."

Whitman's use of "secret" was rather unusual. The term seems to have been seldom used by his Christian contemporaries but there is ample precedent for speaking of spiritual "secrets" in Emerson. For instance, in "The Poet" Emerson exclaims of the few known spiritual truths: "by what accident is it that these are exposed, when so many secrets sleep in nature!"[43] In "New England Reformers," he instructs the reformer that he must provide a "secret" that will enlarge the souls of his auditors before they will rally to the reformer's cause: "We are haunted with a belief that you have a secret, which it would highliest advantage us to learn, and we would force you to impart it to us, though it should bring us to prison, or to worse extremity."[44]

Whitman introduces his secret love early in the *Leaves*. In "Starting from Paumanok" he promises that he will reveal an "undemonstrable" spiritual truth which will unite poet and reader in a bond of love:

> O something ecstatic and undemonstrable! O music wild!
> O now I triumph—and you shall also;
> O hand in hand—O wholesome pleasure—O one more desirer and lover!
> (ll. 267–69)

In "Song of Myself" this motif is continued. The poet informs his readers, both male and female, that he has an ineffable love to share with them, and that it is integrally related to his soul, or to the mysterious spiritual principle of his being:

> Man or woman, I might tell how I like you, but cannot,
> And might tell what it is in me and what it is in you, but cannot,
> And might tell that pining I have, that pulse of my nights and days.
> (ll. 991–93)

So in the opening poem of "Calamus," when Whitman promises that he will "tell the secret of my nights and days," he has prepared his readers to expect that he will now reveal a love which will unite them to him in a bond of mystical love. Then he discloses this secret in the only way he can—through hints; and he expects the active reader to discover elements of his own experience which will supplement or fulfill the suggestions in the poetry. Finding these, the readers will successively intuit the poet's meanings until they fully share his love. In one of the sequence's closing poems, "Among the Multitude," this dynamic is described as a process of detecting the poet's secret signs and progressively knowing him until both reader and poet become united in mystical love:

> Among the men and women the multitude,
> I perceive one picking me out by secret and divine signs,
> Acknowledging none else, not parent, wife, husband, brother, child, any nearer
>   than I am,
> Some are baffled, but that one is not—that one knows me.
>
> Ah lover and perfect equal,
> I meant that you should discover me so by faint indirections.

This passage must be related to Whitman's recurring usage of "secret"; it describes the ideal poet-reader relationship in which the reader's soul, joined to the poet's in a bond of mystical love, is actively engaged in the process of unlocking the poet's secrets and entering more fully into his vision.

Another adjective Whitman uses to describe this love is "manly" ("In Paths Untrodden," "For You O Democracy," and "I Saw in Louisiana"). Unlike "electric," "athletic," and "secret," this term did not have a special religious meaning, but in the mid-nineteenth century it did carry connotations of moral and civic virtue that are lost to modern readers. During the Revolutionary era "manly" was an antonym of servile or slavish; a "manly" person was someone who openly and boldly resisted oppression. John Adams paid tribute to the courage of the early Puritans by asserting that "no fear of punishment, nor even death itself" could conquor the "steady, manly, pertinaceous spirit with which they had opposed the tyrants of those days in church and state."[45] Benjamin Franklin described his Puritan grandfather's essay for religious tolerance as "written with a good deal of decent plainness and manly freedom."[46] After the Revolution, "manly" came to suggest the qualities of candor and courage that were to characterize the good republican. This usage appears in the hard question with which Channing pricks his audience to a deeper concern over the actual fruits of American liberty: "Does it exalt us in manly spirit, in public virtue, above countries trodden under foot by despotism?"[47] In "Remarks on National Literature," he asserts that "a people whose institutions demand for their support a free and bold spirit . . . should be able to subject to a manly and independent criticism whatever comes from abroad."[48] "Manly" also conveyed the idea of simplicity and the absence of artifice, corruption, or degeneracy. Henry Ward Beecher contrasted the French language, "the dialect of refined sensualism and of licentious literature" to "the dignity and manliness of our English language which has never grown supple to twine around brilliant dissipation."[49] In "Manners," Emerson also contrasts manliness with degeneracy: "Fashion, though in a strange way, represents all manly virtue. It is virtue gone to seed: it is a kind of posthumous honor."[50] In the lexicon of the Civil War clergy, "effeminacy" and "manliness" were key terms, according to the study of James H. Moorhead. The former indicated the "softness, love of ease, materialism, and selfishness of a degenerate citizenry"; the latter suggested "those qualities of frugality, self-sacrificing simplicity, and heroic loyalty that befitted true patriots rightly esteeming the divine government."[51]

We can easily detect these layers of ethical and political meaning in Whitman's usage. An *Aurora* editorial argued that the Tammany party needed "a newspaper bold, manly, able, and American in its tenor."[52] In a piece of Whitman's early fiction, "The Last of the Sacred Army," the various expressions of gratitude men and women pay to the last survivor of the Revolutionary War "spring from the fairest and manliest traits in the soul."[53] In his correspondence, Whitman described the hospitalized Union soldiers as "full of manly independence";[54] and he spoke of one in particular as "so sensible, [with] such decent manly ways, nothing shallow or mean."[55] By describing the "Calamus" love as "manly," Whitman was linking it with the honesty, courage, and simplicity that were the hallmarks of good citizenship. Awareness of the term's historical meaning raises the question of whether it is likely that Whitman would have elected to use it and then gone about covertly imbedding a theme of homosexual love.

Excursus: An Example

After dealing rather hurriedly with the special vocabulary Whitman uses to indicate the spiritual dynamics of the poet-reader relationship, let me alter my pace and provide an intensive analysis of one of the more enigmatic love songs, "Earth, My Likeness." My purpose is to reinforce the preceding discussion by showing how the poem draws upon Whitman's religious vocabulary and contributes to his spiritual vision; conversely, interpretations that overlook the spiritual significance of Whitman's language will misread the poem as little more than an expression of homosexuality.[56]

    (1) Earth, my likeness,
    (2) Though you look so impassive, ample and spheric there,
    (3) I now suspect that is not all;
    (4) I now suspect there is something fierce in you eligible to burst forth,
    (5) For an athlete is enamour'd of me, and I of him,
    (6) But toward him there is something fierce and terrible in me eligible to burst
        forth,
    (7) I dare not tell it in words, not even in these songs.

The poem expresses the inner tension which Whitman felt in regard to his poetic method: on the one hand, he keenly desired to articulate his love in a more direct manner; on the other hand, he knew that this was impossible because his meaning was ineffable. He also felt that to be more explicit would be improper, because the reader, if he were to acquire a conceptual understanding of this love, might not go on to bring it to full existential realization.

The lines are most immediately related to other poems in "Calamus." In "Recorders Ages Hence," Whitman informed his future biographers not to be misled by his "impassive exterior" because beneath it was a "measureless ocean of love" and he "freely pour'd it forth." In "Not Heat Flames Up and Consumes," the poet depicts his desire for the reader's love to be as relentless as the sea-waves ("Does the tide hurry, seeking something, and never give up? O I the same") and as consuming as flame ("O none of these more than the flames of me, consuming, burning for his love whom I love"). Yet despite the intensity of his desire, he refused to declare his love fully, for he realized it could only be appreciated by an active and spiritually prepared soul that related the poem's suggestions to its own religious experience:

> Love-buds put before you and within you whoever you are,
> Buds to be unfolded on the old terms,
> If you bring the warmth of the sun to them they will open and bring form, color,
>   perfume, to you.
>
> ("Roots and Leaves Themselves Alone")

"Earth, My Likeness" rests upon a comparison which continues and expands these motifs. The poet notes that the earth has an impassive exterior, and this leads him to suspect that it contains a "fierce" and hidden love "eligible to burst forth" to the active soul, because the poet also has an impassive exterior and it covers a "fierce and terrible" love eligible for the spiritually athletic reader. But the content of the poem is denser than this; to be fully appreciated it must be related to the terrestrial symbolism and the terms "fierce" and "terrible" as they are developed throughout the *Leaves.*

For Whitman, the earth was a cardinal religious symbol. He perceived it as revealing a host of spiritual meanings; there were, to mention a few, "the amplitude of the earth, and the coarseness and sexuality of the earth, and the great charity of the earth, and the equilibrium also" ("Kosmos"). In short, the earth was a veritable thesaurus of religious values which the religious poet had to realize and somehow incorporate into his work: "The workmanship of souls is by those inaudible words of the earth, / The masters know the earth's words and use them more than audible words" ("A Song of the Rolling Earth," ll. 15–16). The great poet or "true son of God" would be able to "speak the secret of impassive earth" and thus justify the "whole earth, this cold, impassive, voiceless earth" ("Passage to India," ll. 95, 110–11).

But the poet must not only understand the earth, he must also imitate its indirect manner of speaking. As the above quotations indicate, this was one of its meanings; the "impassive" earth spoke in an "inaudible" and "voiceless" manner. This was the language not only of the earth, but of all nature: "The earth is rude, silent, incomprehensible at first, Nature is rude and incomprehensible at first" ("Song of the Open Road," l. 117), but with the earth, this meaningful silence was especially noticeable. Mother earth was the "eloquent dumb great mother" ("Song of the Rolling Earth," l. 41) whose indirection was paradigmatic for the poet. Though full of meanings, the earth refused to argue or assert; rather it presented itself as the holder of inexpressible truths: "The truths of the earth continually wait, they are not so conceal'd either. / They are calm, subtle, untransmissable by print" ("Rolling Earth," ll. 22–23). It waited for the developed soul to discover its significance: "I swear the earth shall surely be complete to him or her who shall be complete" ("Rolling Earth," l. 90). From contemplating the example of the earth, Whitman learned that in communicating religious meanings it was best to have a few secrets or to leave some things untold: "I swear I will never henceforth have to do with the faith that tells the best, / I will have to do only with that faith that leaves the best untold" ("Rolling Earth," ll. 119–20). Thus, in "Earth My Likeness," Whitman emphasizes that his love is like the secret meanings of the earth; it is ample, yet word-defying, and it waits for the athletic reader to whom it is "eligible to burst forth."

Whitman perceived the earth's silent, impassive face and its willingness to wait as a manifestation of the immensity and omnipotence of the divine mind as it deliberately worked out the cosmic plan for evolutionary ascent and spiritual development. His response was a sense of awe before the infinitude and perfection of the divine consciousness. It is this state of mind which underlies his description of his love as "fierce and terrible." "Terrible" has the positive connotation of reverent fear before the mysterious and sublime. Thus Whitman elsewhere speaks of being terrified by the earth's impassive manner, "Now I am terrified at the Earth, it is that calm and patient" ("This Compost," l. 42). Whitman's characterization of his love as fierce is closely related to this meaning of "terrible"; it is employed to convey his sense of how the divine consciousness regulated the cosmos with inexorable and undeviating laws. This usage frequently prompts the poet to term the divine sea, with its inevitable recall of all finite reality to its spiritual source, as a "fierce old mother." Similarly, he conceived of the soul as lured or impelled through life by the attraction of eternal spiritual mysteries; and, because they exercised a persistent and unyielding attraction, he addresses them as "ye aged fierce enigmas" ("Passage to India," l. 230).

Thus when the fierce and terrible love of "Earth My Likeness" is placed within the context of related elements throughout the *Leaves*, its primary theme appears to be a commentary upon the religious character of the poet's method. In likening his expression to that of the earth's, Whitman is assimilating both his love and his poetic practice to the activity of the divine consciousness, with its indirect statement and willingness to wait on the one hand, and its ample, powerful meanings and certitude of eventual success on the other. The poem's central message is the poet's assertion that his love calmly waits for the spiritual athlete to discover its inexorable power and awesome meaning.

Other Evidence for a Homosexual Reading

When sufficient attention is given to the religious dimensions of "Calamus," much of the evidence routinely cited in support of a homosexual reading either becomes problematic or must be rejected as unconvincing. But the above discussion has not done justice to the argument for Whitman's homosexuality and the presence of a homosexual theme in "Calamus" and the *Leaves*. A full discussion of the topic must also consider relevant biographical materials, revisions of the manuscripts and printed texts, and an analysis of selected aspects of Whitman's style. Without attempting an exhaustive review of this evidence, I will try to present the most compelling information and also to indicate its limitations.

Whitman's biography provides no clear evidence of his having ever engaged in a homosexual affair, but it presents a lot of ambiguous materials as well as convincing evidence of his homosexual inclinations. The evidence most suggestive of sexual relations with other men can be briefly summarized. In notebook-diaries of 1862-63, Whitman made brief entries about men he had met in New York City, Brooklyn, and Washington, D.C., and in four cases he recorded having slept with them:

> *Dan'l Spencer* (Spencer, pere, 214 44th st. & 59 William somewhat feminine—
> 5th av. (44) (May 29th)—told me he had never been in a fight and did not drink
> at all gone in 2d N.Y. Lt Artillery deserted, returned to it slept with me Sept.
> 3d. (*NPM*, II, 487)

> *David Wilson* night of Oct. 11, '62, walking up from Middagh—slept with me—
> works in blacksmith shop in Navy Yard—lives in Hampden st.—walks together
> Sunday afternoon & night—is about 19. (*NPM*, II, 496)

> Horace Ostrander Oct. 22 '62 24 4th av. from Otsego co. 60 miles west of Al-
> bany was in the hospital to see Chas. Green) about 28 y'rs of age—about 1855
> went on voyage to Liverpool—his experiences as a green hand (Nov. 22 16 4th
> av.) slept with him Dec. 4 '62. (*NPM*, II, 497)

> Jerry Taylor, (NJ.) [October 9, 1863; Washington, D.C.] of 2d dist. reg't slept
> with me last night weather soft, cool enough, warm enough, heavenly. (*NPM*,
> II, 537)

In addition there is the intense relationship Whitman developed with the ex-Confederate soldier Peter Doyle whom he met in 1865 and with whom he enjoyed a close relationship for eight years. Four of Whitman's notebook entries, apparently written in 1870, indicate that he himself recognized that his affection for Doyle exceeded the bounds of conventional male friendship. The first and third of these are made more revealing by the fact that a close analysis of the handwriting reveals that the pronouns were originally masculine and then erased and written over as feminine.

Cheating, childish abandonment of myself, fancying what does not really exist in another, but is all the time in myself alone— utterly deluded & cheated by *myself* & my own weakness—REMEMBER WHERE I AM MOST WEAK, & most lacking. Yet always preserve a kind spirit & demeanor to 16 [presumably the 16th letter of the alphabet, "P," for Peter Doyle]. BUT PERSUE HER NO MORE. (*NPM*, II, 887)

June 17—
It is IMPERATIVE, that I obviate & remove myself (& my orbit) *at all hazards*, from this incessant *enormous & abnormal* PERTURBATION (*NPM*, II, 887)

July 15—1870
TO GIVE UP ABSOLUTELY *& for good, from the present hour, this* FEVER-ISH, FLUCTUATING, *useless* UNDIGNIFIED PURSUIT *of* 16.4 [numerical code for the letters P & D, the initials of Peter Doyle]—*too long, (much too long)* persevered in,—so humiliating—*It must come at last &* had better come now—(*It cannot possibly be a success*). LET THERE FROM THIS HOUR BE NO FALTERING, NO GETTING *at all henceforth*, (NOT ONCE, UNDER *any circumstances)—avoid seeing her, or meeting her, or any talk or explanations—or* ANY MEETING WHATEVER, FROM THIS HOUR FORTH, FOR LIFE

> July 15 '70
> (*NPM*, II, 888-89)

> Depress the adhesive nature /
> It is in excess—making life a torment /
> Ah this diseased, feverish disproportionate adhesiveness /
> (*NPM*, II, 889–90)

Whitman also established a passionate friendship with the semi-literate Harry Stafford in the late 1870s. Its nature is indicated in the following line from a letter Whitman wrote him in June 1877 (Stafford was then nineteen years old): "Dear son, how I wish you could come in now, even if but for an hour & take off your coat, & sit down on my lap—"[57] In responding to an invitation to visit John H. Johnston in New York, Whitman disingenuously referred to Harry as his nephew and stated that "when traveling [we] always share the same room together & the same bed."[58]

   Crucial as this material is to an understanding of Whitman's personality, its exact meaning and relevance to his poetry remains unclear. That Whitman slept with other men is not compelling evidence of his having had sexual relations with them. That he took the precaution of introducing Stafford as his nephew indicates how he feared their relationship might be construed, but at the same time the fact that he could openly assert that they slept together suggests that it was not uncommon for men to share a bed in Victorian America. Whitman's anguished reflections, erasures, and use of numerical code indicate his awareness of the homosexual nature of his feelings for Peter Doyle, but they also suggest that the affection was not mutual and there is no evidence of a sexual relationship.

The most interesting fact about Whitman's notebook jottings of 1870 is not that they reveal his homosexual inclinations, but that they disclose his evaluation of them as abnormal and to be corrected. This calls into question the recent homosexual interpretation that Whitman was fully aware of his sexual identity in the 1850s and had thought it through so carefully that he developed a highly original and complex poetic for celebrating it as an important theme in his poetry for more than a decade. If this were the case, it hardly seems credible that Whitman would then begin to conceive of it in such negative terms and to feel the need to hide his feelings even in his private notebooks. Furthermore, if he had developed such an artful code for talking about his homosexuality, he would not resort to such bush-league tactics as poorly concealed erasures and a numerical code for the alphabet. The manner in which he characterizes his love for Doyle and his clumsy efforts at concealment strongly suggest that the Whitman of 1870, far from being a seasoned homosexual who had bravely pioneered ways to proclaim his homosexual identity, was still trying to repress and deny this central element of his identity.

Whitman's Revisions

According to proponents of a gay reading, Whitman revised his poetry to disguise or delete the homosexual theme. Some of the alterations cited in support of this contention are manuscript revisions made before publication; most, however, occurred in the later editions, and these are seen as part of the older Whitman's design to hide his earlier unconventional ways. It has even been asserted that this effort at self-censorship was the cause for the decline in Whitman's creativity in his later years.[59] A thorough review of these revisions would require a separate study, but I wish to discuss a few of the principal pieces of evidence in order to point out their problematic and unconvincing aspects.

After asserting that the "Calamus" poems are "the most overtly homosexual of Whitman's poems," Alan Helms argues that "it is there we find the process of revision and self-censorship most clearly taking place." As a prime example, Helms maintains that Whitman dropped three of the "most intimate and revealing poems" for the 1867 edition:

> "Long I thought that knowledge alone would suffice" ("Calamus" 8) in which he announces that he will sing the songs of America no longer, for "One who loves me is jealous of me, and withdraws me from all but love"; "Hours continuing long, sore and heavy- hearted" ("Calamus" 9) in which he laments being abandoned by his lover ("Is there even one other like me—distracted—his friend, his lover, lost to him?"); and "Who is now reading this?" ("Calamus" 16) in which he expresses puzzlement at himself, along with intense shame and guilt ("(O conscience-struck! O self-convicted)").[60]

It is difficult to believe that Whitman felt compelled to drop these poems as too revealing in light of others which were retained. For instance, elsewhere in "Calamus" Whitman depicts himself with "my dear friend my lover" sleeping "under the same cover" with "his arm lightly around my breast" ("When I Heard at the Close of the Day"). Helms's characterization of these deletions is accurate only if he refers to emotional and not sexual intimacy, for they provide no conclusive information about Whitman's personal life or about whether "Calamus" is intended to endorse homosexuality. Furthermore, as is true throughout "Calamus," even rejected poems are primarily important for their spiritual meaning.

Read within the larger context of "Calamus," poems 8 and 9 dramatize the spiritual lesson, later repeated more powerfully in "Out of the Cradle," that the inevitable frustration of earthly love should lead to a more mature understanding of the needs of the human heart. It should teach the lover to fixate not upon the human object but upon the experience of love so as to initiate the soul's ascent to a higher state of consciousness in which it has the sense of participating in attributes of divinity itself. This theme is, of course, a traditional religious idea which manifests itself in the poetry of religious romanticism. For instance, in "Give All to Love," Emerson instructs his reader (who is assumed to be male) to sacrifice all—property, fame, family and friends, and even the muse—to love, for it is an avenue to a transcendent realm or (in Emerson's words) a "god" which "dives into noon" and knows "the outlets of the sky." But at the same time he warns the reader to love the emotion or experience of love, not the beloved, because the "maid" will inevitably discover "a joy apart from thee"; then the reader can shift his affection from its human object to a fuller participation in love itself, which is, in fact, a participation in divinity:

> Though thou loved her as thyself,
> As a self of purer clay,
> Though her parting dims the day,
> Stealing grace from all alive;
> Heartily know,
> When half-gods go,
> The gods arrive.[61]

Similarly, in "Calamus" 8 and 9 Whitman establishes human love as the highest earthly aspiration and then points to the soul's need for a transcendent love. First, he lists his earlier goals in life: to be distinguished for learning, to become a public orator, to be a courageous hero, and then to be a national poet. But when he discovers love, all other pursuits, even the pursuit of the muse, become "empty and tasteless" as Whitman professes to be " . . . indifferent to my own songs—I will go with him I love, / It is to be enough for us that we are together—We never separate again."[62] But this is Whitman dramatizing an erroneous sense of the sufficiency and security of a human relationship, just as he does with the two birds in "Out of the Cradle" who in their love are "*Singing all time, minding no time, / While we two keep together.*" Just as their happiness is immediately dashed by the death of the she-bird, so in the very next poem, "Calamus" 9, Whitman reports the departure of his love: "Hours discouraged, distracted—for the one I cannot content myself without, soon I saw him content himself without me." Whitman's error has been to attempt to satisfy an infinite desire with a finite object, instead of recognizing, as he does in "Out of the Cradle" and in "Song of Myself," that the proper object is "The great Camerado, the lover true."

As in "Out of the Cradle," in "Calamus" Whitman also uses the experience of frustrated love as the material for poetic production:

> But now I think there is no unreturn'd love, the pay is certain one way or another,
> (I loved a certain person ardently and my love was not return'd,
> Yet out of that I have written these songs.)
>
> ("Sometimes with One I Love")

But as the content of the songs indicates, the experience has involved more than a transmutation of emotion into art; it has also led Whitman to a higher wisdom of love—an understanding of human love as a proleptic form of the more satisfying love he will know in the afterlife.

A closer analysis of "Calamus" 16 discloses that it is neither especially personal nor revealing, at least in regard to manly love:

> Who is now reading this?
> May-be one is now reading this who knows some wrong-doing of my past life,
> Or may-be a stranger is reading this who has secretly loved me,
> Or maybe one who meets all my grand assumptions and egotisms with derision,
> Or maybe one who is puzzled at me.
> As if I were not puzzled at myself!
> Or as if I never deride myself! (O conscience-struck! O self-convicted!)
> Or as if I do not secretly love strangers! (O tenderly, a long time, and never avow it;)
> Or as if I did not see, perfectly well, interior in myself, the stuff of wrong-doing,
> Or as if it could cease transpiring from me until it must cease.

There is an inherent contradiction in Helms's judgment that Whitman is conscience-stricken about his homosexuality. For if Helms maintains that Whitman was celebrating his homosexuality in 1860, then he would not speak of this as a wrongdoing, for this would undercut the alleged argument for its morality. Rather than a veiled admission of homosexuality, the poem appears to be Whitman's general statement that even though he is presenting a version of himself as exemplary, he is acutely aware both of the discrepancy between his ideal and his actual selves and of his incomplete self-understanding. In short, the poet is a self-critical prophet, and this vague confessional emphasizes that the reader's faith must be so strong and properly rooted in spiritual values that it will not be undermined by the discovery of any mistakes or imperfections in Whitman's personal faith or behavior.

In addition to disagreeing with Helms's reading of these poems, I believe there are other possible explanations for their deletion. For instance, Whitman may have dropped 8 and 9 because they are of questionable literary merit and express an insecurity, frustration, and possessiveness that is out of keeping with the sequence's emphasis upon the freedom and calm induced by manly love. Also, it is relevant to recall that 16 was originally composed in late 1856 or early 1857; some two years later when Whitman conceived of the idea of a cluster of poems on manly love, he added it to this grouping.[63] Its subsequent removal may be explained by the fact that it had neither significant aesthetic value nor special relevance to the sequence. The fact is that the motivation for these changes in "Calamus," as is so often the case with authorial revisions, remains largely unclear, and any arguments based on them are at best conjectural.

Helms also asserts that Whitman revised his poetry to reduce the number of references to homosexual cruising. For instance, "A Song of Joys" originally contained this line which was excised in 1871: "O of men—of women toward me as I pass—the memory of only one look—the boy lingering and waiting." When "A Noiseless Patient Spider" was first published in 1871, it no longer contained these lines from the 1862-63 draft: "Oh I saw one passing alone, saying hardly a word—yet full of love I detected him, by certain signs / O eyes wishfully turning! O silent eyes."[64] But Helms takes these lines out of the context of the larger religious vision, thus overlooking Whitman's belief that the spiritually integrated person exercised an attractive influence over others. In "Song of Myself" (section 39) Whitman depicts a "friendly and flowing savage," uncorrupted by civilization, as possessing this type of spiritual power:

> Wherever he goes men and women accept and desire him,
> They desire he should like them, touch them, speak to them, stay with them,
> . . . .
> He is one of those who is beautiful and happy, he is one of those that to look
> upon and be with is enough.

The Indian woman in section 6 of "The Sleepers" enthralls Whitman's mother with her very presence:

> My mother look'd in delight and amazement at the stranger,
> . . . .
> The more she look'd upon her she loved her,
> Never before had she seen such wonderful beauty and purity.

Whitman's anticipated noble American, the culmination of evolution and history, is described in a similar manner: "The guest that was coming, he waited long, he is now housed, / He is one of those who are beautiful and happy, he is one of those that to look upon and be with is enough" ("To Think of Time," ll. 79–80). In "Think of the Soul," later excluded from the *Leaves*, readers were admonished to attend to their spiritual development not only because the soul continues "somehow to live in other spheres," but also because "you can interfuse yourself with such things that everybody that sees you shall look longingly upon you" (ll. 2, 5). In his real life, Whitman seems to have had a magnetic personal presence, and in his poetry he appropriately exaggerated his attractive power because he was presenting himself as a prototype of the ideal American.

This charismatic power functions in several ways in Whitman's spiritual poetic. As part of his strategy for developing his readers' souls, Whitman wanted to give them a mystical appreciation of the beauty and mystery of what might be called, for want of a better term, human facticity. "There is," he proclaimed, "something in staying close to men and women and looking on them, and in the contact and odor of them, that pleases the soul well" ("Song of the Body Electric," l. 49). Exactly what this "something" was, Whitman could not say precisely because, like all spiritual experience, it was too fundamental and complex. Accordingly, its power to charm the soul was one of the great "inaudible words" that the master-poet, in imitation of the earth's indirect manner, merely hinted at, expecting the reader to unlock its meaning in her or his experience: "The charms that go with the mere looks of some men and women, are sayings and meanings also. / The workmanship of souls is by those inaudible words of the earth" ("Song of the Rolling Earth," ll. 14–15). By attributing to himself a marked degree of personal charisma, Whitman not only reinforces his claim to having the requisite spiritual development to be America's poet-prophet, but also further defines, as in the following passage from "Crossing Brooklyn Ferry," the timeless fascination he hopes to exercise over future readers: "What is more subtle than this which ties me to the woman or man that looks in my face? / Which fuses me into you now, and pours my meaning into you?" (ll. 96-97). That Whitman's attractive power is not homosexual is indicated by the fact that it exists for both sexes and is capable of assuming the form of a mystical bond between poet and readers. But taken out of its spiritual context, it can be easily mistaken for homosexual behavior.

Some recent critics have seen the homosexual theme to be significant if not dominant in such poems as "The Sleepers," "Song of Myself," and "Drum Taps." These interpretations cannot be fairly summarized, so I will instead cite some of the evidence that might be found most convincing. Martin, who has made extended readings of several of Whitman's major poems as homosexual literature, sees these lines from "Song of Myself" (sections 28 & 29) as referring to homosexual anal intercourse:

> You villain touch! what are you doing? my breath is tight in its throat,
> Unclench your floodgates, you are too much for me.
>
> Blind loving wrestling touch, sheath'd hooded sharp-tooth'd touch!
> Did it make you ache so, leaving me?[65]

In the following passage from "Song of Myself," (the end of section 21 and beginning of 22, according to the later numbering), the fifth and sixth lines, present in the versions of 1855, 1856, and 1860 and subsequently deleted, are also said to refer to anal intercourse between men:

> Far-swooping elbowed earth! Rich apple-blossomed earth!
> Smile, for your lover comes!
>
> Prodigal! you have given me love!. . . . therefore I to you give love!
> O unspeakable passionate love!
>
> Thruster holding me tight and that I hold tight!
> We hurt each other as the bridegroom and the bride hurt each other!
>
> You sea! I resign myself to you also. . . . I guess what you mean.[66]

In addition, Martin argues that the following passage, which appeared in the 1855 version of "The Sleepers," depicts homosexual fellatio and was later dropped to make the poem's homosexual theme less obvious:

> The cloth laps a first sweet eating and drinking,
> Laps life-swelling yolks . . . laps ear of rose-corn, milky and just ripened:
> The white teeth stay, and the boss-tooth advances in darkness,
> And liquor is spilled on lips and bosoms by touching glasses, and the best liquor
>   afterward.[67]

Some of Martin's interpretations strike me as wrong and none provide certain evidence of intended homosexual meaning. For instance, as indicated in my reading of "Song of Myself," I think that the sexuality in sections 28-29 is better understood as masturbation and that the "ache" refers to the pain of ejaculation. Whitman had ample reason for deleting the pair of lines from section 22 for they seem inappropriate if not ludicrous. If Whitman wanted to suggest the intensity of his love for the creation by using a metaphor of sexual intercourse with the entire earth, it is simply better to have left the specifics of this passionate coupling comfortably vague. Even a little vivid detail leaves the reader with some ridiculous imagery. Furthermore, Martin asserts that the "thruster" is necessarily masculine ("an unmistakeable image of the male lover"), but this is an unwarranted assumption, especially so in light of Whitman's concern to create athletic women who fully acknowledged and expressed their sexuality. Nor does the passage in the "Sleepers" necessarily refer to fellatio. It can be interpreted as referring to intercourse; for instance, the first three lines may be describing sensuous delight in eating a meal that is a prelude to lovemaking, the third line to kissing and male sexual arousal, and the last to a slightly inebriated toast that is to be followed by sexual intercourse ("the best liquor afterward"). Furthermore, there is no indication of the gender of the lovers and so no clear evidence of homosexuality.

Finally, it is argued that in order to disclose his homosexuality to other sympathetic readers without incurring the wrath of the larger society Whitman developed several artistic strategies of simultaneous revelation and concealment: the use of an indirect method in which meanings are only suggested or hinted; the depiction of sexual relations in which the gender of the beloved is not specified; the exploitation of conventional same-sex situations, for example, the use of the soldier- comrade motif and elegiac convention in "Drum-Taps" to "state homosexual feelings openly and yet 'safely'."[68] This argument cannot, of course, provide conclusive evidence of Whitman's homosexuality because it rests upon the assumption that Whitman exploited the possibilities of ambiguous methods and materials. Furthermore, as the argument itself implies, all of these elements of Whitman's style can be accounted for without recourse to his alleged homosexuality. For instance, Whitman's indirections were dictated by the ineffable nature of religious experience and his emphasis upon reader involvement. The occasional silence about genders may be adequately accounted for by hypothesizing that it never occurred to Whitman that his audience would assume anything other than that these were depictions of heterosexual love. Finally, expressions of intense male comradeship are appropriate in war poetry, and this is especially the case for Whitman who became so personally involved with ministering to the injured and wounded. In sum, the argument for Whitman's homosexuality based upon the ambiguities of his style does disclose new possibilities of meaning which may complicate our reading of the poetry, but it does not provide definitive evidence for an intended homosexual theme.

The Quietness of Manly Love

Another set of revisions that have been frequently cited as evidence of Whitman's concern to camouflage his homosexuality are the changes made in the manuscript of "Once I Passed through a Populous City." Originally conceiving of the poem as an example of manly love, Whitman subsequently changed the gender of his lover to a woman and published the poem in "Children of Adam." Thus quoting from the fourth line, Cady asserts that the "woman who passionately clung" to Whitman was originally a man.[69] But this phrase did not occur in the original manuscript which read:

> But now of all that city I remember only the man who wandered with me, there, for love of me.
> Day by day, and night by night, we were together.

This was changed to:

> Day by day and night by night we were together,—All else has long been forgotten by me.
> And I remember I say only that woman who passionately clung to me.[70]

It is important to call attention to this change because it points to a consistent pattern. In the poems of male comradeship, even when the men are embracing or sleeping together, there is a notable absence of physical passion. This is most clearly indicated by several passages in "Children of Adam" which are, with slight but significant differences, paralleled in "Calamus." These differences suggest that the love of the first sequence is sexual and that of the second, spiritual. For example, in "Children" Whitman proclaims his desire as the "greed that eats me day and night with hungry gnaw" ("Spontaneous Me," l. 42) and "the hungry gnaw that eats me night and day" ("From Pent-up Aching Rivers," l. 10). Contrasting with the carnal connotations of these lines, in "Calamus," when he refers to his love as "the secret of my nights and days" ("In Paths Untrodden"), there is no suggestion of sexual desire. Also, both sequences present lovers in bed, but Whitman carefully avoids any implication of physical passion in portraying the male lovers. In "Children" he describes the "bedfellow's embrace in the night," with "bending curve and the clinch" ("From Pent-up Aching Rivers") and he depicts "Two sleepers at night lying close together as they sleep, one with an arm slanting down across and below the waist of the other" ("Spontaneous Me"). But in the most intimate "Calamus" poem, when the poet describes himself sleeping with a comrade, the emphasis is upon "stillness," not sexual energy and activity; also the lover's arm is placed around the poet's breast, not "below the waist":

> . . . the one I love most lay sleeping by me under the same cover in the cool night,
> In the stillness in the autumn moonbeams his face was inclined toward me,
> And his arm lay lightly around my breast—and that night I was happy.
> ("When I Heard at the Close of the Day")

Even after his sustained attempt at a homosexual reading, Martin includes the incongruous (for his argument) summary observation: "Although there are many passages in praise of the phallus and of sexuality in *Leaves of Grass,* 'Calamus' is devoted almost exclusively to the celebration of being together; the lovers kiss and embrace, they sleep together, but they are not depicted in actual sexual acts. . . . 'Calamus' is largely a sequence of artistic and psychological significance, in which the learning of affection has primary place."[71]

Ultimately the strongest argument against a homosexual reading is that throughout "Calamus" comradeship finds its fulfillment not in an eruptive ecstasy of sexual love but in moments of spiritual serenity:

> . . . how calm, how solemn it grows to ascend to the atmosphere of lovers.
> ("Scented Herbage," l. 13)

> When the subtle air, the impalpable, the sense that words and reason hold not,
>   surround us and pervade us,
> Then I am charged with untold and untellable wisdom, I am silent, I require
>   nothing further.
> ("Of the Terrible Doubt of Appearances")

> Of a youth who loves me and whom I love, silently approaching and seating
> himself near, that he may hold me by the hand,
> . . . .
> Then we two, content, happy in being together, speaking little, perhaps not a
> word.
>
> ("A Glimpse")

Sexual excitement appears to be antithetical to the essence of comradeship, which is a stillness of spirit in which the male lovers are enveloped in a sense of well-being and love.

Keeping in mind that some contemplative traditions, for example, Buddhism and Christianity, have encouraged separate male and female communities, it seems possible that Whitman's belief in the spiritual superiority of love between members of the same gender may be giving fresh expression to an older religious insight. This leads to two possible lines of speculation. One is that because male-female friendships are frequently subject to sexual tension, same-sex relationships may be more conducive to the type of spiritual calm that promotes spiritual development. The other is that in cultures where there is a great deal of gender differentiation, it may be that members of the same sex are able to bond more deeply because of the greater similarity of their life experience.

"Calamus" and Cultural Needs

Another consideration that conflicts with the recent readings of "Calamus" as poetry of gay liberation is the seldom discussed but significant fact of the sequence's sexism. If Whitman had come to a full realization and acceptance of his homosexuality, it seems that he would also have written poems of lesbian love. There is special reason to believe this since he promised to sing the female equally with the male and since, as the expositors of the homosexual reading maintain, the process of coming to grips with one's homosexual identity creates a radically subversive consciousness and a sympathy for other marginalized groups. The fact that there are no poems of lesbian love suggests that Whitman went through no such process of self-realization. The apparent reason "Calamus" is directed toward male readers, and that there is no balancing sequence for women, is that Whitman never fully incorporated an attitude of gender equality into his vision of an ideal polity. Troubled by the vulgar crudeness of American life, and conceiving of males as the principal participants in his new society, he composed his images of manly love not to encourage homosexuality but to correct a perceived deficiency in the personality of American males so as to make them better citizens. In a letter to Rudolph Schmidt in 1874 Whitman lamented the "'*hardness*,' crudeness, worldliness—absence of the spiritual" in American democracy but argued that this might be offset by the "eligibility to manly & loving comradeship, very marked in American young men."[72] On his rounds in the Civil War hospitals, Whitman had seen ample evidence of this potential for masculine comradeship:

> Above all the poor boys welcome magnetic friendship, personality (some are so fervent, so hungering for this) . . . . O how one gets to love them, often, particular cases, so suffering, so good, so manly & affectionate . . . lots of them have grown to expect as I leave at night that we should kiss each other . . . poor boys, there is little petting in a soldier's life in the field, but . . . I know what is in their hearts, always waiting, though they may be unconscious of it themselves—[.][73]

But Whitman had discovered this capacity for loving male friendship before the Civil War; as he succinctly stated in a small poem of 1860, "To the East and to the West":

> . . . the germs are in all men,
> I believe the main purport of these States is to found a superb friendship, exaltè,
> previously unknown,
> Because I perceive it waits, and has been always waiting, latent in all men.

In "Calamus" he tried to call forth this repressed tenderness and make it the hallmark of the new American man, the guarantor of political unity, and both the means to and crowning achievement of American spiritual democracy.

Whitman's call for masculine love must also be seen as a protest against contemporary gender stereotypes, especially as they had developed in response to the social and economic impact of emerging capitalism. Prior to the early nineteenth century most women were essential co-workers with their husbands in maintaining largely self-sufficient rural homesteads. But by the mid-1800s this situation was rapidly disappearing. Men were increasingly employed as wage-earners and profit-makers in work which was acknowledged to desecrate the human spirit. To ease the emotional and cultural strain, women were increasingly defined as the repositories of traditional values. They were to be pious, pure, submissive, and domestic, providing an emotional sanctuary to which husbands could return after struggling for their livelihood. As women's economic contribution declined, a canon of domesticity arose which stressed that their power resided in superior delicacy and morality. These gender-specific functions created a psychological distance between the sexes and strong emotional bonds between members of the same sex.[74]

Whitman was probably not fully aware of these economic determinants, but he was consciously responding to this excessive sexual differentiation. In *Democratic Vistas* he calls for "the entire redemption of woman out of these incredible holds and webs of silliness, millinery, and every kind of dyspeptic depletion" (*PW*, 372), and in his notes he asserts that the reigning feminine "modesties and prohibitions" prevent "love and comradeship" so that a man frequently loves another man "with more passionate attachment than he ever bestows on any woman, even his wife" (*NPM*, I, 341). Whitman prized the

direct, genuine affection he experienced with some men. Writing to the hospitalized Elijah Douglas Fox, he describes the accomplishments of his New York
friends but then tells the uneducated soldier: "You are so much closer to me
than any of them . . . there is something that takes down all artificial accomplishments, & that is a manly & loving soul."[75] "Calamus" calls for this freer
form of love that Whitman had experienced with some of his male friends.
As developed in "Children of Adam," heterosexual attraction is a form of religious experience, but as is made clear in "Fast Anchor'd Eternal O Love," the
manly comradeship of "Calamus" is a higher and more satisfying form of spirituality:

> Fast-anchor'd eternal O love! O woman I love!
> O bride! O wife! more resistless than I can tell, the thought of you!
> Then separate, as disembodied or another born,
> Ethereal, the last athletic reality, my consolation,
> I ascend, I float in the regions of your love O man,
> O sharer of my roving life.

Whitman emphasizes the spiritual and non-sexual character of this love by describing it as "ethereal" and himself as "disembodied or another born," that
is, spiritually reborn. Clearly Whitman conceives of manly love as an experience of the soul.

Conclusion

The fact that the religious themes in "Calamus" have been largely ignored
and that a homosexual reading has dominated Whitman scholarship for several decades is to be explained in part by the two reasons already mentioned:
critics have not related the poems to Whitman's larger religious vision and they
have ignored his special vocabulary. In some respects the homosexual interpretations reveal more about our current intellectual and spiritual milieu than
about the poetry itself. The earlier criticism reflects our culture's distrust of
male affection, and the later readings are expressions of the gay subculture's
understandable search for its own history and heroic figures. Also the homosexual theme could not have become dominant without the assistance of a secularism which has made many readers both insensitive to and uninterested in
the complexities of religious experience and expression.

Yet while insisting upon the primacy of the religious theme in "Calamus"
and the *Leaves* and questioning the evidence for the current homosexual interpretation, I am not necessarily rejecting the possibility for such a reading (if
made in a more convincing manner that acknowledges Whitman's pervasive
spirituality). There clearly seems to be a pattern of homosexual desire trying
to find expression in both Whitman's life and art, but the question is the degree
of awareness and acceptance this personality trait acquired in Whitman's con-

sciousness. One possibility is that Whitman was never fully aware of his homosexuality. Accordingly, the recurring homosexual motif in his poetry is often the product of unconscious activity; and even when this dimension of his sexuality sometimes became partially conscious, it was so effectively sublimated that Whitman never had to acknowledge its true meaning. Another possibility is the recent gay reading that Whitman subtly but intentionally celebrated homosexuality as an important element of his new American personality and democratic polity. The theme was artfully encoded to avoid social ostracism and literary censorship, but it is nevertheless there for the reader who "has loved as I [Whitman] have loved" (that is, who shares Whitman's homosexual orientation and outlook). But if this position is maintained, I think it must also be conceded that the experience of gays and non-gays is sufficiently different to make this theme much less obvious to many non-homosexual readers, and thus its presence cannot be objectively demonstrated. A third possibility is that Whitman was fully aware of his homosexuality but uncertain if his personal proclivity was either ethical or likely to receive widespread social acceptance in the future. Consequently, as with his treatment of the relationship between heterosexual love and marriage, he chose to make his treatment of manly love ambiguous and leave the issue's final resolution to future generations. Without further evidence than now exists, it seems impossible to decide with certainty between these alternatives, and so prudence dictates that all opinions on the subject be voiced with moderation.

Keeping this caveat in mind, I think the evidence is most supportive of the viewpoint that Whitman was a repressed homosexual who had inklings of his homosexuality but never allowed this self-understanding to reach full consciousness. For reasons cited in the preceding discussion — the Platonic nature of "Calamus" with its emphasis upon spiritual calmness, the failure to write poems advocating lesbianism, the rejection of his excessive "adhesiveness" in the notebook entries of 1870 — it seems necessary to reject the notion that for ten or twenty years in the 1850s and 1860s Whitman assumed a homosexual identity and boldly integrated it into his personality and poetry. In keeping with this viewpoint, some combinations of poetic imagery that might be read as consciously conveying a subtle theme of homosexuality, for example, the phallic imagery of the calamus combined with the reference to something "fierce and terrible in me eligible to burst forth" in "Earth My Likeness" and the assertion of the "sexuality of the earth" in "Kosmos," are best interpreted as unintended patterns — possible instances of failed repression. Other passages, such as the picture of two male lovers tenderly embracing ("When I Heard at the Close of the Day"), disclose a poet trying to convince himself that his secret desires, although unorthodox, are nevertheless platonic, spiritual and exemplary for future democratic citizenship. The very daringness of the usage was intended to function as an exorcism of self-doubt. But both Whitman's instincts and his doubts remained. Far from being a brave pioneer of gayness, he continued to repress a discomforting part of himself. Contemporary readings which hail Whitman as a modern gay prophet argue that the lyrics of manly love demonstrate his supreme mastery of his materials, but it seems more likely that precisely in this area he wrote with the most uncertainty and lack of conscious control.

Modern views of human sexuality suggest that the popular stereotype of the homosexual and heterosexual as polar opposites is misleading. Perhaps most, if not all, individuals have at least some capacity for both heterosexual and homosexual love. Furthermore, many people may be bisexual or feel that their sexual preference is not clearly differentiated in their own consciousness. In integrating their sexuality with the other dimensions of their lives, some people with relatively strong homosexual preferences may, with greater or lesser degrees of self-understanding, choose to repress or sublimate these desires in order to avoid conflict with their own superegos or the larger society. As a means of compensation, many of these individuals may make career choices, pursue avocations and develop friendships and ideals that allow for the platonic expression of their homosexual inclinations. Relating these comments to Whitman, I would suggest that he possessed strong homosexual tendencies which he neither fully understood nor accepted but instead sublimated into forms of conduct and belief that, while giving an unusual degree of emphasis to male friendship, were nevertheless sufficiently conventional to be acceptable to the standards of his own conscience and those of the larger society.[76]

Various elements in Whitman's historical context conspired to make it relatively easy for him to keep his homosexuality from coming to full consciousness. He could interpret his longing to touch and embrace other men as a corrective to the culture's repression of male affection, and he could conceive of his preference for male friendships as natural in a society that imposed crippling role expectations upon women, making them less than satisfactory companions. In addition, in the decades before the Civil War, both a growing competitive capitalism and an increasingly rancorous sectionalism impressed Whitman with the need for greater friendship and unity among the American people. Finally, Whitman shaped a religious vision that conceived of comradeship as essential to the soul's full development. All of these factors enabled him to sublimate his homosexuality and to interpret it in ways acceptable to his superego. This is not to say that repressed homosexuality is the key to Whitman's personality and vision, but it does shed light upon the genesis, content, and intensity of the "Calamus" theme. Conversely, an awareness of how Whitman's cultural background and vision encouraged him to sublimate his homosexuality helps to explain why it could be a pronounced element in his personality and yet remain largely unconscious to him.

VIII

POETRY AND POLITICS
A NEW PUBLIC FAITH

At the beginning of this century, George Santayana, in an essay entitled "The Poetry of Barbarism," expressed his conviction that the poetic imagination, no longer disciplined by either Christianity or classicism, had "relapsed into barbarism." A prime specimen of this intellectual deterioration was Walt Whitman who possessed "the corrupt desire to be a primitive" and offered to his readers an "abundance of detail without organization."[1] Subsequent scholarship has made a more sympathetic evaluation of Whitman, seeing him as a noble primitive who possessed the power to reacquaint overcivilized society with the instinctive, especially the sexual, roots of human nature; or he is, with his realistic imagery and free verse, hailed as the unpolished progenitor of modern American poetry. This criticism does not, however, disagree with Santayana's charges of irrationality and incoherence, and Santayana's indictment has never received the refutation that it deserves. The proper rejoinder is that Whitman, too, observed the waning power of the inherited symbols and belief, but instead of joyfully embracing barbarism, he set about to construct the foundations for a new cultural order. To be sure, he aspired to a primitive relationship with nature—as did Wordsworth, Carlyle, Emerson, Thoreau, and a host of lesser Romantics—but this was more than an act of psychological and cultural regression. His goal was to descend anew into the sources of idealism in raw or preconceptualized religious experience; and then, as difficult and presumptuous as the endeavor might seem, he wanted to express these experiences in a new religious vision that would incorporate the other forms of modern culture. As indicated in the preceding chapters, Whitman did, in fact, succeed in fusing a traditional religious cosmology with evolutionary science and a millennial theory of history to create a coherent world view which presented progress, both evolutionary and historical, as a movement of divine immanence toward reunion with its transcendent source. All of Whitman's major subthemes—political freedom, democracy, sex, love, and death—and his chief symbols such as the waters, stars, earth, and grass are integrated into this central vision.

The present critical assessment of Whitman as an inspired but incoherent

primitive reflects, in part, scholarship's failure to disclose the unity of his vision. But even if Whitman's new myth were better understood, the current division of academic labor does not encourage a reasoned response to its claims
for acceptance. Once his work was placed in the bailiwick of English departments, it was predictable that Whitman would receive careful literary scrutiny
but that his potential religious and political significance would be largely ignored. Whitman sometimes anticipated such a future in which the *Leaves*
would be taken hold of by the "literary, professional fellows," and found it
cause for near despair. "I confess I shrink from it with horror," he told Traubel
(*Camden*, IV, 145). The problem with critics, he explained in another of his
anti-literary stews, was that "probably three-quarters, perhaps even more, of
them do not take the trouble to examine what they start out to criticize—to
judge a man from his own standpoint, to even find out what that standpoint
is" (*Camden*, IV, 41).

Literary scholars have conveniently dismissed such fulminations with a pa-
tronizing indulgence but the history of Whitman's reception makes clear that
his worries were justified. Seldom have professional critics given serious consideration to the principal assumptions of Whitman's poetic: (1) Every society
needs a shared religious faith; and (2) American artists and intellectuals must
take up the challenge of forging a new national vision that will unify and guide
the American people. Yet these ideas are arguably sound and receive support
from a considerable body of respected contemporary scholarship. For instance,
to quote Robert Bellah: "It is one of the oldest of sociological generalizations
that any coherent and viable society rests on a common set of moral understandings about good and bad, right and wrong, in the realm of individual
and social action. It is almost as widely held that these common moral understandings must also in turn rest upon a common set of religious understandings
that provide a picture of the universe in terms of which the moral understandings make sense."[2] Bellah and others who hold this view do not argue that
a society must subscribe to a traditional religious faith with supernatural prem-
ises, but only that a viable society does require a more or less coherent set of
ideals which have a character of ultimacy and are so widespread and deeply
engrained in the personalities of the citizenry that they constitute a common
religious faith.

Additional support for Whitman's position could also be derived from the
fact that our increasingly secular and pluralistic society shows many of the classical symptoms of cultural degeneration: dependency upon alcohol and drugs,
widespread violence, disregard of traditional sexual mores, and public corruption. At the same time, there is a perceived need for a shared vision that will
promote greater economic and political justice in both our domestic and foreign policies and will enable us to address urgent global concerns of hunger,
dwindling nonrenewable resources, destruction of the biosphere, and the terror
of nuclear armaments. So it might be said that the present crisis proves the

correctness of Whitman's call for a new civil faith that would protect against political fragmentation and moral decay.

These opening remarks about the truth, or at least plausibility, of the basic assumptions of Whitman's poetic lead to two possible conclusions. The first is that despite its considerable aesthetic merit, Whitman's attempt to start a new myth is so farfetched in its conception and/or such a failure in its appeal to our political and spiritual needs that Whitman is of no ongoing religious significance and so he deserves to be perceived, as he currently is, as a figure—most assuredly a revered one—in the history of our literary culture. The second possible conclusion is that despite Whitman's failure to provide a dominant myth, there are, nevertheless, elements in his mythpoetics and vision itself that are germane to our current need for a new civic faith, and so Whitman should also be placed in the context of our religious and political culture in order that his potential service to our public religious life can be clearly perceived.

The second possibility deserves fresh consideration because simple justice to Whitman demands that we interrogate him on his own terms. Furthermore, Whitman's more than literary intentions should be examined because many of his better and more important readers—the subsequent American poets who were to justify him—have responded to him as more than a conventional literary figure. In order to understand both Whitman's purposes and his enduring appeal, it is necessary to approach him not just as a poet, or even as an interpreter of the needs and aspirations of our private souls, but as the prophet of the political and spiritual possibilities of our national community.

Any assertion of Whitman's possible contribution to our civic faith must, of course, be uttered with considerable caution lest one be placed in the camp of his early disciples who, ascribing to their prophet an exaggerated significance, are today dismissed with contumely as "Whitmaniacs." Clearly Whitman's proposed new religion has failed to become our regnant myth, and it is certain that this will not happen in the future. Furthermore, the very complexity of the subject calls for caution. It is commonplace to lament the fact that we live in the interstice of two epochs: the old vision no longer suffices and the new is not yet. No one knows how this cultural impasse is to be surmounted or even if it can be. Yet having said this, it also seems appropriate, after having explicated Whitman's poetry as an effort to create a new religion appropriate for modern America, to attempt some explanation for its failure to become a controlling myth, to survey the nature and degree of influence it has had and to inquire about its potential utility for our public life.

Whitman's Failure

A crucial cause for Whitman's inability to establish a new religious vision was his appallingly inaccurate perception of the lasting appeal of Christianity.

Allied with this was his apparent ignorance of the extent to which cultural systems depend upon supporting educational institutions. Whitman naively proclaimed: "There will soon be no more priests. Their work is done" (1855 Preface, *PW*, 456). He anticipated a quick end to Christianity, for he believed "The soul of the people . . . have [sic] irrevocably gone from those churches!" (*NPM*, VI, 2086). Visiting the United States in the 1830s, Alexis de Tocqueville more accurately observed that there was "no country in the world where the Christian religion retains a greater influence over the souls of men."[3] Propagators of the Protestant vision had, in comparison to Whitman's effort to proclaim a new gospel, the easier task of nurturing their religion among those who were either already church members or at least accustomed to the vocabulary and claims of Christianity. In addition, Protestantism was supported by the churches, schools, and colleges, and it developed other effective organizations and strategies for outreach such as revivals, tract societies, and home missions. In wanting to start an institutionless religion, Whitman naively assumed that a new faith could, merely through the power of the printed word and the individual's response to it, quickly conquer an established and well-institutionalized competing belief system and become disseminated among tens of millions of citizens until, finally, it would naturally inform the nation's daily life and institutional structures.

Nor was Whitman successful in the virtually superhuman task he set for himself of forging an alternative to the Judeo-Christian world view. In his efforts to re-conceive the universe, he profited greatly from the influence of deism and Emersonian Transcendentalism. Both convinced him that Christianity did not have a monopoly on religious truth and thus freed him from an uncritical allegiance to the particular form of religion in his time. But there was also implicit in deism, and explicit in Emerson, the challenge to create a post-Christian vision adequate to the spiritual needs of the modern world. It is undoubtedly unfair to criticize Whitman for failing to succeed at this awesome task, and yet in analyzing the reasons for the failure of his myth it is necessary to note the fundamental inadequacy of his basic theology. Central to Whitman's new vision is a rather traditional, but non-biblical, theism to which is grafted the idea of inevitable evolutionary and historical progress. Ultimately this ends up pleasing virtually no one. The rejection of biblical supernaturalism is offensive to traditional Christians and Jews. At the same time, the theism is incompatible with contemporary secularism and personal religions which reject all explicit assertions of supernaturalism. As a result Whitman ends up in limbo: a heretic to traditionalists and an anachronism to modernists.

Whitman should be given credit for recognizing that his new religion must somehow incorporate process thought, and his attempt to account for evolution and history by viewing them as a progressive movement toward perfection in God's immanent nature perhaps entitles him to be conceived of as a crude forerunner of more recent process theologians such as Alfred North Whitehead or Teilhard de Chardin. A difficulty with Whitman's process world view, however, is that it makes historical progress inevitable and denies the possibility of irreversible evil in the world. This seems simplistic to modern readers sensitive to the very real possibilities of large-scale ecological disaster and nuclear holocaust. The problem is not that Whitman believed in divine providence but that he expected future readers to be able to look at the course of history for a confirmation of his optimistic faith. Whitman's solution to the problem of evil, which is essentially to deny its ultimate significance, is certainly no improvement over the voice from out of the whirlwind that addressed Job or other traditional Judeo-Christian formulations, and not surprisingly, this aspect of Whitman's thought has often been subjected to trenchant criticism.

Another reason for the small success of Whitman's religion stems from his overly optimistic view of human nature. One aspect of this error is that Whitman overestimated his readers. Subscribing to antebellum beliefs in millennialism and perfectionism, he anticipated a growing audience of moral athletes who, bent upon their spiritual development, would willingly devote themselves to unlocking the secrets of his enigmatic text. But Whitman's expectations were unrealistic, and so the result has been not a new race of mystics bound to their prophet in bonds of mystical sympathy but successive generations of puzzled readers.

A second liability stemming from Whitman's perfectionism is that subsequent readers, even sympathetic poets who have wanted to build upon his beginning, have charged him with having an excessive faith in the goodness of the common people. In the words of Edwin Markham:

> You laud "the average man," and yet his feet
> Are mired in clay, his soul beholds no star,
> Hears only a far faint music from the skies.

What Whitman overlooked, according to Markham, was the "something wild in the world" that meant "Even Christ found here no place to lay his head."[4] More recently Louis Simpson has dryly observed that Whitman's optimism about the masses "seems out of place in our century" in which "the masses elect mass-murderers."[5] Or again, Dave Smith responds to Whitman with an image of contemporary Americans that stands in biting contrast to the heroic citizens announced in the *Leaves*. In visiting the Civil War battlefield at Fredericksburg, rather than seeing "the Christ divine" in the faces of his fellow Americans, as Whitman had in looking upon the war's injured and dying soldiers, Smith saw only the tamed spirits of courteous and satisfied consumers attuned not to Whitman's patriotic chants but to the blandishments of the car dealer:

> they wear the green clothes of Park Rangers
> the polite smile of Toledo, and one
> thinks you sold him a Buick.[6]

Because of Whitman's insistence upon the dignity of the working class and the need to struggle against all forms of oppression, he has generally been praised by Marxist critics, but some readers have rightly criticized his failure to develop an incisive class consciousness. The ramifications of an emerging class system were explored by many of Whitman's nineteenth-century contemporaries ranging from Melville, whose writings began to treat the issue in the early 1850s, to Carnegie who in the 1880s described society as a system of "rigid castes" in which each class is "without sympathy with the other." The result was "friction between the employer and the employed, between capital and labor, between rich and poor."[7] An entrenched class structure with alienation between the classes was clearly antithetical to Whitman's dream of a loving democracy dominated by common men and women. Whitman also made some efforts at developing a class analysis in his journalism, and in the postwar years he became profoundly troubled by the conflict between labor and capital. But his belief in individual freedom and a laissez-faire economy made him unable to formulate a political response. Accordingly Whitman's poetry never confronts the new political problems created by urbanization, the industrial revolution, and the increasing political and economic power of the capitalist class. This oversight has proved even more glaring in the twentieth century. In the midst of the Great Depression, Stephen Vincent Benet resuscitated the persona of Whitman to have him inquire: "Is it well with these States?" In response Benet describes what happens when a nation's abundance is controlled by a system that puts profits before distributive justice:

> They [the capitalists] burn the grain in the furnace while men go hungry.
> They pile the cloth of the looms while men go ragged.
> We walk naked in our plenty.[8]

In the post-World War II era, Kenneth Patchen makes this absence of a class consciousness glaringly evident by indicating how even as a child (of an Ohio coal-mining family) he found Whitman's political vision irrelevant to his experience when striking miners found the power of government clearly allied with the owners:

> . . . and I went down through the woods
> To the smelly crick with Whitman
> In the Haldeman-Julius edition,
> And I just sat there worrying my thumbnail
> Into the cover—What did he know about
> Orange bears with their coats all stunk up with soft coal
> And the National Guard coming over
> From Wheeling to stand in front of the Millgates
> With drawn bayonets jeering at the strikers?[9]

   In sum, in his transcendentalist metaphysics, millennialist faith in progress, perfectionist anthropology, and personalist approach to politics, Whitman's poetic and vision are clearly captive to antebellum culture. David Ignatow undoubtedly speaks for many other contemporary readers when he protests that despite a near-filial devotion to Whitman he cannot "accept his acceptance of Nineteenth Century piety in relation to a godhead, nor to a vision of so-called progress, nor a vision of the perfection of man, nor of man's ultimate union in brotherhood.[10]

Whitman's Achievement

. . . a hundred years later our poets still talk about,
talk to, talk back to Walt Whitman.
—Ed Folsom[11]

D. H. Lawrence chastised Americans for being "not worthy of their Whitman," asserting that they take him "like a cocktail, for fun";[12] but at least two groups of Americans have made a more authentic response, wrestling with Whitman's meanings in something like the manner he wished. The first of these would be the innumerable political and religious radicals and come-outers of assorted stripes who found in the *Leaves* at least some of the inspiration for their dreams and struggles. For the most part this group has left no record of its indebtedness to the poet who saluted the "ever-welcome defiers." But the second group, "our poets," have left ample record not only of Whitman's unique influence upon subsequent American literature but also of the kind of power that he has exercised over many of his best readers. As Folsom suggests, American poets have often had a mixed reaction to Whitman: unable to accept the total vision, they have, nevertheless, gone on to confess admiration for much of his achievement. Best known in this regard is the "pact" Ezra Pound made once he was "old enough now to make friends." Pound's acceptance of his "pig-headed father" contains more than the willingness of a son, after having found his identity, to make peace with his father, acknowledging his merits and accepting his weaknesses. There is also Pound's recognition that his incisive imagination must work with the timber felled by Whitman's powerful broadax: "It was you that broke the new wood, / Now is the time for carving."[13] Despite their large differences in style and temperament, Pound realized that if he was to be an American poet in the sense of trying to help define America's meaning and realize its potential, he must build upon Whitman's beginning.

That Whitman did carve out some such foundational position is clearly attested to by his unique impact upon subsequent poets. Roy Harvey Pearce exaggerated Whitman's influence, but only slightly, when he asserted that "all American poetry . . . is, in essence, if not in substance, a series of arguments with Whitman."[14] Pearce's statement is largely true if we interpret "American" to mean not poetry written by Americans but poetry that treats, either implicitly or explicitly, aspects of American democracy. Whitman transcends the limitations of his vision because he was the first to formulate a comprehensive democratic poetics and use it to create a vision of democracy. If for no other reason than this, subsequent writers who treat of American democracy are in some sense responding to Whitman's beginning, but of course this in itself does not adequately explain Whitman's subsequent appeal.

Nor is it enough to add that Whitman expressed his vision with great artistry; yet to understand the influence he has exercised over his best readers, it is necessary to call attention to an aspect of his art which might be termed a poetics of personal intimacy. The factors that contribute to this are manifold, but three interrelated elements are of special importance. Most obvious is Whitman's decision to use an autobiographical persona and to shape his life to this persona. Another is the unquestionable sincerity of Whitman's concern for democracy which is attested to by his journalism and political activities, his four-decade effort to create a new order of democratic poetry, and perhaps most important for the present discussion, his selfless hospital service during the Civil War. Harold Bloom rightly comments that no other Western writer "of anything like Whitman's achievement . . . ever gave himself or herself up so directly to meeting the agonized needs of the most desperate."[15] Finally, there is Whitman's effective use of the timeless or non-temporal character of religious experience to establish a sense of mystical union with his readers. Whitman recognized that a deeply felt sense of union with earlier exemplary figures of a moral tradition is crucial to the dedication of later members, especially when their commitment to this tradition causes them to reject the values of their culture, thus denying themselves the material rewards and the emotional support that comes from integration with the status quo. Much as a sense of mystical union with Christ inspires an occasional Luther or John Woolman or Martin Luther King, Jr., so Whitman intended for future poet-prophets and other spiritual athletes of his democratic faith to turn to him for both an exemplary model and perfect comrade:

> Here to put your lips upon mine I permit you,
> With the comrade's long-dwelling kiss or the new husband's kiss,
> For I am the new husband and I am the comrade.
>   ("Whoever You Are Holding Me Now in Hand")

No other author has been able to establish the personal relationship that Whitman enjoys with his sympathetic readers. Numerous people have attested to having received from the *Leaves* a sense of loving fellowship which inspires them to take up Whitman's revolutionary agenda. Perhaps Hart Crane gives best expression to the combination of intimacy and inspirational power that informs Whitman's verse:

> And it was thou who on the boldest heel
> Stood up and flung the span on even wing
> Of that great Bridge, our Myth, whereof I sing!
> . . . .

> Yes, Walt,
> Afoot again, and onward without halt,—
> Not soon, nor suddenly,—no, never to let go
> My hand
> in yours,
> Walt Whitman—
>
> so—[16]

Just as some devout Christians take their walk through life with Christ, so some of Whitman's readers, including some important writers, have traversed the open road hand-in-hand with their poet-prophet.

Part of Whitman's power also comes from the fact that despite the errors of his vision his poetry does contain a number of themes and symbols which continue to address important needs in modern American culture. Several of these deal with gender roles and the sexual dimension of our personalities.

Whitman's treatment of women is a mixture of traditional and progressive elements. Some of the views expressed in his journalism are surprisingly conventional. For instance, in the July 24, 1846 *Brooklyn Daily Eagle*, he presents the accepted view of women as divinely ordained to occupy the domestic sphere, preserve the most refined cultural values, and transmit them to the next generation:

> Retired from the stern conflicts of the world — from the chaffering, grosser strife — women seem to be selected by Providence, as the depositories of the germs of the truest Truth and the fairest Beautiful. In their souls is preserved the ark of the covenant of purity. To them is given the mission of infusing some portion of those good things in the minds of all young children. . . .[17]

Even as late as 1857, after the first two editions of the *Leaves*, Whitman editorialized in the *Brooklyn Daily Times* against the use of female boarding schools because women possessed weaker minds or consciences. "Educate them [your daughters] at home," he insisted, to avoid their corruption by "a thousand evil influences." If some withstood these temptations, it was only because they "must necessarily possess minds strong beyond the generality of womankind."[18] With these remarks in mind, it is not surprising that in 1856 Whitman describes the female form as symbolizing traditional female attributes:

> As I see my soul reflected in Nature,
> As I see through a mist, One with inexpressible completeness, sanity, beauty,
> See the bent head and arms folded over the breast, the Female I see.
> ("I Sing the Body Electric," ll. 72–74)

In contrast, the male symbolizes "action and power," "Scorn . . . appetite and defiance," the "wildest largest passions," "full-spread pride" and "Knowledge" (ll. 76–81).

It must be recognized that for the modern reader, and even for the more progressive reader of Whitman's day, the radical expectations established by his opening declaration — "The Female equally with the Male I sing" ("One's-Self I Sing") — are sometimes disappointed by the subsequent poetry. As usual, Whitman is most radical in his treatment of sexuality, and so women are most nearly equal to men in "children of Adam" where they are depicted as strong, passionate, sexual beings. In light of this equal treatment, there is a good deal of propriety in the way Whitman positions Eve relative to himself in the sequence's opening poem: "By my side or back of me Eve following, / Or in front, and I following her just the same" ("To the Garden the World"). Yet one could find traditional sexism implicit in the title, "Children of Adam," which suggests that offspring belong to the male parent. Much more upsetting is the fact that the ensuing "Calamus" poems are directed to men and the *Leaves* contains no corresponding poems for women. In his catalogic poetry, Whitman includes numerous women in various activities, but there are no references to women pioneering in new areas: no reformers, no journalists, no organizers, no feminists. When Whitman's catalogs turn to the "large hearts of heroes, / The courage of present times and all times" ("Songs of Myself," ll. 822–23), there are no examples of female heroism. These splendid opportunities were missed. Of course, it is to be expected that Whitman's imagination would be limited by the sexism of his time, but it is also important to acknowledge that his treatment of women is not completely appropriate for our times and to note that while Whitman was a gifted visionary and prophet, his politics were often not radical but moderately progressive.

But in general Whitman is forward-looking in his depiction of women. He thoroughly rejected the idea that women were to be passive and sheltered, subordinate to and dependent upon men. To be "fit for These States," a girl was to be "free, capable, dauntless, just the same as a boy" ("Poem of Remembrance for a Girl or Boy of These States," l. 17), and women should "know how to swim, row, ride, wrestle, shoot" ("A Woman Waits for Me," l. 18). Whitman's emphasis upon equality extended to marriage and the family; a wife was "not one jot less than the husband" and a daughter "just as good as the son" ("A Song for Occupations," ll. 33–34). Nor was a woman to be restricted to the domestic sphere. The *Leaves* depicts "athletic girls, new artists, musicians, and singers" ("A Woman Waits for Me," l. 34), and "Democratic Vistas" describes a woman employed in a "mechanical business" as a fit model for American women and an apt subject for artists (*PW*, 400). In the same essay, on the question of whether women were to be enfranchised and assume positions of leadership, Whitman is cautiously affirmative, suggesting that women could, if properly nurtured, "become the robust equals, workers, and, it may be, even practical and political deciders with the men" (*PW*, 389). The time is coming, he predicted, when these issues "may be put to decision, and real experiment" (*PW*, 401). If Whitman was less progressive than the radical feminists of his day, he nevertheless still provides the earliest firm foundation for a feminist tradition in American poetry.

Whitman was also prophetic in his recognition in numerous poems, but especially in the "Calamus" sequence, of the need for greater tenderness in the American male personality and greater comradeship between men. Some readers may still find his pictures of manly love somewhat startling, for instance his dream of "the new city of Friends" where "the quality of robust love" could be "seen every hour in the actions of men . . . / And in all their looks and words" ("I Dream'd in a Dream"), but surely these images provide a needed corrective to a culture in which male violence is glorified and gentleness is taboo. Furthermore, although I do not think Whitman necessarily intended this, many modern readers can find in his poetry an affirmation of homosexual love as being both wholesome and holy.

In contrast to the inherited Christian and Victorian attitudes which jar with the modern affirmation of sexuality, Whitman provides the earliest, yet perhaps still unsurpassed, pictures in American literature of the beauty and mystery of heterosexual love (as perceived from a masculine perspective), capturing what he terms its "mystic deliria" in images that lean toward neither prudery nor pornography:

> This is the female form,
> A divine nimbus exhales from it from head to foot,
> It attracts with fierce undeniable attraction,
> . . . .
> Mad filaments, ungovernable shoots play out of it, the response likewise ungovernable,
> Hair, bosom, hips, bend of legs, negligent falling hands all diffused, mine too diffused,
> Ebb stung by the flow and flow stung by the ebb, love-flesh swelling and deliciously aching,
> Limitless limpid jets of love hot and enormous, quivering jelly of love, white-blow and delirious juice,
> Bridegroom night of love working surely and softly into the prostrate dawn,
> Undulating into the willing and yielding day,
> Lost in the cleave of the clasping and sweet-flesh'd day.
> ("I Sing the Body Electric," 5)

A second set of Whitman's themes are highly relevant to current debate regarding our national priorities and purpose. In contrast to a policy of escalating the arms race while Americans go hungry and homeless and one-quarter of the world lives in absolute poverty, Whitman's succinct definition of our national mission is refreshingly sane: it is "not to become a conqueror nation, or to achieve the glory of mere military, or diplomatic, or commercial superiority—but to become the grand producing land of nobler men and women—of copious races, cheerful, healthy, tolerant, free—to become the most friendly nation" (1872 Preface, *PW*, 460). Furthermore, in an age of growing global interdependence that is marked by increasing economic stratification both between and within nations, there is a special timeliness to Whitman's insistence that human rights are not the special privilege of a particular nation, gender, race or class. Instead he avowed: "By God! I will accept nothing which all cannot have their counterpart of on the same terms" ("Song of Myself," l. 507). You will be able to tell the "words of the true poems," he asserted, by whether or not they "balance ranks, colors, races, creeds, and the sexes" ("Song of the Answerer," ll. 75 & 77). In light of passages such as these, Langston Hughes comments that Whitman's "all-embracing words lock arms with workers and farmers, Negroes and whites, Asiatics and Europeans, serfs, and free men, beaming democracy to all."[19]

Hughes is correct in stressing Whitman's preference for the working class, his militant opposition to class divisions, and his hearty encouragement of social solidarity. In respect to race, however, Whitman's sentiments are sufficiently complex to require further discussion. An analysis of Whitman's journalism reveals that he strongly oppposed slavery as a violation of both moral and republican principles. Accordingly, he consistently denounced the institution of slavery and backed the Wilmot Proviso which sought to prohibit its extension into new territories. But he was willing to tolerate slavery where it already existed in the South because it was legalized by the Constitution. Slaves would simply have to wait for their freedom until the Southern states voluntarily agreed to emancipation. So while favoring abolition as an ultimate goal, Whitman disapproved of the abolitionist movement as "mad fanaticism" or a "dangerous fanatical insanity" because, in addition to an apparent personal discomfort with all forms of radical political activism, he feared the tactics of the abolitionists would further alienate existing sectional differences and lead to civil war.[20]

As with his treatment of women, Whitman's journalism reveals that his racial thought was captive to contemporary complacency, stereotype and myth. In the April 2, 1842 *Aurora* Whitman describes a lithograph of a slave family in their shanty being visited by a "gentleman and lady, with two children" and approvingly comments that "Every thing [sic] bears the impress of cheerfulness and content."[21] A May 14, 1857 *Daily Times* editorial criticizes the abolitionist movement as extremist and comfortably opines that slavery "will certainly, before a hundred years have rolled on, become extinct in everyone of the United States." Furthermore Whitman argues that the "institution of slavery is not at all without its redeeming points."[22] The following year he approved of Oregon's constitution which prohibited blacks, disclosing his subliminal hope that they might go back to Africa, or at least somehow leave the United States: "Who believes that the Whites and Blacks can ever amalgamate in America? Or who wishes it to happen? Nature has set an impassable seal against it. Besides, is not America for the Whites? And is it not better so? As long as the Blacks remain here how can they become anything like an independent and heroic race? There is no chance for it." On the other hand, if given "some secure and ample part of the earth" where they could develop their potential and form their own nation, then blacks "would take no mean rank among the peoples of the world."[23]

Although Whitman believed that all races had equal promise, the white race was historically the most advanced, and it was most developed in America where the mass of ordinary men and women were, for the first time in history, being provided the opportunity to realize their full potential. But the presence of the less developed blacks threatened the progress of the white working class by degrading the dignity of their labor. Thus Whitman contrasted the "sturdy independence" of the workingmen of New York, Pennsylvania, and Ohio with the "miserable, ignorant, and shiftless" poor southern whites.[24] In the North manual labor had dignity. But in the South the existence of a genteel white class that was above working with its hands and a black slave class that was condemned to manual labor created a culture in which ordinary work was devalued. For poor whites to do it was to risk being reduced to the lowest caste in society. After the Civil War blacks continued to be relegated to the lowest forms of labor, and so Whitman probably continued to see them as a threat to the dignity and purity of his beloved white working class.

It is, of course, possible that a sensitivity to the opinions of his publishers and readers influenced Whitman to adopt a more conservative position on racial issues than was his own inclination.[25] Yet Whitman's opposition to amalgamation and the very presence of African-Americans seems to have been a deep-seated personal conviction, for in 1888 he forcefully reiterated these views to Traubel: "I don't believe in it [amalgamation]—it is not possible. The nigger like the Injun, will be eliminated." Drawing upon his experience in New Orleans, Whitman went on to explain that the French, Spanish, and Indians will marry blacks and "achieve equally fine reproductivities" but the "American white and the Southern black will *mix* but not ally." Preventing this were "psychologies, physiologies, some deeper fact" (*Camden*, II, 283, Whitman's emphasis). This insistence, which seems a veiled wish that blacks and Indians would disappear, along with his inclination to distinguish the French and Spanish subcultures from white America, raises the suspicion that always nestled someplace in Whitman's mind was a vision of an ideal America populated by Anglo-Saxon and Teutonic stock.

In contrast to the journalism of the 1840s and 1850s, the poetry of the 1850s (which is the poetry most concerned with race) exudes compassion, brotherhood, and inclusiveness. Describing a runaway slave coming to his house, Whitman gives him "a room that enter'd from my own" and has him "sit next me at table" ("Song of Myself," ll. 194, 198). Of "cotton-field drudge or cleaner of privies," he proclaims, "On his right cheek I put the family kiss, / And in my soul I swear I will never deny him" ("Song of Myself," ll. 1003–1005). In the slave-auctions depicted in "I Sing the Body Electric" (sections 7 & 8), Whitman emphasizes that all human bodies—"red, black, or white"—are sacred: the exquisite products of aeons of divinely directed evolution (ll. 95–128). Among a list of various races and nationalities in section 11 of "Salute au Monde!" Whitman merely names most groups, but he makes a special point of stressing the divinity and equality of blacks: "You dim-descended, black, divine-soul'd African, large, fine-headed, nobly-form'd, superbly destin'd, on equal terms with me!" In the conclusion of the catalog, these sentiments are reinforced: "Each of us limitless—each of us with his or her right upon the earth" and "Each of us here as divinely as any is here." Evidently Whitman believed that the members of all races, including blacks, had equal potential for limitless spiritual development and a moral claim to equal political rights.

The poetry and prose are not easily reconciled. It is significant that the poetry, like the editorial on the Oregon constitution, implies that blacks, while potential equals, were spiritually less advanced than whites, by frequently listing them with the moral dregs of American society: "The black with his woolly head, the felon, the diseas'd, the illiterate person" ("Song of the Open Road," l. 19) or "The kept-woman, sponger, thief, are hereby invited, / The heavy-lipped slave is invited, the venerealee is invited" ("Song of Myself," ll. 375–76). Again, as with Whitman's treatment of women, the modern reader is disappointed that the poetry is not more progressive in depicting nineteenth-century blacks of unusual achievement: for example, orators, abolitionists, educators, and statesmen. But unlike the journalism, the poetry does not argue that blacks should be excluded or leave but rather stresses their divinity and potential. Despite his unresolved personal feelings about race relations and the role of black people in America's future, it seems Whitman kept in mind that the *Leaves* was for the ages. Accordingly, he affirmed his general theological belief in the sanctity and propriety of all of the creation, including the various races, and his general political values of freedom and equality. But rather than advocating specific racial policies, he chose, as he did in a number of other areas, to remain vague so that the *Leaves* would prove relevant to a range of possible future developments. Thus in contrast to his journalism and private conversation, the poetry allows for the type of optimistic reading that Hughes makes.

But Whitman's utility derives from more than the fact that he is America's first, most intimately beloved and prophetic poet of democracy. Informing all of these is a fourth factor that is indispensable to an understanding of Whitman's unique power, namely, his absolute faith in human potential and democratic ideals. Muriel Rukeyser has contrasted Melville and Whitman in this respect, pointing out that whereas the former is "the poet of outrage of his century in America, Whitman is the poet of possibility."[26] It might be added: not only of their century but also of ours. Each of these writers has assumed a position as chief expositor of a philosophical outlook or a possibility of human existence as it may be lived under the conditions of American culture and institutions. A Melvillian pessimism reappears in such writers as the later Twain, Stephen Crane, Nathanael West, O'Neill, Hemingway, and Albee; Whitman's optimism finds expression in, among others, Sandburg, Hart Crane, the progressive Dos Passos, the late Dreiser, Hughes, Roethke, and Ginsberg. Since World War I Americans, especially intellectuals and artists,

have increasingly recognized the validity of Melville's anatomy of the patholo-
gies of the American system and psyche. In contrast, Whitman enlarged upon
even the early Emerson's sense of possibility. It is this unchecked optimism
which raises the question of Whitman's relevance to a century that has experienced the Great Depression, two world wars, and now our present sense of
appalling economic injustice and manifold threats to human survival. Yet
Whitman's optimism transcends the particular, dated formulation it receives
in his larger vision because a considerable degree of faith is necessary to a political system like ours which invests the citizenry with so much freedom and
responsibility. Furthermore, it is also true that the darker the historical moment, the greater the need for faith. For these reasons Whitman is indispens
able to democracy and especially relevant to our present time.

A Melvillian corrective to earlier Protestant and Transcendental millennialism provides a sense of limitation that needs to be retained, but now
there is a new paradoxical openness to optimism in response to the recognition
that any future, even one bleaker than Melville's bleakest imaginings, is threatened. In our present situation an unmitigated pessimism seems psychologically
infantile, morally self-serving, and politically self-destructive. Today there is
a need for the conviction, however muted and painfully earned, of possibility
that empowers people to work for political renewal. Ellen Wade has effectively
pointed to this newly emerging mood in reflections upon her undergraduate
education:

> In college . . . my education was dominated by modernist thinkers and artists
> who taught me that the supreme imperative was courage to face the awful truth,
> to scorn the soft-minded optimism of religious and secular romantics as well as
> the corrupt optimism of governments, advertisers, and mechanistic or manipula-
> tive revolutionaries. I learned that lesson well. . . . Yet the modernists' once-
> subversive refusal to be gulled or lulled has long since degenerated into a ritual
> despair at least as corrupt, soft-minded, and cowardly—not to say smug—as the
> false cheer it replaced. The terms of the dialectic have reversed: now the subver-
> sive task is to affirm an authentic postmodernist optimism that gives full weight
> to existent horror and possible (or probable) apocalyptic disaster, yet insists—
> credibly—that we can, well, overcome.[27]

Despite Whitman's conscious efforts to include the full reality of evil, his vision
does not provide an "authentic postmodernist optimism" that is adequate to
our understanding of the ambiguities of human nature and the tragedy of modern history. Yet the response of many subsequent writers demonstrates that
in times of political crisis Whitman does have the power to instill a functional,
if not fully satisfactory, sense of possibility. In the darkness of the Great Depression Sherwood Anderson called for "a return to Whitman, to his songs,
his dreams, his consciousness of the possibilities of the land that was his land
and is our land."[28] This appeal to Whitman's example of faith continues today.
Robert Creeley echoes Anderson by asserting, "If our America now is a petty

shambles of disillusion and violence, the dreams of its possibility stay actual
in Whitman's words."[29] In his "Populist Manifesto," a serio-comic jeremiad,
Lawrence Ferlinghetti, pointing to the seriousness of the times ("San
Francisco's burning / Mayakovsky's Moscow's burning"), exhorts his fellow
poets to "Stop mumbling and speak out / with a new wide-open poetry" to
"Whitman's wild children still sleeping there":

> Of your own sweet Self still sing
> yet utter "the word en-masse"—
> Poetry the common carrier
> for the transportation of the public
> to higher places.[30]

Whitman continues as the exemplary model for American poets who decide
to join in the struggle for liberation from the oppressive forces of their historical situation. Thus June Jordan presents Whitman as the archetypal New
World poet and defines this tradition as including Whitman and "all of the
poets whose lives have been baptized by witness to blood, by witness to cata-
clysmic, political confrontations from the Civil War through the Civil Rights
Era, through the Women's Movement, and on and on through the conflicts
between the hungry and the fat, the wasteful, the bullies."[31]

Minor Prophet

In "The Poet" Emerson declares: "All that we call sacred history attests that
the birth of a poet is the principal event in chronology." Implicit in this large
assertion is his hopeful anticipation, made explicit later in the essay, of an
American poet-prophet who will inaugurate a new religious era. Whitman responded to this summons, using it to define his sense of vocation; and his
hyper-venerating disciples were so enamoured of his achievement that they
proclaimed him the Christ of the modern world. Yet Whitman himself was
more cautious in his self-evaluation, especially as he grew older. His swollen
early ambition, ever-present in "Song of Myself," is well summed up in a note
written in the middle of 1857: "The Great Construction of the New Bible. Not
to be diverted from the principal object—the main life work—the three hundred and sixty-five."[32] But even in these initial years Whitman was unsure
about how to define his project: Was he composing the new Scripture or was
he only writing its preface—providing some ideas and symbols for a new age
of the spirit? This tension is encapsulated in two brief passages from "Starting
from Paumanok," which first appeared in the 1860 *Leaves*:

> I too, following many and follow'd by many, inaugurate a religion, I descend
>   into the arena,
> (It may be I am destin'd to utter the loudest cries there, the winner's pealing
>   shouts,

Who knows? they may rise from me yet, and soar above every thing.)

Know you, solely to drop in the earth the germs of a greater religion,
The following chants each for its kind I sing.[33]

(ll. 102–4 and 129–30)

Whitman is clear about his intention to inaugurate a new religion. But he is
uncertain about his own role: is he to be the major figure, "destin'd to utter
the loudest cries"? or is he merely to plant the beginnings or "germs of a
greater religion" and leave, as he suggests in another 1860 poem, the main
creation to others?

> Poets to come! orators, singers, musicians to come!
> . . . .
> Arouse! for you must justify me.
> . . . .
> Leaving it to you to prove and define it.
> Expecting the main things from you.
>
> ("Poets to Come")

In his final years, Whitman approved of M. D. Conway's understanding of his
effort: "Conway you will notice," he told Traubel with whom he was discussing Conway's letter, "does not call the *Leaves* a new Bible but the genesis of
a new Bible. That's more like sense than to make monopolistic claims." Then
Traubel interjected, "No matter what has come more is yet to come." Whitman
responded: "That's what I would have said, Horace, if you'd given me time"
(*Camden*, II, 285).

The old poet's crotchety endorsement of the assessment of his tediously
eager Boswell is certainly a more reasonable estimate than the inflated claims
of the early disciples. Yet it is also clear that this greatly reduced claim still
exaggerates Whitman's influence upon our culture. Whitman is not a new
Christ or even a lesser but major prophet of a new religion. Yet the fact remains
that his vision of American possibility continues to have an inspirational effect
upon many readers that is unique in our literature. The political nature of this
influence in combination with the pervasively religious character of Whitman's
undertaking suggests that he should be viewed as an early minor prophet of
a needed but largely inchoate civil faith—a faith that would not replace Judeo-
Christianity, as Whitman anticipated, but rather coexist with it.

Exactly how much influence this new order of democratic poetry might have
upon our society is a question to be answered by the future, and it will likely
be determined less by literary events than by the degree of political activism
and spiritual awareness in the larger culture. Whitman wrote in an age of intense religious ferment and political reform, and he appeals most strongly to
readers who have been caught up in currents of social commitment. If there
develops a substantial progressive movement for political renewal in America,
and if this struggle draws upon and appeals to our religious idealism, as has

been true in our previous periods of marked social change, then the importance of Whitman's poetry and example may grow. It is germane to note the remarkable popularity of the *Leaves* in Russia during the period of revolution: translations were published in 1914, 1918, and 1919—the last a printing of 50,000 copies by the Petrograd Soviet of Workers and Red Army Deputies.[34] Surely in favorable times Whitman's poetry should have even greater appeal to American readers. Yet as this example from Soviet history suggests, the success or failure of Whitman's effort to nurture political idealism does not rest solely with the adequacy or inadequacy of his achievement. It is also contingent upon whether or not readers develop an appropriate consciousness and respond with imagination and integrity to the challenges of their historical situation. There is considerable truth in Whitman's declaration, "To have great poets there must be great audiences too." A would-be prophet such as Whitman is recognized not simply because of the quality of his utterance. Acceptance comes in great part from a people's willingness to make a worthy response to him.

NOTES

Abbreviations

Camden	Horace L. Traubel, *With Walt Whitman in Camden*. Vol. I, Boston, 1906. Vol. II, New York, 1908. Vol. III, New York, 1914. Vol. IV, Philadelphia, 1953. Vol. V, Carbondale, Ill., 1964.
NPM	*Notebooks and Unpublished Prose Manuscripts*, 6 vols., ed. Edward F. Grier. *The Collected Writings of Walt Whitman*. New York, 1984.
PW	*Prose Works 1892*, 2 vols., ed. Floyd Stovall. *The Collected Writings of Walt Whitman*. New York, 1963 and 1964.
Workshop	*Walt Whitman's Workshop*, ed. Clifton Joseph Furness. Cambridge, 1928.

Unless otherwise indicated, references to Whitman's poetry are from *"Leaves of Grass": Comprehensive Reader's Edition*, ed. Harold W. Blodgett and Sculley Bradley. *The Collected Writings of Walt Whitman*. New York, 1963.

1. Reconsidering Whitman's Intention

1. J. H. Clifford, Letter, *The Conservator* 10 (July 1899), 72; as quoted in Charles B. Willard, *Whitman's American Fame*, (Providence, R.I.: Brown Univ. Press, 1950), p. 72.

2. *Walt Whitman* (Boston: Houghton Mifflin, 1906), p. 308.

3. *The Conservator* 18 (November 1906), 139 & 140.

4. London: C. W. Daniel, 1921.

5. Willard, *Whitman's American Fame*, p. 32.

6. Gay Wilson Allen, *Walt Whitman as Man, Poet, and Legend* (Carbondale: Southern Illinois Univ. Press, 1961), pp. 107–108.

7. "A Woman's Estimate of Walt Whitman," *In Re Walt Whitman*, ed. Richard M. Bucke et al. (Philadelphia: David McKay, 1893), p. 42.

8. *The Changing Order* (Chicago: Charles H. Kerr, 1906), pp. 264–65.

9. *Walt Whitman* (London: John C. Nimmo, 1893), p. 159.

10. The three most important psychoanalytic studies are Edwin Haviland Miller, *Walt Whitman's Poetry: A Psychological Journey* (New York: Houghton Mifflin, 1968); Stephen Black, *Whitman's Journeys into Chaos* (Princeton, N.J.: Princeton University Press, 1975), and David Cavitch, *My Soul and I: The Inner Life of Walt Whitman* (Boston: Beacon Press, 1985). This criticism sees little that is religious in Whitman's personality and poetry and even less evidence of a prophet deeply engaged with his historical environment in an effort to influence the course of American culture. For example, Miller, asserting that he does not hear a "consistently prophetic voice" and that "the external world is of little importance" in Whitman's poetry, argues that the *Leaves* is essentially an inner psychological drama best understood in terms of the "brilliant insights of Freud"; not surprisingly, the product of Whitman's poetic imagination is viewed as "regressive imagery, fantasy, and [the] reactivation of infantile longings," but Whitman, nevertheless, lays claim to our attention by the "profundity" of his "intuitive insights" and his "ability to put into artistic order what remains inarticu-

late and formless for lesser minds and sensibilities" (pp. 3, 8, & vii-viii). Miller's study has many merits, chief among them being his use of psychoanalytic theory to speculate, often quite cogently, on the psychic roots of Whitman's mature themes and symbols and his insistence upon the importance of Whitman's sexuality to an understanding of both the production and content of his poetry. But psychoanalytic studies such as Miller's suffer from the absence in Freud of an adequate conceptual understanding of the relationship between infantile imagery and the religious personality's subsequent investment of this imagery with mature religious intentions; accordingly Whitman's religious symbols are reduced to little more than obscure expressions of libidinal longing. Also, while an approach such as Miller's rightly claims that to deny "the sexual component in art is to indulge in cultural castration" (p. 4), it is equally true that an exclusive focus on the inner life completely uproots Whitman from his cultural context.

This tendency to de-historicize and secularize Whitman is continued by Black and Cavitch. For instance, the latter's recent study begins by declaring that it takes history seriously (p. xiv), but it soon becomes clear that the interest is largely limited to Whitman's family history; Cavitch quickly shows his lack of interest in Whitman's religious experience and purposes by defining Whitman not as a religious poet but as a poet who uses traditional sacred language to express a modern secular psychology. After describing Whitman's account of a mystical experience in section 5 of "Song of Myself" (which includes lines such as "And I know that the hand of God is the promise of my own, / And I know that the spirit of God is the brother of my own. . . ."), Cavitch acknowledges that the ecstasy "resembles the holy passion of a Christian conversion or the transfiguration of a mystic." But he then goes on to argue that Whitman asserts that this experience "has an *internal* cause; and God does not do anything or play a necessary part in Whitman's explanation." Referring to "the utter naturalness of the experience," Cavitch maintains that Whitman holds "a wholly secular attitude toward the world" (p. 49).

Without denying the value of such psychoanalytic studies or the skill of the practitioners, it must still be argued that their interpretations inevitably lead to partial and distorted views of Whitman. Assuming that it is unnecessary to discover Whitman's own understanding of his religious experience because religion is really something else and ignoring Whitman's social, political, economic, and religious concerns because it is also assumed that the public world is ultimately not important to an understanding of the inner life, this criticism does not provide a picture of the complete Whitman but of the poet who is most amenable to a particular psychoanalytic methodology.

11. In a 1932 article, Floyd Stovall provided a framework for much subsequent criticism by dividing Whitman's career into three periods: the first Whitman (1855–59) was a "sensualist," "materialist," and "egotist"; the second (1859–65) underwent the experiences of love and death and became "humble, melancholy and perplexed"; the third (1866-death) "retained and expanded" the ideas of the second and emphasized immortality and "thoughts of the spiritual side of life." According to Stovall, Whitman's spiritual interests first emerge in the second phase and only become fully pronounced in the third. Thus Whitman's claim in the 1872 Preface that the underlying principle of *Leaves of Grass* had always been religious ("one deep purpose underlay the others, and has underlain it and its execution ever since—and that has been the religious purpose") is referred to and explicitly denied: "I can find no slightest trace of a religious purpose in these early poems [of the first stage], unless the joyous and sensuous love of life may be called religious" ("Main Drifts in Whitman's Poetry," *American Literature* 4, [March 1932], 8).

In the early 1960s a group of important and frequently reprinted essays by Stephen Whicher, Roy Harvey Pearce, R. W. B. Lewis, and Clark Griffith both built upon and altered Stovall's interpretation to establish the current general conception of Whitman's development which I have stated in the text. Whicher's essay, "Whitman's Awakening to Death: Toward a Biographical Reading of 'Out of the Crade Endlessly Rocking'," was first delivered at the 1960 English Institute and was subsequently published in *Studies in Romanticism* 1 (Autumn 1961), 9–28; *The Presence of Walt Whitman*, ed. R. W. B. Lewis (New York: Columbia Univ. Press, 1962), pp. 1–27; *A Century of Whitman Criticism*, ed. Edwin Haviland Miller (Bloomington: Indiana Univ. Press, 1969), pp. 285–92; *"Out of the Cradle Endlessly Rocking"*, ed. Dominick P. Consolo (Columbus, Ohio: Charles E. Merrill, 1971), pp. 85–103; *Critics on Whitman*, ed. Richard H. Rupp (Coral Gables, Fla.: Univ. of Miami Press, 1972), pp. 61–65; and *Walt Whitman: A Collection of Criticism*, ed. Arthur Golden (New York: McGraw-Hill, 1974), pp. 77–96. Pearce's article, "Whitman Justified: The Poet in 1860," was also delivered at the 1960 English Institute and subsequently appeared in *Minnesota Review* 1 (1961), 261–94; *The Presence of Walt Whitman*, pp. 72–109; and *Whitman: A Collection of Critical Essays*, ed. Roy Harvey Pearce (Englewood Cliffs, N. J.: Prentice-Hall, Inc., 1962), pp. 37–59. An altered version of the article was used as the introductory essay to *Leaves of Grass: Facsimile Edition of the 1860 Text* (Ithaca, N.Y.: Cornell Univ. Press, 1961). Lewis's essay first appeared as an introduction to Whitman in *Major Writers of America*, ed. Perry Miller (New York: Harcourt, Brace and World, 1962), vol. I, pp. 969–87; it was reprinted in Lewis, *Trials of the Word: Essays in American Literature and the Humanistic Tradition* (New Haven: Yale Univ. Press, 1965), pp. 3–35; *Major Writers of America: Shorter Edition*, ed. Perry Miller (New York: Harcourt, Brace and World, 1966), pp. 567–83; and *Walt Whitman: Modern Critical Views*, ed. Harold Bloom (New York: Chelsea House Publishers, 1985), pp. 99–125. Griffith's "Sex and Death: The Significance of Whitman's 'Calamus' Themes" appeared in *Philological Quarterly* 39 (January 1960), 18–38; and *"Out of the Cradle Endlessly Rocking,"* pp. 69–76.

While these articles are not completely consistent with one another, their combined effect was to shift the locus of critical attention from the final to the 1860 (and to a lesser extent the 1867) edition of the *Leaves*, to view the stages in Whitman's development not as an orderly, consistent progression (as Stovall had maintained) but rather as radical transformations, and to deemphasize further the religious dimensions of the *Leaves* by viewing them as emendations introduced in the final period of Whitman's career which distorted the earlier, genuine Whitman and the best poetry. For example, Pearce distinguished between the earlier "poetic" and later "prophetic" Whitmans and argued for the superiority of the 1860 *Leaves*, reading it as an archetypal biography of the Romantic poet. Noting Whitman's assertion in "A Backward Glance" of more than literary purposes ("No one will get at my verses who insists upon viewing them as a literary performance, or attempt at such performance, or as aiming mainly toward art or aestheticism"), Pearce dismisses this as a later innovation, arguing that it is not true of "the earlier Whitman, I daresay the authentic Whitman, whose verses did aim mainly toward art and aestheticism, toward a definition of the vocation of the poet in that part of the modern world which was the United States." Acknowledging that Whitman does in fact announce a new religion in "Starting from Paumanok" (1860), Pearce asserts that he really means something different: "he gives no indication that it is to be a religion of anything else but the poet's universalized vocation. (My misuse of the word 'religion' is his.)," *Facsimile Edition*, pp. xvii-xviii and xxviii. This depreciation of Whitman's religious intention as a later imposition upon the earlier poetry has continued in subsequent criticism. For instance, E.H. Miller and Jerome Loving dismiss Whitman's 1872 claim that his poetry had always possessed an underlying religious purpose as "feeble rationalizations" or a "fabrication" (Miller, *Walt Whitman's Poetry*, p. 222; Loving, *Emerson, Whitman, and the American Muse* [Chapel Hill: Univ. of North Carolina Press, 1982], pp. 188–89).

12. I use this third approach to characterize the treatment of Whitman's spirituality in the two most important studies of the last forty years, Roger Asselineau's *The Evolution of Walt Whitman*, 2 vols. (Cambridge: Harvard Univ. Press, 1960–1962) and Gay Wilson Allen's *The Solitary Singer* (New York: New York Univ. Press, 1955, rev. 1967). In contrast to proponents of the "phases" interpretation, Asselineau and Allen correctly read the *Leaves* as having an important religious dimension from its inception. Also, while both conceive of Whitman as going through an emotional crisis in the late 1850s, neither sees this experience as destroying his earlier optimism to such an extent that the 1860s *Leaves* has a decidedly different philosophical vision.

My reading of Whitman differs from those of Asselineau and Allen in part because they employ a different methodological approach in pursuit of a different objective. Their studies are critical biographies which correlate the content of Whitman's poetry to his personal life and surrounding cultural and intellectual influences. Primarily concerned to elucidate the sources and development of Whitman's ideas, they understandably give less attention to analyzing the meaning of his poems and the unity of his vision. Nevertheless, I would argue that both studies provide a misleading account of the nature and development of Whitman's life and poetry because they present his spirituality as a discrete part of his intellectual belief system (a set of ethical and metaphysical ideas) rather than seeing it as the fundamental dimension of his consciousness that informs his personality and unites all of his experience and poetic themes. Thus Whitman is presented, for instance, as a democratic, scientific, and religious poet rather than as a religious poet whose spirituality permeates and integrates his scientific and political ideas.

13. I am using the term "phenomenology of religion" to refer to a distinctive method of studying religion and the body of scholarship it has produced. Phenomenologists intentionally ignore the issue of the truth or falsehood of religious propositions and instead use a method of intuition and careful analysis to describe the life world, the inner dynamics and existential values, of the religious consciousness. Some phenomenological studies limit themselves to an examination of the moments of religious experience in a particular religious personality. But a more common form of scholarship describes the essential structure and meanings of an aspect of religious life, e.g., the phenomenon of spiritual rebirth or the experiencing of stars as religious symbols, which recurs in the religions of different cultures and historical periods. The chief phenomenologists of religion are relatively few: Rudolf Otto, Gerardus van der Leeuw, W. Brede Kristensen, Paul Tillich, Paul Ricoeur, and Mircea Eliade. In addition, one might add Evelyn Underhill and William James, whose studies of mysticism, while not consciously employing a phenomenological method, nevertheless provide careful analyses of various recurring structures of religious experience. The work of these scholars is generally recognized as providing the best existing discussion of religious experience and its expression in myth and symbol.

14. *American Renaissance* (New York: Oxford Univ. Press, 1941), Preface, p. xi.

15. Of course, this must be done with care to avoid imposing extraneous meanings upon the poetry. Ideas brought to the *Leaves* must help to account for its language and to disclose patterns of imagery and thought which could only exist as a result of the poet's conscious arrangement of his materials. My goal has been to determine the unique characteristics of Whitman's thought and feeling, but it is beneficial if the discussion of a particular religious element in the *Leaves* also indicates its essential or recurring meaning. This discloses what Whitman's spirituality shares with other religious visions, and at the same time it highlights what is distinctive or innovative in the *Leaves*, thus providing a basis for judging the poet's thoughtfulness and creativity.

16. *Walt Whitman's Leaves of Grass: The First (1855) Edition* (New York: Viking Press, 1959), Introduction, pp. xiv & xxii.

17. Lincoln: Univ. of Nebraska Press, 1964.

18. Miller, *A Critical Guide to "Leaves of Grass"* (Chicago: Univ. of Chicago Press, 1957); Crawley, *The Structure of "Leaves of Grass"* (Austin: Univ. of Texas Press, 1970).

19. Hutchinson, *The Ecstatic Whitman: Literary Shamanism & the Crisis of the Union* (Columbus: Ohio State Univ. Press, 1986).

20. *Camden*, I, 105 and 271–72; II, 115, 297, 373 and 512; III, 320–21.

21. *A Reader's Guide to Walt Whitman* (New York: Farrar, Straus & Giroux, 1970), p. 148.

22. *American Visionary Poetry* (Baton Rouge: Louisiana State Univ. Press, 1982), pp. 28–29.

23. *Evolution of Walt Whitman*, vol. I, pp. 10 & 12. Elsewhere Asselineau asserts that Whitman's poetry "continually implies a confused and complex metaphysic upon which, at first, it seems impossible to impose an order"; however, "the contradictions are explained and the logic of his position becomes evident if one considers, instead of the present totality of *Leaves of Grass*, the temporal succession of the ideas which Whitman in turn tried to express" (*The Evolution of Walt Whitman*, vol. II, pp. 21–22). These statements imply that there is a unity, or at least a logic, in Whitman's thought, but that it cannot be discerned from the analysis of any single edition, even the final one. Rather it only becomes clear from a longitudinal study of the various editions placed within the context of Whitman's other writings. Asselineau uses this approach skillfully to make exhaustive chronological surveys of selected themes, for instance, "democracy" or "industrialism," which have greatly contributed to an understanding of the evolution of Whitman's thought. However, such an approach does not lend itself to discovering the underlying unity in Whitman's vision or the relationship between various ideas. In addition, it can also lead to misreadings of individual poems or passages by taking them out of the larger context of the *Leaves*.

In addition to disagreeing with Asselineau's judgment about the disunity of the *Leaves*, I also believe his effort to describe Whitman's world view ("The Implicit Metaphysics," *The Evolution of Walt Whitman*, vol. II, pp. 21–77) is wrong or inadequate in several fundamental respects. For instance, it characterizes Whitman's view of God's relationship to the world as pantheistic whereas it should be seen as theistic, and this fundamental misunderstanding leads to distortions of other aspects of Whitman's thought. Asselineau also incorrectly attributes to Whitman a doctrine of metempsychosis rather than seeing that Whitman conceived of the soul as following a course of progressive development toward higher forms of spiritual organization. More important, it may be said as a general statement that Asselineau fails to recognize how Whitman's world view is unified around a belief in progress: the progressive evolution of nature, the millennial movement of history, and the soul's ascent toward divinity.

24. Oscar L. Triggs, "The Growth of *Leaves of Grass*," *The Complete Writings of Walt Whitman* (New York, 1902), vol. X, p. 101.

25. Another reason for choosing the final edition is that it is the only text to which most readers of Whitman have easy access. However, at times it has been necessary to refer to earlier editions either because my argument discusses passages or poems that were later deleted or because I argue that the evidence for my interpretation of a particular poem or aspect of Whitman's vision was present not only in the final edition but also in earlier editions. For instance, in analyzing "Song of Myself" I cite the final edition, but I also argue that the evidence for my religious reading of the poem was already present in the 1855 edition. To demonstrate this point and to deal with possible objections to this part of my argument, I maintain a running commentary on the 1855 text in my footnotes that indicates relevant deletions, additions, and other alterations. Similarly, in my less frequent references to *Prose Works 1892*, I have cited the honored text

which is based upon Whitman's *Complete Prose Works* of 1892, but whenever my argument is based upon an earlier edition of the text, I have always checked the editorial notes to ascertain that the material cited was present (without substantive change) in the earlier version.

2. A New Religion: Fusing the Real and the Modern

1. *The Sacred and the Profane* (New York: Harper and Row, 1959), pp. 12 & 13.
2. Ibid., p. 202.
3. *Love Letters of Nathaniel Hawthorne* (Chicago: Society of the Dofobs, 1907), p. 121.
4. Prior to publication of the first edition of the *Leaves*, it was possible for Whitman to have become familiar with the following works by Emerson: *Nature* (1836), *Essays, First Series* (1841), *Essays, Second Series* (1844), *Poems* (1847), *Nature, Addresses, and Lectures* (1849), and *Representative Men* (1849). The best account of the history of Whitman's growing acquaintance with Emerson's thought is Jerome Loving's highly readable *Emerson, Whitman, and the American Muse* (Chapel Hill: Univ. of North Carolina Press, 1982). Loving's study substantiates the earlier critical opinion that Whitman was introduced to Emerson's thought in 1842, but that Emerson's influence upon Whitman only became significant much later, for as "late as 1848 he [Whitman] was in no clear sense a Transcendentalist, in spite of the impact of Emerson's 1842 lecture and whatever he read of Emerson's shortly afterward" (p. 60).
5. Gay Wilson Allen, Jospeh J. Rubin, Charles H. Brown, Alvin Rosenfeld, and Jerome Loving have all argued that Whitman probably first became acquainted with some of Emerson's ideas by attending one or two programs of the latter's New York lecture series of March 3–14, 1842, which consisted of "The Times," "The Poet," "The Conservative," "The Transcendentalist," "Manners," and "Prospects" (see Rosenfeld's unpublished dissertation, "Emerson and Whitman: Their Personal and Literary Relationships," Brown University, 1967, chap. 2, and Loving, *Emerson, Whitman, and the American Muse*, pp. 7–22 & 62–67. On Monday, March 7, Whitman wrote a two-paragraph article in the *Aurora* reporting Emerson's Saturday evening lecture on "Poetry and the Times" (*Walt Whitman of the New York Aurora*, ed. Joseph Jay Rubin and Charles H. Brown, [State College, Pa.: Bald Eagle Press, 1950], p. 105). Despite Whitman's exposure to Emerson's thought approximately one month before writing the articles I cite in notes 6 and 7, it is unlikely that his brief encounter with Emerson affected Whitman seriously at the time. No scholar has argued that Emerson had any significant influence upon Whitman at this early date.
6. "Dreams," April 23, 1842, *Walt Whitman of the New York Aurora*, pp. 132–33.
7. "Life and Love," April 20, 1842, *Walt Whitman of the New York Aurora*, p. 129.
8. For instance, see Paul Tillich, *Systematic Theology*, vol. I (Chicago: Univ. of Chicago Press, 1951), pp. 79–81, 108–18, 211–18; Eliade, *The Sacred and the Profane*, pp. 12–13; and Nicholas Berdyaev, *Freedom and the Spirit* (New York: Charles Scribner's Sons, 1935), p. 9.
9. Of the major categories used to describe God and his relationship to the world—deism, pantheism, and theism—Whitman's theological orientation is best classified as theistic. Consistent with the classical formulation of theism, Whitman's God is both transcendent and immanent. On the one hand, God is the creator of the world, who remains distinct from and superior to it; on the other hand, God is immanently present in the world, sustaining the creation and revealing divine attributes through it.
As the discussion of Whitman's inner cosmology shows, the very structure of the poet's world view is theistic. Furthermore, a survey of Whitman's writings reveals that he never denies God's transcendence and he frequently explicitly affirms it. See *The*

Uncollected Poetry and Prose, ed. Emory Holloway (Garden City, N.Y.: Doubleday, Page and Company, 1921), vol. II, p. 86; "Starting from Paumanok," 9; "Passage to India," 8; and the statement, cited later in this chapter, in which Whitman affirms that "the main meaning of all the material world is the invisible and spiritual world . . . and back of it all is what I may call the almighty."

Yet it is nevertheless true that the subject of God's transcendence receives relatively little attention in the *Leaves*; and even when mentioned, it is never elaborated upon. Instead Whitman stresses God's immanent presence. This relative distribution of emphasis helps explain why the poet has been mistakenly labeled a pantheist, but it does not, of course, justify such a judgment. Rather it indicates his desire to provide his readers not with a conceptual understanding of divine transcendence but with a vital experience of God's immanence which would lead to a belief in divine transcendence. Also, it indicates that Whitman should be numbered among those mystics who insist that the experience of God is a dark knowledge, surpassing human powers of understanding and articulation. As he proclaims in "Passage to India," "Ah more than any priest O soul we too believe in God, / But with the mystery of God we dare not dally." For a more thorough discussion of this issue, see David Kuebrich, "Whitman's New Theism," *ESQ: A Journal of the American Renaissance* 24 (4th quarter 1978), 229–41.

10. *In Re Walt Whitman*, ed. Horace L. Traubel, Richard Maurice Bucke, Thomas B. Harnad (Philadelphia: David McKay, 1893), p. 350.

11. *Essays, Second Series, The Collected Works of Ralph Waldo Emerson*, vol. III (Cambridge: Harvard Univ. Press, 1983), pp. 105–106.

12. *Nature, Addresses, and Lectures, The Collected Works of Ralph Waldo Emerson*, vol. I (Cambridge: Harvard Univ. Press, 1971), p. 193.

13. Ibid., p. 137.

14. "The Over-Soul," *Essays, First Series, The Collected Works of Ralph Waldo Emerson*, vol. II (Cambridge: Harvard Univ. Press, 1979), p. 168.

15. Allen suggests that contemporary astronomy's use of Immanuel Kant's "theory of eternal cycles of cosmic evolution and devolution" might have influenced Whitman to conceive of an afterlife in which souls would "migrate from one cosmic system to another to continue their evolutionary growth in the 'orchards of God'." But then Allen seems to reject this interpretation: "To construct a mythology of the 'spheres' to which Whitman expects his soul to migrate is to interpret his metaphors too literally and simple-mindedly. He had *hope* [Allen's emphasis] of some kind of spiritual life after his mortal end, but his imagination was unequal to visualize it with the vitality of a Blake or a Swedenborg" (*The New Walt Whitman Handbook* [New York: New York University Press, 1975], pp. 198 & 200). As my discussion shows, there were a number of sources from which Whitman might have have acquired a belief in the soul's ongoing development in the celestial regions. While he apparently wanted to avoid constructing an elaborate system of heavenly spheres in the manner of Emanuel Swedenborg or Andrew Jackson Davis, it does nevertheless seem that astronomical theory positing an evolving and seemingly infinite universe led him to conceive of the stellar heavens as both a symbol of the soul's endless growth and as the habitat where this development would occur.

16. *Concerning the Earths in Our Solar System* (Boston: Otis Clapp, 1839), pp. 20 & 21. Before composing the *Leaves*, Whitman could also have acquired these ideas from Swedenborg's *Heaven and Its Wonders, The World of Spirits, and Hell* (New York: American Swedenborg Printing and Publishing Society, 1851), pp. 77 and 222–27. Floyd Stovall suggests that Whitman probably never read any of Swedenborg's books but that he may have become acquainted with his ideas in newspaper and magazine articles because "Swedenborgianism was much talked and written about in this country during the 1840's and 1850's "(*The Foreground of "Leaves of Grass"* [Char-

lottesville: Univ. of Virginia Press, 1974], p. 229). In 1856 Whitman made the acquaintance of a neighbor, John Arnold, who was an adherent of Swedenborgianism, and the two often discussed Swedenborg's ideas (Gay Wilson Allen, *The Solitary Singer* [New York: New York Univ. Press, 1967], p. 199). Whitman wrote an article for the June 15, 1858 Brooklyn *Daily Times* entitled "Who was Swedenborg?" with the surprising prediction that the Swedish mystic "will probably make the deepest and broadest mark upon the religions of future ages here, of any man that ever walked the earth" (*Uncollected Poetry and Prose*, vol. II, pp. 17–18). Both the conversations with Arnold and this unrestrained praise, which seems to reflect a passing enthusiasm, occurred after the first edition of the Leaves, and it remains a matter of conjecture whether and to what extent Whitman was influenced by Swedenborg when he developed his understanding of immortality.

17. *The Philosophy of a Future State* (Brookfield, Mass.: E. & G. Meriam, 1830), p. 52. Dick's theory of the soul's ongoing development also appears in several of his other works: *The Sidereal Heavens and Other Subjects Connected with Astronomy, Celestial Scenery*, and *The Christian Philosopher*. Apparently quite popular, these works were published by several American publishers in the decades just before the first edition of the *Leaves* was published.

18. *Celestial Wonders and Philosophy* (Philadelphia: Printed for the Central University of Illinois, 1838), pp. 72 & 75. Allen speculates that Whitman may have drawn upon the figurative language of *Celestial Wonders* for ll. 798–99 of "Song of Myself" (*The Solitary Singer*, pp. 123–24).

19. "The Book of Abraham," *Holy Scriptures of the Church of Jesus Christ of Latter-Day Saints* (Salt Lake City: Deseret Book Company, 1959), pp. 29–42. The King Follett discourse may be found in *Immortality: Famed Discourses on Eternal Progression and Future Existence* (Salt Lake City: Deseret Book Company, 1974), pp. 53–80. According to Fawn Brodie, Smith was reading Dick's *Philosophy of a Future State* at the time that he alleged to have deciphered the hieroglyphs of the Egyptian papyri, discovering them to be writings of Abraham and Joseph. See Brodie, *No Man Knows My History: The Life of Joseph Smith the Mormon Prophet*, 2nd ed. (New York: Alfred A. Knopf, 1971), pp. 171–72.

20. The Mormons proved highly newsworthy during their years at Nauvoo, Illinois in the early 1840s, and their activities were reported nationally. In New York papers, they received the greatest attention in the *New York Herald*, whose editor, James Gordon Bennett, penned a number of articles on the Mormons in the winter of 1841–42 that created considerable excitement in both New York and Nauvoo. These were followed in the summer of 1842 by a series of sensational articles devoted to the allegations of John C. Bennett, a recently excommunicated Mormon leader, who charged Smith with being a charlatan, a despot, a libertine, and a murderer in a series of letters reprinted or reported in papers across the country. Later in the same year this long catalog of accusations was published as *The History of the Saints* (New York: Bradbury, Soden and Company, 1842). Bennett discusses the Mormon doctrine of the soul's progress to divinity on page 172. The Mormons became still more newsworthy in 1844 with Smith's decision to run for president of the United States and his subsequent assassination. For a discussion of the reportage in the *Herald* and the Bennett affair and its coverage in the nation's press, see Donna Hill, *Joseph Smith: The First Mormon* (Garden City, N.Y.: Doubleday, 1977), pp. 292–93, 300–303, 316–20.

21. Before 1855 Whitman could have read Davis's theory of the soul's ongoing development in *The Principles of Nature, the Divine Revelation, and a Voice to Mankind* (New York: S. S. Lyon & W. Fishbough, 1847), pp. 643–77); *The Philosophy of Spiritual Intercourse* (New York: Fowlers and Wells, 1851); *The Great Harmonia*, vol. 1,

The Physician (Boston: B. B. Mussey, 1851), pp. 157–90; vol. II, *The Teacher* (Boston: B. B. Mussey, 1852), pp. 243–54; vol. III, *The Seer* (Boston: B. B. Mussey, 1852), pp. 64–65; and *The Present Age and Inner Life* (Hartford, 1853), pp. 268–81. Fowlers and Wells published *The Philosophy of Spiritual Intercourse* in 1851 and 1854 and *The Seer* in 1852. Because Davis established a considerable reputation as a clairvoyant and healer in 1846, Whitman probably became somewhat informed about him at this time. If not, he surely learned about Davis the following year when his first book, *The Principles of Nature*, received advance publicity in the New York papers in the late summer, and then its merits were intensely debated upon publication. See Robert W. Delp, "Andrew Jackson Davis: Prophet of American Spiritualism," *Journal of American History* 54 (June 1967), 43–56. Davis's possible influence upon Whitman is discussed further in chapter 4.

22. "Uncollected Manuscript Fragments," *Leaves of Grass: Norton Critical Edition*, ed. Sculley Bradley and Harold W. Blodgett (New York: W. W. Norton & Co. 1973), p. 702.

3. Interpeting History's Meaning: Whitman's Post-Christian Millennialism

1. The references to American materialism are from *Walt Whitman of the New York Aurora*, ed. Joseph Jay Rubin and Charles H. Brown (State College, Pa.: Bald Eagle Press, 1950), p. 41 and *The Uncollected Poetry and Prose of Walt Whitman*, ed. Emory Holloway (Garden City, N. Y.: Doubleday, Page and Company, 1921), vol. I, p. 124. For Whitman's journalism on the condition of workers, see *The Gathering of the Forces*, ed. Cleveland Rodgers and John Black (New York: G. P. Putnam's Sons, 1902), pp. 148–58. His discussion of the New York City housing crisis is presented in *New York Dissected*, ed. Emory Holloway and Ralph Adimari (New York: R. R. Wilson, 1936), pp. 92–102. Treatment of the slave trade and slavery are in *The Gathering of the Forces*, pp. 187–218; *New York Dissected*, pp. 105–14; and *I Sit and Look Out*, ed. Emory Holloway and Vernolian Schwartz (New York: Columbia Univ. Press, 1932), pp. 86–90.

2. Perry Miller, *The Life of the Mind in America* (New York: Harcourt, Brace and World, 1965), provides a convenient discussion of early nineteenth-century America's belief in progress. For the influence of science upon Whitman's thought, see Joseph Beaver, *Walt Whitman—Poet of Science* (New York: King's Crown Press, 1951) and Gay Wilson Allen, *The New Walt Whitman Handbook* (New York: New York Univ. Press, 1975), pp. 181–88. Allen summarizes earlier scholarship pertaining to Whitman's knowledge of Hegel, *Handbook*, pp. 257–60. More recently Norma Jean Chalfin and Stephen L. Tanner have again argued that Hegel was the chief influence upon Whitman's understanding of history. The fatal defect in this argument is that even its proponents concede that Whitman did not become familiar with Hegel's thought before 1854 and perhaps not until the later 1860s, but the following discussion will show that Whitman's philosophy of history became well developed in the 1840s and early 1850s. Because both American religious nationalism and Hegel conceived of an individual nation as leading the march of universal history, Whitman could later latch on to Hegel's philosophy of history to provide intellectual support for his view of America as God's chosen agent for introducing the millennium. See Chalfin, *Walt Whitman's Philosophy of History* (Dissertation, University of Southern California, 1975), and Tanner, "Religious Attitudes toward Progress: Whitman and Berdyaev," *Cithara* 17 (November 1977), 4–16.

3. My general discussion of American millennialism is indebted to Ernest L. Tuveson, *Redeemer Nation: The Idea of America's Millennial Role* (Chicago: Univ. of Chicago Press, 1968); Nathan Hatch, *The Sacred Cause of Liberty* (New Haven: Yale

Univ. Press, 1977); Edwin S. Gaustad, ed. *The Rise of Adventism: Religion and Society in Mid-Nineteenth Century America* (New York: Harper & Row, 1974).

4. *The Great Awakening, The Works of Jonathan Edwards*, ed. C. C. Goen (New Haven: Yale Univ. Press, 1972), vol. IV, pp. 355–58.

5. For a discussion of the development of American civic millennialism between the Great Awakening and the Revolution, see Hatch, *Sacred Cause*, especially chapters 1–3; J. F. Maclear, "The Republic and the Millennium," in *The Religion of the Republic*, ed. Elwyn A. Smith (Philadelphia: Fortress Press, 1971), pp. 183–216; Stephen J. Stein, "An Apocalyptic Rationale for the American Revolution," *Early American Literature* 9 (1975), 211–25.

6. "Dissertation on the Canon and the Feudal Law," *The Works of John Adams* (New York: AMS Press, 1971), vol. III, pp. 449, 451, 464.

7. *God's New Israel: Religious Interpretations of American Destiny*, ed. Conrad Cherry (Englewood Cliffs, N.J.: Prentice-Hall, 1971), pp. 83, 84, & 91.

8. Ibid., pp. 119, 120.

9. *Lectures on Revivals of Religion* (Cambridge: Harvard Univ. Press, 1960), p. 306.

10. *The Perfect Life* in *The Works of William E. Channing* (Boston: American Unitarian Association, 1888), p. 954.

11. *A Treatise on the Millennium* (New York: J. & J. Harper, 1832), p. vii. Henry Dana Ward complained: "so firmly planted has this new faith [millennialism] become in all the churches of America, that never a religious newspaper of high standing with its own sect can easily be found, in New York or Boston, to admit an article in their columns, boldly questioning this proud Philistine, which has seized the ark of our faith," in *History and Doctrine of the Millennium* (Boston, 1840), p. 59; as quoted in Tuveson, *Redeemer Nation*, p. 54.

12. As quoted in Ronald G. Walters, *American Reformers, 1815–1860* (New York: Hill and Wang, 1978), pp. 149. For a discussion of the relations between American millennialism, communitarianism and reform, see Walters, especially pp. 21–29 and Alice Felt Tyler, *Freedom's Ferment* (New York: Harper and Row, 1944), pp. 1– 224.

13. Howard Kerr, *Mediums, and Spirit-Rappers, and Roaring Radicals: Spiritualism in American Literature, 1850–1900* (Urbana: Univ. of Illinois Press, 1972), pp. 10–11.

14. Gay Wilson Allen, *The Solitary Singer*, rev. ed. (New York: New York Univ. Press, 1967), pp. 9–20; Joseph Jay Rubin, *The Historic Whitman* (University Park: Pennsylvania State Univ. Press, 1973), pp. 17 and 356n7; Floyd Stovall, *The Foreground of "Leaves of Grass,"* (Charlottesville: Univ. of Virginia Press, 1974), pp. 24–26.

15. Charles I. Foster, *An Errand of Mercy: The Evangelical United Front, 1790–1837* (Chapel Hill: Univ. of North Carolina Press, 1960), p. 119.

16. "American Sunday School Union," *The American Sunday School Magazine* 1 (July 1824), 1. The first issue of the Episcopal Sunday school magazine indicates that its editors had an equally high opinion of the Sunday school's ability to effect the millennium: "It would seem as though the spirit of God has now put into the hands of men the instrument [the Sunday school] which was to be more successful than any other in bringing about the blessed era, when 'all shall know the Lord from the *least* unto the greatest,'" "Sunday Schools Prospectively Considered," *The Sunday School Visitor* 1 (February 1835), 44.

17. *The Uncollected Poetry and Prose of Walt Whitman*, ed. Emory Holloway (Garden City, N.Y.: Doubleday, Page and Company, 1921), vol. II, p. 293. Whitman's reminiscences about the revival services leave the time of his attendance unclear. Rubin, *The Historic Whitman*, pp. 17, 25, implies Whitman attended as a boy; Stovall, *The*

Foreground of "Leaves of Grass," p. 25, believes it "more probable" that Whitman went as a young adult, sometime after 1845.

18. Winthrop S. Hudson, *Religion in America* (New York: Charles Scribner's Sons, 1981), 3rd ed., pp. 198–201; Martin Marty, *Righteous Empire: The Protestant Experience in America* (New York: Dial Press, 1970), pp. 89–99.

19. Rubin, *The Historic Whitman*, pp. 80–81.

20. Allen (*Solitary Singer*, p. 134) asserts that Whitman began writing the *Leaves* in the late 1840s; Edward F. Grier ("Walt Whitman's Earliest Known Notebook," *PMLA* 83 [Oct. 1968], pp. 1453–56) argues for a date at least as early as mid-April 1847.

21. Walt Whitman, *New York Dissected: A Sheaf of Recently Discovered Newspaper Articles by the Author of "Leaves of Grass"*, ed. Emory Holloway and Ralph Adimari (New York: R. R. Wilson, 1936), p. 44.

22. Rubin, *The Historic Whitman*, p. 215.

23. *Uncollected Poetry and Prose*, vol. I, pp. 234–35. It seems especially likely that Whitman would have been aware of the millennialist views of Lyman and Henry Ward Beecher because they were both preachers of national stature who spent considerable parts of their lives on Long Island. It was as a minister over the Presbyterian Church at East Hampton (1799–1810) that the elder Beecher became famous as a revival preacher and reform leader. Later, after leaving Long Island, he became one of the most prominent ministers of the Second Great Awakening, a leading spokesman for the more Arminian New Haven theology of Nathaniel Taylor which was replacing Calvinist orthodoxy, and a catalyst for various evangelical reforms, including the widespread temperance movement. After retiring from the presidency of Lane Seminary in Cincinnati in 1850, Beecher returned to Long Island, spending his last years at the home of Henry Ward in Brooklyn, where he died in 1863. The son, an even more conspicuous public figure than his father, quickly acquired his position as America's leading clergyman during the early years of his long ministry (1847–1887) to the Congregational Plymouth Church of Brooklyn. By 1849 his weekly congregation was averaging about 2,500 people, and his sermons were printed each week and widely distributed in pamphlet form. Whitman would also have been interested in Beecher because of his prominent role in the abolitionist movement. He openly opposed the Compromise of 1850, and campaigned for Fremont in 1856 and Lincoln in 1860 (*Dictionary of American Biography*, vol. I, pp. 135–36 & 129–35).

One of Whitman's earliest extant letters (June 20, 1857) refers to both of the Beechers: "Mrs. Price and Helen [neighbors of the Whitmans] had been out all day with the sewing machine, at Mr. Beecher's—either Henry Ward's, or his father's" (*The Correspondence*, ed. Edwin Haviland Miller [New York: New York Univ. Press, 1961], vol. I, p. 42). This casual reference suggests that Whitman was well aware of the Beechers, seemingly considering them a familiar part of his local environment.

24. *Uncollected Poetry and Prose*, vol. I, p. 234, No. 1.

25. "Introduction," *The United States Magazine and Democratic Review* 1 (October 1837), 1–15; reprinted in *Social Theories of Jacksonian Democracy*, ed. Joseph Blau (New York: Hafner, 1947), pp. 32, 33. It is uncertain when Whitman began reading the *Democratic Review*. Rubin suggests that he was reading it regularly by 1839 (*The Historic Whitman*, p. 45). Stovall notes that he was a regular reader from 1841–47 (*The Foreground to "Leaves of Grass,"* p. 143). Whitman contributed three pieces to the *Review* in 1841, five in 1842, and two more in 1845. Although Whitman was only eighteen when O'Sullivan began the journal, he had already served as a printer's devil for two Democratic papers and was a committed Democrat, active in party politics by this time. So it is possible that he read O'Sullivan's declaration of political faith as early as 1837. Even if he did not, he probably would have encountered it at

a later date, for O'Sullivan and William Leggett were the chief political mentors in the later 1830s for the liberal ("Locofoco") branch of the Democratic party which Whitman supported.

Whitman could also have garnered the principles of O'Sullivan's millennial ideology from subsequent issues of the *Review*, for O'Sullivan continued to expound his belief that the United States was chosen by God to be an engine of progress and freedom that would regenerate humanity and establish God's kingdom on earth. For instance, a September 1839 article, "The Course of Civilization," describes the "history of humanity" as "the record of a grand march, more or less rapid . . . at all times tending to one point—the ultimate perfection of man" (pp. 208–209). Divine providence, itself "committed to the restless workings of that principle of progression," had designated the United States to be "the birth-place of a new society"; the American Revolution had initiated "a reform destined to cease only when every man in the world should be finally and triumphantly redeemed" (pp. 208, 213). In "The Progress of Society" (July 1840), O'Sullivan describes history as "the record of man's efforts at progress" and divides universal history into three overlapping epochs: from the creation to the age of Socrates, from Greek civilization to the establishment of Christianity as a state religion under Constantine, and from "the promulgation of the glad tidings of the Gospel by the Saviour to the American Revolution, which events may be deemed the two most important in the history of the world" (pp. 70–71). The "eyes of the world" were "fixed upon the citizens of this young republic" because America was "placed in the forefront of the battle" which the human race was waging against all forms of oppression. A careful reading of the "many and prominent signs" of the times disclosed that victory was imminent and entrance into the long-promised land would soon be achieved: "There are many who believe that the good yet in store for our race is not remote—that, though our feet are not permitted to enter the happy precincts of the promised land, yet we have gained a Pisgah height . . . and that the day when admission to it shall end man's weary pilgrimage through this wilderness of thorns is not far off" (p. 87). An August 1842 essay entitled "Democracy and Literature" asserts that the study of history "effectually demonstrates the progress of the democratic principle" (p. 198). The "spirit of Literature" and the "spirit of Democracy" are pronounced identical because "both speak to the instinctive aspirations of the human soul after liberty of thought and freedom of expression" (p. 196). The American Revolution was nothing less than "a baptism of a great nation, the political regeneration of a great people" (p. 200). In a June 1843 review of William E. Channing's "A Statement of the Principles of the Christian Union" (the Union was a society devoted to advancing the millennium), O'Sullivan proclaims that democracy and Christianity, previously estranged, now share the "joint and blessed mission" of applying Christian principles "to the regeneration of human society, to realize . . . the coming of the Kingdom of God upon the earth" ("The Christian Union," p. 567).

26. Ibid., p. 28.

27. Ibid., p. 32.

28. *Walt Whitman of the New York Aurora*, ed. Joseph Jay Rubin and Charles H. Brown (State College, Pa.: Bald Eagle Press, 1950), p. 64.

29. "American Futurity," *The Gathering of the Forces*, ed. Cleveland Rodgers and John Black (New York: G. P. Putnam's Sons, 1920), vol. I, p. 28.

30. "Our Territory on the Pacific," *Gathering of the Forces*, vol. I, pp. 246–47.

31. Untitled editorial, *Gathering of the Forces*, vol. I, pp. 253–54.

32. For discussions of the revivalists' tendency to view the temperance pledge as a sign of conversion, see W. J. Rorabaugh, *The Alcoholic Republic: An American Tradition* (New York: Oxford Univ. Press, 1979), pp. 208–9; John Allen Krout also discusses this point as well as the identification of temperance with the millennium in *The*

Origins of Prohibition (New York: Alfred A. Knopf, 1925), pp. 113–23. A brief sampling of contemporary temperance literature readily shows the widespread practice of linking universal temperance with the millennium. The executive committee of the American Temperance Union declared their cause "must and will universally prevail before the world shall be filled with the knowledge and glory of God"; they asked Christian ministers to "co-operate with us in a work which more than any other will help you in redeeming this world from sin and woe, and bringing it home to God" ("Address," *Journal of the American Temperance Union* 1, (January 1837), 5). The Reverend Austin Dickinson closed his temperance sermon by exhorting the young to work for temperance with "moral courage, intelligence, and purity; and with corresponding effort, say to the whole earth, *the hour of her redemption is come.*" Then happy would be their children who would "like the rainbow above the retiring cloud, reflect from one end of the earth to the other, the glories of a millennial sun ("Appeal to American Youth on Temperance," *The Temperance Union: Embracing the Temperance Tracts of the American Tract Society*, [New York: D. Fanshaw, 1834], p. 120). In another appeal to America's young, Edward Hitchcock, a professor at Amherst College, predicted that the "intelligent youth of our land" will "take the high vantage-ground of total abstinence" and provide "a noble example for all the world" so that "soon would Millennial Temperance reign in all the earth, and Millennial Happiness follow in the train!" (*An Argument for Early Temperance Addressed to the Youth of the United States* [New York: Scofield and Voorhies, 1837], p. 89). Reverend Lebbeus Armstrong, an original member of what was perhaps the first American Temperance Society, founded in Moreau, New York, in 1808, conceived of a millennial history in which the temperance movement was the decisive happening. There were the "dark ages of Popery; the Protestant Reformation; the subsequent persecution of the church, and her second flight into the wilderness; (doubtless, of, then, savage America;) the new stratagem of Satan to destroy the church by intemperance . . . and the Standard of the Lord lifted up against the enemy, comprising the Temperance Reformation." These were "all foretold as events which are to come to pass previous to the overthrow of the Antichrist, at the Lord's great battle day, preparatory to the Millennium" (*The Temperance Reformation of this XIXth Century: The Fulfillment of Divine Prophecy* [New York: Putney, Hooker & Russell, 1845]. As a final example, Chancellor Walworth of New York entreated fellow laborers in the cause to persevere "until 'total abstinence' shall be inscribed upon the banner of every state and nation of this world. Then, and not till then, shall the peaceful reign of the kingdom of the Messiah commence and be extended to the ends of the earth" (*Massachusetts Spy*, August 24, 1836, as quoted in Krout, *Origins of Prohibition*, p. 123).

33. "Franklin Evans or The Inebriate," *The Early Poems and the Fiction*, ed. Thomas L. Brasher (New York: New York Univ. Press, 1963), pp. 221.

34. Thomas L. Brasher discusses this issue and the various stories of what liquors Whitman may or may not have been drinking when he composed "Franklin Evans," in *The Early Poems and the Fiction*, pp. 124–26.

35. Whitman's knowledge of phrenology is discussed by Edward Hungerford, "Walt Whitman and His Chart of Bumps," *American Literature* 2, (1931), 350–84; Thomas L. Brasher, "Whitman's Conversion to Phrenology," *Walt Whitman Newsletter* 4 (March 1958), 95–97; Madeleine B. Stern, *Heads and Headlines: The Phrenological Fowlers* (Norman: Univ. of Oklahoma Press, 1971), pp. 99–123; Arthur Wrobel, "Whitman and the Phrenologists: The Divine Body and the Sensuous Soul," *PMLA* 89 (1974), 17–23; and Harold Aspiz, *Walt Whitman and the Body Beautiful*, (Urbana: Univ. of Illinois Press, 1980), pp. 113–17.

36. *American Phrenological Journal* 8 (July 1846), pp. 200–203.

37. Ibid. 10 (June 1848), 190–91.

38. Ibid. 9, (March 1847), 73–74.

39. *The Principles of Nature* (New York: S. S. Lyon & Wm. Fishbough, 1847), p. 745.

40. Ibid., p. 779.

41. Whitman wrote himself the following cautionary note: "Remember in scientific and similar allusions that the theories of Geology, History, Language, &c., &c., are continually changing. Be careful to put in only what *must* be appropriate centuries hence" (*Notes and Fragments*, ed. Richard Maurice Bucke [London, Ontario: A. Talbot & Co. 1899], p. 55). Whitman seems to have followed his self-advice rather successfully. As Beaver has demonstrated in *Walt Whitman—Poet of Science*, Whitman's poetry does conform to the general principles and some of the particular discoveries of nineteenth-century science, especially in geology and astronomy. Aspiz and others make a convincing case for Whitman's indebtedness to phrenology for his sense of vocation and his use of phrenological ideas and language in the *Leaves* (*Walt Whitman and the Body Beautiful*, pp. 109–33), but it seems that Whitman avoided drawing upon ideas and minutiae specific to phrenology, so that even when it proved to be a pseudoscience, the ideas informing these parts óf the poetry were not dated. Spiritualism (a "science" to the extent that it drew upon the ideas of mesmerism or animal magnetism), however, appears to have enjoyed a considerably lower status in Whitman's mind, for as Aspiz points out, the *Leaves* only draws upon selected ideas and vocabulary, mainly using them as a source of metaphor (p. 164). It is likely that Whitman's belief in spiritualism was short-lived.

42. As quoted in Aspiz, *Walt Whitman and the Body Beautiful*, p. 154.

43. *American Phrenological Journal* 22 (October 1855), 90.

44. These ideas are repeated with slight variations in most of Davis's major works. See *The Principles of Nature* and *The Great Harmonia*, vols. I-III. Except for Stovall, who speculated that Whitman may have read volumes II and III of *The Great Harmonia* (*The Foreground of "Leaves of Grass,"* p. 155), scholars had not linked Davis and Whitman until Aspiz pointed to a number of rather close parallels between Jackson's and Whitman's descriptions of their inspired or clairvoyant states (*Walt Whitman and the Body Beautiful*, pp. 162, 164, 169–78). Davis would have been a most likely source for Whitman's belief in spiritualism for he was the most popular and prolific "philosophical" spiritualist (Jackson's term to distinguish his theories from the more sensational, spirit-rapping spiritualism of the Fox sisters and their numerous emulators). Surely Aspiz is correct in stating that Whitman never subscribed to the specific beliefs of Davis or any of the other spiritualists (p. 164). This judgment is confirmed in a letter Whitman wrote to Sarah Tyndale in 1857 which contains, I believe, the only reference to Davis in Whitman's writings: "Andrew Jackson Davis puts *matter* as the subject of his homilies, and the primary source of all results—I suppose the soul among the rest. Both [Davis and Cora L.V. Hatch, another spiritualist] are quite determined in their theories. Perhaps when they know much more, both of them will be much less determined" (*The Correspondence*, vol. I, p. 43).

45. *Essays, First Series, The Collected Works of Ralph Waldo Emerson*, (Cambridge: Harvard Univ. Press, 1979), vol. II, p. 48.

46. "Nature," *Nature, Addresses, and Lectures, The Collected Works of Ralph Waldo Emerson*, (Cambridge: Harvard Univ. Press, 1971), vol. I, p. 43.

47. *Essays, First Series*, p. 5.

48. "Politics," *Essays, Second Series, The Collected Works of Ralph Waldo Emerson*, (Cambridge: Harvard Univ. Press, 1983), vol. III, p. 121.

49. "Experience," *Essays, Second Series*, p. 34.

50. Ibid., p. 40.

51. Ibid., p. 41.

52. "Nature" *Nature, Addresses, and Lectures*, p. 7.
53. "Divinity School Address," *Nature, Addresses, and Lectures*, p. 84.
54. *Essays, Second Series*, pp. 7 & 21.
55. Similarly, in his letter to Emerson which served as the 1856 Preface, Whitman speaks of America as the "grandest of lands in the theory of its politics, in popular reading, in hospitality, breadth, animal beauty, cities, ships, machines, money." To these achievements is to be added a new American literature for the development of the American people: "The time is at hand when inherent literature will be a main part of These States, as general and real as steam-power, iron, corn, beef, fish. First-rate American persons are to be supplied," *Leaves of Grass: Norton Critical Edition*, ed. Harold W. Blodgett and Sculley Bradley (New York: W. W. Norton & Co., 1973), pp. 734–35. The 1872 Preface declares that the basis for the ideal American society is already established in "boundless products for feeding, clothing, sheltering everybody . . . and with civil and ecclesiastical freedom." Upon this foundation, Whitman declared, a "modern image-making creation is indispensible to fuse and express the modern political and scientific creations—and then the trinity will be complete" (*PW*, 461).
56. *Leaves of Grass: Norton Critical Edition*, pp. 739–40.
57. In *Walt Whitman and the Body Beautiful*, pp. 192–236, Aspiz demonstrates the remarkable extent to which Whitman's poems of heterosexual love draw upon nineteenth-century eugenic theory. Aspiz proves the correctness of John Burroughs's observation, inspired if not written by Whitman himself, that "Children of Adam" was composed "mainly with reference to offspring, and the future perfection of the race, through a superior fatherhood and motherhood" (*Notes on Walt Whitman as Poet and Person* [New York: American News Co., 1867], p. 28; as quoted in Aspiz, p. 195).
58. As quoted in Thomas B. Harned, "Walt Whitman and Oratory," *The Complete Writings of Walt Whitman*, ed. Richard Maurice Bucke et al. (New York: G. P. Putnam's Sons, 1902), vol. 8, p. 245.
59. Chalfin's analysis of Whitman's philosophy of history, which is derived mainly from his later prose, especially *Democratic Vistas*, supports this reading of his millennial caste of mind in the years after the Civil War. Chalfin concludes that the theory of personalism outlined in *Democratic Vistas* was "Whitman's definition of a final stage of the dialectical process. . . . Personalism is the culmination of world cultures, even as democracy is the culmination of previous political systems" (*Walt Whitman's Philosophy of History*, pp. 214–15).
60. *Lectures on Revivals of Religion*, p. ix.
61. Ibid., p. xi.
62. As quoted in William G. McLoughlin, Introduction, *Lectures on Revivals of Religion*, p. xxix.
63. *Lectures to Professing Christians* (Oberlin, Ohio: E. J. Goodrich, 1880), p. 341.
64. "The Nature, Importance, and Means of Eminent Holiness," *The American National Preacher* 10 (June-July 1835), 195.
65. Ibid., p. 198.
66. *The Way of Holiness* (Putney, Vt.: J. H. Noyes and Co., 1838), p. 36.
67. *The Liberator* 11 (October 15, 1841), p. 167
68. Timothy L. Smith, *Revivalism and Social Reform in Mid-Nineteenth-Century America* (New York: Abingdon Press, 1957), p. 7.
69. Timothy L. Smith, *Called Unto Holiness; The Story of the Nazarenes: The Formative Years* (Kansas City, Mo.: Nazarene Publishing House, 1962), p. 11.
70. Ibid.
71. "The Millenium" [sic], 8 (July 1846), p. 199.
72. "Republicanism the True Form of Government," 9 (March 1847), p. 74.
73. Ibid., p. 76.

74. *The Principles of Nature*, p. 782. In *The Philosophy of Spiritual Intercourse*, Davis closes on a similar note: "Ignorance, bigotry, skepticism, fanaticism, intolerance, spiritual depression, and all slavery, the great evils which now beset mankind—are rapidly dispersing; they shall recede entirely from the earth, never again to enslave and degrade humanity. This world of thought and affection, and of social relations, shall be progressively purified, until there shall be unfolded a new heaven and a new earth wherein dwelleth righteousness" (p. 176).

75. *Essays, First Series*, pp. 48–49.

76. M. Wynn Thomas describes the effect of emerging urban-commerical capitalism upon antebellum culture in general and Whitman's poetry in particular in *The Lunar Light of Whitman's Poetry* (Cambridge: Harvard Univ. Press, 1987). For a discussion of the threat posed by the Civil War to the public faith of Whitman and other Americans, see George B. Hutchinson, *The Ecstatic Whitman: Literary Shamanism and the Crisis of the Union* (Columbus: Ohio State Univ. Press, 1986), pp. 1–25.

77. *The Patriot Citizen* (Hanover, N.H., 1842), as quoted in John R. Bodo, *The Protestant Clergy and Public Issues, 1812–1848* (Princeton: Princeton Univ. Press, 1954), p. 53.

78. "The Necessity of Education in a Republican Government," *Lectures on Education* (Boston: Ide & Dutton, 1855), p. 124.

79. Ibid., p. 157.

80. "Human Government," *Lectures on Systematic Theology*, ed. J.H. Fairchild (Oberlin, Ohio: E. J. Goodrich, 1878), p. 222.

81. "The Nature, Importance, and Means of Eminent Holiness," pp. 202, 217.

82. "Spiritual Freedom: Discourse Preached at the Annual Election, May 26, 1830," *Works of William E. Channing* (Boston: American Unitarian Association, 1888), pp. 183–84.

83. Ibid., p. 174.

84. "Introduction," *The United States Magazine and Democratic Review* in *Social Theories of Jacksonian Democracy*, ed. Blau, pp. 28–29, 32–33.

85. "Some Plain Paragraphs, For Plain People" in Thomas L. Brasher, *Whitman as Editor of the Brooklyn Daily Eagle* (Detroit: Wayne State Univ. Press, 1970), p. 103.

86. "Legislation and Morality," *Walt Whitman of the New York Aurora*, p. 100.

87. Florence Bernstein Freedman, *Walt Whitman Looks at the Schools* (New York: Columbia Univ. Press, 1950), p. 126.

88. "Force in Government," *Gathering of the Forces*, vol. I, p. 55.

89. "You Cannot Legislate Men Into Virtue," *Gathering of the Forces*, vol. I, p. 60.

90. Ibid., p. 59.

91. "Abolition," *Gathering of the Forces*, vol. I, p. 193.

92. "Self-Reliance," *Essays, First Series*, p. 30.

93. Ibid., p. 42.

94. Ibid., p. 37.

95. *Essays, Second Series*, pp. 127–28.

96. Ibid., pp. 128–29.

97. Ibid., p. 129.

98. Sydney Ahlstrom, *A Religious History of the American People* (New Haven: Yale Univ. Press, 1972), p. 476; A. Leland Jamison, "Religions on the Christian Perimeter," *The Shaping of American Religion*, ed. A. Leland Jamison and James Ward Smith (Princeton: Princeton Univ. Press, 1961), pp. 197–98.

99. *The Solitary Singer*, p. 13.

100. Ibid., pp. 7, 8, 22, & 140.

101. Floyd Stovall discusses Whitman's reading of Coleridge and Carlyle in *The Foreground of "Leaves of Grass,"* pp. 104–12.

102. *Sartor-Resartus, The Works of Thomas Carlyle,* vol. I (New York: AMS Press, 1974), pp. 155, 179.

103. John Townsend Trowbridge, *My Own Story: With Recollections of Noted Persons* (Boston: Houghton Mifflin, 1903), pp. 366–67.

104. *The Freedom of Man in Myth* (Nashville: Vanderbilt Univ. Press, 1968), p. 110.

4. Style: From Silence to Symbol

1. The division of the Christian mystical way into the stages of Purgation, Illumination, and Union first appears in the writings of the Syrian monk Dionysius the Areopagite (writing between 475 and 525). Much of his mystical vocabulary was adopted by later contemplatives, including the Franciscan Saint Bonaventure (1221–1274) whose explanation of the mystical stages strongly influenced the important mystical schools of fourteenth-century Germany and England, thus permanently establishing the three stages as a staple of Christian mystical literature. For further discussion, see Evelyn Underhill, *Mysticism* (London: Methuen and Company, 1911), pp. 167–75; F. C. Happold, *Mysticism* (Baltimore: Penguin, 1970), pp. 56–99; and Louis Dupre, *The Other Dimension* (New York: Doubleday, 1972), pp. 523–45. As these scholars indicate, the stages provide a helpful way of understanding the Christian mystic's development, but they cannot be rigidly applied to each mystic. I am not arguing that the stages provide a chronology of Whitman's spiritual maturation but simply that his mysticism contains corresponding elements.

2. Thomas, *The Lunar Light of Whitman's Poetry* (Cambridge: Harvard Univ. Press, 1987), especially chapter 2.

3. *Practical Mysticism* (New York: E. P. Dutton, 1915), p. 24.

4. Ibid., p. 84.

5. Ibid., p. 99.

6. Ibid., pp. 95, 97.

7. Ibid., p. 91.

8. C. F. Kelley, *The Spirit of Love* (New York: Harper and Row, 1951), p. 83.

9. Happold, *Mysticism,* p. 371.

10. "Whitman and the Phrenologists: The Divine Body and the Sensuous Soul," *PMLA* 89 (January 1974), 17–23.

11. Underhill, *Practical Mysticism,* pp. 90, 105–7. A study that in many ways parallels my use of the phenomenology of religion to interpret Whitman is Catherine Albanese's study of American Transcendentalism, *Corresponding Motion: Transcendental Religion and the New America* (Philadelphia: Temple Univ. Press, 1977), which makes extensive use of phenomenological scholarship to elucidate the religious world view and psychological dynamics of the correspondential vision. Albanese also discusses how the Transcendentalists forged a new vocabulary to relate the inherited theory and symbols of correspondence, with their assumption of a static universe, to nineteenth-century America's belief in science and progress. Similarly, at the end of this chapter and at later points, I consider Whitman's effort to adapt traditional religious symbols to his vision of evolutionary and historical progress.

12. *Symbolism and American Literature* (Chicago: Univ. of Chicago Press, 1953).

13. Miller, *Walt Whitman's Poetry: A Psychological Journey* (New York: Houghton Mifflin, 1968); Black, *Whitman's Journeys into Chaos* (Princeton: Princeton Univ. Press, 1975).

14. See Paul Tillich, *The Dynamics of Faith,* (New York: Harper & Row, 1958), chapter V.

15. In contrast to Christianity which has taken most of its symbols from history, the *Leaves* draws its symbols mainly—although by no means exclusively—from the realm of nature; and when it does employ historical symbols, it takes them from American history. Feeling that his readers were culturally alienated from the Bible not only because of its antiquated world view but also because of the temporal and geographical remoteness of its setting, Whitman wanted to provide them with new symbols that were as immediate and American as Abraham Lincoln or the calamus grass that surrounded the pond waters in the northeastern states.

In turning to nature as his primary source of symbols, Whitman could, in theory, pick any object or event. Since he believed that God was immanent throughout nature, any part of it, rightly perceived, was symbolic of divinity. However, Whitman felt that some natural phenomena spoke to the soul more effectively than others. As he states in "To the Sun-Set Breeze," "Thou hast, O Nature! elements! utterance to my heart beyond the rest—and this [sunset breeze] is of them." In addition to creating some new symbols such as the calamus grass, Whitman's imagination was also arrested by several "privileged" segments of the cosmos—the stars, the waters, the earth, the sun, the moon, the seasons, the night—which the religious imagination has repeatedly selected as the natural phenomena which best reveal certain important spiritual truths. In the *Leaves*, these natural symbols express the same general meanings they have had in other religions. Yet Whitman consciously invests some of these symbols with significant levels of new meaning because, in attempting to reconcile reason and religion, he recognized the need to adapt these traditional symbols to the evolutionary world view of modern science. Seen from the perspective of the history of religions, this effort to modernize traditional religious symbols is perhaps Whitman's most significant achievement.

16. It is a partial illustration because while I draw upon Eliade's phenomenology of aquatic symbolism and consider Whitman's use of this symbol throughout the *Leaves*, I do not at this point attempt an extended analysis of any particular instance of Whitman's symbolism in an effort to intuit his unstated meaning. In chapter 6, I do make a brief phenomenological analysis of the symbolic meaning of the sea in "Out of the Cradle Endlessly Rocking."

17. *Patterns in Comparative Religion* (Cleveland: World Publishing Co., 1958), p. 212.

5. The Principal Poem

1. Emerson's letter to Whitman, *Critical Essays on Walt Whitman*, ed. James Woodress (Boston: G. K. Hall, 1983), p. 17; Thoreau's letter to Harrison Blake, *Critical Essays*, p. 40.

2. Chase, *Walt Whitman Reconsidered* (New York: William Sloane Associates, 1955), pp. 58–59; Miller, *Walt Whitman's Poetry* (Boston: Houghton Mifflin, 1968), pp. 85–114; Black, *Whitman's Journeys into Chaos* (Princeton: Princeton Univ. Press, 1975), pp. 88–118; Cavitch, *My Soul and I: The Inner Life of Walt Whitman* (Boston: Beacon Press, 1985), pp. 45–71; Miller, *A Critical Guide to "Leaves of Grass"* (Chicago: Univ. of Chicago Press, 1957), pp. 6–35; *Walt Whitman's "Leaves of Grass": The First (1855) Edition*, ed. Cowley (New York: Viking Press, 1959), pp. xv & xxii; Middlebrook, *Walt Whitman and Wallace Stevens* (Ithaca: Cornell Univ. Press, 1974), pp. 72–73, 93, & 103; Hutchinson, *The Ecstatic Whitman* (Columbus: Ohio State Univ. Press, 1986), pp. 67–94.

3. The effort to analyze the poem in terms of a logical or thematic structure began with Carl F. Strauch. "The Structure of Walt Whitman's 'Song of Myself,'" *English Journal* 27 (September 1938), 597–607. Other notable interpretations of the poem's structure include Miller, *A Critical Guide*, pp. 6–35; *Walt Whitman's "Leaves of Grass,"* ed. Cowley, pp. 17–20; Earl Tannenbaum, "Patterns in Whitman's 'Song of

Myself'," *CLA Journal* 6 (Sept. 1962), 44–49; F. DeWolfe Miller, "The Partitive Studies of 'Song of Myself'," *American Transcendental Quarterly* 12 (Fall 1971), 11–17; J. Albert Robbins, "The Narrative Form of 'Song of Myself,'" *American Transcendental Quarterly* 12 (Fall 1971), 17–20; E. Fred Carlisle, *The Uncertain Self: Whitman's Drama of Identity* (East Lansing: Michigan State Univ. Press, 1973), pp. 177–204; Alfred S. Reid, "The Structure of 'Song of Myself' Reconsidered," *Southern Humanities Review* 8 (Fall 1974), 507–14; and Ivan Marki, *The Trial of the Poet* (New York: Columbia Univ. Press, 1976), pp. 91–227.

Strauch divides the poem into five parts: 1–18, 19–25, 26–38, 39–41, 42–52; Miller suggests seven: 1–5, 6–16, 17–32, 33–37, 38–43, 44–49, 50–52; Cowley sees nine: 1–4, 5, 6–19, 20–25, 26–29, 30–38, 39–41, 42–50, 51–52; Tannenbaum, F. D. Miller, and Robbins argue for five, but each differs as to where they occur: 1–6, 7–15, 16–33, 34–42, 43–52 (Tannenbaum); 1–7, 8–23, 24–38, 39–47, 48–52 (Miller); 1–5, 6–32, 33–38, 39–50, 51–52 (Robbins); Carlisle divides the poem into six stages: 1–5, 6–17, 18–32, 33–37, 38–51, 52; Reid cites five: 1–7, 8–19, 20–25, 26–47, 48–52; and Marki makes nine: 1–4, 5–7, 8–16, 17–19, 19–24, 24–32, 33–38, 38–50, 51–52.

In response to absence of agreement about the poem's structure, some critics have argued that it has no traditional logical, thematic, or narrative form; for example, see Roy Harvey Pearce, *The Continuity of American Poetry* (Princeton: Princeton Univ. Press, 1961), pp. 74–75, and V. K. Chari, *Walt Whitman in the Light of Vedantic Mysticism* (Lincoln: Univ. of Nebraska Press, 1965), p. 124. Instead of looking for a structural pattern, a number of recent critics, following the lead of Thomas Rountree, have chosen to examine Whitman's strategies for involving the reader: Rountree, "Whitman's Indirect Expression and Its Application to 'Song of Myself'," *PMLA* 73 (1958), 549–55; David Robinson, "The Poetry of Dialogue in 'Song of Myself'," *American Poetry & Poetics* 1 (Fall 1974), 34–50; Donald D. Kummings, "The Vernacular Hero in Whitman's 'Song of Myself,'" *Walt Whitman Review* 23 (March 1977), 23– 34; and George Y. Trail, "'Song of Myself': Events in the Microstructure," *Walt Whitman Review* 25 (September 1979), 106–13.

There are, however, two strong reasons for continuing the above efforts at a partitive analysis. First, the disagreements about the poem's structure are fewer and less significant than initially appears to be the case. Most critics see transitions occurring between sections 5 and 8, between 15 and 19, 32 and 34, 37 and 39, and 48 and 51. This is a goodly amount of agreement, especially given that the poem's form is organic not architectonic, so one movement does not end and another begin at a specific point. Rather, all the themes are present in most parts of the poem, with each receiving emphasis during a particular movement and then gradually subsiding with the concomitant emergence of another. Given this type of thematic development, one would not expect unanimity about exactly when one theme supersedes another. Second, analysis of *how meaning is developed* in a literary work requires discussing it in terms of some pattern. The choice is not a matter of seeing or not seeing a pattern but simply of how clear one makes the terms of the discussion. Accordingly, I have chosen to discuss the poem explicitly as consisting of seven movements: 1–6, 7–17, 18–22, 23–32, 33–38, 39–45, 46–52.

4. In discussing "Song of Myself," as throughout my study, I cite the final edition. Whitman's alterations after the 1855 version were relatively minor (especially in light of his lifelong reworking of the *Leaves*) and never substantially altered either the poem's structure or its thematic meaning. The passages I cite are either identical with the 1855 text or differ from it in relatively minor respects, for example, the alteration of a word or brief phrase or emendations of words, spelling, punctuation, and typography. If I do cite a passage that, in my judgment, sufficiently differs from the 1855 text as possibly to allow for conflicting readings, I have also provided the original version in a footnote.

5. The phrases cited in this sentence were not in the 1855 edition. Sometime after 1871 Whitman added the following 8 lines after line 5:

My tongue, every atom of my blood, form'd from this soil, this air,
    Born here of parents born here from parents the same, and their parents the same,
    I, now thirty-seven years old in perfect health begin,
    Hoping to cease not till death.

    Creeds and schools in abeyance,
    Retiring back a while sufficed at what they are, but never forgotten,
    I harbor for good or bad, I permit to speak at every hazard,
    Nature without check with original energy.

These lines help to clarify and emphasize Whitman's mystical orientation and prophetic intentions, but they do not alter the basic tenor of the poem's opening movement.

6. In the 1855 text the second line read: "As God comes a loving bedfellow and sleeps at my side all night and close on the peep of the day." In 1860 the line appeared as "As the hugging and loving Bed-fellow sleeps at my side through the night, and withdraws at the peep of the day"; and in 1871 Whitman added "with stealthy tread."

7. "Some Lines from Walt Whitman," *Poetry and the Age* (New York: Alfred A. Knopf, 1953); rep. *Leaves of Grass: Norton Critical Edition*, p. 883.

8. Antebellum Christians had a ready stock of biblical passages to draw upon for their martial imagery. For instance, Paul conceived of the individual Christian life as a moral battle, urging Timothy to "wage the good warfare, holding faith and a good conscience" (I Tim. 1:19) and the church at Ephesus to "Put on the whole armor of God" (Eph. 6:13). In Revelations John predicted that the forces of Satan "will make war on the Lamb, and the Lamb will conquer them (Rev. 17:14) and recounts how he saw "the beast and the kings of the earth with their armies gathered to make war against him who sits upon the horse and against his army" (Rev. 19:19). Such passages had a special relevance to millennial-minded Christian leaders who were encouraging strenuous moral effort in the churches' organizations for evangelization and reform. Edward Beecher cautioned his readers: "he who reads and believes the word of God should . . . arouse himself at once, gird on his armor . . . for who can tell how near the day may be, even the GREAT DAY OF THE BATTLE OF GOD ALMIGHTY?" ("The Nature, Importance, and Means of Eminent Holiness Throughout the Church," *American National Preacher* 10 [June-July 1835], 206). In declaring that the *Liberator* would also be an organ for the doctrine of non-resistance, Garrison condemned existing governments as agents of "brute force" and called his readers to become citizens of the kingdom of the Lord who would participate in the "government of the law of love" and be "clad in the whole armor of God" (*The Liberator* 7 [December 15, 1837], p. 203). William Boardman described the Protestant Evangelical Alliance as presenting the "imposing spectacle of a single front, and the invincible strength of an undivided line of battle" (*The Higher Christian Life* [New York: D. Appleton and Co., 1859], p. 228). In his conflict with the better educated, more conservative seminary professors who opposed his new methods, Finney once compared the revival movement to a battlefield and his opponents to superannuated generals: "Those fathers who have the training of our young ministers are good men, but they are ancient men, men of another age and stamp, from what is needed in these days of excitement. . . . And it is as dangerous and ridiculous for our theological professors, who are withdrawn from the field of conflict, to be allowed to dictate, in regard to measures and movements of the church, as it would be for a general to sit in his bed-chamber and attempt to order a battle" (*Lectures on Revivals of Religion* [Cambridge: Harvard Univ. Press, 1960], p. 192).

9. In Luke 14:21 the master of the house instructs his servant: "Go out quickly

into the streets and lanes of the city, and bring in hither the poor, and the maimed, and the halt and the blind"; see also Luke 15:2, "and the Pharisees and scribes murmured, saying, This man receiveth sinners, and eateth with them." See Bruce A. Bergquist, *Walt Whitman and the Bible: Language, Echoes, Images, Allusions and Ideas* (Dissertation, Univ. of Nebraska, 1979), pp. 180–81.

10. Coming immediately after this passage in the 1855 text were the following two lines: "Thruster holding me tight and that I hold tight! / We hurt each other as the bridegroom and the bride hurt each other." Deleted in 1866, these two lines (discussed in chapter 7) are of possible relevance to Whitman's "Calamus" theme, but their presence or absence does not significantly change the meaning of this part of the poem.

11. The 1855 version of this passage read:

I hear the trained soprano . . . she convulses me like the climax of my love-grip;
The orchestra whirls me wider than Uranus flies,
It wrenches unnamable ardors from my breast,
It throbs me to gulps of the farthest down horror,
It sails me. . . . I dab with bare feet. . . . they are licked by the indolent waves,
I am exposed. . . . cut by bitter and poisoned hail,
Steeped amid honeyed morphine. . . . my windpipe squeezed in the fakes of death.

The most important later changes were the explicit comparison introduced in the first line, which creates greater parallelism between the passages dealing with seeing, hearing, and feeling, and the deletion of the puzzling fourth line, a change which gives the passage a more positive tone but does not seem to alter its essential meaning.

12. The idea that sexual excitement culminates in spiritual ecstasy receives further development in "Children of Adam" where Whitman repeatedly depicts sexual experience as a form of religious experience; see chapter 7.

13. For more information on these three historical episodes which Whitman incorporates into "Song of Myself," see Blodgett and Bradley's footnotes to ll. 832, 875, & 899 (pp. 66–69).

14. After 1871 Whitman added this line: "A few large stars overhead, silent and mournful shining."

15. In 1866 Whitman sharpened the transition between what became sections 37 and 38 by dropping two lines at the end of the catalog of suffering in 37 ("I rise extatic [sic] through all, and sweep with the true gravitation, / The whirling and whirling is elemental within me.") and adding the new line at the beginning of 38, "Enough! enough! enough!" The end of section 38 originally read:

Eleves I Salute you,
I see the approach of your numberless gangs. . . . I see you understand yourselves
    and me,
And know that they who have eyes are divine, and the blind and lame are equally
    divine,
And that my steps drag behind yours yet go before them,
And are aware how I am with you no more than I am with everybody.

In 1871 Whitman further emphasized his role as teacher by shortening the passage to simply read: "Eleves, I salute you! come forward / Continue your annotations, continue your questionings."

16. Many of the early Transcendentalists, including Emerson, Thoreau, Alcott, and Francis, spoke of creating a "world bible" consisting of selections from the scriptures of the East and West. Theodore Parker left unfinished a serious comparative study of world religions aimed at showing their progressive evolution toward one perfect religion. These interests were continued by later Transcendentalists, culminating in three

works of the 1870s: Moncure Conway's *The Sacred Anthology: A Book of Ethnical Scriptures* (New York: H. Holt & Co., 1874), the best of the attempts to edit a world bible; James Freeman Clarke's *Ten Great Religions: An Essay in Comparative Theology* (Boston: James R. Osgood, 1871), a popular study which treated non-Christian faiths as imperfect religions to be eventually replaced by the perfection of Protestant Christianity; Samuel Johnson's *Oriental Religions and Their Relation to Universal Religion*, 3 vols. Boston: J. R. Osgood, 1872–85), a study of the religions of China, India, and Persia which, like Parker's uncompleted work, viewed them as advancing toward a complete religion. For a full discussion of this subject, see Carl T. Jackson, *The Oriental Religions and American Thought* (Westport, Conn.: Greenwood Press, 1981), especially pp. 45–84 and 103–40.

Like Parker and Johnson, Whitman believed that religious history was progressing toward a perfect faith. Earlier religions were the creations of partially developed souls, and a more developed soul could comprehend and transcend all the faiths of the past: "I say to you that all forms of religion, without excepting one, any age, any land, are but mediums, temporary yet necessary, fitted to the lower mass-ranges of perception of the race—part of its infant school—and that the developed soul passes through one or all of them, to the clear homogeneous atmosphere above them" (*Workshop*, p. 44). As one such "developed soul," Whitman presents himself in "Song of Myself" as the first prophet of a new religion which included and improved upon the spiritual insights of the past.

17. Originally this passage was even more audacious, having a third line (deleted in 1871) which read: "The most they offer for mankind and eternity less than a spirt of my own seminal wet." Perhaps Whitman felt this line was too cavalier in its dismissal of earlier religions, but it also has considerable merit, being both thematically appropriate and full of condensed wit. Elsewhere in the poem Whitman emphasizes the parental and procreative aspects of his prophetic role, even likening his poetic production to sexual ejaculation, so in addition to the line's literal meaning, Whitman exploits the poem's ongoing sexual symbolism, claiming that a "spirt" of his semen, i.e., a part of his new religious vision which affirms human perfectibility and the soul's ongoing development toward divinity in the afterlife, offers more to his readers than all previous religions which had less exalted views of human nature and immortality.

18. *The Sacred and the Profane* (New York: Harper & Row, 1959), p. 138.

19. See Joseph Beaver, *Walt Whitman—Poet of Science* (New York: King's Crown Press, 1951), pp. 71–72; Beaver's study, still the standard discussion of Whitman's use of science, also discusses previous scholarship. For a discussion of Laplace's nebular theory and the development of evolutionary geology and pre-Darwinian biology, see William C. Dampier, *A History of Science* (Cambridge: Cambridge Univ. Press, 1948), pp. 443–44 and 270–76.

20. There is a pleasant irony in Whitman's description of an "expanding, always expanding" universe, for surely he spoke more wisely than he knew. Contrary to what the poetry implies, the idea was not part of contemporary astronomical theory. Yet Whitman's error was a *felix culpa*, for today the notion of an expanding universe is widely maintained. The hypothesis is based upon the fact that light emitted by a receding object appears more red than the light from a stationary source; and the light from the stars of distant galaxies exhibits this red shift. See E. B. Uvarov and D. R. Churchman, *A Dictionary of Science*, 4th rev. ed. (Baltimore: Penguin, 1971), p. 116 and the articles in Section IV, *Theories of the Universe*, ed. Milton K. Munitz, (Glencoe, Ill.: Free Press, 1957), pp. 271–429. Section 45 also contains a second error. Whitman depicts the sun as one member of a binary star system ("My sun has his sun and round him obediently wheels"), but the sun is not a binary but a single star. There is no existing evidence for attributing these mistakes to Whitman's sources, for these ideas are

not in any of the astronomy books listed in Beaver's bibliography. Significant as these two errors are, they discredit neither Beaver's nor my thesis that scientific theory plays an important functional role in Whitman's poetry, but they do indicate that Whitman's understanding of contemporary cosmology was less precise than Beaver suggests.

21. See Dampier, *A History of Science*, pp. 434–35; also M. A. Hoskin, "Herschel, William," *Dictionary of Scientific Biography* (New York: Scribner's, 1972), vol. VI, pp. 328–36.

22. (New York: Greeley & McElrath, 1848), p. 30.

23. *The Sacred and the Profane*, pp. 118–21, and *Patterns in Comparative Religions* (Cleveland: World Publishing Co., 1958), pp. 38–41 & 109–11.

6. Anticipations of Immortality

1. *Walt Whitman: The Critical Heritage*, ed. Milton Hindus (London: Routledge & Kegan Paul, 1971), p. 39.

2. Major analyses which read "Out of the Cradle" as affirming the finality of death include Leo Spitzer, "*Explication de Texte* Applied to Walt Whitman's Poem 'Out of the Cradle Endlessly Rocking'," *ELH: Journal of English Literary History* 16 (September 1949), 229–49; Charles C. Walcutt, "Whitman's 'Out of the Cradle Endlessly Rocking'," *College English* 10 (February 1949), 277–79; Clark Griffith, "Sex and Death: The Significance of Whitman's 'Calamus' Themes," *Philological Quarterly* 39 (January 1960), 18–38; Stephen Whicher, "Whitman's Awakening to Death: Toward a Biographical Reading of 'Out of the Cradle Endlessly Rocking'," *Studies in Romanticism* 1 (Autumn 1961), 9–27; Roy Harvey Pearce, "Introduction," *Leaves of Grass: Facsimile Edition of the 1860 Text* (Ithaca: Cornell Univ. Press, 1961), pp. 39–47; Paul Fussell, Jr., "Whitman's Curious Warble: Reminscence and Reconciliation," *The Presence of Walt Whitman*, ed. R. W. B. Lewis (New York: Columbia Univ. Press, 1962), pp. 28–51; Richard Chase, "'Out of the Cradle' as Romance," *The Presence of Walt Whitman*, pp. 52–71; Horace M. Kallen, "Of Love, Death, and Walt Whitman," *Walt Whitman Review* 15 (September 1969), 171–80, rep. in *Leaves of Grass: Norton Critical Edition* (New York: W. W. Norton, 1973), pp. 979–90.

The articles of Whicher, Pearce, and Kallen also interpret Whitman's "Lilacs" elegy as denying immortality, as do Richard P. Adams, "Whitman's 'Lilacs' and the Tradition of Pastoral Elegy," *PMLA* 72 (June 1957), 479–87, and Evelyn J. Hinz, "Whitman's 'Lilacs': The Power of Elegy," *Bucknell Review* 20 (Fall 1972), 35–54. Several psychoanalytic critics see no belief in immortality in "Out of the Cradle," "Lilacs," or elsewhere in the *Leaves*: Edwin Haviland Miller, *Walt Whitman's Poetry* (Boston: Houghton Mifflin, 1968), especially pp. 173–86 and 186–98; Stephen Black, *Whitman's Journeys into Chaos* (Princeton: Princeton Univ. Press, 1975), pp. 66–76 and 234–44; David Cavitch, *My Soul and I* (Boston: Beacon Press, 1985), pp. 145–53 and 162–69. In the *Uncertain Self* (East Lansing: Michigan State Univ. Press, 1973), pp. 142–75, E. Fred Carlisle argues that some of Whitman's poems do affirm personal immortality but that this is not true of his two major poems on death.

A much smaller body of criticism reads the Lincoln elegy and "Out of the Cradle" as expressing a belief in personal immortality. Both Allen (*The Solitary Singer*, [New York: New York Univ. Press, 1967], pp. 231–36 and 353–57) and Asselineau (*The Evolution of Walt Whitman* [Cambridge: Harvard Univ. Press, 1962], vol. II, 61–68) do, but they do not provide close readings. Allen and Charles T. Davis make a pithy analysis of "Out of the Cradle" as resolving itself with a belief in immortality in *Walt Whitman's Poems* (New York: New York Univ. Press, 1955), pp. 164–67. In his *Critical Guide to "Leaves of Grass"* (Chicago: Univ. of Chicago Press, 1957), pp. 104–10 and 111–19, James E. Miller, Jr., discusses both poems as concluding with an affirmation of immortality.

3. When the death poems and "Calamus" are properly interpreted, then "As I Ebb'd with the Ocean of Life," which is the other major poem cited as evidence of the skeptical or tragic Whitman, appears not as a symptom of Whitman's loss of faith but as a confession of his inability to do justice to the nature of his poetic undertaking. Fully cognizant of the mystery and grandeur of the divine nature, Whitman describes his effort to build bridges between the natural world and its transcendent source as little more than debris washed upon the shoreline—a strikingly apt image, in terms of the *Leaves'* recurrent aquatic symbolism, of Whitman's fear of failing to create lasting images for mediating between the natural world and its transcendental source.

4. I have quoted from the final edition. These lines were revised, apparently chiefly for stylistic reasons, but the idea of immortality is clearly present in these passages as they appeared in the 1860 *Leaves*. The following quotations are from the 1860 *Facsimile Edition*:

> O the beautiful touch of Death, soothing and benumbing a few moments for
> reasons;
> O that of myself, discharging my excrementitious body, to be burned, or ren-
> dered to powder, or buried,
> My real body doubtless left to me for other spheres.
>
> ("Poems of Joys")

> How can the real body ever die, and be buried?

> Of your real body, and any man's or woman's real body, item for item, it will
> elude the hands of the corpse-cleaners, and pass to fitting spheres, carrying
> what has accrued to it from the moment of birth to the moment of death.
>
> ("Proto-Leaf")
> I feel like one who has done his work—I progress on,
> The unknown sphere, more real than I dreamed, more direct, darts awakening
> rays about me—*So long*!
>
> ("So Long!")

5. After this passage the original version contained these lines which were deleted in 1881:

> Oh a word! O what is my destination?
> O I fear it is henceforth chaos!
> O how joys, dreads, convolutions, human shapes, and all shapes, spring as from
> graves around me!
> O phantoms! You cover all the land, and all the sea!
> O I cannot see in the dimness whether you smile or frown upon me;
> O vapor, a look, a word! O well-beloved!
> O you dear women's and men's phantoms!
>
> (*Facsimile Edition*)

It is frequently argued that this passage is crucial proof of Whitman's new metaphysical questioning and acceptance of the tragic reality of death in the middle period, and its excision is seen as evidence of Whitman's later effort to cover over his period of lapsed faith. Apart from the obvious difficulty of simply making a convincing interpretation of these lines, there are two crucial weaknesses with this position. First, the lines are not central to the poem's resolution. As is usually suggested, they do seem to intensify the child-adult poet's expression of fear or doubt, but their presence or absence does not alter the poem's conclusion. Second, if Whitman began his process of revision in the late '60s and this passage was so clearly antithetical to his newly embraced faith, then it is unlikely that he would have waited for over a decade to make this change.

A more probable explanation is that the passage is not crucial to the poem and Whitman dropped it to achieve greater economy, clarity, and unity of tone.

6. Allen, *Solitary Singer*, p. 332.

7. "Eulogy," *A Memorial of Abraham Lincoln*, compiled by Boston City Council (Boston: J. E. Farwell 1865), p. 91.

8. *The Martyr President* (New York: Carleton, 1865), pp. 10–11.

9. *In Memoriam*, compiled by Buffalo citizens (Buffalo: Matthews & Warren, 1865), p. 29.

10. Ibid., p. 13.

11. Ibid., pp. 20, 21.

12. "The Assassination of President Lincoln," *The Nation's Loss: A Poem on the Life and Death of the Hon. Abraham Lincoln* (Newark: N. J.: F. Starruch, 1866), pp. 10–11.

13. Reverend Dr. Allen of Northampton, Mass. in B. F. Morris, ed., *Memorial Record of the Nation's Tribute to Abraham Lincoln* (Washington, D.C.: W. H. & O. H. Morrison, 1865), p. 220.

14. "The Death of Lincoln," *Lincoln and the Poets*, ed. William W. Betts, Jr. (Pittsburgh: Univ. of Pittsburgh Press, 1965), p. 4.

15. "Abraham Lincoln," *The Complete Works of Ralph Waldo Emerson*, vol. XI (Cambridge: Riverside Press, 1904), pp. 336–37.

16. Buffalo citizens, *In Memoriam*, p. 23.

17. Ibid., p. 27.

18. *Nation's Tribute*, p. 220.

19. Ibid., p. 230.

20. Allen, *Solitary Singer*, p. 328.

21. *The Gathering of the Forces*, eds. Cleveland Rodgers and John Black (New York: G. P. Putnam's Sons 1920), vol. I, pp. 206, 209, 210–11.

22. In a similar manner, Thoreau also designates a swamp as a holy place, perceiving it as the symbol of the spiritual power that informs nature: "I enter a swamp as a sacred place, a sanctum sanctorum. There is the strength, the marrow, of nature" ("Walking").

7. The Ecstasy and Quiet of Religious Love

1. Quoted in Edwin Haviland Miller, *A Century of Whitman Criticism* (Bloomington: Indiana Univ. Press, 1969), pp. 5–6.

2. Unsigned reviews in the *Critic* (April 1, 1856) and the *Christian Examiner* (June 1856); as quoted in Milton Hindus, ed., *Walt Whitman: The Critical Heritage* (New York: Barnes and Noble, 1971), pp. 56 & 63.

3. See Numa Praetorius, "Storm over Whitman," in *Homosexuality and Creative Genius*, ed. Hendrik Ruitenbeek (New York: Astor-Honor 1967), pp. 128, 130–31.

4. Miller, *A Critical Guide to Leaves of Grass* (Chicago: Univ. of Chicago Press, 1967), pp. 52–79; Freyre, "Camerado Whitman," trans. Benjamin M. Woodbridge, Jr., in *Walt Whitman Abroad*, ed. Gay Wilson Allen (Syracuse, N. Y.: Syracuse Univ. Press, 1955), pp. 223–34; Thomas Crawley, *The Structure of Leaves of Grass* (Austin: Univ. of Texas Press, 1970), pp. 103– 20.

5. Arvin, *Whitman* (New York: Macmillan, 1938), pp. 272–78; Van Doren, *The Private Reader* (New York: H. Holt & Co., 1942), p. 82; Griffith, "Sex and Death: The Significance of Whitman's *Calamus* Themes," *Philological Quarterly* 39 (Jan. 1960), 18–38; Whicher, "Whitman's Awakening to Death: Toward a Biographical Reading of 'Out of Cradle Endlessly Rocking'," in *The Presence of Walt Whitman*, ed. R. W. B. Lewis (New York: Columbia Univ. Press, 1962), pp. 1–27; Asselineau, *The Evolution of Walt Whitman* (Cambridge: Harvard Univ. Press, 1960), vol. I, pp.

108–28; Allen, *Walt Whitman as Man, Poet, and Legend* (Carbondale: Southern Illinois Univ. Press, 1961), pp. 144–45 and *The Solitary Singer* (New York: New York Univ. Press, 1967), pp. 222–26 and 253–57; Cowley, ed. *The Works of Walt Whitman* (New York: Funk & Wagnalls, 1968), vol. I, pp. 12–21; Miller, *Walt Whitman's Poetry* (Boston: Houghton Mifflin, 1968), pp. 140–70; Golden, ed., *Walt Whitman's Blue Book* (New York: New York Public Library, 1968), vol. II, pp. xxii–xxvii.

6. These critics tend to see the homosexual theme as central not only to "Calamus" but also to other poems and sequences, especially "Song of Myself," "Sleepers," and "Drum Taps." See Martin, "Whitman's 'Song of Myself': Homosexual Dream and Vision," *Partisan Review*, 42 (1975), 80–96; Cady, "Not Happy in the Capitol: Homosexuality and the 'Calamus' Poems," *American Studies* 19 (1978), 5–22; Martin, *The Homosexual Tradition in American Poetry* (Austin: Univ. of Texas Press, 1979), pp. 3–89; Keller, "The *Whitman* Issue in American Literature: A Review Essay," *Texas Studies in Literature and Language* 22 (Winter 1980), 575–86; and "Walt Whitman and the Queening of America," *American Poetry* 1 (Fall 1983), 4–26; Killingsworth, "Sentimentality and Homosexuality in Whitman's 'Calamus'," *ESQ: Journal of the American Renaissance* 29 (1983), 144–53; Helms, "Whitman Revised," *Études Anglaises* 37 (1984), 257–71; Cady, "'Drum Taps' and Nineteenth-Century Male Homosexual Literature," in *Walt Whitman: Here and Now*, ed. Joann Krieg (Westport, Conn.: Greenwood Press, 1985), pp. 49–59. (Earlier versions of the articles by Killingsworth and Helms also appear in *Walt Whitman: Here and Now*, a volume containing papers delivered at a colloquium held at Hofstra University in 1980 but not published until 1985.) Also, Killingsworth, "Whitman's Sexual Themes During a Decade of Revision: 1866–76," *Walt Whitman Quarterly Review* 4 (Summer 1986), 7–15.

7. Martin, *The Homosexual Tradition*, pp. 51–52.

8. First published in the 1860 edition, these sequences did not acquire new or substantially different religious import as a result of Whitman's subsequent additions, changes, and deletions. There is no critical dispute over the spiritual meaning of "Children of Adam" because this dimension of the poetry has been largely overlooked. Nevertheless it might be noted that all but two of the passages cited to support my reading are present in the 1860 text and subsequently received only minor changes in punctuation, capitalization, etc. Both exceptions pertain to "One Hour to Madness and Joy", discussed later in this chapter; in 1867 Whitman added the phrase "one hour to madness and joy!" to form the beginning of line 1, and changed the wording of line 12 from "to be absolved from previous follies and degradations" to "to be absolv'd from previous ties and conventions." Similarly, with one exception, all the passages referred to in my discussion of the religious meaning of "Calamus" were present in the 1860 text and subsequently received only minor changes. The "exception" is "The Base of All Metaphysics" which was added in 1871. As I argue in this chapter, the later inclusion of this poem and deletion of several others may further emphasize Whitman's religious purposes and affect the tone of the sequence, but these changes do not fundamentally alter the sequence's original meaning.

9. Harold Aspiz, *Whitman and the Body Beautiful* (Urbana: Univ. of Illinois Press, 1980), pp. 183–209.

10. "1856 Preface," *Leaves of Grass: Norton Critical Edition*, p. 739.

11. Ibid. pp. 739–40.

12. The quotation, from *Notes and Fragments Left by Walt Whitman*, ed. Richard Maurice Bucke (London, Ontario: A. Talbot & Co., 1899), p. 169, is discussed by Fredson Bowers, *Whitman's Manuscripts: Leaves of Grass (1860): A Parallel Text* (Chicago: Univ. of Chicago Press, 1955), pp. lxxiii. The suggestion that "Children of Adam" was written to mask the homosexual theme in "Calamus" is made by Miller, *Walt Whitman's Poetry*, pp. 140–41.

13. *A Lecture to Young Men, on Chastity* (Boston: C. H. Peirce, 1848), pp. 87, 88–139. Also see Aspiz, *Whitman and the Body Beautiful*, pp. 207–8.

14. Ibid., pp. 198–207.

15. See ibid., pp. 202–3.

16. I have been unable to locate any detailed records of Warren's views on marriage. His championing of free love is referred to by Walters, *American Reformers, 1815–1860* (New York: Hill & Wang, 1978), pp. 73–74. Resemblances between Whitman's perhaps limited reservations regarding marriage and those of Noyes are superficial at best. Sexual relations at Oneida were very carefully regulated and the practical-minded Noyes, faced with the responsibilities of overseeing his community, advocated ideas that clash with Whitman's songs of freedom. Noyes clearly recognized the need for repression: "Nay, it is the glory of man to control himself, and the Kingdom of Heaven summons him to self-control in ALL THINGS." In opposition to Whitman's images of sexual abandon, Noyes advocated "male continence" (intercourse without ejaculation), and he justified this position with language that runs counter to Whitman's unqualified appreciation of motherhood and sexual release: "In the first place, it [male continence] secures women from the curses of involuntary and undesirable procreation; and, secondly, it stops the drain of life on the part of man." Also, in contrast to Whitman's seeming approval of sexual fidelity in marriage, Noyes clearly opposed an exclusive marital relationship, asserting that "complex marriage" was necessary to free love from an unhealthy possessiveness. See *Male Continence* (Oneida, N.Y.: Office of Oneida Circular, 1872), pp. 9–10 & 13.

17. *The Letters of John Addington Symonds*, ed. Herbert M. Schueller and Robert L. Peters (Detroit: Wayne State Univ. Press, 1969), vol. III, pp. 818–19. Symonds began posing tactful questions about the meaning of "Calamus" as early as 1871, but Whitman never responded to these inquiries until 1890. In his study of Whitman, Symonds declared: "Had I not the strongest proof in Whitman's private correspondence with myself that he repudiated any such deductions [of a homosexual theme] from his 'Calamus', I admit that I should have regarded them as justified; and I am not certain whether his own feelings upon this delicate topic may not have altered since the time when 'Calamus' was first composed" (London: John C. Nimmo, 1893, p. 76).

18. Whitman's letter to Symonds has been lost. But a draft of it may be found in *Walt Whitman: The Correspondence* (New York: 1969), vol. V, pp. 72–73.

19. Cady, "Not Happy in the Capitol," pp. 10–11; Martin, *The Homosexual Tradition*, pp. 52–59, and "Conversion and Identity: The 'Calamus' Poems," *Walt Whitman Review* 25 (June 1979), 59–66.

20. Fredson Bowers, ed., *Whitman's Manuscripts* (Chicago: Univ. of Chicago Press, 1955), pp. lxiii and lxxi-lxxiii.

21. Griffith, "Sex and Death," pp. 20–23; Whicher, "Whitman's Awakening to Death," pp. 95–96; Cady, "Not Happy in the Capitol," pp. 13–15; Martin, *The Homosexual Tradition*, 59–63.

22. *The Correspondence*, vol. V, p. 168.

23. *Uncollected Poetry and Prose*, vol. II, p. 81.

24. Martin, *The Homosexual Tradition*, p. 63.

25. *The Correspondence*, vol. I, p. 347.

26. *The Dialogues of Plato*, trans. Benjamin Jowett (New York: Boni & Liveright, 1927), p. 232.

27. See footnote 4 above. For other Marxist studies of Whitman, see Stephen Stephanchev, "Whitman in Russia," and D. Mirsky, "Poet of American Democracy," *Walt Whitman Abroad*, ed. Allen, pp. 144–45, 169–86.

28. "The Spirit of the Pilgrims," as quoted in Perry Miller, *The Life of the Mind in America* (New York: Harcourt, Brace & World, 1965), p. 36.

29. "The Nature, Importance, and Means of Eminent Holiness Throughout the Church," *The American National Preacher* 10 (June-July 1835), 217.

30. *The Stone and the Image* (Philadelphia: Higgins & Perkinpine, 1856), p. 198.

31. *The Tongue of Fire* (New York: Harper & Brothers, 1857), pp. 123–24.

32. *The Kingdom of Christ on Earth* (Andover: Warren F. Draper, 1874), p. 4.

33. I have not made a comprehensive survey of the interpretation of these terms in Whitman criticism, but as examples of their being read with no apparent awareness of their spiritual meaning, see Cady's use of "manly" and "athletic" in "Not Happy in the Capitol," pp. 11–13 and 18; Helms's use of "secret" in "Whitman Revised," pp. 257 and 267; and Martin's reading of "athlete" and "secret" in *The Homosexual Tradition*, pp. 84–88.

34. Barbara Kroll surveyed Whitman's use of "electric" and conjectured that he acquired the term from contemporary physics, "Meaning in Whitman's Use of 'Electric'," *Walt Whitman Review* 19 (December 1973), 151–53. In a discussion that focused upon "I Sing the Body Electric," Myrth Jimmie Killingsworth, "Another Source for Whitman's Use of 'Electric'," *Walt Whitman Review* 23 (September 1977), 129–32, argued instead that Whitman "borrowed the concept of 'sexual electricity' from the medical writers of sex education literature." In the most complete discussion, Aspiz, *Walt Whitman and the Body Beautiful*, pp. 143–79, has demonstrated the widespread usage of electrical theory and terminology in the mid-century, and argues convincingly that the most important sources of Whitman usage were contemporary writings on mesmerism and spiritualism.

35. *Six Lectures on the Philosophy of Mesmerism* (New York: Fowlers & Wells, 1854), pp. 37–38.

36. In *The Philosophy of Spiritual Intercourse* (New York: Fowlers & Wells, 1851), Andrew Jackson Davis approvingly quotes a succinct statement of this article of the spiritualist faith from the *Messenger* (Springfield, Mass.): " . . . let it first be understood that each created thing sustains certain electrical relations to all other things; that all *higher* forms of development sustain *positive* relations to all *lower* forms—as the vegetable to the mineral, the animal to the vegetable, and MAN to all the lower kingdoms in nature. Ascending still further in the scale of progression, the rule will hold good; and hence it is evident that the *spirit-world* sustains a *positive* electrical relation to the *natural world*, of which it is a *higher form*—a further and more perfect development" (pp. 26–27).

37. *The Philosophy of Spiritual Intercourse*, p. 20.

38. John W. Edmonds and George J. Dexter, *Spiritualism*, vol. I (New York: Partridge & Brittan, 1853), p. 132.

39. Charles Grandison Finney, *Lectures on Revivals of Religion* (Cambridge: Harvard Univ. Press, 1960), pp. 398, 460.

40. *The Tongue of Fire*, p. 135.

41. *The Way of Holiness* (New York: G. Lane & C. B. Tippett, 1845), p. 79.

42. *The Higher Christian Life* (New York: D. Appleton & Co. 1859), p. 321.

43. *Essays, Second Series, The Collected Works of Ralph Waldo Emerson*, p. 23.

44. Ibid., p. 163.

45. "Dissertation on the Canon and the Feudal Law," *The Works of John Adams*, vol. III (Free Port, N. Y.: AMS Press, 1971), p. 452.

46. *The Autobiography of Benjamin Franklin* (New York: Macmillan 1967), p. 6.

47. "Spiritual Freedom," *The Works of William E. Channing* (Boston: American Unitarian Association, 1888), p. 186.

48. Ibid., p. 131.

49. *Lectures to Young Men* (New York: M. H. Newman, 1851), p. 172.

50. *Essays, Second Series*, p. 76.

51. *American Apocalypse: Yankee Protestants and the Civil War, 1860–1869* (New Haven: Yale Univ. Press, 1978), p. 146.

52. *Walt Whitman of the New York Aurora*, p. 62.

53. *Uncollected Prose and Poetry*, vol. I, p. 77.

54. *Walt Whitman: The Correspondence*, ed. Edwin H. Miller (New York, 1961), vol. I, p. 160.

55. Ibid., p. 147.

56. Two such recent misreadings are in Miller, *Walt Whitman's Poetry*, p. 167, and Martin, *The Homosexual Tradition*, p. 84.

57. *The Correspondence*, vol. III, p. 86.

58. Ibid., p. 68.

59. Helms, "Whitman Revised," pp. 261, 264–65, 271.

60. Ibid., p. 265.

61. *Poems of Ralph Waldo Emerson* (New York: Thomas Y. Crowell, 1965), pp. 80–82.

62. The texts of these deleted poems are in Pearce, *Leaves of Grass: Facsimile Edition of the 1860 Text* (Ithaca: Cornell Univ. Press, 1961), pp. 354–56 & 361–62.

63. Bowers, *Whitman's Manuscripts*, pp. xxxiii-xli.

64. "Whitman Revised," pp. 269–70.

65. *Homosexual Tradition*, p. 27.

66. Ibid., pp. 23–24.

67. Ibid., pp. 10–11.

68. Ibid., p. 17; Cady, "'Drum-Taps' and Nineteenth-Century Male Homosexual Literature," pp. 51–52; Helms, "Whitman Revised," pp. 258–59.

69. "Not Happy in the Capitol," p. 6.

70. Bowers, *Whitman's Manuscripts*, p. 64.

71. *Homosexual Tradition*, p. 83.

72. *The Correspondence*, vol. II, p. 288.

73. Ibid., vol. I, p. 162.

74. The antebellum feminine ideal and its relationship to social and economic change is discussed by Barbara Welter, "The Cult of True Womanhood: 1820–1860," *American Quarterly* 18 (Summer 1966), 151–166, 171–74; see also Nancy F. Cott, *The Bonds of Womanhood: "Women's Sphere" in New England, 1780–1835* (New Haven: Yale Univ. Press, 1977); and Ann Douglas, *The Feminization of American Culture* (New York: Avon Books, 1977).

75. *The Correspondence*, vol. I, p. 187.

76. An illuminating parallel can be drawn between Whitman and the recent Democratic party activist and congressman from New York, Allard Lowenstein. Like Whitman, Lowenstein was vain about his body and physical appearance, preferred the companionship of young men, and actually slept with them. It seems that both men used these friendships to satisfy their needs for physical and emotional affection. Yet both denied that they were gay, and in neither case is there evidence of actual homosexual relations. It is rumored that before his violent death in 1980, Lowenstein became influenced by the growing gay rights movement, confidentially admitted his gayness, and planned to make this public. See David Harris, *Dreams Die Hard: Three Men's Journeys Through the Sixties* (New York: St. Martin's/Marek, 1982), pp. 109–10, 259, 316–18. However, unlike Lowenstein, Whitman lived in a period of unremitting homophobia. In the absence of any public support for gay rights, it seems likely that he never allowed his homosexuality to come to full consciousness, let alone decide to go public with his gayness.

8. Poetry and Politics: A New Public Faith

1. *Interpretations of Poetry and Religion* (New York: Charles Scribner's Sons, 1900), pp. 173, 185 and 180.

2. Robert Bellah, *The Broken Covenant: American Civil Religion in Time of Trial* (New York: Seabury Press, 1975), p. ix. Alfred North Whitehead makes a similar observation: "Religion has been and is now the major source of those ideals which add to life a sense of purpose that is worthwhile." It follows, he adds, that "apart from religion, expressed in ways generally intelligible, populations sink into the apathetic task of daily survival, with minor alleviations"; as quoted in Sidney Mead, *The Old Religion in the Brave New World* (Berkeley: Univ. of California Press, 1977), p. 63. In making his argument for the indispensable social function of religion, Mead supports his position by citing, among others, Ruth Benedict, Edward Shils, Talcott Parsons, and Paul Tillich (pp. 58–80).

3. Alexis de Tocqueville, *Democracy in America* (New York: Random House, 1981), p. 182.

4. "Walt Whitman" in *Walt Whitman: The Measure of His Song*, ed. Jim Pearlman, Ed Folsom, and Dan Campion (Minneapolis: Holy Cow! Press, 1981), p. 77. Readers of Whitman are indebted to the editors for compiling this lively collection of poems and essays illustrating the "tolerance, empathy, family feeling both affectionate and irascible, deadeyed analysis, and freedom" with which subsequent writers have responded to Whitman "Preface," p. xvii. Unless otherwise indicated, subsequent footnotes in this chapter refer to this anthology.

5. "Honoring Whitman," p. 260.

6. "With Walt Whitman at Fredericksburg," p. 263.

7. Andrew Carnegie, "The Gospel of Wealth," *The Gospel of Wealth and Other Timely Essays* (Cambridge: Harvard University Press, 1965), p. 16.

8. "Ode to Walt Whitman," pp. 84–85.

9. "The Orange Bears," p. 101.

10. "Son to Father," p. 178.

11. "Talking Back to Walt Whitman: An Introduction," p. xxi.

12. *The Symbolic Meaning: The Uncollected Versions of Studies in Classic American Literature*, ed. Armin Arnold (London: Centaur Press, Ltd., 1962), pp. 262–63.

13. "A Pact," p. 29.

14. *The Continuity of American Poetry*, (Princeton: Princeton Univ. Press, 1961), p. 57.

15. *Walt Whitman: Modern Critical Views* (New York: Chelsea House Publishers, 1985), p. 4.

16. "Cape Hatteras," pp. 64–65.

17. "Women," *The Gathering of the Forces*, ed. Cleveland Rogers and John Black (New York: G. P. Putnam's Sons, 1920), vol. II, pp. 88–89.

18. "Our Daughters," *I Sit and Look Out*, ed. Emory Holloway and Vernolian Schwarz (New York: Columbia Univ. Press, 1932), pp. 55–56.

19. "The Ceaseless Rings of Walt Whitman," p. 96.

20. *Gathering of the Forces*, pp. 187–218 (references to abolitionism, pp. 192 & 194); *I Sit and Look Out*, pp. 86–90.

21. "Black and White Slaves," *Walt Whitman of the New York Aurora*, ed. Joseph Jay Rubin and Charles H. Brown (State College, Pa.: Bald Eagle Press, 1950), p. 126.

22. "Abolition Convention," *I Sit and Look Out*, pp. 87–88.

23. "Prohibition of Colored Persons," *I Sit and Look Out*, p. 90.

24. "American Workingmen, Versus Slavery," *Gathering of the Forces*, pp. 208–209.

25. Oscar Cargill argues that hopes for political appointment caused Whitman to

keep his *Eagle* editorials in line with the Free Soil wing of the Democratic Party; see "Walt Whitman and Civil Rights," *Essays in American and English Literature Presented to Bruce Robert McElderry, Jr.*, ed. Max F. Schulz, William D. Templeman, and Charles R. Metzger (Athens: Ohio Univ. Press, 1967), pp. 50 & 56.

26. "Whitman and the Problem of Good," p. 109.

27. *Beginning to See the Light: Pieces of a Decade* (New York: Alfred A. Knopf, 1981), p. 80.

28. "Walt Whitman," p. 70.

29. "Introduction," p. 200.

30. "Populist Manifesto," pp. 201, 203, 204.

31. "For the Sake of a People's Poetry: Walt Whitman and the Rest of Us," p. 351.

32. *Notes and Fragments*, p. 57.

33. In the 1860 text these lines appeared as follows:

> I too, following many, and followed by many, inaugurate a Religion—I too go
>   to the wars,
> It may be I am destined to utter the loudest cries thereof, the conqueror's shouts,
> They may rise from me yet, and soar above every thing.
> . . . .
> O I see the following poems are indeed to drop in the earth the germs of a greater
>   Religion.
>
> ("Starting from Paumanok, sections 25 & 33)
>
> Poets to come!
> . . . .
> You must justify me
> . . . .
> Leaving it to you to prove and define it,
> Expecting the main things from you.
>
> ("Poets to Come")

There is no significant difference in the general content of the 1860 and 1892 versions of these lines; for our purposes, perhaps the most significant change was Whitman's later addition of "solely" (to what became line 129 of the final edition) which called greater attention to his religious purpose.

34. Stephen Stepanchev, "Whitman in Russia," *Walt Whitman Abroad*, ed. Gay Wilson Allen (Syracuse, N. Y.: Syracuse Univ. Press, 1955), p. 150.

WORKS CITED

Works by Whitman

Whitman, Walt. *The Collected Writings of Walt Whitman*. General editors, Gay Wilson Allen and Sculley Bradley. New York: New York Univ. Press, 1961–84.

———. *The Complete Writings of Walt Whitman*. 10 vols. Ed. Richard Maurice Bucke, Thomas B. Harned, and Horace Traubel. New York: Putnam's Sons, 1902.

———. *The Correspondence*. 6 vols. Ed. Edwin Haviland Miller. *The Collected Writings of Walt Whitman*. New York: New York Univ. Press, 1961–69, 1977.

———. *The Early Poems and the Fiction*. Ed. Thomas L. Brasher. *The Collected Writings of Walt Whitman*. New York: New York Univ. Press, 1963.

———. "An English and an American Poet. *The American Phrenological Journal* 22 (October 1855), 90–91.

———. *The Gathering of the Forces: Editorials, Essays, Literary and Dramatic Reviews and Other Material Written by Walt Whitman as Editor of the Brooklyn Daily Eagle in 1846 and 1847*. 2 vols. Ed. Cleveland Rodgers and John Black. New York: G. P. Putnam's Sons, 1920.

———. *I Sit and Look Out; Editorials from the Brooklyn Daily Times*. Ed. Emory Holloway and Vernolian Schwarz. New York: Columbia Univ. Press, 1932.

———. *"Leaves of Grass": Comprehensive Reader's Edition*. Ed. Harold W. Blodgett and Sculley Bradley. *The Collected Writings of Walt Whitman*. New York: New York Univ. Press, 1964.

———. *Leaves of Grass: Facsimile Edition of the 1860 Text*. Ed. Roy Harvey Pearce. Ithaca: Cornell Univ. Press, 1961.

———. *Leaves of Grass: Norton Critical Edition*. Ed. Harold W. W. Blodgett and Sculley Bradley. New York: W. W. Norton & Co., 1973.

———. *New York Dissected*. Ed. Emory Holloway and Ralph Adimari. New York: R. R. Wilson, 1936.

———. *Notebooks and Unpublished Prose Manuscripts*. 6 vols. Ed. Edward F. Grier. *The Collected Writings of Walt Whitman*. New York: New York Univ. Press, 1984.

———. *Notes and Fragments*. Ed. Richard M. Bucke. London, Ontario: A. Talbot and Company, 1899.

———. *Prose Works 1892*. 2 vols. Ed. Floyd Stovall. *The Collected Writings of Walt Whitman*. New York: New York Univ. Press, 1963, 1964.

———. *The Uncollected Poetry and Prose of Walt Whitman*. 2 vols. Ed. Emory Holloway. Garden City, N. Y.: Doubleday, Page and Company, 1921.

———. *Walt Whitman of the New York Aurora*. Ed. Joseph Jay Rubin and Charles H. Brown. State College, Pa.: Bald Eagle Press, 1950.

———. *Walt Whitman's Blue Book*. 2 vols. Ed. Arthur Golden. New York: New York Public Library, 1968.

———. *Walt Whitman's Leaves of Grass: The First (1855) Edition*. Ed. Malcolm Cowley. New York: Viking Press, 1959.

———. *Walt Whitman's Poems*. Ed. Gay Wilson Allen and Charles T. Davis, New York: New York Univ. Press, 1955.

———. *Walt Whitman's Workshop*. Ed. Clifton Joseph Furness. Cambridge: Harvard Univ. Press, 1928.

———. *Whitman's Manuscripts: Leaves of Grass (1860): A Parallel Text.* Ed. Fredson Bowers. Chicago: Univ. of Chicago Press, 1955.

———. *The Works of Walt Whitman.* 2 vols. Ed. Malcolm Cowley. New York: Funk & Wagnalls, 1968.

Works about Whitman

Adams, Richard P. "Whitman's 'Lilacs' and the Tradition of Pastoral Elegy." *PMLA* 72 (June 1957), 479–87.

Allen, Gay Wilson. *The New Walt Whitman Handbook.* New York: New York Univ. Press, 1975.

———. *A Reader's Guide to Walt Whitman.* New York: Farrar, Straus & Giroux, 1970.

———. *The Solitary Singer.* New York: New York Univ. Press, 1967.

———, ed. *Walt Whitman Abroad.* Syracuse, N. Y.: Syracuse Univ. Press, 1955.

———. *Walt Whitman as Man, Poet, and Legend.* Carbondale: Southern Illinois Univ. Press, 1961.

Arvin, Newton. *Whitman.* New York: Macmillan, 1938.

Aspiz, Harold. *Walt Whitman and the Body Beautiful.* Urbana: Univ. of Illinois Press, 1980.

Asselineau, Roger. *The Evolution of Walt Whitman.* 2 vols. Cambridge: Harvard Univ. Press, 1960, 1962.

Beaver, Joseph. *Walt Whitman—Poet of Science.* New York: King's Crown Press, 1951.

Bergquist, Bruce A. *Walt Whitman and the Bible: Language, Echoes, Images, Allusions and Ideas.* Dissertation, Univ. of Nebraska, 1979.

Black, Stephen A. *Whitman's Journeys into Chaos.* Princeton, N. J.: Princeton Univ. Press, 1975.

Bloom, Harold, ed. *Walt Whitman: Modern Critical Views.* New York: Chelsea House Publishers, 1985.

Brasher, Thomas L. *Whitman as Editor of the Brooklyn Daily Eagle.* Detroit: Wayne State Univ. Press, 1970.

———. "Whitman's Conversion to Phrenology." *Walt Whitman Newsletter* 4 (March 1958), 95–97.

Bucke, Richard M. Traubel, Horace, and Harned, Thomas B., eds. *In Re Walt Whitman.* Philadelphia: David McKay, 1893.

Cady, Joseph. "Not Happy in the Capitol: Homosexuality and the 'Calamus' Poems." *American Studies* 19 (1978), 5–22.

Cargill, Oscar. "Walt Whitman and Civil Rights." *Essays in American and English Literature: Presented to Bruce Robert McElderry, Jr..* Ed. Max F. Schulz, William D. Templeman and Charles R. Metzger. Athens: Ohio Univ. Press, 1967, pp. 48–58.

Carlisle, E. Fred. *The Uncertain Self: Whitman's Drama of Identity.* East Lansing: Michigan State Univ. Press, 1973.

Cavitch, David. *My Soul and I: The Inner Life of Walt Whitman.* Boston: Beacon Press, 1985.

Chalfin, Norma Jean. *Walt Whitman's Philosophy of History.* Dissertation, Univ. of Southern California, 1975.

Chari, V. K. *Whitman in the Light of Vedantic Mysticism.* Lincoln: Univ. of Nebraska Press, 1964.

Chase, Richard. *Walt Whitman Reconsidered.* New York: William Sloane Associates, 1955.

Clifford, J. H. "Letter." *The Conservator* VI (1895), 59.

Consolo, Dominick P., ed. *"Out of the Cradle Endlessly Rocking."* Columbus, Ohio: Charles E. Merrill, 1971.

Coffman, Stanley K., Jr. "Crossing Brooklyn Ferry: A Note on the Catalogue Technique in Whitman's Poetry." *Modern Philology* 51 (May 1954), 225–32.

Crawley, Thomas. *The Structure of "Leaves of Grass."* Austin: Univ. of Texas Press, 1970.

De Selincourt, Basil. *Walt Whitman: A Critical Study.* New York: Mitchell Kennerly, 1914.

Freedman, Florence Bernstein. *Walt Whitman Looks at the Schools.* New York: Columbia Univ. Press, 1950.

Furness, Clifton Joseph. "Walt Whitman's Politics." *American Mercury* 16 (April 1929), 459–66.

Golden, Arthur. ed. *Walt Whitman: A Collection of Criticism.* New York: McGraw-Hill, 1974.

Grier, Edward F. "Walt Whitman's Earliest Known Notebook." *PMLA* 83 (October 1968), 1453–56.

Griffith, Clark. "Sex and Death: The Significance of Whitman's 'Calamus' Themes." *Philological Quarterly* 39 (January 1960), 18–38.

Hayes, Will. *Walt Whitman.* London: C. W. Daniel Ltd., 1921.

Helms, Alan. "Whitman Revised." *Etudes Anglaises* 37 (1984), 247–71.

Hindus, Milton, ed. *Walt Whitman: The Critical Heritage.* London: Routledge & Kegan Paul, 1971.

Hinz, Evelyn J. "Whitman's 'Lilacs': The Power of Elegy." *Bucknell Review* 20 (Fall 1972), 35–54.

Hungerford, Edward. "Walt Whitman and His Chart of Bumps." *American Literature* 2 (1931), 350–85.

Hutchinson, George B. *The Ecstatic Whitman: Literary Shamanism and the Crisis of the Union.* Columbus: Ohio State Univ. Press, 1986.

Kallen, Horace M. "Of Love, Death, and Walt Whitman." *Walt Whitman Review* 15 (September 1969), 171–80.

Keller, Karl. "The *Whitman* Issue in American Literature: A Review Essay." *Texas Studies in Literature and Language* 22 (Winter 1980), 575–86.

———. "Walt Whitman and the Queening of America." *American Poetry* 1 (Fall 1983), 4–26.

Kennedy, William Sloane. *The Fight of a Book for the World.* West Yarmouth, Mass.: Stonecraft Press, 1926.

Killingsworth, Myrth Jimmie. "Another Source for Whitman's Use of 'Electric'." *Walt Whitman Review* 23 (September 1977), 129–32.

———. "Sentimentality and Homosexuality in Whitman's 'Calamus'." *ESQ: Journal of American Renaissance* 29 (1983), 144–53.

———. "Whitman's Sexual Themes During a Decade of Revision: 1866–76." *Walt Whitman Quarterly Review* 4 (Summer 1986), 7–15.

Krieg, Joann, ed. *Walt Whitman: Here and Now.* Westport, Conn.: Greenwood Press, 1985.

Kroll, Barbara. "Meaning in Whitman's Use of 'Electric'." *Walt Whitman Review* 19 (December 1973), 151–53.

Kuebrich, David. "Whitman's Politics: Poetry and Democracy." *Literature and History.* Ed. Harry R. Garvin. Lewisburg, Pa.: Bucknell Univ. Press, 1977, pp. 116–30.

———. "Whitman's New Theism." *ESQ: Journal of the American Renaissance* 24 (4th Quarter 1978), 229–41.

Kummings, Donald. "The Vernacular Hero in Whitman's 'Song of Myself'." *Walt Whitman Review* 23 (March 1977), 23–34.

Lewis, R. W. B., ed. *The Presence of Walt Whitman*. New York: Columbia Univ. Press, 1962.

———. "Walt Whitman: Always Going Out and Coming In." *Trials of the Word: Essays in American Literature and the Humanistic Tradition*. New Haven: Yale Univ. Press, 1965, pp. 3–35.

Loving, Jerome. *Emerson, Whitman, and the American Muse*. Chapel Hill: Univ. of North Carolina Press, 1982.

Marki, Ivan. *The Trial of the Poet: An Interpretation of the First Edition of Leaves of Grass*. New York: Columbia Univ. Press, 1976.

Martin, Robert L. "Conversion and Identity: The 'Calamus' Poems." *Walt Whitman Review* 25 (June 1979), 59–66.

———. *The Homosexual Tradition in American Poetry*. Austin: Univ. of Texas Press, 1979.

———. "Whitman's 'Song of Myself': Homosexual Dream and Vision." *Partisan Review* 42 (1975), 80–96.

Middlebrook, Diane. *Walt Whitman and Wallace Stevens*. Ithaca: Cornell Univ. Press, 1974.

Miller, Edwin Haviland, ed. *A Century of Whitman Criticism*. Bloomington: Indiana Univ. Press, 1969.

———. *Walt Whitman's Poetry: A Psychological Journey*. Boston: Houghton Mifflin, 1968.

Miller, F. DeWolfe. "The Partitive Studies of 'Song of Myself'." *American Transcendental Quarterly* 12 (Fall 1971), 11–17.

Miller, James E., Jr. *A Critical Guide to "Leaves of Grass."* Chicago: Univ. of Chicago Press, 1957.

Murray, J. Middleton. "Walt Whitman: The Prophet of Democracy." *Pacific Spectator* 9 (Winter 1955), 32–57.

Nagle, John M. "Toward a Theory of Structure in 'Song of Myself'." *Critics of Whitman*. Ed. Richard H. Rupp. Coral Gables, Florida: Univ. of Miami Press, 1972.

Pearce, Roy Harvey, ed. *A Collection of Critical Essays*. Englewood Cliffs, N. J.: Prentice-Hall, 1962.

———. "Whitman Justified: The Poet in 1860." *Minnesota Review* 1 (1961), 261–94.

Perlman, Jim, Ed Folsom, and Dan Campion, eds. *Walt Whitman: The Measure of His Song*. Minneapolis: Holy Cow Press, 1981.

Perry, Bliss. *Walt Whitman*. Boston: Houghton Mifflin, 1906.

Reid, Alfred, S. "The Structure of 'Song of Myself' Reconsidered." *Southern Humanities Review* 8 (Fall 1974), 507–14.

Robbins, J. Albert. "The Narrative Form of 'Song of Myself'." *American Transcendental Quarterly* 12 (Fall 1971), 17–20.

Robinson, David. "The Poetry of Dialogue in 'Song of Myself'." *American Poetry and Poetics* 1 (Fall 1974), 34–50.

Rountree, Thomas. "Whitman's Indirect Expression and Its Application to 'Song of Myself'." *PMLA* 73 (1958), 549–55.

Rubin, Joseph Jay. *The Historic Whitman*. University Park: Pennsylvania State Univ. Press, 1973.

Rupp, Richard H., ed. *Critics on Whitman*. Coral Gables, Fla: Univ. of Miami Press, 1972.

Sixbey, George L. "'Chanting the Square Deific'—A Study in Whitman's Religion." *American Literature* 9 (May 1973), 171–95.

Spitzer, Leo. *"Explication de Texte* Applied to Walt Whitman's Poem 'Out of the Cradle Endlessly Rocking'." *ELH: Journal of English Literary History* 16 (September 1949), 229–49.

Stovall, Floyd. *The Foreground of "Leaves of Grass."* Charlottesville: Univ. of Virginia Press, 1974.

———. "Main Drifts in Whitman's Poetry." *American Literature* 4 (March 1932), 3–21.

Strauch, Carl F. "The Structure of Walt Whitman's 'Song of Myself'." *English Journal* 27 (September 1938), 597–607.

Symonds, John Addington. *Walt Whitman.* London: John C. Nimmo, 1893.

Tannenbaum, Carl. "Patterns in Whitman's 'Song of Myself'—A Summary and a Supplement." *College Language Association Journal* 6 (1962–63), 44–69.

Tanner, Stephen L. "Religious Attitudes toward Progress: Whitman and Berdyaev." *Cithara* 17 (November 1977), 4–16.

Thomas, M. Wynn. *The Lunar Light of Whitman's Poetry.* Cambridge: Harvard Univ. Press, 1987.

Trail, George Y. "'Song of Myself': Events in the Microstructure." *Walt Whitman Review* 25 (September 1979), 106–13.

Traubel, Horace L. *With Walt Whitman in Camden.* Vol. I, Boston: Small, Maynard, 1906. Vol. II, New York: Appleton, 1908. Vol. III, New York: M. Kennerly, 1914. Vol. IV, Ed. Sculley Bradley, Philadelphia: Univ. of Pennsylvania Press, 1953. Vol. V, Ed. Gertrude Traubel, Carbondale: Southern Illinois Univ. Press, 1964.

———. Rev. of *Walt Whitman,* by Bliss Perry. *The Conservator* 18 (1906), 139–40.

Van Doren, Mark. *The Private Reader.* New York: H. Holt & Co., 1942.

Walcutt, Charles C. "Whitman's 'Out of the Cradle Endlessly Rocking'." *College English* 10 (February 1949), 277–79.

Whicher, Stephen E. "Whitman's Awakening to Death: Toward a Biographical Reading of 'Out of the Cradle Endlessly Rocking'." *Studies in Romanticism* 1 (Autumn 1961), 9–27.

Willard, Charles B. *Whitman's American Fame.* Providence, R. I.: Brown Univ. Press, 1950.

Woodress, James, ed. *Critical Essays on Walt Whitman.* Boston: G. K. Hall, 1983.

Wrobel, Arthur, "Whitman and the Phrenologists: The Divine Body and the Sensuous Soul." *PMLA* 89 (1974), 17–23.

Religious Studies and Religion in America

Adams, John. "Dissertation on the Canon and the Feudal Law." *The Works of John Adams.* Vol. III. New York: AMS Press, 1971.

Ahlstrom, Sydney E. *A Religious History of the American People.* New Haven: Yale Univ. Press, 1972.

Albanese, Catherine. *Corresponding Motion: Transcendental Religion and the New America.* Philadelphia: Temple Univ. Press, 1977.

Allred, Gordon, ed. *Famed Discourses on Eternal Progression and Future Existence.* Salt Lake City: Hawkes Publishers, 1974.

Anonymous. "Sunday Schools Prospectively Considered." *The Sunday School Visitor* 1 (February 1835), 44.

————. "American Sunday School Union." *The American Sunday School Magazine* 1 (July 1824), 1.

Armstrong, Lebbeus. *The Temperance Reformation of this XIXth Century: The Fulfilment of Divine Prophecy*. New York: Pudney, Hooker & Russell, 1845.

Arthur, William. *Tongue of Fire; or, the True Power of Christianity*. New York: Harper & Brothers, 1857.

Beecher, Edward. "The Nature, Importance, and Means of Eminent Holiness Throughout the Church." *The American National Preacher* 10 (June-July 1835), 193–224.

Beecher, Henry Ward. *Lectures to Young Men*. New York: M. H. Newman, 1851.

Bellah, Robert. *The Broken Covenant: American Civil Religion in Time of Trial*. New York: Seabury Press, 1975.

Bennett, John C. *The History of the Saints*. New York: Bradbury, Soden & Co., 1842.

Berdyaev, Nicolas. *Freedom and the Spirit*. Trans. Oliver Clarke. New York: Charles Scribner's Sons, 1935.

Berg, Joseph F. *The Stone and the Image or, The American Republic, The Bane and Ruin of Despotism*. Philadelphia: Higgins & Perkinpine, 1856.

Boardman, W. E. *The Higher Christian Life*. New York: D. Appleton & Co., 1859.

Bodo, John R. *The Protestant Clergy and Public Issues, 1812–1848*. Princeton: Princeton Univ. Press, 1954.

Bolle, Kees. *The Freedom of Man in Myth*. Nashville: Vanderbilt Univ. Press, 1968.

Boynton, Jeremy. *Sanctification Practical: A Book for the Times*. New York: Foster and Palmer, Jr., 1867.

Brodie, Fawn. *No Man Knows My History: The Life of Joseph Smith the Mormon Prophet*. 2nd ed. New York: Alfred A. Knopf, 1971.

Bucke, Richard M. *Cosmic Consciousness*. New York: E. P. Dutton, 1969.

Bush, George. *The Millennium of the Apocalypse*. New York: J. & J. Harper, 1832.

————. *A Treatise on the Millennium*. New York: 1832.

Channing, William Ellery. *Self-Culture: An Address Introductory to the Franklin Lectures*. Boston: Dutton & Wentworth, 1838.

————. *The Works of William E. Channing*. Boston: American Unitarian Association, 1888.

Cherry, Conrad, ed. *God's New Israel: Religious Interpretations of American Destiny*. Englewood Cliffs, N.J.: Prentice-Hall, 1971.

Church of Jesus Christ of Latter-Day Saints. *Holy Scriptures of the Church of Jesus Christ of Latter-Day Saints*. Salt Lake City: Deseret Book Company, 1960.

Clarke, James Freeman. *Ten Great Religions: An Essay in Comparative Theology*. Boston: James R. Osgood, 1871.

Conway, Moncure. *The Sacred Anthology: A Book of Ethnical Scriptures*. New York: H. Holt & Co., 1874.

Davis, Andrew Jackson. *The Principles of Nature, the Divine Revelation, and a Voice of Mankind*. New York: S. S. Lyon & Wm. Fishbough, 1847.

————. *The Philosophy of Spiritual Intercourse: Being an Explanation of Modern Mysteries*. New York: Fowlers & Wells, 1851.

————. *The Great Harmonia: Being a Philosophical Revelation of the Natural, Spiritual and Celestial Universe*. Vols. I–III. Boston: B. B. Mussey, 1851–52.

Delp, Robert W. "Andrew Jackson Davis: Prophet of American Spiritualism." *Journal of American History* 54 (June 1967), 43–56.

Dick, Thomas. *Celestial Scenery: or, The Wonders of the Planetary System Displayed; Illustrating the Perfections of Deity and a Plurality of Worlds*. New York: Harper & Brothers, 1838.

———. *The Christian Philosopher; or the Connection of Science and Philosophy with Religion.* New York: G. & C. & H. Carvill, 1829.

———. *The Philosophy of a Future State.* Brookfield, Mass.: E. & G. Meriam, 1830.

———. *The Sidereal Heavens and Other Subjects Connected with Astronomy, as Illustrative of the Character of Deity, and of an Infinity of Worlds.* New York: Harper & Brothers, 1840.

Dickinson, Austin. "Appeal to American Youth on Temperance." *The Temperance Union: Embracing the Temperance Tracts of the American Tract Society.* New York: D. Fanshaw, 1834.

Dods, John Bovee. *Six Lectures on the Philosophy of Mesmerism.* New York: Fowlers & Wells, 1854.

Dupre, Louis. *The Other Dimension.* New York: Doubleday, 1972.

Edmonds, John W. and Dexter, George T. *Spiritualism.* Vol. 1. New York: Partridge & Brittan, 1853.

Edwards, Jonathan. *The Great Awakening. The Works of Jonathan Edwards.* Ed. C. C. Goen. Vol. IV. New Haven: Yale Univ. Press, 1972.

Eliade, Mircea. *Images and Symbols.* Trans. Philip Mairet. London: Harvill Press, 1961.

———. *Patterns in Comparative Religion.* Trans. Rosemary Sheed. New York: Sheed and Ward, 1958.

———. *The Sacred and the Profane.* Trans. Willard R. Trask. New York: Harcourt, Brace and Co., 1959.

———. *The Two and the One.* Trans. J. M. Cohen. New York: Harper & Row, 1965.

Eliade, Mircea and Kitagawa, Joseph, eds. *The History of Religions: Essays in Methodology.* Chicago: Univ. of Chicago Press, 1959.

Finney, Charles Grandison. *Lectures on Revivals of Religion.* Ed. William G. McLoughlin. Cambridge: Harvard Univ. Press, 1960.

———. *Lectures on Systematic Theology.* Oberlin, Ohio: E. J. Goodrich, 1878.

———. *Lectures to Professing Christians.* Oberlin, Ohio: E. J. Goodrich, 1880.

Foster, Charles I. *An Errand of Mercy: The Evangelical United Front 1790–1837.* Chapel Hill: Univ. of North Carolina Press, 1960.

Fowler, Orson Squires. "The Millennium." *The American Phrenological Journal* 8 (July 1846), 200–210. Also "Republicanism the True Form of Government: Its Destined Influence," 9 (March 1847), 73–76; "Progression: A Law of Things—Its Application to Human Improvement, Collective and Individual," 10 (June 1848), 189–92.

Garrison, William Lloyd. *The Liberator* 7 (December 15, 1837), p. 203, and 11 (October 15, 1841), p. 167.

Gaustad, Edwin S., ed. *The Rise of Adventism: Religion and Society in Mid-Nineteenth Century America.* New York: Harper & Row, 1974.

Happold, F. C. *Mysticism.* Baltimore: Penguin, 1970.

Harris, Samuel. *The Kingdom of Christ on Earth.* Andover: Warren F. Draper, 1874.

Hatch, Nathan. *The Sacred Cause of Liberty.* New Haven: Yale Univ. Press, 1977.

Hill, Donna. *Joseph Smith: The First Mormon.* Garden City, N. Y.: Doubleday, 1977.

Hitchcock, Edward. *An Argument for Early Temperance Addressed to the Youth of the United States.* New York: Scofield & Voorhies, 1837.

Hudson, Winthrop S. *Religion in America.* 3rd edition. New York: Charles Scribner's Sons, 1981.

Jackson, Carl T. *The Oriental Religions and American Thought.* Westport, Conn.: Greenwood Press, 1981.

James, William. *The Varieties of Religious Experience*. New York: Collier Books, 1961.

Jamison, A. Leland. "Religions on the Christian Perimeter." *The Shaping of American Religion*. Ed. James Ward Smith and A. Leland Jamison. Princeton: Princeton Univ. Press, 1961, pp. 162–231.

Johnson, Samuel. *Oriental Religions and their Relation to Universal Religion*. 3 vols. Boston: J. R. Osgood & Co., 1872–75.

Jones, Donald G. and Richey, Russell E., eds. *American Civil Religion*. New York: Harper & Row, 1974.

Jung, Carl. *Psychology and Religion*. New Haven: Yale Univ. Press, 1938.

Kelly, C. F. *The Spirit of Love*. New York: Harper & Row, 1951.

Kerr, Howard. *Mediums, and Spirit-Rappers, and Roaring Radicals: Spiritualism in American Literature, 1850–1900*. Urbana: Univ. of Illinois Press, 1972.

Maclear, James F. "The Republic and the Millennium." *The Religion of the Republic*. Ed. Elwyn A. Smith. Philadelphia: Fortress Press, 1971, pp. 183–216.

Marty, Martin E. *Righteous Empire: The Protestant Experience in America*. New York: Harper & Row, 1970.

Mead, Sydney. *The Old Religion in the Brave New World*. Berkeley: Univ. of California Press, 1977.

———. *The Nation with the Soul of a Church*. New York: Harper & Row, 1975.

Moorhead, James H. *American Apocalypse: Yankee Protestants and the Civil War, 1860–1869*. New Haven: Yale Univ. Press, 1978.

Noyes, John Humphrey. *The Way of Holiness*. Putney, Vt.: J.H. Noyes & Co., 1838.

Otto, Rudolf. *The Idea of the Holy*. Trans. John W. Harvey. New York: Oxford Univ. Press, 1925.

———. *Mysticism East and West*. Trans. Bertha L. Bracey and Richenda C. Payne. New York: Macmillan, 1960.

Palmer, Phoebe. *The Way of Holiness*. New York: G. Lane & C. B. Tippett, 1845.

Perry, Lewis. *Radical Abolitionism: Anarchy and the Government of God in Antislavery Thought*. Ithaca, N. Y.: Cornell Univ. Press, 1973.

Santayana, George. *Interpretations of Poetry and Religion*. New York: Charles Scribners, 1900.

Schlesinger, Arthur M., Sr. "A Critical Period in American Religion, 1875–1900." *Religion in American History*. Ed. John M. Mulder and John F. Wilson. Englewood Cliffs, N.J.: Prentice-Hall, 1978, pp. 302–17.

Smith, Timothy L. *Called Unto Holiness; the Story of the Nazarenes: The Formative Years*. Kansas City, Missouri: Nazarene Publishing House, 1962.

———. *Revivalism and Social Reform in Mid-Nineteenth-Century America*. New York: Abingdon Press, 1957.

Stein, Stephen J. "An Apocalyptic Rationale for the American Revolution." *Early American Literature* 9 (1975), 211–25.

Swedenborg, Emanuel. *Concerning the Earths in Our Solar System*. Boston: Otis Clapp, 1839.

———. *Heaven and Its Wonders, The World of Spirits, and Hell*. New York: American Swedenborg Printing & Publishing Society, 1851.

Tillich, Paul. *The Dynamics of Faith*. New York: Harper & Row, 1958.

———. *Systematic Theology*. Vol. I. Chicago: Univ. of Chicago Press, 1951.

———. *Theology of Culture*. Ed. Robert C. Kimball. New York: Oxford Univ. Press, 1959.

Tuveson, Ernest L. *Redeemer Nation: The Idea of America's Millennial Role*. Chicago: Univ. of Chicago Press, 1968.

Underhill, Evelyn. *Mysticism*. London: Methuen & Co., 1911.

———. *The Mystics of the Church*. New York: Schocken Books, 1964.
———. *Practical Mysticism*. New York: E. P. Dutton, 1915.

Other

American Temperance Union, Executive Committee. "Address," *Journal of the American Temperance Union* 1, no. 1 (January 1837), 2–8.

Arnold, Armin, Ed. *The Symbolic Meaning: The Uncollected Versions of Studies in Classic American Literature*. London: Centaur Press, 1962.

Betts, William W., Jr., ed. *Lincoln and the Poets*. Pittsburgh: Univ. of Pittsburgh Press, 1965.

Blau, Joseph, ed. *Social Theories of Jacksonian Democracy*. New York: Hafner, 1947.

Boston City Council. *A Memorial of Abraham Lincoln*. Boston: J. E. Farwell, 1865.

Brown, Richard D. *Modernization: The Transformation of American Life, 1600–1865*. New York: Hill & Wang, 1976.

Buffalo Citizens. *In Memoriam*. Buffalo: Matthews & Warren, 1865.

Carlyle, Thomas. *Sartor-Resartus, The Works of Thomas Carlyle*. Vol. I. New York: AMS Press, 1974.

Carnegie, Andrew. *The Gospel of Wealth and Other Timely Essays*. Cambridge: Harvard Univ. Press, 1965.

Carpenter, Frederic Ives. *Emerson Handbook*. New York: Hendricks House, 1953.

Churchman, D. R. and Uvarov, E. B. *A Dictionary of Science*. 4th rev. ed. Baltimore: Penguin, 1971.

Cott, Nancy F. *The Bonds of Womanhood: "Woman's Sphere" in New England, 1780–1835*. New Haven: Yale Univ. Press, 1977.

Dampier, William C. *A History of Science*. Cambridge: Cambridge Univ. Press, 1948.

Douglas, Ann. *The Feminization of American Culture*. New York: Avon Books, 1977.

Emerson, Ralph Waldo. *The Collected Works of Ralph Waldo Emerson*. Vols. I–III. Cambridge: Harvard Univ. Press, 1971–.

———. *The Complete Works of Ralph Waldo Emerson*. Vol. XI. Cambridge: Riverside Press, 1904.

Fiedelson, Charles, Jr. *Symbolism in American Literature*. Chicago: Univ. of Chicago Press, 1953.

Franklin, Benjamin. *The Autobiography of Benjamin Franklin*. New York: Macmillan Co., 1967.

Graham, Sylvester. *A Lecture to Young Men, on Chastity*. Boston: C. H. Peirce, 1848.

Hawthorne, Nathaniel. *Love Letters of Nathaniel Hawthorne*. Chicago: Society of the Dofobs, 1907.

Hoskin, M. A. "Herschel, William." *Dictionary of Scientific Biography*. Vol. VI. New York: Charles Scribner's Sons, 1972, pp. 328–36.

Krout, John Allen. *The Origins of Prohibition*. New York: Alfred A. Knopf, 1925.

Mann, Horace. *Lectures on Education*. Boston: Ide & Dutton, 1855.

Matthiessen, F. O. *American Renaissance*. New York: Oxford Univ. Press, 1941.

Miller, Perry. *The Life of the Mind in America*. New York: Harcourt, Brace & World, 1965.

———. *Nature's Nation*. Cambridge: Harvard Univ. Press, 1967.

Mitchell, O. M. *A Course of Six Lectures on Astronomy.* New York: Greeley McElrath, 1848.

Morris, B. F., ed. *Memorial Record of the Nation's Tribute to Abraham Lincoln.* Washington, D.C.: W. H. & O. H. Morrison, 1865.

Munitz, Milton K., ed. *Theories of the Universe.* Glencoe, Ill.: Free Press, 1957.

Newell, R. H. *The Martyr President.* New York: Carleton, 1865.

Noyes, John Humphrey. *Male Continence.* Oneida, N. Y.: Office of Oneida Circular, 1872.

O'Sullivan, John L. "Introduction." *The United States Magazine and Democratic Review* 1 (October 1827), 1–15. Also "The Course of Civilization," 6 (September 1839), 208–17; "The Progress of Society," 8 (July 1840), 67–87; "Democracy and Literature," 11(August 1842) 196–200; "The Christian Union," 12 (June 1843), 563–67.

Pearce, Roy Harvey. *The Continuity of American Poetry.* Princeton: Princeton Univ. Press, 1961.

Peters, Robert L. and Schueller, Herbert M., eds. *The Letters of John Addington Symonds.* Vol. III. Detroit: Wayne State Univ. Press, 1969.

Plato. *The Dialogues of Plato.* Trans. Benjamin Jowett. New York: Boni & Liveright, 1927.

Rhodes, Jacob. *The Nation's Loss: A Poem on the Life and Death of the Hon. Abraham Lincoln.* Newark, N.J.: F. Starruch, 1866.

Rorabaugh, W. J. *The Alcoholic Republic: An American Tradition.* New York: Oxford Univ. Press, 1979.

Ruitenbeek, Hendrik, ed. *Homosexuality and Creative Genius.* New York: Astor-Honor, 1967.

Stern, Madeleine B. *Heads and Headlines: The Phrenological Fowlers.* Norman: Univ. of Oklahoma Press, 1971.

Tocqueville, Alexis de. *Democracy in America.* New York: Random House, 1981.

Triggs, Oscar Lovell. *The Changing Order.* Chicago: Charles H. Kerr, 1906.

Trowbridge, John Townsend. *My Own Story: With Recollections of Noted Persons.* Boston: Houghton Mifflin, 1903.

Tyler, Alice Felt. *Freedom's Ferment.* New York: Harper & Row, 1944.

Waggoner, Hyatt H. *American Visionary Poetry.* Baton Rouge: Louisiana State Univ. Press, 1982.

Wallace, Anthony F. C. "Revitalization Movements." *American Anthropologist 58* (1956), 264–81.

Walters, Ronald G. *American Reformers, 1815–1860.* New York: Hill & Wang, 1978.

Welter, Barbara. "The Cult of True Womanhood: 1820–1860." *American Quarterly* 18 (Summer 1966), 151–66, 171–74.

Willis, Ellen. *Beginning to See the Light: Pieces of a Decade.* New York: Alfred A. Knopf, 1981.

Woodress, James, ed. *American Literary Scholarship: An Annual.* Durham, N. C.: Duke Univ. Press, 1969.

INDEX

Adams, John: American Revolution and millennialism, 32; use of term "manly," 156
American Phrenological Journal: millennialism, 37–38; perfectionism, 51–52
American Renaissance: literature and symbolic imagination, 72
American Sunday School Union: millennialism, 34–35
American Temperance Union: millennialism, 205n
Animal-magnetism: Whitman and spiritualism, 38. *See also* Mesmerism
Aquatic imagery: Whitman's symbolism, 74–78, 94; symbol of divinity, 126
Arminianism: Protestantism and perfectionism, 49
Armstrong, Lebbeus: temperance and millennialism, 205n
Arnold, John: Whitman and Swedenborgianism, 200n
Arthur, William: love and community, 151; athletics and spiritual activity, 154
Astronomy: Whitman's concept of soul, 25, 199n; astral symbolism, 105–107; Whitman's concepts and scientific error, 214n–215n
Athletes and athletics: Whitman's depiction of self, 110; metaphor and spiritual activity, 154–55
Augustine: allegorical millennialism, 31
Aurora: early development of Whitman's theory of the soul, 14–15; reports on churches, 35; United States and world history, 36; perfectionism, 53; republicanism, 59; use of term "manly," 157; racism, 186; on Emerson, 198n
Autobiography: Whitman's persona, 182

Banquet: symbolism, 92
Beecher, Edward: perfectionism, 50; revivalism and republicanism, 57–58; love and fellowship, 151; martial imagery, 212n
Beecher, Henry Ward: admired by Whitman, 35; use of term "manly," 156; Whitman and millennial views, 203n
Beecher, Lyman: republican government and millennialism, 33, 151; Whitman and millennial views, 203n
Bennett, John Cook: Whitman's knowledge of Mormonism, 26, 200n

Berg, Joseph: love and fellowship, 151
Bible: aquatic symbolism, 75; "Calamus" and love, 149–50; nature symbolism, 210n; martial imagery, 212n
Biography: disciples and collection of materials, 2; evidence for homosexuality, 160–62; criticism, 196n
Birds: symbolism, 117, 125–26
Boardman, William: athletic metaphor for spiritual activity, 154; martial imagery, 212n
Body: celebration as means to religious experience, 95–99; sexuality, 134; as religious symbol, 135–36
"A Broadway Pageant": American millennialism, 46
Bryant, William Jennings: religious response to Lincoln's assassination, 121
Bush, George: American Protestantism and millennialism, 33

"Calamus": aquatic imagery, 76–77; homosexuality, 130–32, 139–40, 160–62; spiritual love, 140–50; political love, 150–52; poetic love, 152–57; homosexuality and self-censorship, 162–68; quietness and manly love, 168–70; cultural needs, 170–72; criticism and homosexuality, 172–74
Calamus grass: symbol of immortality, 125, 142; as key symbol of new religion, 147–49
Calvinism: Protestantism and perfectionism, 49; Whitman's rejection of, 92
Capitalism: Whitman and millennialism, 48; status of women, 171; failure of Whitman's new religion, 180
Carlyle, Thomas: influence on Whitman, 64; Whitman on death of, 106, 113
Channing, William Ellery: American Protestantism and millennialism, 33; revivalism and republicanism, 58; use of term "manly," 156
"Children of Adam": sexuality and religious vision, 132–39
Christ: second coming and perfectionism, 50–51; Whitman's new religion, 146
Christianity: Whitman's rejection of traditional vocabulary, 5; theism, deism, and Whitman's cosmology, 19; nineteenth-century American millennialism, 29; Whitman's post-Christian millennialism, 42; war imagery, 92; doctrine of personal immortality and